ETHICAL HACKING

ETHICAL HACKING

Alana Maurushat

University of Ottawa Press
2019

Les **Presses** de l'Université d'Ottawa
University of Ottawa **Press**

The University of Ottawa Press (UOP) is proud to be the oldest of the francophone university presses in Canada and the only bilingual university publisher in North America. Since 1936, UOP has been "enriching intellectual and cultural discourse" by producing peer-reviewed and award-winning books in the humanities and social sciences, in French or in English.

Library and Archives Canada Cataloguing in Publication

Title: Ethical hacking / Alana Maurushat.
Names: Maurushat, Alana, author.
Description: Includes bibliographical references.
Identifiers: Canadiana (print) 20190087447 | Canadiana (ebook) 2019008748X | ISBN 9780776627915
    (softcover) | ISBN 9780776627922 (PDF) | ISBN 9780776627939 (EPUB) | ISBN 9780776627946 (Kindle)
Subjects: LCSH: Hacking—Moral and ethical aspects—Case studies. | LCGFT: Case studies.
Classification: LCC HV6773 .M38 2019 | DDC 364.16/8—dc23

Copy editing   Robbie McCaw
Proofreading   Robert Ferguson
Typesetting   CS
Cover design   Édiscript enr. and Elizabeth Schwaiger
Cover image   *Fragmented Memory* by Phillip David Stearns, n.d., Personal
                   Data, Software, Jacquard Woven Cotton. Image © Phillip David
                   Stearns, reproduced with kind permission from the artist.

The University of Ottawa Press gratefully acknowledges the support extended to its publishing list by Canadian Heritage through the Canada Book Fund, by the Canada Council for the Arts, by the Ontario Arts Council, by the Federation for the Humanities and Social Sciences through the Awards to Scholarly Publications Program, and by the University of Ottawa.

ONTARIO ARTS COUNCIL
CONSEIL DES ARTS DE L'ONTARIO
an Ontario government agency
un organisme du gouvernement de l'Ontario

Canada Council   Conseil des arts
for the Arts   du Canada

Canadä

uOttawa

Table of Contents

CHAPTER I

Why Ethical Hacking?

This book aims to explore the issue of ethical hacking from an unconventional and unique viewpoint, one that draws upon my own vast experience in this area. My background spans seventeen years and has incorporated roles as a law and cyber-security professor, human-rights activist, cyber-policy consultant, technology developer, and cybercrime investigation advisor. It is this experience that I will draw upon to form the pillars of the book, which departs from some of the conventional thinking in this area. This is not a book about Anonymous or about hacking organizations per se, though case studies from various incidences are certainly explored. This book is about various types of activities that are often referred to as "ethical hacking"—hacking for an ethical reason—whereby it will be argued that law and policy ought not to be the same here as for those hacking activities that are purely for economic gain or to cause harm or mischief. As will be seen, I have grouped ethical hacking into five groups:

- online civil disobedience;
- hacktivism;
- penetration testing and security-vulnerability disclosure;
- counterattack/hackback; and
- security activism.

Let us start this journey first by talking briefly about you, about me, and then a lot about ethical hacking.

1.1 You

The book is designed to cater to a broad spectrum of readers, ranging from cyber-security experts and policy-makers to academics. Despite its intended primary audience, the book has also been written in such a manner as to make it accessible not only to university students but the broader general public. The complexity and rate of change seen within areas of technology, cyber security, and ethical hacking make it essential not to assume that you are across all terminology. There are many terms that common media and blogs use incorrectly or interchangeable, such as "computer virus," which turns out to be a "computer worm." Other new methods of malicious-software propagation may emerge that a reader would not necessarily be familiar with. In general, ethical hacking involves many technical terms that require a foundational level of understanding in order to better understand policy and other issues. For example, a denial-of-service attack is potentially lawful if your own device is used to participate in an online political protest. It would not be lawful to use a botnet that connects to unknown or third-party devices to participate in the same protest. The aim is to provide you with digestible material that demonstrates concepts through engaging case studies. These case studies of ethical hacking, spanning the last twenty years, are dissected and catalogued in a manner that identifies the groups and movements, their motivations, and the techniques they used. You will see some of the most notorious of these incidences explored referenced in chapters 4–6, then selected incidences are looked in context and by issues in chapters 7–13.

If you are a policy-maker, chapters 3–7 and 14 are essential reading. Chapter 3 provides the only publicly available quantitative analysis of ethical hacking in the world. The stark numbers contained within this chapter will assist you in demonstrating why the decisions and policies you recommend are fundamentally essential. As a policy-maker, you are all too aware that in a world of cleverly masked sensationalism posing as substantive information it has become difficult to discern what information can be trusted. Chapters 4–6 table legal cases and selected noteworthy incidences from the quantitative analysis. Throughout chapters 7–13 I aim to provide you with intricate and, at times, intimate looks at the world of ethical hacking, which will assist you in generating well-informed and robust policy. Chapter 14 discusses the required frameworks and changes required as a matter of both policy and law.

If you are a cyber-security expert or consider yourself a hacktivist, there are ethical and legal issues contained within this book that are essential reading. This includes policy and legal lines to be cautious of, which could easily see you cross from that of "ignore action with caution" to one of "prosecute" by authorities. These cautionary tales are drawn from my experience undertaking a large range of roles, as described above.

As I know all too well, the issues surrounding cyber security have garnered interest from a broad demographic of society, and is not limited to just policy-makers, experts, and academics. Even if you do not fit within any of the three later categories, I would still love for you to drop me a line at alanacybersecurity.com and let me know your background. While I keep analytics on how many people visit the site, and the general geographic area of the IP addresses, this will give me an opportunity to engage with you and understand the broader community interests. But please remember that if you are looking at the site or wish to contact me about a private or sensitive matter, this site offers no anonymity to you. So, connect with a VPN, proxy or other anonymizer such as TOR.

www.alanacybersecurity.com

There is also the option of communicating later using encryption and, for journalists, I have and use Signal.

1.2 Me

I have a confession: I am an ethical hacker. *I use technology in a non-violent way in the pursuit of a cause, political or otherwise, which is often legally and morally ambiguous.* I don't intentionally break the law. Many of the actions I take are assumed by politicians, lawmakers, and people around the globe to be legal because there are few to no legal precedents and scant reportage. The law is written broadly, in a way that captures far more than one might expect. Part of my motivation for writing this book is to highlight how desperately new law and policy are required for ethical hackers.

As a human-rights activist I work to educate and protect online civil liberties globally, but more specifically for the jurisdictions in which I have lived and worked, namely Canada, Hong Kong, and Australia. When I lived in Hong Kong I provided research assistance for the OpenNet Initiative (a collaborative partnership between the Citizen Lab at the University of Toronto, the Berkman Center for Internet & Society at Harvard Law School, and the Advanced Network Research Group at the Cambridge Security Programme, Cambridge University) to examine how Chinese authorities filtered the Internet in 2003–2005. The testing of which sites were blocked in the Chinese firewall meant that a host of domestic Chinese laws were violated, even though the object was merely to provide an accurate reflection of what types of sites were blocked, along with where, when, and possibly why these sites were filtered. I continue to be involved in research efforts addressing civil liberties and Internet freedom for the nongovernmental Freedom House, a liberty watchdog. I was the researcher and author of the Australian Internet Freedom portion of the annual Freedom House Report, *Freedom on the Net* (2011–2017). *Freedom on the Net* is the most widely utilized worldwide resource for activists, government officials, journalists, businesses, and international organizations aiming to understand the emerging threats and opportunities in the global Internet landscape, as well as policies and developments in individual countries.

I am a professor and researcher above all else—I currently am the Professor of Cybersecurity and Behaviour at Western Sydney University. I am in the privileged position of leading multidisciplinary research and lecturing teams across a range of cyber-security projects and courses. I work with industry, government, and civil society on a daily basis. But my views about ethical hacking can be traced to a time and place long before I became a professor of cyber security. Here is a bit more about what informs the research, analysis, and opinions represented in this book.

I was a key researcher with the law and policy division of the Data to Decisions Cooperative Research Centre (D2DCRC). The D2DCRC specializes in big data/artificial intelligence for national-security purposes. The centre involved multiple computer scientists and data scientists from universities, industry (e.g., Palantir and SASS) along with governmental departments predominantly in Australia but also in Canada and the United Kingdom. With the D2DCRC, we worked on confidential matters where we helped groups make informed decisions on how new technologies were being built and how they would function based on proposed new legal and policy frameworks.

From an international perspective, I was fortunate enough to be asked to speak at a United Nations workshop in China on cyber security and human rights, where the majority of attendees were students and professors in the cyber-security division of the People's Liberation Army's National Defence University. The questions asked and views imparted to me were enlightening, and reminded me how much misinformation there is in cyber security and ethical hacking. My research from my honours in law, masters, and PhD degrees—and indeed my current research—has been entirely interdisciplinary, as has my work with government, law firms, and later with universities. For my PhD I worked with underground security-activist groups concerned with botnets, conducted empirical qualitative research, and worked closely with the technical community to deepen the research. I worked with individuals and organizations in Europe, Asia, North America, and Australia. This included dialoguing and consulting with individuals from Internet-service providers, the Australian Communications and Media Authority, computer emergency response teams (in Australia, Canada, and Estonia), cyber-security journalists, Shadowserver, various computer-science researchers, and the National Cyber-Forensic Training Alliance (an FBI and Carnegie Melon cybercrime training and investigative service, located in Pittsburgh). The thesis could best be described as in the field of cyber security, using methods and analysis from criminology, economics, information systems, and the law. This book borrows from my graduate work in botnets, especially in the chapter on security activism.

I am on the board of directors and am the special cyber adviser for the investigation firm IFW Global. IFW is an investigation firm specializing in cybercrime and intelligence. My advisory work has involved performing a variety of tasks, including surveillance advice, developing protocols for sensitive investigations in foreign countries, providing legal information on investigative procedures and contracting with intelligence units, as well as writing memoranda for arbitration disputes involving counterfeit engineering products. Our investigations have involved online fraud and malicious online conduct, which has led us to cooperate with cybercrime and anti-money laundering divisions of the FBI, CIA, Interpol, the

AFP, the New South Wales Police Force, and Thai and Philippines police. Our investigatory work on one cybercrime case led to corruption investigations and charges against certain members of the Queensland police force. IFW is globally renowned for shutting down and recovering funds from sophisticated online organized crime, including payment-diversion fraud and boiler-room and binary-option scams.

Payment-diversion fraud typically involves a situation where a network and/or devices on a network are compromised, a criminal watches the actions of the company over time and is able to divert payment due to a supplier to an unknown third party. This is also known as compromised supply-chain fraud.

A boiler-room scam typically refers to a call centre selling questionable investments over the phone, and nearly almost always with legitimate looking fake websites.

Binary options involve a highly speculative form of trading where you don't trade on a market but you often trade against a binary-option "company" (in market parlance, a bucket shop)—effectively, an illegitimate broker. The binary-option broker has a backdoor into an online trading platform, where the broker can manipulate prices while you, the potential customer, is trading—ensuring that you don't win too often, or win just enough to draw you in to want to invest more. The chances of a payout are remote (one in several million), yet people are lured into investing due to premises of a big payout. Kind of like someone inciting you to invest a large sum of money on a horse race with poor odds. The difference, however, is that the odds are so remote that this type of investment is illegal in many jurisdictions. Additionally, the scammers are actively manipulating prices as you engage and invest, luring you into losing more money. Communication is often done through highly encrypted apps such as Signal, and money is exchanged and funnelled through money-laundering processes and, increasingly, through cryptocurrencies. It is extremely difficult to recover money laundered through encrypted cryptocurrencies, making this type of online fraud a lucrative business.

I provide legal and ethical information to computer-security experts (and almost certainly some hackers) on a wide range of topics, such as deviation of application program interfaces (APIs), data crawling on the Deep Web, sale of vulnerabilities and bugs, copyright issues in proof-of-concept videos, subverting national firewalls, disclosure of corrupt practices, and hacking targets. I do know that requests for information have come from Russia, Estonia, China, Jordan, Saudi Arabia, Australia, and Canada, but possibly too from anywhere as people tend to use anonymizing technology to contact me to reduce risk of identification. One person goes so far as to only send me hard documents by post.

Lastly, I have done consultancies for government and industry. In fact, this book is largely the product of research/consultancy work on ethical hacking for Public Safety Canada in 2010. Public Safety Canada engages and works with various departments on a range of cybersecurity issues and also houses the Canadian Cyber Incident Response Centre. As you can see, my understanding of cyber-security behaviour and ethical hacking is based on first-hand knowledge as well as research. That's more than enough about me; let's move onto the topic of the book: ethical hacking.

1.3 Ethical Hacking

What is ethical hacking? My definition differs from the computer-science terminology (which only covers penetration/intrusion testing and vulnerability discovery), whereby I include online civil disobedience, hacktivism, penetration/intrusion testing and vulnerability discovery, counterattack/hackback, and security activism.

Ethical hacking is the non-violent use of a technology in pursuit of a cause, political or otherwise, which is often legally and morally ambiguous.

This book examines five types of ethical hacking: online civil disobedience, hacktivism, penetration/intrusion testing and vulnerability discovery, counterattack/hackback, and security activism. I have briefly defined these below. Controversial aspects of my definitions are examined in chapter 2.

Online civil disobedience is the use of any technology that connects to the Internet in pursuit of a political end. Civil disobedience involves a just cause, where specific technology use is often legal.

Hacktivism is a clever use of technology that involves unauthorized access to data or a computer system in pursuit of a cause or political ends.[1]

Penetration/intrusion testing is a type of information-systems security testing on behalf of the system's owners. This is known in the computer-security world as ethical hacking. There is some argument, however, as to whether penetration testing must be done with permission from a system's owners or whether a benevolent intention suffices in the absence of permission. Whether permission is obtained or not, however, does not change the common cause: improving security.

Vulnerability discovery is the process of finding weaknesses and ways in a network, device, or within the organization themselves that are capable of being exploited by others (sometimes for nefarious reasons). Vulnerability discovery is often done with the authorization of the owner/operator of a network or device, but not always.

Counterattack/hackback is also referred to as strikeback. Counterattack is when an individual or organization that is subject to an attack on their data, network, or computer takes similar measures to attack back at the "hacker/cracker" (see ch. 2 for definitions). For example, when an individual or organization is subject to a denial-of-service attack, that organization might initiate their own denial-of-service attack on the responsible party's website.

Security activism is similar to penetration/intrusion testing in that the cause is to improve security. Security activism goes beyond mere testing of security, however, to gather intelligence on crackers and to launch active attacks to disrupt criminal online enterprises. One example is the taking down of a botnet.

There is no clear line between ethical hacking and vigilantism. Indeed, the water is murky, and what many might characterize as ethical others might see as a form of unwanted vigilantism. Vigilantism is understood to be outside of the state or beyond legal, or extra-state or extra-legal. Vigilantism may involve citizens acting in a manner they believe the state should permit yet currently sanctions. Often a vigilante will break the law, often in response to the state's own violation of laws. There may be a sense that justice under due course will not occur, hence reaction to an action is required. Some might classify this as a valid or even ethical action under the circumstances, while others would paint the same act in a negative fashion, as vigilantism. Cyber vigilantism is similar to traditional forms of vigilantism. Traditional vigilantism might involve the planning of an act, use or threat of force, reaction to a crime or other social act, and the notion of personal and collective security.[2] Cyber vigilantes, as argued by Trottier, are individuals with computer-science skills who respond to cybercrime and cyber security.[3] In this sense they might use an invasive "traceback" search, shut down a website, issue a distributed denial-of-service protest/ attack, and hack into databases to expose corrupt practices. Or perhaps they take down botnets.

But before we delve further into the world of botnets, cryptocurrency, Dark-Net forums, and hackers let's begin with a tale of civil disobedience in 1960, with Martin Luther King Jr. and the civil rights fight for equality and justice for African-American people. From there we look at what some see as Julian Assange's first escapade into hacktivism, with the use of the WANK worm to protest NASA's use of nuclear fuel in rocket ships in the 1980s. You see, hacktivism isn't as new as one might think, but it has and will continue to take new forms and be a prevalent form of protest and activism.

Forcing the Line of Transparency[4]

Civil activists in the 1960s and 1970s had sit-ins and protests for civil rights and against war. Many people thought that civil disobedience would lead to change. Change would lead to rational and critical discussion of citizens with governments in a move toward more open and transparent democratic governance. In the late 1970s and early 1980s, many governments enacted laws around freedom and access to information to better ensure open disclosure and government transparency. Prior to such enactment of freedom and access to information laws, it was difficult to obtain copies of government documents. These laws were devised in an attempt to move the disclosure of information default from private to public. In this sense, a government employee would not ask when something should be made public but, rather, when something should be made private (in other words, transparency by default).

While freedom and access-to-information laws have shifted the line of transparency, they did not achieve transparency by default. Internal guidelines for when information should remain private or public were muddled with bureaucratic wording. The result was that government employees began to self-censor. This took place in two main ways. The first, employees erred on the side of caution when classifying documents, and thus over-classified documents as private/secret and under-classified documents as public/transparent. The second, when access-to-information requests were granted, documents were often so blacked out that it was difficult to ascertain with any certainty what decision or policy was adopted, or why. The "black pen" effect began.

The early twenty-first century will likely be seen as an era when ethical hackers opened governments. The line of transparency is moving by force. The Twitter page for WikiLeaks demonstrates this ethos, through its motto ("We Open Governments") and its location ("Everywhere"). Hacktivism is a form of civil-rights activism in the digital age. In principle, hacktivists believe in two general but spirited principles: respect of human rights and fundamental freedoms, including freedom of expression and personal privacy; and the responsibility of government to be open, transparent, and fully accountable to the public. In practice, however, hacktivists are as diverse in their backgrounds as they are in their agendas.

Ethical hacking is not new. In the late 1980s Australian hacktivists penetrated a NASA network releasing a computer worm known as WANK—Worms Against Nuclear Killers.[5] The worm was written and released as a form of protest against the NASA launch of the Galileo rocket, which was to navigate itself to Jupiter using nuclear energy. The infamous German hacker group Chaos Computer Club (CCC) was also busy in the late 1980s, attacking German government systems to protest the collection and storage of census information; the groups believed that the state should not amass the personal information of its citizens.[6]

Moving forward to the first decade of the twenty-first century, ethical hacking, while not new, had fundamentally changed in one distinct manner—the ability to participate in attacks (denial of service) is no longer limited to an elite group of people with excellent computer skills; the technology is available to the masses in an accessible format for those with limited technical skill. People follow the tweet feeds of Anonymous and Lulz Security (LulzSec), two hacktivist groups, where hacking operations are communicated. One can simply click the download button for open-source LOIC (Low Orbit Ion Canon) software, select the demonstration one wishes to participate in by typing in the URL, then click again. *Fait accompli.* One is now participating in a denial-of-service attack. It must be noted that denial-of-service attacks using LOIC require a critical mass to be effective. This means that many people must participate in the event.

People around the globe are participating in denial-of-service attacks on many types of websites for a variety of causes. Major websites that have been attacked include those of the Australian Parliament, PayPal, MasterCard, paedophilia websites, the New York

Stock Exchange, the Toronto Stock Exchange, *News of the World*, Oakland City Police, the governments of Mexico, Ecuador, and Peru. The list goes on.

One of the most well-known hacktivism groups is Anonymous. The word "group" here is arguably used incorrectly as Anonymous is more like an umbrella name for a decentralized collective of participants and operations. In addition to performing denial-of-service attacks, members of some of the smaller Anonymous groups participate in more sophisticated forms of hacktivism that require a higher range of computer skills. Instances of these more sophisticated attacks include the release of names and details of the Mexican drug cartel Los Zetas, the names and details of consumers of child-pornography sites, and the capturing of secret documents held by governments around the world—some of these documents are then given and released by WikiLeaks.

Hacktivism isn't limited to attacking information systems and retrieving documents. It also extends to finding technical solutions to mobilize people. At the height of the Egyptian e-revolution the major Internet-service providers and mobile-phone companies shut down Internet traffic, preventing people from using the Internet and mobile phones. This, in turn, affected people's ability to mobilize. Anonymous worked around the clock to ensure that images from the revolution were still being sent to the international press. Hacktivists have worked to penetrate the Iranian government's firewall to tunnel passages allowing Iranian citizens to view blocked sites. I was involved with a similar firewall penetration when I organized some of the internal testing of the Chinese firewall for the OpenNet Initiative.[7] There are similar initiatives for Saudi Arabia and other parts of the world with strong censorship. Keeping secrets and preventing citizens from accessing information may no longer be an achievable goal. The question becomes, should governments adopt heavy-handed policies and laws to investigate and prosecute ethical hackers, to deter such activity and keep the status quo? Or should governments enact an appropriate legislative response that reflects the reality of this new era—the forced line of transparency?

Other forms of ethical hacking are rooted in ensuring the security of networks. This has taken shape in four main ways. The first is through intrusion or penetration testing, where experts are invited to expose the security vulnerabilities of an organization's network. The second is somewhat more controversial as it involves hackers who, without authorization, illegally access a network, software, or hardware to expose security vulnerabilities. Sometimes these hackers will go so far as to fix the vulnerability or to report it to the system's owner. Third, there is a growing concern that many organizations, including corporations and governments, are engaging in counterattack efforts to deter attacks to their systems. This is known as hackback or counterattack. Increasingly, attacks have moved into the corporate world, where organizations are moving from defensive protection against cyber threat to responding with similar measures. There is growing momentum in some jurisdictions to legalize hackback, including a recent United States bill for its legalization (see ch. 10). Last, many security experts are forming self-organized security communities to actively engage in intelligence gathering and counterattacks—here called security activism.

How courts and governments will deal with hacking attempts that operate in grey areas of the law, and where different ethical views collide, remains to be seen. There are no exceptions to the cybercrime/computer-crime provisions for security research or for the public interest in most jurisdictions. The US bill on hackback remains controversial. Equally difficult is how civil rights apply to hacktivism. This question is shrouded with uncertainty. How will governments and courts manoeuvre in this new era of digital activism within the boundaries of protected civil liberties?

As will be seen throughout this book, online protests are and will continue to increase, and the type and size of such attacks will escalate in order to, in part, capture the interest of the media.

There is a growing movement in some online communities (hackers) to ensure that "back doors" (ways to exploit a program) are inserted into computer programs and then kept quiet as a means of ensuring access to future information (especially government websites). These types of "attacks" are not done for media attention.

Technologies such as LOIC will evolve to allow for encryption and anonymity. This will parallel similar developments that took place with peer-to-peer file-sharing networks. We are already seeing groups of hackers come together in countries without extradition treaties with the United States, or to protect vulnerable investigative journalists and whistle-blowers. These groups are at the forefront of encryption expertise and data and identity protection.

As will be seen in the data-analysis chapter (ch. 3), the most popular discussion threads in hacking forums are "beginner hacking" and "hacking tools and programs," indicating the likelihood of increased hacking, both ethical and for criminal purposes. United Nations–sponsored research on hackers demonstrated that legal deterrence only works with beginners and with young hackers (under aged twenty-five).[8] These individuals will generally quit illegal hacking after a first conviction. The law does not have a deterrent effect for highly skilled and often older hackers (over twenty-five). This United Nations Commission on International Trade Law study, however, did not address hacktivism, nor motivation or deterrence, as hacktivism didn't become popular until 2011, with the UN quantitative and qualitative study being performed in the early 2000s. More recent studies on hacktivism are qualitative, not quantitative.

This book looks at qualitative studies, but it is also the first and only study of its kind to have performed quantitative analysis of emerging ethical-hacking events. While there are many academics writing on this topic, no one to my knowledge is performing metrics. There are, therefore, no current reliable open metrics for government to make decisions (it is an assumption only that intelligence is more knowledgeable on point). Many law-enforcement agencies, for example, are not authorized to run analytics on the dark Web (see ch. 2) as their work must be tied to a specific investigation or operation. While a law-enforcement agency can seek authorization to go onto Dark-Net forums, what they can do once there is limited to their enabling statute coupled with privacy restrictions. The importance of the study of ethical hacking on the dark Web is intuitive—evidence-based policy relies on evidence. If evidence is limited to media reports and police investigations, policy-makers and experts may be able to apply a corollary to a specific incidence, but they will not be aware of the extent to which citizens are increasingly taking to ethical hacking as a means of political and social discourse, or as a means of vigilantism. This book, therefore, has a distinct benefit in using three different measurements to look at ethical hacking from 1999 to 2018.

My team of researchers has been cataloguing the most interesting case law and ethical-hacking incidences for the past twenty years. The case law spans multiple jurisdictions and is included in grouped table format in chapter 4. Over 200 ethical-hacking incidences from around the world are presented, classified first by organization (e.g., Anonymous, CCC, etc.), in chapters 5 and 6. Chapters 7 through 13 then take a sample of incidences and cases and probe the incidences in detail, dissecting policy, motivation, ethical, and other considerations.

As will be seen in the case studies, some individuals involved in hacking are considered as having an addiction similar to gambling, video games, drugs, or alcohol. The role of hacking addiction in sentencing has been mentioned in a few key legal decisions, but there has been no detailed analysis of how a proper framework might be established to address technology addiction.

As will also be seen through an examination of emerging events, a significant portion of corporations and organizations are engaged in some form of counterattack/hackback, though this is not widely known and rarely spoken of publicly. On a computer network, intrusion-detection software not only detects denial-of-service attacks but also automatically initiates counter-denial-of-service attacks. There are no legal exemptions for these types of counterattacks. The problem of corporate hackback, while still controversial, is increasingly being recognized as an issue that requires new law and policy. Both governments and corporations are moving from a defensive cyber-threat posture to one of mitigation of threat, and often moving to the offensive or active cyber-security posture.

Other ethical-hacking incidents are closely tied with the objective of protecting human rights and promoting an open, transparent democracy. Many ethical hackers view their work as acts of civil disobedience, and align their actions with traditional civil disobedience as espoused by Ghandi, King, and Henry David Thoreau. Other hackers identify with an ethos of hacking that developed in the 1980s, and look to technical gurus and to the writings of "Hacktivismo Declaration" by the Cult of the Dead Cow, "The Hacker Manifesto," "The Anonymous-Anonops," the Electrohippies collective's "Client-Side Distributed Denial-of-Service," and the "Gospel According to Tux." Other groups are less ideal in their philosophy, citing motivation as "for the laughs." However, further probing of such hackers reveals that their hacking is done out of "a sense of wrongdoing," without always being able to clearly articulate what that wrongdoing is.

Denial-of-service attacks by movements such as Anonymous require critical mass for success. As will be seen, there is often a correlation between the number of participants in a denial-of-service attack and the worthiness/morality of the cause. Which causes will acquire critical mass is unpredictable, though it may be possible in future research to use a machine-learning approach across social media and Dark-Net forums to predict which causes are likely to acquire critical mass.

Explored in depth throughout the book is the concept of assumptions as dangerous. For example, it would be incorrect for governments or organizations to assume that members of ethical-hacking groups come from one type of community, race, or age demographic. Many ethical hackers are not aware that their activities are illegal, especially those participating in politically motivated denial-of-service attacks. The analytics performed in our qualitative and quantitative analysis demonstrates that this is a global trend, and not one limited to those with technical skills and prowess; the ease and affordability of hiring someone to perform acts makes ethical hacking appealing. Further, the risk of "getting caught" for many of these activities is extremely low for some acts (e.g., corporate hackback) but is quite high for other activities, especially where hacktivism targets an entity with deep pockets or where there is a strong desire to use the law as a deterrence. This has been the case with some politically sensitive acts of Anonymous. While most instances of ethical hacking are illegal, it is interesting to note that some methods used by law enforcement and by security firms contracted to perform criminal-intelligence gathering may also be illegal, or at best highly controversial. The legal framework is a blunt object that is rarely applied to certain acts, but it remains deliberately broad to allow the prosecution of an individual when political appetite changes. This, as will be seen throughout the book, makes working in cyber security—expert or not—an ever-changing field of play in which what is low risk one day is high risk the next.

This book concludes by providing a series of detailed recommendations to:

- Develop and publicize guidelines and public policy for online civil disobedience and hacktivism. In the United States, recent Department of Justice guidelines related to vulnerability and "bug bounty" programs such as HackerOne is an excellent example of government-led policy that clarify exemptions to criminal and civil law when security activities are performed within certain parameters. The guidelines promote online bug-bounty programs wherein companies pay individuals—hackers—for revealing software defects/bugs in their networks or products. The guidelines not only encourage these types of programs but recommend legal immunity in such matters. This means that a hacker who discovered a bug would be shielded from criminal and civil-law sanctions. This could be a model explored for some forms of ethical hacking.

- Run an education campaign once these guidelines are finalized.
- Allow and encourage a legitimate "space" for virtual protests.
- Implement a security-research exemption for computer offences.
- Further consider the idea of a public-interest exemption for hacking offenses. This could be done in a multi-party working group for both security-research and public-interest exemptions.
- Develop a code of conduct for counterattack and have a legislative review of how principles of self-defence might apply to a counterattack situation.
- Treat any governmental engagement with ethical hacking as legal and transparent. These activities should not be contracted out to security firms unless they are closely scrutinized and held accountable in some form of safeguard or compliance mechanism.
- Review the insecure practices of corporations and organizations that hold sensitive personal data, and consider implementing more effective legislation, such as data-breach notification—but significantly more important is the obligation to encrypt all personal information held by such entities and to encourage data minimization.
- Ensure that data owned or generated by Canadians is protected and that such data, if collected and stored, is deleted after a reasonable period when using foreign services such as Google, Facebook, and Twitter (US-based). Currently, any person who uses Google, Facebook, Twitter and similar services is subject to US Internet monitoring by governments and law enforcement, and potentially is exposed to subpoenas to release personal information even in the *absence* of a criminal investigation.

Each of these recommendations are explored in further detail in the final chapter: Toward an Ethical Hacking Framework.

On a final note: this book was conceived with web viewing in mind. As a result, many of the illustrations are less conducive to the printed format. However, since they are key to understanding the material, we have decided to include all figures and illustrations in both the print and the digital versions.

Notes

1. Samuel 2004.
2. Johnston 1996.
3. Trottier 2016.
4. The introduction is taken with permission from Maurushat 2012 ("Forced Transparency: Should We Keep Secrets in Times of Weak Law, and Should the Law do More?," *Media & Arts Law Review* 17.2).
5. Dreyfus and Assange 2011.
6. Dreyfus and Assange 2011.
7. OpenNet Initiative.
8. Chiesa, Ducci, and Ciappi 2009.

CHAPTER II

Essential Terms and Concepts

This chapter contains definitions and explanations of essential terms and concepts for those with a minimal knowledge of cyber security. As a wide readership is anticipated for the book, it is essential that terms and concepts are explained. Those with more experience in cyber security may want to either skim or go to the next relevant chapter, based on your interest. Essential terms are grouped and discussed by category:

1. Types of ethical hackers
2. Definitions and typology of ethical hacking
3. Conventional computer-security model
4. Common methods
5. Other relevant terms

These terms will be used throughout the book and explained further, where relevant to a specific context. Nonetheless, the reader is encouraged to engage with this chapter to ensure a fuller understanding of the ethical-hacking landscape.

2.1 Types of Ethical Hackers

The terminology around ethical hacking is confusing as terms mean different things according to their disciplines, and often these terms are used interchangeably. For instance, the technical world distinguishes between a hacker and a cracker, whereas the mainstream media lump both terms under the umbrella of hacker. Expressed differently, the distinction is sometimes made by referencing "black-hat," "grey-hat," and "white-hat" hackers. For clarity, these terms are defined below:

Hacker: "A person who delights in having an intimate understanding of the internal workings of a system, computers and computer networks in particular. The term is often misused in a pejorative context, where 'cracker' would be the correct term."[1]

Cracker: "A cracker is an individual who attempts to access computer systems without authorization. These individuals are often malicious, as opposed to hackers, and have many means at their disposal for breaking into a system."[2]

Black-hat hacker: (also referred to as a cracker), is "someone who uses his computer knowledge in criminal activities in order to obtain personal benefits. A typical example is a person who exploits the weaknesses of the systems of a financial institution for making some money."[3]

White-hat hacker: "Although white hat hacking can be considered similar to a black hacker, there is an important difference. A white hacker does it with no criminal intention in mind. Companies around the world, who want to test their systems, contract white hackers."[4] They will test the security of a system, and are often hired to make recommendations to improve such systems.

Grey-hat hacker: "A grey hat hacker is someone who is in between these two concepts. He may use his skills for legal or illegal acts, but not for personal gains. Grey hackers use their skills in order to prove themselves that they can accomplish a determined feat, but never do it in order to make money out of it. The moment they cross that boundary, they become black hat hackers."[5]

People who participate in ethical hacking do not fit neatly into set categories. The differentiation, however, between hackers, crackers, and hat colours plays little importance when looking at these concepts from a legal perspective. Any form of unauthorized access, modification, or impairment of data, network, or computer is a crime. There are no exemptions in most jurisdictions; hackers and crackers alike rely on the discretion of law enforcement as to whether to prosecute or turn a blind eye. Another fallacy in classifying hackers is that an individual falls solely into one definition. Each attack must be individually characterized, not the individual behind the attack. For example, you might have a hacker who predominantly breaks into systems to learn, sometimes she might even fix a security flaw in a system. The same hacker might also break into a system to collect data on individuals who are actively engaged in child pornography, and then make this data publicly available to law enforcement and the public. Yet this same hacker might also accept a fee to break into a corporation's (one they may view as unethical) database and steal a trade secret that is handed over to a competitor. Each of these examples involves unauthorized access. The difference with each attack goes to intent and motive, and involves the individual's subjective notion of what is ethical or moral. Ethical hacking, therefore, is difficult to define.

2.2 Definitions and Typology of Ethical Hacking

Ethical hacking is also a term that is used interchangeably with hacktivism in the media, but which has a distinct meaning in the computer-science discipline. For example, in the computer sciences "ethical hacking" is used to describe what is known as penetration or intrusion testing (white-hat hacking). Similarly, someone who merely participates in a denial-of-service attack for political reason would not be considered a hacker within the computer-sciences community. This type of action would be more akin to online civil disobedience.

For this book, "ethical hacking" will be used in its broadest sense to include the following activities:

Online civil disobedience: the use of any technology that connects to the Internet in pursuit of a cause or political end.

Hacktivism: the clever use of technology that involves unauthorized access to data or a computer system in pursuit of a cause or political end.[6]

Penetration/intrusion testing: is a type of information-systems security testing on behalf of the system's owners. This is known in the computer-security world as ethical hacking. There is some argument, however, as to whether penetration testing must be done with permission from a system's owners or whether a benevolent intention suffices in the absence of permission. Whether permission is obtained or not, however, does not change the common cause: improving security.

Vulnerability discovery: is the process of finding weaknesses and ways in a network, device, or within an organization that are capable of being exploited by others (sometimes for nefarious reasons). Vulnerability discovery is often done with the authorization of the owner/operator of a network or device, but not always.

Counterattack: is also referred to as hackback or strikeback. Counterattack is when an individual or organization who is subject to an attack on their data, network, or computer takes similar measures to attack back at the hacker/cracker. For example, when an individual or organization is subject to a denial-of-service attack, that organization might initiate their own denial-of-service attack on the responsible party's website.

Security activism: is similar to penetration/intrusion testing in that the cause is to improve security. Security activism goes beyond mere testing of security, however, to gather intelligence on crackers, and to launch active attacks to disrupt criminal online enterprises. One example is the taking down of a botnet (see definition below).

My definition of ethical hacking potentially includes all the above, though ethical-hacking incidences are, like most things, contextual and fact-specific. I have chosen not to require that an act be "legal" as all the case studies discussed in this book are captured as illegal under hacking provisions that adopt a strict liability approach. For example, when access or use of data, network, or computer is unauthorized it is captured under criminal provisions. Some jurisdictions, as will be seen in the book, require intent to commit a criminal act, other jurisdictions have hacking provisions with no mention of intent or motive. The absence of intent in a criminal provision is known as a strict liability offence.

Ethical hacking, then, is the non-violent use of a technology in pursuit of a cause, political or otherwise, which is often legally and morally ambiguous.[7]

The use of a technology that resulted in acts of violence or physical harm would fall outside the scope of ethical hacking. Cyber jihadism, controversially, is included under this definition if the actions do not result in violence or physical harm, though arguably this is difficult to measure.

2.3 Conventional Computer-Security-Threat Model

The conventional computer-security model is adopted whereby threatening events impinge on vulnerabilities to cause harm. Safeguards are then used to prevent or ameliorate that harm. At least that is the theory. Some ethical-hacking incidences do not cause harm, or at least not in the conventional way. Nonetheless, these incidences are often treated as falling within the standard computer-security-threat model. More fully:

Threat: A threat is a circumstance that could result in harm or damage and may be natural, accidental, or intentional. A party responsible for an intentional threat is referred to as an attacker.

Threatening event: A threatening event is an instance of a generic threat (such as malicious code) that may cause harm or damage.

Harm: Harm is anything that has deleterious consequences, which includes injury to persons, damage to property, financial loss, loss of value of an asset, and loss of reputation and confidence. Harm arises because a threatening event impinges on a vulnerability.

Vulnerability: A vulnerability is a feature or weakness that gives rise to susceptibility to a threat. Vulnerabilities exist in software and hardware.

Exploit: An exploit is the implementation, in software, of a vulnerability.

Safeguard: A safeguard is a measure intended to avoid or reduce vulnerabilities. Safeguards may or may not be effective and may be subject to countermeasures.

A functioning cyber-security ecosystem has an attack-safeguard-countermeasures cycle. Increasingly, as will be seen in the book, there is the need to identify and remedy threats and vulnerabilities before attacks may be instigated.

The question becomes to what extent does ethical hacking challenge the conventional computer-security-threat model? This question is explored in a variety of contexts, drawing on case studies throughout the book.

2.4 Common Methods Used in Ethical Hacking

The following section provides explanations of some of the most common methods used in ethical hacking.

SQL injection: Defacing a website involves the insertion of images or text into a website. This is often done via a SQL (structured query language) injection. A SQL injection is an attack in which computer code is inserted into strings that are later passed to a database.[8] A SQL injection can allow someone to target a database giving them access to the website. This allows the person to deface the website with whatever images or text they wish.

DNS hijacking: DNS (domain name system) hijacking allows a person to redirect web traffic to a rogue domain name server.[9] The rogue server runs a substitute IP address to a legitimate domain name. For example, www.alanna.com's true IP address could be 197.653.3.1, but the user would be directed to 845.843.4.1 when they look for www.alanna.com. This is another way of redirecting traffic to a political message or image.

Adware: Adware refers to any software program in which advertising banners are displayed as a result of the software's operation. This may be in the form of a pop-up or as advertisements displayed on the side of a website, such as on Google or Facebook.

Phishing: Phishing refers to the dishonest attempt to obtain information through electronic means by appearing to be a trust-worthy entity.

Ransomware: Ransomware is a type of malicious software that prevents the user from accessing or using their data (often through encrypting the data), whereby a fee must be paid or service per-formed before the user's data is decrypted.

Malware: A simplistic definition of malware is malicious software. Malware, for the purpose of this research, is defined as potentially harmful software or a component of software that has been installed without authorization to a third-party device.[10]

Virus: A virus is a "block of code that inserts copies of itself into other programs." Viruses generally require a positive act by the user to activate the virus. Such a positive act would include opening an email or attachment containing the virus. Viruses often delay or hinder the performance of functions on a computer, and may infect other software programs. They do not, however, propagate copies of themselves over networks. Again, a positive act is required for both infection and propagation.[11]

Worm: A worm is a program that propagates copies of itself over networks. It does not infect other programs, nor does it require a positive act by the user to activate the worm. It replicates by exploit-ing vulnerabilities.

Zero day: Zero day is an exploit or vulnerability that is exploited against a target on the day on which public awareness of the existence of the vulnerability occurs (i.e., zero days have elapsed between the awareness and the use). These vulnerabilities are typically considered to be the most valuable as the utility and value of an exploit or vulnerability markedly decreases once it is known, as vendors produce patches or users reconfigure their systems to ameliorate the effect of the vulnerability.[12]

Back door: A back door is a method of accessing a computer program or network that circumvents security mechanisms. Sometimes a programmer will install a back door so that the programmer can accesses the program to perform security patches, troubleshoot, or monitor use. Attackers, however, can also use back doors that they discover (or install themselves) as part of an exploit.[13]

Distributed denial of service (DDoS): A DDoS attack is the most common form of online civil protest. A denial-of-service attack is distributed when multiple systems flood a channel's bandwidth and/or flood a host's capacity (e.g., overflowing the buffers).[14] This technique renders a website inaccessible.

DDoS attacks are performed with a botnet, with several of the compromised computers sending packets to the target computer simultaneously. A DDoS attack may also be distributed by use of peer-to-peer nodes.[15] The importance of botnets is explained below.

A botnet is comprised of core elements.[16] They are defined below for clarity and will be re-examined in more specific contexts in the analysis that follows this section.

Botnet: A botnet is a collection of compromised computers that are remotely controlled by a bot master.

Compromised computer: The term "compromised computer"[17] is commonly used interchangeably, and in some cases wrongly, in the literature with "zombie," "bot," and "bot client," which confuses hardware with software, creates inconsistency of usage, and may be confusing to users. Herein, a "compromised computer" is a computer that is connected to the Internet (an internet is any network of any size that uses the protocol TCP/IP, and the Internet is the largest such internet)[18] and on which a bot is installed.[19] The computer is thus said to be compromised.

Bot: A bot is software that is capable of being invoked from a remote location in order to provide the invoker with the capacity to cause the compromised computer to perform a function.[20] Botnets have a modular structure whereby modules (bots) may be added or taken away from each bot to add to it new exploits and capabilities. This ensures a botnet master's ability to rapidly respond to technical measures set up to infiltrate and take down the botnet.[21]

Bot server and command-and-control (C&C) source: C&C refers to the communications infrastructure of a botnet. A botnet master issues commands and exercises control over the performance of bots. Bots fetch data from a pre-programmed location, and interpret that data as triggers for action and instructions on what function to perform. The pre-programmed location is known as the bot server or C&C source. C&C is achieved by means of a bot server. The term "server" refers to any software that provide services on request by another piece of software, which is called a client. The bot requests and the server responds. Where the client is a bot, the server is reasonably enough called a bot server. Common bot servers are IRC servers, HTTP servers, the DNS (by means of TXT records), peer-to-peer nodes, cloud nodes, and increasingly devices otherwise known as the Internet of things (e.g., Xbox).

Traffic between the C&C source and its bots may be in clear or encrypted form. For example, IRC is an open-network protocol that can also be used with SSL (Secure Sockets Layer). SSL enables the establishment of an encrypted channel. Where the C&C of a botnet occurs in IRC alone, the information is openly available for viewing and tracking. When SSL is used in conjunction with IRC, the information is encrypted and is, therefore, not visible to anyone who lacks access to the relevant decryption key. For the purpose of clarity, there will be no further reference to the term "bot server" here unless in a quote. Rather, "C&C source" will be the term used throughout.

Multihoming: Involves the configuration of a domain to have several IP addresses. If any one IP address is blocked or ceases to be available, the others essentially back it up. Blocking or removing a single IP address, therefore, is not an effective solution to removing the content. The content merely rotates to another IP address.

Dynamic DNS: A service that enables the domain name entry for the relevant domain name to be updated very promptly, every time the IP address changes. A dynamic DNS provider enables a customer to either update the IP address via the provider's web page or using a tool that automatically detects the change in IP address and amends the DNS entry. To work effectively, the time-to-live value for the DNS entry must be set very short, to prevent cached entries scattered around the Internet serving up outdated IP addresses. Chapter 7 will explore DNS policy to prevent dynamic DNS being used by botnet masters.

Fast flux: A particular, dynamic DNS technique used by botnet masters whereby DNS records are frequently changed. This could be every five minutes.[22] Essentially, large volumes of IP addresses are rapidly rotated through the DNS records for a specific domain. This is similar to dynamic DNS tactics. The main difference between dynamic DNS and fast flux is the automation and rapidity of rotation with a fast-flux botnet.[23] Some fast-flux botnets rotate IP addresses every five minutes, and others every hour. Introducing a policy whereby IP addresses are not allowed to quickly rotate at the DNS level will be explored in chapter 7.[24]

Distributed Command and Control (or super botnets): A type of botnet that draws on a small botnet comprised of fifteen to twenty bots. The botnet herders may have anywhere from 10,000 to 250,000 bots at their disposal but use a select few for a particular purpose. The smaller botnet is then used to issue commands to larger botnets (hence the term "distributed command and control").[25]

Encryption: Encryption is the conversion of plain text into "ciphertext," encrypted information. Encryption acts to conceal or prevent the meaning of the data from being known by parties without decryption codes. Botnet instructions commonly use encryption. Encrypted instruction can then not be analyzed, making investigating, mitigation, and prevention much more difficult. Public-key cryptography is often used. In public-key cryptography, a twin pair of keys is created: one is private, the other public. Their fundamental property is that, although one key cannot be derived from the other, a message encrypted by one key can only be decrypted by the other key.

Proxy servers: Proxy servers refer to a service (a computer system or an application) that acts as an intermediary for requests from clients by forwarding requests to other servers. One use of proxy servers is to get around connection blocks such as authentication challenges and Internet filters. Another is to hide the origin of a connection. Proxy servers obfuscate a communication path such that user M connects to a website through proxy server B, which again connects through proxy server Z, whereby the packets appear to come from Z not M. Traceback to Z yields information of an additional hurdle, however, as packets also appear to come from B. Other proxy servers such as Tor are anonymous. Tor is also known as an onion router. Tor is described as follows:

Tor protects you by bouncing your communications around a distributed network of relays run by volunteers all around the world: it prevents somebody from watching your Internet connection from learning what sites you visit, and it prevents the sites you visit from learning your physical location.[26]

Tor is described as onion routing due to the use of multiple layers of proxy servers, similar to the multiple layers of an onion. Tor is used by users in heavily Internet-censored countries, like China and Iran, to access blocked websites, as well as by some criminals to prevent law enforcement from traceback to the source.

Virtual private network (VPN) service: A VPN is a network that uses a public telecommunications infrastructure (usually the Internet) to connect remote sites or users together.[27] This connection allows secure access to an organization's network. Instead of a dedicated, real-world connection such as a leased line, a VPN uses virtual connections "routed through the Internet from an organization's private network to the remote site or employee."[28] VPN is made secure through cryptographic tunnelling protocols that provide confidentiality by blocking packet sniffing and interception software. VPN is used by many companies and government agencies, as well as by cybercriminal gangs such as will be seen in section 2.6 with the Mariposa botnet.

Rootkits: Rootkits are software or hardware devices designed to gain administrator-level control and sustain such control over a computer system without being detected.[29] A rootkit is used to obscure the operation of malware or a botnet from monitoring and investigation.

Peer-to-peer (P2P) communications: P2P "is any distributed network architecture composed of participants that make a portion of their resources (such as processing power, disk storage or network bandwidth) directly available to other network participants, without the need for central coordination instances."[30] Famous botnets such as Waledac, Torpig, and Mariposa use P2P protocol as their backup C&C. A P2P network relies on the capacity of multiple participants' computers, each of which has both client and server capabilities. This differs from conventional client-server architectures, where a relatively low number of servers provide the core function of a service or application.[31] Such networks are useful for many purposes, such as sharing of scientific information among researchers, file-sharing of videos and music, and for telephone traffic. P2P operates on peer nodes.[32] P2P may be used to send content in clear or encrypted format. The ad hoc distribution of P2P makes it an ideal server location for C&C. The use of P2P channels allows an additional layer of rapid IP-address fluctuation. For this reason, botnets that use P2P channels are seen as offering the equivalent of "double fast-flux." The diagrams in figure 1 explain a botnet.

In step 1, the botnet herder needs to install bots on computers and thereby acquire compromised computers in order to build his/her botnet.

In step 2, the botnet master then makes content available to the bots, which causes them to perform actions. The botnet master may or may not be the botnet herder who builds the botnet. The botnet master could, for example, hire the use of the botnet.

There are three ways of using a botnet to perform a denial-of-service attack:

Make the botnet. In the first, a person would have to physically make a botnet through painstaking hours of labour, as it would involve compromising several hundred, if not thousands, of computers. This type of botnet would require the botnet master to have a high level of computer skills.

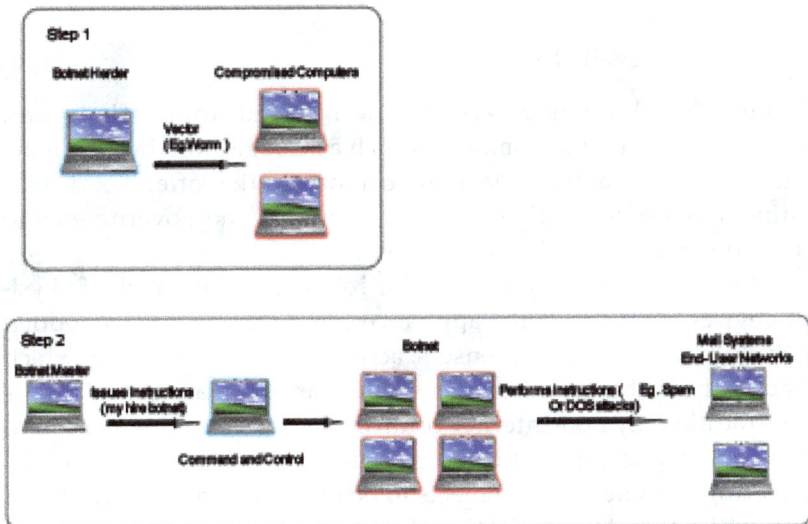

Figure 1. Steps in Procuring and Using a Botnet.

Hire/rent a botnet. The second type involves simply hiring someone to execute a denial-of-service attack. This requires no computer skills, but for the ability to use a search engine (such as Google). Bot-agent design and bot delivery have become a commoditized service industry.[33] A small botnet is sufficient to launch an effective denial-of-service attack causing much damage, and costs as little as US$200 for a twenty-four-hour attack.[34] A person does not require any special computer skills to use a botnet to commit a crime. Figure 10 later in the book sketches the commercialization of denial-of-service attacks with a botnet. The customer would merely specify the targeted website to attack, pay a nominal fee of US$200, and a denial-of-service attack would be launched for twenty-four hours against the website.

LOIC. The third type is where the user allows their device to become part of a botnet for the purpose of participating in a DDoS protest with LOIC (as expressed above, Low Orbit Ion Canon) or similar software. LOIC is a free software program and is used for most of the denial-of-service attacks performed by members of Anonymous, for example. Use of LOIC requires minimal computer skills. One googles LOIC, downloads the software with a click, types in the URL (e.g., www.paypal.com), and presses start. The denial-of-service attack then commences and people from all over the world may join in using LOIC.

2.5 Other Relevant Terms

Cloud: The cloud is a term for web-based applications and data-storage solutions. Companies such as Google, Microsoft, Yahoo, and Amazon are among the many companies that offer cloud computing services for individuals, corporations, and governments to store and access their data online, on the cloud.[35]

Internet of things (IoT): The IoT refers to "the network of physical devices, vehicles, home appliances, and other items embedded with electronics, software, sensors, actuators, and connectivity which enables these things to connect, collect and exchange data."[36] IoT sees traditionally non-Internet-connected devices or objects becoming connected to Internet-connected devices in a network, thereby rendering such devices or objects to be monitored and controlled.

API keys: An application programming interface (API) key "is a code passed in by computer programs calling an application programming interface...to identify the calling program, its developer, or its user to the website. API keys are used to track and control how the API is being used, for example to prevent malicious use or abuse of the API (as defined perhaps by terms of service)."[37]

Surface Web: "The Surface Web is the portion of the Web that has been crawled and indexed (and thus searchable) by standard search engines such as Google or Bing via a regular web browser."[38]

Deep Web: The Deep Web refers to non-indexed websites (websites which do not appear in your web page browser's search engine results). This can include publicly accessible online databases, pay-to-access databases, subscription-based services, and webpages located behind password-protected web pages.[39]

Dark Web: Deeper than the Deep Web, the dark Web is accessible via software such as Tor, which enables users to anonymously connect to web pages. The dark Web is a space for political dissidents, whistle-blowers, and journalists to communicate with others, but it is also a space for cybercriminals to operate in due to its somewhat anonymizing features and degrees of anonymity.[40]

Internet protocol (IP) address: "An Internet Protocol address (IP address) is a numerical label assigned to each device connected to a computer network that uses the Internet Protocol for communication. An IP address serves two principal functions: host or network interface identification and location addressing."[41]

URL: "A Uniform Resource Locator (URL), colloquially termed a web address, is a reference to a web resource that specifies its location on a computer network and a mechanism for retrieving it. A URL is a specific type of Uniform Resource Identifier (URI), although many people use the two terms interchangeably. URLs occur most commonly to reference web pages (http), but are also used for file transfer (ftp), email (mailto), database access (JDBC), and many other applications."[42]

Notes

1. RFC 1392 Internet Users Glossary.
2. RFC 1392 Internet Users Glossary.
3. Hacking Alert, "White Hat and Grey Hat Hacking."
4. Hacking Alert, "White Hat and Grey Hat Hacking."
5. Hacking Alert, "White Hat and Grey Hat Hacking."
6. Samuel 2004.

7. Samuel 2004.

8. Security Spotlight 2010.

9. Security Spotlight 2010.

10. Clarke 2009.

11. Pfleeger 2006.

12. Oremus 2013.

13. Rouse 2007.

14. For more, see Wikipedia, "Denial of Service Attack (distributed)."

15. Athanasopoulos, Anagnostakis, and Markatos 2006.

16. Solomon and Evron 2008.

17. The term "compromised computer" has been selected over the term "compromised device." A computer may be as little as a processor (a personal computer will often contain multiple processors) or may be the world's largest computer. The term "computer" is used here to refer to any computing device, even if it is commonly called by some other name, and includes current and future devices with computing capabilities which may be connected to the Internet, including mobile phones, tablets, surveillance cameras, controllers for ADCs (analogue-digital converters) such as monitoring water levels, etc. For this reason, Clarke, for example, prefers "device." I have chosen "compromised computer," however, because it reflects the terminology used in computer science and information studies on botnets.

18. TCP/IP is often used as a single acronym when in fact it references two key protocols. TCP refers to transmission control protocol. TCP is a connection-oriented protocol that establishes a communication channel, known as a data stream, between two network hosts. IP refers to Internet protocol and is an identification and addressing scheme that, in the case of the latter, links distinct numerical labels as IP addresses. See Pfleeger and Pfleeger 2006.

19. A computer may still be compromised in the absence of a botnet master. Where a controller is gone but where a botnet continues to infect computers, it is referred to as an "orphan botnet." See Gutman, "The Commercial Malware Industry."

20. Modified definition of Clarke's (2009), where he defines bots as "(Generally, a program that operates as an agent for a user or another program. More specifically:) software that is capable of being invoked remotely in order to perform a particular function."

21. Dunham and Melnick 2009.

22. See "How Fast-Flux Service Networks Work" at http://www.honeynet.org/node/132.

23. Dunham and Melnick 2009.

24. L. Gaaster, *GNSO Council Issues Report on Fast Flux Hosting,* March 31, 2008, available at https://gnso.icann.org/sites/default/files/filefield_5868/gnso-issues-report-fast-flux-25mar08.pdf.
25. Barakat and Khattab, "A Comparative Study of Traditional Botnets Versus Super-Botnet," in INFOSEC 2010.
26. Tor Project, "Anonymity Online." Tor is available at https://www.torproject.org. There are many other types of anonymizing proxy servers and similar technologies, such as Phantom Access Agent.
27. Wikipedia, "Virtual Private Network."
28. Tyson 2010.
29. Pfleeger and Pfleeger 2006.
30. The author looked at many different definitions of P2P and found the Wikipedia definition had the best description; see Wikipedia "Peer-to-peer."
31. Clarke 2004.
32. Oram 2001.
33. Ollmann, cited in Greenberg 2010.
34. Ollmann, cited in Greenberg 2010.
35. Soghoian 2009.
36. Wikipedia, "Internet of Things."
37. Wikipedia, "Application Programming Interface Key."
38. Rudesill, Caverlee, and Sui 2015.
39. Rudesill, Caverlee, and Sui 2015, 8.
40. Rudesill, Caverlee, and Sui 2015, 8.
41. Wikipedia, "IP Address."
42. Wikipedia, "URL."

CHAPTER III

Methodology and Quantitative Studies of Ethical Hacking: Evidence-Based Decision and Policy-Making

This chapter features additional research by Kevin Kim, Adrian Agius, and Richard Li.

3.1 Report for Public Safety Canada, 2011

As mentioned in chapter 1, some of this book is based on a report that was commissioned in the fall of 2010 by Public Safety Canada. The report—*Ethical Hacking*—was finalized in 2011.[1] The report was not made available to the public at the time but was subject to freedom-of-information requests. Generously, Public Safety Canada has allowed me to retain intellectual property to publish the research. The bulk of the report, therefore, has found its way into this book.

The 2011 report examined five types of ethical hacking: hacktivism, online civil disobedience, penetration/intrusion testing, security activism, and counterattack/hackback. Each category was defined and a series of related aspects were examined using the following sub-headings:

- Selected Case Studies
- Motivation
- Main Targets
- Relation Between Targets and Motivations
- Fundamental Principles of "Hacker Ethics"

- Perceptions of the Illegality of Activity
- Deterrence Effects of Case Law and Convictions
- Relevant Case-Law Convictions
- Observations

The case studies for the report were selected based on a gathering of ethical-hacking incidences globally from 1999 until 2010. An extensive, multidisciplinary literature review (information systems, psychology, fiction, risk management, computer science, law, political science) was conducted and is included in the references at the end of this book. This was a labour-intensive process where we did a comprehensive literature review in three languages—English, French, and Russian. Most of the incidences were discovered due to media coverage of the topic.

The report was written in a few months because I was able to draw on my PhD work in cybercrime, entitled "Botnet Badinage: Regulatory Approaches to Combating Botnets" (PhD diss., University of New South Wales, 2011), where I interviewed people involved in the cyber-security industry (including law enforcement), as well as with some cybercriminals, and attended conferences around the world, including in eastern Europe, the United Kingdom, Canada, Australia, Hong Kong, and the United States. Throughout this process, I was inspired by many of the selfless and brave risks many cyber-security professionals took to help protect and secure networks and infrastructure, and to safeguard users. Their actions were often not done for monetary gain. Their passion for cyber security was undeniable. They worked in silence, with users and organizations, to protect systems all the while unaware of the efforts taken and the self-sacrifices made. And the risks they took were not always proportionate to the benefits gained. Many of these risks involved the uncertainty of legal sanction, whether it be criminal or civil lawsuits. Many of the technical and legal challenges for ethical hacking bare some similarities with hacking activities in general.

At the time, in 2010, there were few interviews or empirical studies on ethical hacking. The studies that existed were purely qualitative. Two of the most significant qualitative studies of ethical hackers were Dr. Suelette Dreyfus and Julian Assange's (2011) book, *Underground*, and Dr. Alexandra Samuel's (2004) PhD thesis on hacktivism and political participation. Dreyfus and Samuel were interviewed for the report.[2]

At the time of writing the report, there were only a few quantitative studies on hacking. The most prominent was a United Nations Interregional Crime and Justice Research Institute (UNICRI) study by Raoul Chiesa, Stefania Ducci, and Silvio Ciappi published in 2009 as *Profiling Hackers: The Science of Criminal Profiling as Applied to the World of Hacking*. The book provided a comprehensive look at hackers globally, using both qualitative and quantitative analysis. However, because hacktivism had not yet become popular there was no differentiation of hacking for political or social cause within the analysis. That is because most forms of ethical hacking, hacktivism, and online civil disobedience did not take flight until after 2011. While the authors were not able to be interviewed for my report, I gratefully borrowed some statistics and other information from *Profiling Hackers*.

While this book borrows heavily from the 2011 report for Public Safety Canada, it will deviate from it in two main ways. First, incidences from 2011 to 2018 are analyzed in this book, which means that new qualitative studies are referenced. Second, this chapter uses three new methodologies to provide a more comprehensive quantitative examination of ethical-hacking incidences around the globe.

In the first instance, we used the global database GDELT Analysis Service to explore incidences between 2013 and 2014. This methodology allowed us to examine incidences reported in a hundred different languages.

Second, we used standard SQL to customize the search queries using Google's BigQuery for the years 2015, 2016, and 2017, and then used the visualization features from Tableau software. This also allowed us to search through a hundred different languages of online media and blog reports of ethical hacking.

Lastly, we wrote python scripts to analyze data from cyber-jihad and hacking forums on the Dark Net to look for hacking incidences (contemplated, planned, or executed) that might have elements of ethical hacking. These data sets run from 2012 to 2016 for most of the hacking forums, while the cyber-jihad forums run from 2000 to 2012.

These methodologies are examined below and in greater detail in sections 3.3 to 3.5. The important findings from the different methodologies are summarized in section 3.2.

3.2 Summary of Findings

My original methodology for the report only allowed the capture of incidences that were reported online through manual searching in the media in English, French, and Russian. Adding GDLET and then SQL using BigQuery did not change the source of incident retrieval as these only pull information from reported online media and blog sites. These methodologies did, however, allow us to discover incidences reported in over a hundred languages, allowing for a picture of how ethical hacking was emerging globally.

The above methodologies are limited as they only allowed us to look at incidences that had been reported online by media and in blogs. This of course left a large gap in accuracy in determining how prevalent ethical hacking was becoming around the world. The opportunity arose where we were able to use publicly available Dark-Net data sets from the AZSecure-data.org involves an online portal that provides access to data collected on the Dark Net. The majority of the forum datasets have been collected by the University of Arizona's Artificial Intelligence Lab. While these data sets were only available in English, they revealed the magnitude and growth of ethical hacking in ways that traditional media analysis could not. Some of the important findings are summarized in table 1.

Future studies should run analytics on Dark Nets in languages other than English where data is available. Equally if not more important is the performance of data analytics for ethical-hacking discussions on social media, and in the hacker communication platform called Internet Relay Chat (IRC).

I have begun to run more data analytics on other Dark-Net forums, as well as in the IRC. For an updated look at ethical hacking, and to use interactive ethical-hacking maps, please visit www.ethicalhackinglaw.org/statistics or you can link to this through www.alanacybersecurity.com.

Table 1. Summary of Findings

Method	Coverage	Estimated Number of Incidences	Notable Differences and Observations
Online media sample (1999 until 2017)	1999–2012	137	English, French, and Russian media and blog postings.
GDLET	2013–2015	10,000	100+ languages, which revealed that ethical hacking was prevalent globally. Could only search with pre-selected terms.
SQL BIGQUERY	2015–2017	50,000	100+ languages which revealed that ethical hacking is prevalent globally. Could search with a variety of terms chosen by the researchers. There was an absence of incidences reported in Vietnam, Malaysia, Mexico and Brazil which may be due to heavy government influence of privatised media, censorship and fear of physical attack of journalists and bloggers. Countries with known heavy state censorship such as China, Iran and Saud Arabia reported many incidences of ethical hacking though these instances were consistently related to patriotic hacking.
Cyber-jihad Dark Net forums	2000–2012	43,000	We only looked a cyber-jihad forums in the English language. False positives were difficult to ascertain.

Method	Coverage	Estimated Number of Incidences	Notable Differences and Observations
Hacking Dark-Net forums	2012–2016	922,000	We could not fully clean the data due to size restrictions, and are therefore unable to isolate return searches that referred to the same incident. Our rates of false positive are unknown. We are likewise unable to provide positive predictive value. We analyzed one string of communications where there were four participants each responding approximately three times. If we performed this sample on the 922,000 the rate of single incidences would be closer to 77,000 separate incidences.

3.3 GDELT Analysis Service—Event Data (with Kevin Kim)

Our previous methodology only allowed us to view incidences reported in English-language media and blogs. With the GDELT research we could see a more global picture of ethical hacking, though the research revealed that there were many countries where no incidences of ethical hacking occurred. Possible reasons why, along with a more nuanced exploration of this research, is found below.

The GDELT Analysis Service is a free cloud-based database that allows you to explore, visualize, and export global event data. No technical expertise is required to use this service. This service does not allow the user to search with free text. The user must choose a theme or combination of themes. GDELT is an open database with approximately 1.5 billion geo-references within its data sets. The references are from media, other open data sets, and blogs across one hundred languages. The references run from January 1, 1979, to the present.

For our purposes, we selected the Events Data Heatmap to perform and visualize our research.

The next step required us to select a search theme or combination of themes (see fig. 2). Ethical hacking, hacktivism, and online civil disobedience were not identified as possible themes. The closest search parameters we could find were "cyber attack" in combination with "civil liberties."

We limited our searches to 2013 and 2015, receiving the data as a heat map with exported CSV (comma-separated values) file in Excel, where the geo-referencing details as well as links to the website or blog reporting the incident—see figure 3.

Each incident reveals the link to the media or blog source. The most prevalent online reporting occurred in the areas coloured red, de-escalating to orange, yellow, green, and blue.

Curiously, there are many countries where no incidences of ethical hacking occur. This indicates that there are some possible inconsistencies. We then compared the heat maps and timelines with *Freedom on the Net* reports from the non-governmental Freedom House. *Freedom on the Net* is the most widely utilized resource worldwide

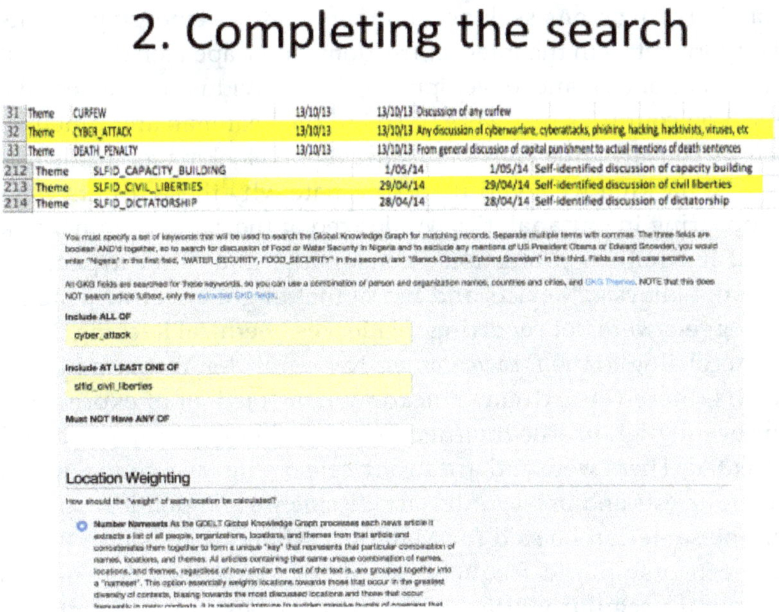

Figure 2. Search Themes.

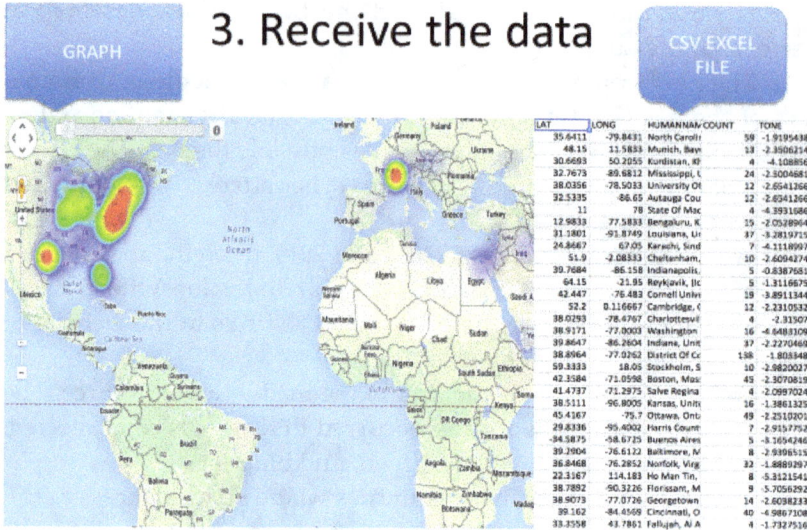

Figure 3. CSV Data Retrieval and Heat Map.

for activists, government officials, journalists, businesses, and inter-national organizations seeking to understand the emerging threats and opportunities in the internet-freedom landscape globally, as well as regards policies and developments in individual countries. We focused on countries that were "cold" in the heat map and timeline. When we consulted the Freedom House reports looking for incidences of ethical hacking we could then speculate why these results were not appearing in our analytics. We looked at the general framework around journalism protections, censorship, and other aspects in Vietnam, Malaysia, Mexico, and Brazil that might affect why media and bloggers were not reporting incidences of ethical hacking.

According to the *Freedom on the Net* report for Vietnam in 2013 and 2014, there was extreme crackdown on freedom of expression, with several high-profile Internet writers and bloggers arrested and prosecuted. There were and are strong censorship laws coupled with strategic arrests and prosecutions for dissidence and political opposi-tion. The same can be said for Malaysia, where there is also heavy media censorship and frequent arrests of journalists. Journalists in Brazil are regularly attacked by corrupt law enforcement and criminal organizations. News media is privately owned but relies heavily on state advertising, which is said to lead to government manipulation of media. The same may be said of Mexico, where journalists and bloggers have been routinely attacked. The government also heavily subsidizes and advertises on the country's biggest media outlets, Televisia and TV Azteca.

Curiously, other countries with strict media censorship, such as China, still reported many incidences of ethical hacking (over 1,000 incidences appear for China from 2013 to 2014). Similarly, in Iran and Saudi Arabia, where there is also strict media control, there were still many incidences of ethical hacking that appeared in our data (Iran had 511 incidences and Saudi Arabia had 110). This discrepancy could be explained by the fact that these countries have excellent engineering and computer-science sectors, with many skilled and savvy computer users who would know how to use proxies and host blogs on sites that are not easily taken down. This discrepancy can also be explained by the deep levels of nationalism and patriotism within these countries. Studies of hacktivism in China[3] found strong correlations between hacktivism and patriotism, especially within the "red hacker" Honker Union, a Chinese group whose own code of conduct includes "Love your country. Strictly forbid attacks against any legitimate institutes within the country…. Uniformly defend the country and respond to defiant acts by foreign countries."[4] While patriotic hacking may not be condoned by the Chinese government, it also isn't censored in Chinese media or blogs.

3.4 Google's BigQuery (with Richard Li)

While the GDELT databases allowed us to capture a more global snapshot of ethical hacking, the process of running the analytics was very slow, requiring systems to run days to deliver basic analytics. Google's BigQuery allowed us to process higher volumes of data. We used the same terminology as we did in GDELT, and the same amount of languages were automatically translated. We captured nearly double the amount of incidences using BigQuery as explored below.

Below are incidences that were captured using a slightly different methodology and visualization. BigQuery is a data-analytics service that allows users to enter their own queries (i.e., not limited to set themes), export the data, and conduct analytics on the data using standard SQL. SQL allows complex search queries returning near-real-time results, as opposed to GDELT, which only allowed searches with pre-determined themes.

The data in GDELT is open and free, but performing search queries using Google's BigQuery is not free. Due to limited funding, we were only able to perform analytics over 2015, 2016, and 2017.

We used the same terms—"cyber attacks" and "civil liberties"— as we had previously done. While we have results for 2015, 2016, and 2017, only the image for 2017 is displayed in figure 4. We were then able to use Tableau software to visualize the incidences.[5]

There were over 50,000 incidences of ethical hacking in 2017 alone. As we will see below, once data other than media and blogs were used, the incidences climb exponentially. Of course, the volume of incidences only shines light on the prevalence of ethical hacking. Understanding motivation, likely targets, the cause and effects of such occurrences can only be found through different data-mining techniques, and through qualitative research.

Figure 4. Ethical Hacking 2017.
Data retrieved and analyzed on May 4, 2017.

3.5 Dark-Net Analysis of Malware and Cyber-Jihad Forums

The data sets being used for this research are broadly categorized as the dark Web or Dark Net. Recall that the surface Web is the layer of the Internet that most people use on a daily basis—it involves using the World Wide Web protocol; it is also indexed, which means that you can use search engines such as Google to find content. The Deep Web is the next layer of the Internet where most data traffic occurs. It is not indexed by search engines; therefore, is unsearchable for the layperson via Google or Bing. One must go to a specific website in order to perform such a search. For example, I cannot access my medical-claim history in Australia through Google. I must first go to the Medibank site, enter my username and password, and then conduct a search. The dark Web or Dark Net is a subset of the Deep Web that can only be accessed by using encrypted services such as a TOR or VPN or both. It is the portion of the Internet where the darkest and most illegal activities occur. It is also not indexed. For our purposes, the dark Web as cited here refers to forum activity captured for the purposes of analyzing malware and the Jihadi social-media movement.

We ran analytics on many Dark-Net forums, which were categorized into two types: cyber-jihad and hacking/malware forums. Each of these are explained in greater detail below.

3.5.1 Cyber-Jihad Forums (with Adrian Agius)

We analyzed data that had been previously collected by the Data Infrastructure and Building Blocks (DIBB) program. The DIBB project is a collaboration between the University of Arizona, Drexel University, University of Virginia, University of Texas at Dallas, and the University of Utah. It is partly funded by the National Science Foundation, an independent US government agency supporting research in non-medical fields of science and engineering. The sets of data collected by the DIBB are forums, threads, and posts scattered across both the public-facing internet and the dark Web. DIBB provides open-source data (i.e., open-source intelligence information) for the intelligence and security informatics community.

For the purposes of streamlining the data processing and cleansing required for analysis, only forums that contained predominantly English-language postings were considered. English categorizations were provided by the DIBB, which greatly assisted in pre-determining sets to be downloaded. Each of the data sets used for analysis was stored on a server operated by the DIBB. Each forum was allocated a text file and was directly downloaded into a local environment for processing.

The python script could not be easily run over the existing data sets without being further cleaned. According to data scientists Rahm and Hai Do:

> *Data cleaning*, also called *data cleansing* or *scrubbing*, deals with detecting and removing errors and inconsistencies from data in order to improve the quality of data. Data quality problems are present in single data collections, such as files and databases, e.g., due to misspellings during data entry, missing information or other invalid data. When multiple data sources need to be integrated, e.g., in data warehouses, federated database systems or global web-based information systems, the need for data cleaning increases significantly. This is because the sources often contain redundant data in different representations. In order to provide access to accurate and consistent data, consolidation of different data representations and elimination of duplicate information become necessary.[6]

Cleaning data is a laborious process. Dark-Web forum data is in an unstructured format, which means that one must clean and categorize the data to render it useful for analytics. In our case, the forum data was already partially cleaned by DIBB, but required further cleaning and categorization for our purposes.

Storing all the data collected into a single repository would make it easier to run any functions or queries required to gain insight into the data set as a whole. Thus, the first python script written to process the data was one which appended each set of forum data into a single file. Each file appended was tagged with its filename, as well as a broad categorization as either a "cyberterror"- or "geoweb"-themed forum. This will provide contextual relevance for later use.

Once collected and tagged appropriately, the consolidated file was then ingested to detect anomalies and remove any problematic lines of data. This included lines where special characters, including Arabic and other special keyboard characters, were present. As a blanket rule, any line of data that contained such characters were deleted from the set of data. (Ideally, in the future we will run data analytics on Chinese-, Russian-, and Arabic-language forums.) We were able to delete entries that were duplicated in order to reduce false positives. Therefore, if the same pseudonym discussed an online ethical-hacking incident, this single incidence would be counted as one, as opposed to being counted as thirty separate incidences due to the pseudonym referencing the same incident thirty times.

The following structure prevailed.

MessageID—ID of forum post
ThreadID—ID of parent thread
ThreadName—Name of parent thread
MemberID—ID of posting member
MemberName—Name of posting member
Message—Content of forum post in question
Pyear—Year of post
Pmonth—Month of post
Pday—Day of post
Pdate—Aggregated field of above three times
ThreadFirstMessageID—ID of first message in thread
Forumname—Generated field, recording name, of originating forum
Classification—Generated field, describing type of message content

To give context to programs analyzing the content stored in the aggregated CSV file, the content contained in each forum post needed to be tokenized. Tokenization is the process of individually segmenting each word within a larger corpus. Tokenization is a fundamental part of natural language processing (NLP), which allows for computers to interpret language to perform various operations to generate insight about what is being said. Given the size of the data set at hand and the inability of a single analyst to traverse each entry, NLP provides for an effective way to analyze this data set.

Tokenizing the current data set required yet another script. Using the Natural Language Toolkit (commonly known as NLTK) developed out of Stanford University, tokenization is made possible. Given that the content of each forum post is what we are required to tokenize, the process of tokenization will only be applied to forum messages. At the conclusion of tokenization, a final field, "tokens," was added to the above-mentioned structure, storing the tokens associated with each message in a structure that preserves its relationship with the original table.

At the conclusion of processing, the working data set was approximately 7.43 gigabytes in size. However, for this analysis we were able to leverage search terms in order to condense to be more specific in our findings. The search terms we used to narrow the collected set were:

Ethical Hacking
Hacktivism
Anonymous
Cyber
DDoS
Lulzsec
Chaos Computer Club
Online
Hacking

The presence of these terms needed to be felt across either the ThreadName or MessageID fields in each post. These searchers resulted in a total data-set size of approximately 256 megabytes, which represents the subset of data used in the analysis below.

The following Dark-Net forums were cleaned and analyzed:

afghanForum
afghanForums
allsomaliforum
ansarl.txt
banadir24
Gawaher.txt
IslamicAwakening.txt
IslamicNetwork.txt
Itdarashag
Karbush
Myiwc.txt
Pastunforums
Somaliaonline
solamliUK
TurtoIslam.txt
Ummah.txt

Figure 5 looks at the frequency of instances in cyber-jihad forums where there are elements of ethical hacking from 2000 to 2012.

There were approximately 43,000 hits on terms related to "ethical hacking" from 2000 to 2012 in the cyber-jihad forums. Many of the conversations, however, had elements of ambivalence where the intended use of hacking remained unclear.

Figure 6 provides an example of content found in the various forums.

This analysis may indicate that cyber-jihad forums are more akin to traditional hacking forums in that they are more oriented around providing general advice and tutorials rather than traditional jihad forums, which focus more around discussing terrorist events and discussions around religious and political issues. As will be seen below, the analysis of hacking forums retrieved very different results from the cyber-jihad groups.

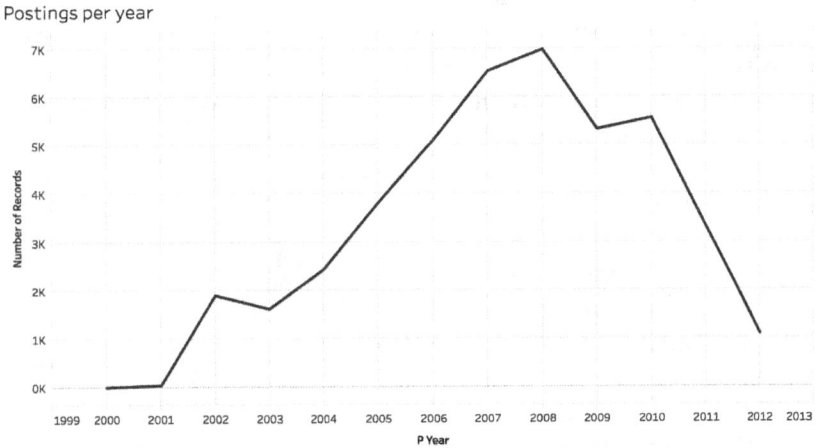

Figure 5. Ethical Hacking in Cyber-Jihad Forums.

Cyber Jihad

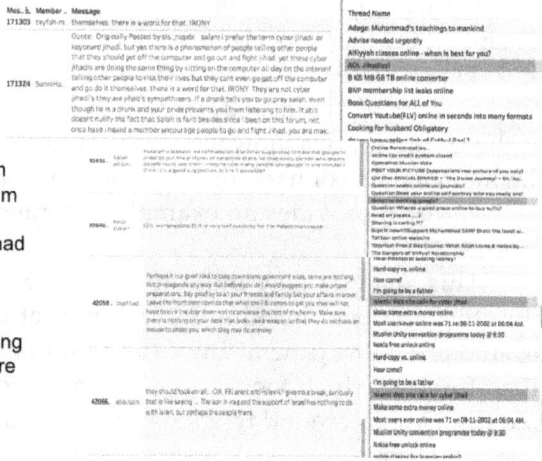

- Small proportion of forum talk around online activism

- Online/cyber forms of Jihad belittled due to removed nature vs physical act

- Discussion around learning to hack and program more prevalent, intended use unclear

Figure 6. Example of Content Found in Forums.

3.5.2 Hacking Forums (with Richard Li)

For the Dark-Net analysis of hacking forums, we used dark-market data sets (forums) that had previously been scraped and, in most instances, cleansed and indexed. The AZSecure data sets were also from the DIBB and were further cleaned as per the same methodology that was used in the cyber-jihad forums. The forums analyzed were:

Dark-Net Market Archives
(https://www.gwern.net/DNM%20archives)
• Grams archive and select dark-market forums used

AZSecure Other Forums
(http://www.azsecure-data.org/other-forums.html)
• Only the English-language forum HackHound used

AZSecure Other Data
(http://www.azsecure-data.org/other-data.html)
• Only network traffic data and websites data used

We did not run analytics on real-time dark-market forum chatter as this was beyond our analytical skills, would require hundreds of hours cleaning and indexing the data, and, most importantly, would require a secure facility/server to process the information, as many of the forums contain live malware.

Some of the forums required us to clean/scrub the data. Other forums were indexed and cleaned. In these instances, we changed the clean-up script to accept multiple file inputs, and added skipping blank lines and initial whites pace—see below.

```
import pandas as pd
import sys

pd.set_option('display.max_rows', None)
pd.set_option('display.max_columns', None)
pd.set_option('display.max_colwidth', -1)

reload(sys)
sys.setdefaultencoding('latin-1')

for line in sys.stdin:
        csvfile = pd.read_csv(line.rstrip(), error_bad_lines=False,
skipinitialspace=True, skip_blank_lines=True)
        csvfile.to_csv("datasetoutput.csv," mode='a', index=False)
```

We then put CSV files into the same directory with script and ran using `ls -p *.csv | python test.py`.

We changed the clean-up script to be recursive, to find and read all CSV files in current directory, then output as a single CSV file (adds date field based on directory name due to schema)—see below.

```python
import pandas as pd
import os
import sys

pd.set_option('display.max_rows', None)
pd.set_option('display.max_columns', None)
pd.set_option('display.max_colwidth', -1)

reload(sys)
sys.setdefaultencoding('latin-1')

path = '.'
count = 0

for dirpath, dirnames, files in os.walk(path):
    for f in files:
        if f.endswith('.csv'):
            #f is csv file name e.g., Valhalla.csv
            #os.path.basename(dirpath) is directory name e.g.,
            2016-04-17

            filepath = os.path.join(dirpath, f)

            df = pd.read_csv(filepath, error_bad_lines=False,
            skipinitialspace=True, skip_blank_lines=True,
            quoting=3)
            df['date'] = os.path.basename(dirpath)

            if (count == 0):
                count += 1
                df.to_csv("datasetoutput.csv," mode='a',
                index=False)
            else:
                df.to_csv("datasetoutput.csv," mode='a',
                header=False, index=False)
```

We only wanted data on forum posts to search for key-words—that is, scrapped forum threads.

We initially patterned extracted forum archives using the command:

```
tar -zxf [forumname].tar.xz --include='[pattern]'
```
(the pattern differed depending on the forum)

The resulting scraped html of forum threads was then parsed by a python script into a CSV file. The python script only outputs data where either the title or post content matched the search terms. To speed up analysis, the actual content of a post is not written to the CSV file after being searched for matching terms.

We open the resulting CSV file (e.g., "datasetoutput.csv") with Tableau, which allowed us to visualize our analytics. We then created a calculated field for content to search; for example, thread title and post content. Afterward, we created a filter for that field with a condition that searches for specified keywords within content.

- Search terms: Ethical Hacking, Hacktivism, Anonymous, Cyber, DDoS, LulzSec, Chaos Computer Club, Online, Hacking.
- Additional search terms: AntiSec, Anti-Sec, CyberBerkut, Ethical Hacker, Hacktivist, Iranian Cyber Army, Syrian Electronic Army, White Hat.

Figure 7. Grams Listings 2014–2016.

Figures 7 and 8 further show the numbers involved with aspects notable to ethical hacking.

The numbers from the Grams data reveal over 922,000 references to ethical hacking. These numbers are further broken down per market below.

Forum data from HackHound retrieved much smaller results than from the Grams data. We used the same-directory CSV-file methodology, and we also had to manually clean up and delete html content that overran a cell. As illustrated in figure 9, we had a total match of 198.

Market Name

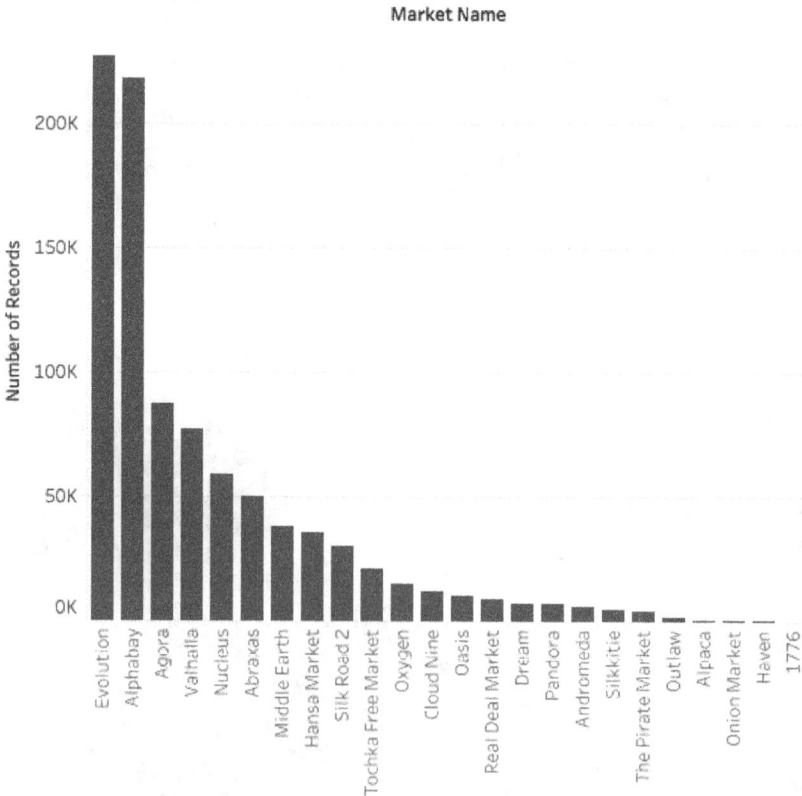

Figure 8. Grams Listings per Market.

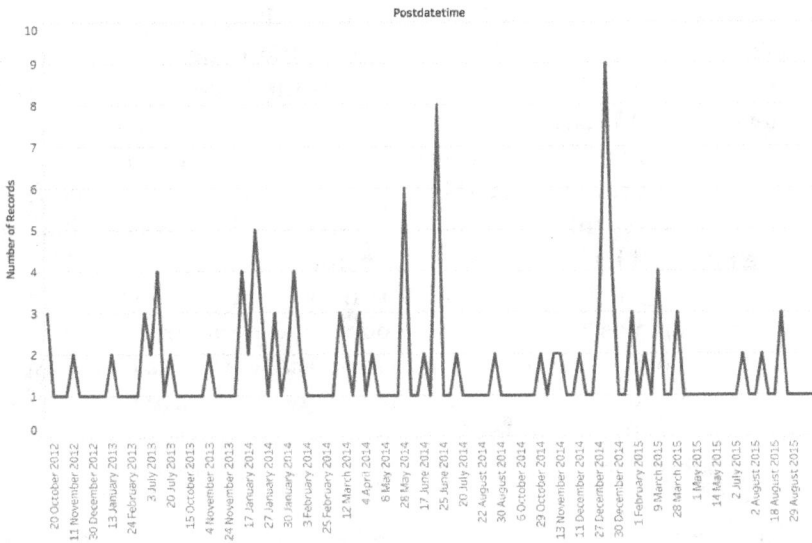

Figure 9. HackHound Forum Incidences 2012–2016.

3.6 Observations

We made use of the Grams archive that had CSV data for dark-market listings over several dark markets (https://www.gwern.net/DNM%20 archives#grams). From there we used multiple-directory CSV-file methodology, resulting in total matches of 922,649. These indicate records, and not separate incidences; therefore, we were unable to cleanse the data to the point where we could infer a record like we were able to when using the cyber-jihad forum data. Due to the other forums being smaller in size, we were able to clean that data to make records of single events related to ethical hacking. This is clearly not an ideal methodology. In fact, the methodology has been developed on a rather ad hoc basis from 2011 to 2017. We have not received any research funding for this project; we have merely done what was within our grasp at the time based on the resources and skills available from students interning with the Cyberspace Law and Policy Centre of the University of New South Wales, along with myself. However, the numbers say something rather significant—that ethical hacking is occurring globally and that it is escalating as a means of both political and social protest.

Our traditional research methodology for the 2011 report included approximately 137 different incidences, while our research using GTELD and SQL BigData query resulted in approximately 50,000 ethical-hacking incidences. With the cyber-jihad forums alone, we retrieved 43,000 records. With the hacking forums, we retrieved close to 922,000 references to ethical-hacking terms. While the 922,000 number does not isolate incidences/records, it is safe to infer that the numbers would be significantly greater than the few hundred hits and the 50,000 hits when the searching was limited to online reported incidences through media and blogs.

Future research would also run analytics on social-media platforms, such as Twitter and Facebook, and popular social-media platforms in other countries, such as in Russia and China (WhatsApp for China, VK for Russia). Indeed, language skills have been a limiting factor to the analytics for dark-market analysis. The GTELD and BigQuery analysis has built-in translation services that provide results in multiple languages, which is a significant advantage. Future research would also be funded and performed with experts in data science.

Methodologies reliant on using manual search queries or data analytics running on media and blogs produce results that can be contextualized. However, they also only pick up a slight portion of the number of ethical-hacking incidences occurring globally, as can be seen with the data analytics run on the dark-market forums. Chapters 4 through 8 look at selected ethical hacking.

Notes

1. A. Maurushat, *Ethical Hacking*. A report for Public Safety Canada (2011).
2. The interview questions appear in the appendix below.
3. Yip and Webber 2011.
4. Honker Union of China.
5. These maps are not interactive in the book. However, the maps are interactive for users on the website http://www.ethicalhackinglaw.org/statistics. You can also link to the ethical-hacking website and information from www.alanacybersecurity.com. On these websites, you can right-click on a blue dot which represents incidences with a link to that geographic location. Right-clicking will provide direct links to incidences reported in media and blogs. A single blue dot could represent hundreds of incidences, or only one. Clicking on the dot, therefore, is important in ascertaining a more accurate picture of the number and source variety of incidences.
6. Rahm and Hai Do 2009.

CHAPTER IV

Legal Cases Around the World

(with Jelena Ardalic)

Extensive case-law review revealed a paucity of reported cases on ethical hacking worldwide. Cases that were reported are published in legal databases. We looked at legal databases for all Commonwealth countries (United Kingdom, Australia, Canada, etc.) as well as the United States, Israel, Indonesia, Japan, Singapore, and Germany. The lack of cases is likely due to three key factors:

1. the currency of the actions (insufficient time for a trial or a decision to have been reported in case-law databases),
2. the accused may have settled the case, or
3. the accused may have agreed to act as an informant in exchange for dropped charges.

The other important factor, as will be explored in chapter 12, is that there are many technical and legal challenges that make investigation and prosecution difficult. Hacking often includes obfuscation technologies routed through multiple jurisdictions. Attribution is the greatest challenge for cybercrime—while you may be lucky enough to trace a communication to a device, device location tracking is often only accurate to a four-block radius, and even if you can drill down to a device, you must prove who the person was who used the device.

This chapter catalogues case law globally, based on jurisdiction, starting with the United States, which has the greatest number of reported cases. We itemize the cases, provide facts, then categorize the case by country, case name, citation, jurisdiction, main URL, charge, legislative provisions, main target, motivation, conviction, sentence, and additional important information.

UNITED STATES

United States of America v. Bradley Manning
The defendant was arrested after allegedly accessing and providing classified US government documents to WikiLeaks. Private First Class Manning was a US Army intelligence analyst based in Iraq and was charged in 2010.

ITEM	NOTES
Case name:	*United States of America v. Bradley Manning*
Citation:	*E., PFC* (2013)
Jurisdiction:	United States Army Military District of Washington
Main URL:	Wikipedia, *United States v. Bradley Manning* (July 25 2018) http://en.wikipedia.org/wiki/United_States_v._Bradley_Manning.
	United States Division—Center, "Soldier Faces Criminal Charges" (media release, no. 20100706-01, July 6, 2010).
	Associated Press, "Panel Says WikiLeaks Suspect is Competent to Stand Trial," *New York Times*, April 29, 2011, available at http://www.nytimes.com/2011/04/30/us/30brfs-PANELSAYSWIK_BRF.html?_r=1&ref=bradleyemanning.
Charged with:	Transferring US government documents to a party not entitled to receive them (Julian Assange of WikiLeaks)
Legislative provisions:	Uniform Code of Military Justice articles 104 (aiding the enemy), 92 (failure to obey a lawful order or regulation), 132 (general article, including counts of offenses against the Computer Fraud and Abuse Act 1986 (18 *United States Code* [hereinafter, U.S.C.] section 1030(a)), and 793 (communicating, transmitting and delivering national defence information to an unauthorized source)
Main target:	US Army and US government
Motivation:	Public disclosure of US government (including foreign policy) documents in order to "change something" (according to the transcript of his chats with hacker Adrian Lamo, see Wikileaks, for example at https://www.youtube.com/watch?v=lzwUeqC8E60)

Convicted of:	Convicted of committing nineteen of the twenty-two charges, but acquitted of aiding the enemy by knowingly providing the enemy with intelligence through indirect means
Sentence:	On August 21, 2013, Manning was sentenced to thirty-five years in prison. On January 17, 2017, then-US President Barack Obama commuted Manning's sentence to a total of seven years' confinement, starting with the initial date of arrest. As a result, Bradley Manning, now known as Chelsea Manning, was released on May 17, 2017
Additional important information:	Twenty-two charges under the Espionage Act, including aiding the enemy and improperly obtaining a classified gunsight video. Proceedings commenced in Forte Mead, Maryland, February 23, 2011. Manning was nominated for a Nobel Peace Prize on February 27, 2011. The increased media attention reflects contemporary attitudes toward hacktivism.

United States of America v. Kevin George Poe

An Anonymous-affiliated Connecticut man, Poe (handle: "spydr101"), was arrested and charged with conspiracy and unauthorized impairment of a protected computer after allegedly disabling rock musician Gene Simmons's website with a denial-of-service attack.

ITEM	NOTES
Case name:	*United States of America v. Kevin George Poe*
Citation:	CR 11 01166
Jurisdiction:	United States District Court for the Central District of California
Main URL:	J. Zand, "Indictment Alleges DDoS Attack on Gene Simmons' Web Site by Anonymous Supporter" on *Justia Law Blog* (December 14, 2011), available at http://techlaw.justia.com/2011/12/14/indictment-alleges-ddos-attack-on-gene-simmons-web-site/. J. Halliday, "Gene Simmons gets kiss of death from notorious web forum," *Guardian*, October 14, 2010, available at http://www.guardian.co.uk/technology/blog/2010/oct/14/gene-simmons-anonymous-attack-filesharing.

	The Smoking Gun, "Plea Deal Struck Over Attack on Kiss Web Sites," February 5, 2013, available at http://www.thesmokinggun.com/documents/gene-simmons-ddos-plea-587912. G. Aegerter, "13 Alleged Members of Anonymous Hacking Group indicted, accused of Participating in Operation Payback," *NBC News*, November 3, 2015, available at https://www.nbcnews.com/news/world/13-alleged-members-anonymous-hacking-group-indicted-accused-participating-operation-flna8C11332039.
Charged with:	Conspiracy and unauthorized impairment of a protected computer
Legislative provisions:	18 U.S.C. sections 371 (conspiracy), 1030(a)(5)(A), (c)(4)(B)(i), (c)(4)(A)(i)(I) (unauthorized impairment of a protected computer)
Main target:	Gene Simmons via his website
Motivation:	Likely to be protest or retribution as the crime occurred shortly after Gene Simmons criticized file sharing and encouraged copyright owners to commence litigation and seek extensive damages against file sharers (see the cited *Guardian* article for screenshot of Anonymous message about Gene Simmons's views)
Convicted of:	Poe pleaded guilty. As part of a plea agreement, he was charged with the reduced impairment count.
Sentence:	Initially, if convicted of both counts, Poe would have faced up to fifteen years in federal prison. However, after pleading guilty to the reduced impairment count and reaching a plea agreement, he was sentenced to home detention and probation
Additional important information:	Used Low Orbit Ion Cannon software to instigate attack

Member of LulzSec Arrested for June 2011 Intrusion of Sony Pictures Computer Systems

"A member of the LulzSec hacking group was arrested…for his role in an extensive computer attack against the computer systems of Sony Pictures Entertainment.… On September 2, 2011, a federal grand jury returned an indictment filed under seal in US District Court in Los Angeles charging [Cody] Kretsinger with conspiracy and the unauthorized impairment of a protected computer" (FBI).

ITEM	NOTES
Case name:	*United States of America v. Kretsinger*
Citation:	2:11-cr-00848
Jurisdiction:	United States District Court, Central District of California (Los Angeles)
Main URL:	FBI, "Member of Hacking Group LulzSec Arrested for June 2011 Intrusion of Sony Pictures Computer Systems" (press release, September 22, 2011), available at http://www.fbi.gov/losangeles/press-releases/2011/member-of-hacking-group-lulzsec-arrested-for-june-2011-intrusion-of-sony-pictures-computer-systems (last accessed October 20, 2011).
	C. Arthur, "Alleged LulzSec hacker of Sony Pictures faces trial data in December," *Guardian*, October 18, 2011, available at http://www.guardian.co.uk/technology/2011/oct/18/lulzsec-alleged-recursion-hacker-trial.
	D. Whitcomb, "Hacker Gets a Year in Prison for Sony Attack," *Sydney Morning Herald*, April 19, 2013, available at https://www.smh.com.au/technology/hacker-gets-a-year-in-prison-for-sony-attack-20130419-2i4hl.html.
Charged with:	Conspiracy and the unauthorized impairment of a protected computer (using an SQL injection and a proxy server)
Legislative provisions:	Most likely to be 18 U.S.C. section 1030(a)(2)
Main target:	Sony Pictures Entertainment's computer systems
Motivation:	Follow-up attack to Sony PlayStation network hack. Proof of ability to exploit global conglomerate with ease: "'From a single injection we accessed EVERYTHING,' the hacking group said in a statement at the time. 'Why do you put such faith in a company that allows itself to become open to these simple attacks'" (Arthur).
Convicted of:	Unauthorized impairment of protected computers
Sentence:	On April 19, 2013, Kretsinger was sentenced to one year in federal prison, along with one year of home detention after the completion of his prison sentence, $605,663 in restitution to Sony Pictures, and 1,000 hours of community service
Additional important information:	Used an "SQL Injection attack" as means of gaining access and gathering information (per Arthur). Kretsinger's handle: "recursion."

United States of America v. Daniel Spitler and Andrew Auernheimer

"Two self-described Internet 'trolls' were arrested...for allegedly hacking AT&T's servers and stealing e-mail addresses and other personal information belonging to approximately 120,000 Apple iPad users who accessed the Internet via AT&T's 3G network" (FBI). The defendants are alleged to be associates of the group Goatse Security, which, according to Wikipedia, is a grey-hat hacker group that exposes security flaws. (So, in this sense, vaguely "ethical.")

ITEM	NOTES
Case name:	United States of America v. Daniel Spitler and Andrew Alan Escher Auernheimer; Appeal: Auernheimer v. United States of America
Citation:	Mag. No. 11-4022 (CCC); Appeal: Third US Circuit Court of Appeals, No. 13-1816
Jurisdiction:	Newark, New Jersey
Main URL:	FBI, "Two Men Charged in New Jersey with Hacking AT&T's Servers" (press release, January 18, 2011), http://www.fbi.gov/newark/press-releases/2011/nk011811.htm.
	Criminal Complaint: http://www.justice.gov/usao/nj/Press/files/pdffiles/2011/Spitler,%20Daniel%20et%20al.%20Complaint.pdf.
	E. Mills, "AT&T-iPad hacker pleads guilty to computer charges," *Cnet*, June 23, 2011, available at http://news.cnet.com/8301-27080_3-20073791-245/at-t-ipad-hacker-pleads-guilty-to-computer-charges/.
	E. Mills, "AT&T-iPad site hacker to fight on in court (exclusive)," *Cnet*, September 12, 2011, available at http://news.cnet.com/8301-27080_3-20105097-245/at-t-ipad-site-hacker-to-fight-on-in-court-exclusive/.
	T. McCarthy, "Andrew Auernheimer's conviction over computer fraud thrown out," *Guardian*, April 12, 2014, available at https://www.theguardian.com/technology/2014/apr/11/andrew-auernheimers-weev-conviction-vacated-hacking.
Charged with:	"Each defendant is charged with one count of conspiracy to access a computer without authorization and...fraud in connection with personal information" (per the FBI)
Legislative provisions:	18 U.S.C. sections 1030(a)(2)(C), I030(c)(2)(B)(ii), and 371
Main target:	AT&T's servers, specifically those handling 3G iPad traffic

Motivation:	Possibly to publicize security faults in AT&T's 3G network, or for "criminal gain or prestige among peers in the cyber-hacking world" (per the FBI)
Convicted of:	Conspiracy to gain unauthorized access to AT&T public servers
Sentence:	"Each count with which the defendants are charged carries a maximum potential penalty of five years in prison and a fine of $250,000" (per the FBI).

Spitler pleaded guilty in June 2011 and was sentenced to three years' probation. Spitler was also ordered to pay $73,167 in restitution.

In 2014, the US Court of Appeals for the Third Circuit Court threw out the convictions against Auernheimer on the basis that the prosecution did not belong in New Jersey. As a result, his November 2012 conviction and forty-one-month prison sentence could not stand. |
| Additional important information: | Andrew Alan Escher Auernheimer's handle: "weev." Daniel Spitler's handle: "JacksonBrown." |

In re § 2703(d) Order (2011)

This was a petition by Twitter users to vacate the so-called Twitter Order granted by a federal court in Virginia upon the US government's *ex parte* motion. The Twitter Order required Twitter to provide the US government information relating to various Twitter accounts, including those of WikiLeaks, Julian Assange, and Bradley Manning. The motion to vacate the order was denied, but the motion to unseal one docket was granted.

ITEM	NOTES
Case name:	Earlier case: *In re § 2703(d) Order* (2011). Later case: *In re § 2703(d) Order* (2013).
Citation:	Earlier case: 830 F. Supp. 2d 114 (US District Court, Eastern District of Virginia, Alexandria Division) November 10, 2011. Later case: No. 11-5151 (US Court of Appeals Fourth Circuit) January 25, 2013.
Jurisdiction:	Earlier case: United States District Court for the Eastern District of Virginia. Later case: United States Court of Appeals, Fourth Circuit.

Main URL:	ACLU Virginia, *In re § 2703(d) Orders*, available at https://acluva.org/en/cases/re-ss2703d-orders.
	Electronic Privacy Information Center, *In re Twitter Order Pursuant to 2703(d)* https://www.epic.org/amicus/twitter/wikileaks/.
	Justia US Law, *In re: 2703(d) Application, No. 11-5151* (Fourth Cir. 2013) https://law.justia.com/cases/federal/appellate-courts/ca4/11-5151/11-5151-2013-01-25.html.
Charged with:	N/A (motion to vacate and motion to unseal)
Legislative provisions:	18 U.S.C. section 2703(d) of the Stored Communications Act
Main target:	N/A (motion to vacate and motion to unseal sought)
Motivation:	Twitter's counsel argued before the US district court that the section 2703(d) order should be vacated on various grounds, such as arguing that the Twitter order violates their fourth amendment right to be free from unreasonable searches and seizures (i.e., disclosure of their IP address should be considered a "search" under the fourth amendment). Also, they argued that the Twitter order violates their constitutional right to procedural due process. As well, it was argued that the Twitter order violates their first amendment rights to free speech and association. Finally, they argued that the court should exercise discretion to deny the Twitter order to avoid the above-mentioned constitutional questions.
Convicted of:	N/A
Sentence:	N/A
Additional important information:	Motion to vacate denied, but motion to unseal granted on one docket. In an update to the case in 2013 at the US Court of Appeals for the Fourth Circuit: "Because the court found that there was no First Amendment right to access such documents, and the common law right to access such documents was presently outweighed by countervailing interests, the court denied the request for relief" (Justia).
	Interesting expansion and appropriation of US constitutional notions of free speech and association, freedom from unreasonable search and seizure and of procedural due process.

United States of America v Dennis Collins, et al. ("PayPal 14")

In December 2013, fourteen individuals connected with Anonymous were arrested in the United States for their alleged roles in cyber attacks against PayPal's website in 2010. The cyber attacks were in response to PayPal's suspension of payments to WikiLeaks and as part of a wider Anonymous campaign, "Operation Payback," which included "Operation Avenge Assange." Two additional individuals were arrested on similar charges.

ITEM	NOTES
Case name:	*United States of America v. Dennis Collins, et al* (2011)
Citation:	No. CR 11-00471 DLJ
Jurisdiction:	United States District Court, Northern District of California, San Jose Division
Main URL:	FBI, "Sixteen Individuals Arrested in the United States for Alleged Roles in Cyber Attacks" (press release, July 19, 2011), available at http://www.fbi.gov/news/ pressrel/press-releases/sixteen-individuals-arrested-in-the-united-states-for-alleged-roles-in-cyber-attacks (last accessed November 10, 2011).
	US Attorney's Office, Northern District of California, "Thirteen Defendants Plead Guilty For December 2010 Cyber-Attack Against PayPal" (press release, December 6, 2013), available at http://www.justice.gov/usao/can/ news/2013/2013_12_06_thirteen.guiltyplea.press.html.
	D. Lucas, "Exclusive: The Legendary #Anonymous PayPal 14 Speak Out Post-Sentencing," *Cryptosphere*, October 31, 2014, available at https://thecryptosphere.com/2014/10/31/ exclusive-the-anonymous-paypal-14-speak-out-post-sentencing/.
Charged with:	California charges: conspiracy and intentional damage to a protected computer.
	For indictment, see http://ia600502.us.archive.org/24/items/ gov.uscourts.cand.242989/gov.uscourts.cand.242989.1.0.pdf.
Legislative provisions:	18 U.S.C. section 1030(b)(felony)—Conspiracy offence 18 U.S.C. section 1030(a)(5)(A)(misd.)—Intentional damage to a protected computer.
Main target:	DDoS attacks on PayPal
Motivation:	Retaliation against PayPal's termination of WikiLeaks's donation account

Convicted of:	With the exception of Valenzuela, Phillips, and Miles, each of the defendants pleaded guilty to one count of conspiracy, in violation of 18 U.S.C. section 1030(b)(felony), and one count of intentional damage to a protected computer, in violation of 18 U.S.C. section 1030(a)(5)(A) (misd.).
	Defendant Valenzuela pleaded guilty to one count of reckless damage to a protected computer, in violation of 18 U.S.C. section 1030(a)(5)(A)(misd.).
	Defendants Phillips and Miles pled guilty to one count each of intentional damage to a protected computer, in violation of 18 U.S.C. section 1030(a)(5)(A)(misd.) only.
Sentence:	In 2014, Collins was the only member charged with involvement with the PayPal 14 and Payback 13, but he was sentenced to house arrest for six months for health reasons.
	Thirteen of the PayPal 14 of Anonymous had their felony charges reduced to a single misdemeanour and were sentenced to probation and $5,600 restitution.
Additional important information:	The individuals named in the San Jose indictment are: • Dennis Collins, aka "Owen" and "Iowa;" • Christopher Wayne Cooper, aka "Anthrophobic;" • Joshua John Covelli, aka "Absolem" and "Toxic;" • Keith Wilson Downey; • Mercedes Renee Haefer, aka "No" and "MMMM;" • Donald Husband, aka "Ananon;" • Vincent Charles Kershaw, aka "Trivette," "Triv" and "Reaper;" • Ethan Miles; • James C. Murphy; • Drew Alan Phillips, aka "Drew010;" • Jeffrey Puglisi, aka "Jeffer," "Jefferp" and "Ji;" • Daniel Sullivan; • Tracy Ann Valenzuela; and • Christopher Quang Vo.
	Dennis Collins was the only member who was charged in relation to both PayPal 14 and Payback 13.
	The chairman of eBay, Pierre Omidyar, called for leniency in the prosecution of those accused of playing a part in DDoS-ing PayPal. He pointed out that the accused were part of thousands who took part in the protest.

United States of America v. Steiger

This case concerns a hacker that obtained evidence that the defendant, Steiger, was producing and collecting child pornography, and passed the evidence to law enforcement in the United States. The issue in this case was whether "the evidence was obtained in violation of the Fourth Amendment as the hacker was a government agent."

ITEM	NOTES
Case name:	*United States of America v. Steiger* (2003)
Citation:	318 F. 3d 1039, Nos. 01-15788, 01-16100 and 01-16269 (January 14, 2003)
Jurisdiction:	United States Court of Appeals, Eleventh Circuit
Main URL:	Case: Available at http://scholar.google.com.au/scholar_case?case=5611821785646747519
Charged with:	Hacker not charged as he was not being prosecuted. The hacker in question was from Turkey. He was merely the source of the information about Stieger's sexual abuse of a young child in the United States
Legislative provisions:	The fourth amendment (right against unreasonable searches and seizures)
Main target:	Steiger—producer and possessor of child pornography
Motivation:	To help law-enforcement officers catch child predators
Convicted of:	N/A
Sentence:	N/A
Additional important information:	For a search by a private person to implicate the fourth amendment, the person must act as an instrument or agent of the government.[1] In 2006, the defendant attempted to convince the court of a motion for a new trial, but failed. As a result, the 2003 judgment still stands (see https://www.gpo.gov/fdsys/pkg/USCOURTS-almd-2_00-cr-00170/pdf/USCOURTS-almd-2_00-cr-00170-0.pdf).

United States of America v. Jarrett

This case concerns a hacker that obtained evidence that the defendant was producing and collecting child pornography, and passed the evidence to law enforcement in the United States. The issue in this case was "whether evidence obtained by a hacker and used in a prosecution implicates the 4th amendment, and there has been communication between the hacker and law enforcement about the evidence."

ITEM	NOTES
Case name:	*United States of America v. Jarrett*
Citation:	338 F. 3d 339, No. 02-4953 (July 29, 2003)
Jurisdiction:	United States Court of Appeals, Fourth Circuit
Main URL:	Case: http://scholar.google.com.au/scholar_case?case= 77043603263711177621
Charged with:	Hacker not charged as he was not being prosecuted in the United States
Legislative provisions:	The fourth amendment (right against unreasonable searches and seizures)
Main target:	Jarrett—producer and possessor of child pornography
Motivation:	To help law-enforcement officers catch child predators
Convicted of:	N/A
Sentence:	N/A
Additional important information:	Whether the hacker's search was a government search turns on "(1) whether the Government knew of and acquiesced in the private search; and (2) whether the private individual intended to assist law enforcement or had some other independent motivation" (*United States of America v. Jarrett*). There must be more than knowledge or acquiescence—there must be participation or affirmative encouragement.

United States of America v. Raynaldo Rivera

Raynaldo Rivera, of Tempe, Arizona—who allegedly used the online nicknames of "neuron," "royal" and "wildciv"—surrendered to police in Phoenix six days after a federal grand jury in Los Angeles produced an indictment accusing Rivera and co-conspirators of stealing information from Sony Pictures Europe's computer systems in May and June 2011 using an SQL injection attack. The SQL injection attack exploits flaws in the handing of data input for databases to take control of a system—in this case, against the studio's website. The indictment says Rivera helped to post the confidential information onto LulzSec's website and announced the intrusion via the hacking group's Twitter account.

ITEM	NOTES
Case name:	*United States of America v. Raynaldo Rivera*
Citation:	CR No. 12- 798-JAK
Jurisdiction:	United States District Court for the Central District of California
Main URL:	C. Arthur, "LulzSec Hacker Arrested Over Sony Attack," *Guardian*, August 29, 2012, available at http://www.guardian.co.uk/technology/2012/aug/29/lulzsec-hacker-arrest-sony-attack.
	Plea agreement, *FreeAnons* https://freeanons.org/wp-content/uploads/court-documents/Raynaldo-Rivera.pdf.
	FBI, "Second Member of Hacking Group Sentenced to More Than a Year in Prison for Stealing Customer Information from Sony Pictures Computers" (FBI press release, August 8, 2013), available at https://archives.fbi.gov/archives/losangeles/press-releases/2013/second-member-of-hacking-group-sentenced-to-more-than-a-year-in-prison-for-stealing-customer-information-from-sony-pictures-computers.
Charged with:	Conspiracy and intent to cause damage without authorization to a protected computer
Legislative provisions:	18 U.S.C. sections 371 and 1030(a)(5)(A), (c)(4)(B)(i), (c)(4)(A)(i)(I)
Main target:	Sony Pictures Europe's computer systems
Motivation:	Unknown, perhaps for the "lulz"
Convicted of:	Conspiracy and intent to cause damage without authorization to a protected computer
Sentence:	Rivera initially faced fifteen years in prison. However, after striking a plea deal, he was sentenced to one year and one day in federal prison by United States District Judge John A. Kronstadt. Rivera was also ordered to serve thirteen months of home detention, to perform 1,000 hours of community service and to pay $605,663 in restitution to Sony Pictures.
Additional important information:	Following the Sony Pictures Europe breach, LulzSec published the names, birth dates, addresses, emails, phone numbers, and passwords of thousands of people who had entered contests promoted by Sony, and publicly boasted of its exploits.

LulzSec released a statement related to the Sony hack. LulzSec said: "From a single injection we accessed EVERYTHING," the hackers said in a statement at the time. "Why do you put such faith in a company that allows itself to become open to these simple attacks?"

A number of arrests followed in the United Kingdom, where six people have been charged with various offences linked to LulzSec's activities.

An accused British hacker, Ryan Cleary, was indicted by a US grand jury on charges related to LulzSec attacks on several media companies, including Sony Pictures.

Cody Kretsinger, who pleaded guilty to the same two charges Rivera faced, was sentenced to one year in federal prison, one year of home detention after the completion of his prison sentence, a fine of $605,663 in restitution to Sony Pictures and 1,000 hours of community service.

Hector Xavier Monsegur, a Puerto Rican living in New York, pled guilty to 12 charges, including three of conspiracy to hack into computers, five of hacking, one of hacking for fraudulent purposes, one of conspiracy to commit bank fraud, and one of aggravated identity theft.

Those charges would attract a total of 124 years in jail, but he arranged a plea bargain with the US government. Monsegur received a six-month reprieve from sentencing in light of his cooperation with the government.

Monsegur, a hacker turned FBI informant, provided the FBI with details enabling the arrest of five other hackers associated with the groups Anonymous, LulzSec and AntiSec.

A court filing made by prosecutors in late May 2014 revealed Monsegur had prevented 300 cyber-attacks in the three years since 2011, including planned attacks on NASA, the US military and media companies.

Monsegur served seven months in prison after his arrest but had been free since then while awaiting sentencing. At his sentencing on May 27, 2014, he was given "time served" for co-operating with the FBI and set free under one year of parole.

Aaron Swartz

Aaron Swartz was facing up to thirty-five years in jail for illegally downloading 4.8 million articles from the JSTOR database in 2011. The Massachusetts Institute of Technology (MIT), whose data network was used in the hack, valued the downloaded information at $50,000. Aaron strongly believed that information, and especially research, should be public and free. Faced with the harsh prison sentence and under the pressure of legal fees, Aaron committed suicide at his home on January 11, 2013.

ITEM	NOTES
Case name:	*United States of America v. Aaron Swartz*
Citation:	1:11-cr-10260
Jurisdiction:	United States District Court for the District of Massachusetts
Main URL:	S. Farberov, H. Pow, and J. Nye, "Revealed: Prosecutors turned down Reddit co-founder Aaron Swartz's request for plea deal over MIT hacking case TWO DAYS before his suicide," *Daily Mail*, January 14, 2013, available at http://www.dailymail.co.uk/news/article-2262137/ Aaron-Swartz-Reddit-founder-request-plea-deal-turned-Massachusetts-prosecutor.html#axzz2KkIHBHh6
Charged with:	Thirteen counts of felony hacking including wire fraud, computer fraud, and unlawfully obtaining information from a protected computer
Legislative provisions:	18 U.S.C. sections 1343, 1030(a)(4), 1030(a)(2), 1030(a)(5)(B), and 2
Main target:	JSTOR database
Motivation:	Swartz believed that academic articles funded by taxpayers' money should be made available for free
Convicted of:	Charges were dismissed following Swartz's death
Sentence:	Faced up to thirty-five years in jail and millions of dollars in fines
Additional important information:	In 2010, Swartz allegedly connected a laptop to MIT's systems through a basement network wiring cupboard. He registered as a guest under the fictitious name, Gary Host—a hacking in-joke in which the first initial and last name spell "ghost." He then used a software program to "rapidly download an extraordinary volume of articles from JSTOR," according to the indictment.

	In the following months, MIT and JSTOR tried to block the recurring and massive downloads, on occasion denying all MIT users access to JSTOR. However, Swartz allegedly got around it, in part, by disguising the computer source of the demands for data.
	It is alleged that on January 6, 2011, Swartz went to the wiring closet to remove the laptop, attempting to shield his identity by holding a bike helmet in front of his face and seeing his way through its ventilation holes. He fled when MIT police tried to question him that day, it is claimed. Legal proceedings followed.

Lauri Love (British) AKA "nsh" "route" "peace" "LOVE"

British citizen Lauri Love is charged with hacking charges in the United States. He is accused of hacking US government departments—stealing the personal details of 5,000 servicemen and women and classified US data by installing hidden "shells" or back doors within the networks.

ITEM	NOTES
Case name:	*Lauri Love v. the Government of the United States of America*
Citation:	[2018] EWHC 172
Jurisdiction:	2013: United States District Court of New Jersey 2014: United States Southern District Court of New York and Eastern District of Virginia 2018: High Court of England and Wales
Main URL:	J. Halliday, "Briton Lauri Love faces hacking charges in US," *Guardian*, October 29, 2013, available at http://www.theguardian.com/world/2013/oct/28/us-briton-hacking-charges-nasa-lauri-love. BBC News, "Lauri Love case: Hacking Suspect Wins Extradition Appeal," February 5, 2018, available at https://www.bbc.com/news/uk-england-42946540. Indictment, https://www.scribd.com/doc/179595899/Love-Lauri-Indictment. Case (High Court of England and Wales), https://freelauri.com/wp-content/uploads/2018/02/lauri-love-v-usa.pdf. D. Pauli, "Aussies Hacked Pentagon, US Army, and Others," IT News, October 29, 2013, available at https://www.itnews.com.au/news/aussies-hacked-pentagon-us-army-and-others-362202.

Charged with:	Violation of 18 U.S.C. sections 371, 1030, and 2
Legislative provisions:	Computer Fraud and Abuse Act, 18 U.S.C. sections 371, 1030, and 2
Main target:	Classified US data—US Army, the Environmental Protection Agency, and NASA
Motivation:	Prosecutors alleged that Love told a colleague in one exchange over IRC: "You have no idea how much we can fuck with the US government if we wanted to…I think we can do some hilarious stuff"
Convicted of:	Love is under indictment in the United States related to a violation of the Computer Fraud and Abuse Act. In 2018, the High Court of England and Wales ruled against extraditing Love to the United States to face trial.
Sentence:	If extradited to the United States, Love would have faced up to ten years' prison time and a fine of $250,000 if found guilty.
Additional important information:	Selected methods of hacking: • Internet Protocol • SQL • SQL Injection Attacks • SQL Injection Strings • HTML • Malware • "Coldfusion" (is a web application and development platform that uses a programming language also referred to as Coldfusion. Adobe later purchased Coldfusion. Coldfusion hacks are those which use the platform to obtain unauthorised access to the backend of a website). • Proxy servers—Used to conceal hacks • IRC "Collectively, the hacks described herein substantially impaired the functioning of dozens of computer servers and resulted in millions of dollars of damages to the Government Victims," US prosecutors claimed (as per IT News). In February 2018, the High Court of England and Wales ruled that Love would not be extradited to the United States to face trial.

Jeremy Hammond AKA "yohoho," "tylerknowsthis," "sup_g," "Anarchaos," "POW," "crediblethreat," "burn," "ghost," "anarchacker" (LulzSec, AntiSec)

Jeremy Hammond leaked millions of emails by Stratfor to WikiLeaks. The emails revealed disturbing evidence of the corruption behind Stratfor, including insider trading techniques, coercive methods, and off-shore share structures (details below).

ITEM	NOTES
Case name:	*United States of America v. Jeremy Hammond*
Citation:	12 Cr. 185 (LAP) (2013)
Jurisdiction:	United States, District Court—Southern District of New York
Main URL:	Case, http://www.justice.gov/usao/nys/pressreleases/May13/HammondJeremyPleaPR/U.S.%20v.%20Jeremy%20Hammond%20S2%20Information.pdf.
	Additional legal documents related to Hammond's case, https://freejeremy.net/category/legal/.
	WikiLeaks, "The Gifiles," https://wikileaks.org/the-gifiles.html.
	J. Kopstein, "Hacker with a cause," *New Yorker*, November 21, 2013, available at http://www.newyorker.com/online/blogs/elements/2013/11/jeremy-hammond-and-anonymous-hacker-with-a-cause.html.
	E. Pilkington, "Jeremy Hammond: FBI directed my attacks on foreign government sites,'" *Guardian*, November 16, 2013, available at http://www.theguardian.com/world/2013/nov/15/jeremy-hammond-fbi-directed-attacks-foreign-government.
Charged with:	He was indicted on six counts, but pled guilty to one: conspiracy to violate the Computer Fraud and Abuse Act.
	The six counts did not come to court, but are worth mentioning.
	Count 1: Conspiracy to commit computer hacking. Count 2: Conspiracy to commit computer hacking—LulzSec. In violation of 18 U.S.C. section 1030(b)—relevant to the cyber attack in June 2011 on computer systems used by the Arizona Department of Public Safety.

	Counts three, four, five, and six: other counts of conspiracy to commit computer hacking in violation of 18 U.S.C. section 1030(b) and substantive computer hacking in violation of sections 1030(a)(5)(A), 1030(b), and 1030(c)(4)(B)(i). Also, conspiracy to commit access device fraud in violation of section 1029(b)(2) and aggravated identity theft in violation of sections 1028A and (2).
	Counts three, four, five, and six are all related to the "Stratfor hack" (discussed below).
Legislative provisions:	Computer Fraud and Abuse Act
Main target:	Stratfor
Motivation:	Corruption of Stratfor, including bribery, insider trading, and corrupt connections with large corporations and government agencies.
	Hammond's sentencing transcript revealed his motivation: "I felt I had an obligation to use my skills to expose and confront injustice—and to bring the truth to light...I have tried everything from voting petitions to peaceful protest and have found that those in power do not want the truth exposed.... We are confronting a power structure that does not respect its own systems of checks and balances, never mind the rights of its own citizens or the international community."
Convicted of:	Pled guilty to conspiracy
Sentence:	Ten years' imprisonment with three years' supervised release
Additional important information:	Counsel for the defendant: Elizabeth Fink US; plaintiff: represented by Rosemary Nidiry, Thomas G. A. Brown Judges: Loretta A. Preska (Chief United States District Judge)
	Note: Preska's husband's email had been leaked with the Stratfor information.
	Hammond also claims that former hacker turned FBI informant, Hector Xavier Monsegur (aka "Sabu"), directed him to attack several government websites.

Anonymous and St0rmyw0rm

Anonymous claims to have temporarily shut down the National Surveillance Agency (NSA) website for hours through a DDoS attack. Both Anonymous and St0rmyw0rm have claimed to have stolen the email addresses of at least 400 NSA workers and sent them "troll" messages.

ITEM	NOTES
Case name:	N/A
Citation:	N/A
Jurisdiction:	United States
Main URL:	RT, "NSA Site went down due to "internal errors," not DDoS attack, agency claims," October 27, 2013, available at http://rt.com/usa/nsa-site-ddos-attack-754/. E. Kovacs, "NSA Website Disrupted Following PRISM Leak, Hackers Want to Troll Agency," Softpedia, June 12, 2013, available at https://news.softpedia.com/news/NSA-Website-Disrupted-Following-PRISM-Leak-Hackers-Want-to-Troll-Agency-360574.shtml.
Charged with:	N/A
Legislative provisions:	Computer Fraud and Abuse Act
Main target:	National Surveillance Agency
Motivation:	Unknown, but it could be to deter the United States from future illegal surveillance
Convicted of:	N/A
Sentence:	N/A
Additional important information:	The NSA claims that an 'internal error', not a DDoS attack, was responsible for the temporary shutdown of their website.

Paracha v. Obama

This case was about an application for immediate access to all publicly available WikiLeaks documents relevant to the petitioner's case. The government opposed the application because there was no emergency, otherwise a requirement for immediate access.

ITEM	NOTES
Case name:	*Paracha v. Obama* (2011)
Citation:	No. 04-2022 (PLF) (April 29, 2011).
Jurisdiction:	United States District Court, District of Columbia
Main URL:	Court order related to the documents, https://scholar. google.com.au/scholar_case?case=7165402973414950017&q= Paracha+wikileaks&hl=en&as_sdt=2006&as_vis=1#r[1]. Petitioner's (Paracha's) emergency application, https://fas.org/sgp/jud/par/042711-access.pdf. Respondents' (Obama et al.'s) response, https://fas.org/sgp/jud/par/061511-response376.pdf.
Cause of action:	Opposition by government of application for immediate access to all publicly available WikiLeaks documents relevant to Saifullah Paracha's case. (The petitioner was a detainee at Guantanamo Bay).
Legislative provisions:	To determine whether an emergency application for immediate access to WikiLeaks documents relevant to Paracha's case is to be granted, the court considered: Executive Order 13,526, section l.1(c) and case law
Main target:	WikiLeaks targeted the US government's confidential files on Guantanamo Bay detention camp detainees. Paracha's counsel wanted access to the documents.
Motivation:	WikiLeaks sought to shine the light of truth on former US President George W. Bush's "war on terror" campaign by seeking to expose files held by the US government on its detainees at Guantanamo Bay. Paracha's counsel filed an emergency application for immediate access to all available WikiLeaks documents relevant to his case.
Convicted of:	Paracha was convicted in 2005 of providing support to al-Qaeda. The case involved an emergency application for immediate access to all publicly available WikiLeaks documents relevant to his case.
Sentence:	The US government opposed Paracha's application because there was no emergency, which is a requirement for immediate access. Also, the US government held that the leaked WikiLeaks documents are to remain classified by the law. Paracha was also denied approval for transfer in April 2016.

Additional important information:	"The Court sees no need for an expedited schedule because...no emergency exists in this litigation, which has been continued pending Mr. Paracha's filing of a status report that was due by April 1, 2011 but has still not been filed" (*Paracha v. Obama*).
	The Justice Department's Court Security Office said that the publicly available WikiLeaks documents remain classified by law.

Bank Julius Baer & Co. Ltd. v. WikiLeaks

This case concerned an allegation that WikiLeaks "had wrongfully published on a website confidential, as well as forged, bank documents belonging to plaintiffs." The court dissolved a previously issued permanent injunction and denied a request for a preliminary injunction (against publication).

ITEM	NOTES
Case name:	*Bank Julius Baer & Co. Ltd. v. WikiLeaks*
Citation:	No. C 08-00824 JSW (February 29, 2008)
Jurisdiction:	United States District Court, Northern District of California
Main URL:	Case provided by the Electronic Frontiers Foundation at https://www.eff.org/files/filenode/baer_v_wikileaks/wikileaks102.pdf
	ACLU Northern California, *Bank Julius Baer & Co. Ltd. v. WikiLeaks* (March 6, 2008) https://www.aclunc.org/our-work/legal-docket/bank-julius-baer-co-ltd-v-wikileaks.
Causes of action:	Unlawful and unfair business practices, declaratory relief, interference with contract, interference with prospective economic advantage, conversion, and injunctive relief
Legislative provisions:	California Business and Professions Code section 17200 and the first amendment
Main target:	It is alleged that a former Baer employee stole and leaked client data. WikiLeaks published it.
Motivation:	WikiLeaks published leaked documents that exposed off-shore tax evasion and money laundering by Baer's wealthy clients
Convicted of:	N/A
Sentence:	N/A

Additional important information:	Initially, Baer obtained a permanent injunction against the domain registrar Dynadot, LLC, shutting down the domain name wikileaks.org. However, the American Civil Liberties Union (ACLU), the Electronic Frontier Foundation (EFF), and others filed a motion to intervene the injunction and they were successful. The ACLU and EFF persuaded the court to dissolve an order that sought to take down the domain name wikileaks.org.
	The court held that (1) it might not have had jurisdiction over the injunction due to the nature of the plaintiffs (some being foreign citizens and entities) and their varying physical addresses; (2) the injunction could impede on free speech under the first amendment to the United States Constitution; (3) the injunction that was issued had the opposite effect as was intended; and (4) the plaintiffs did not adequately show that the injunction would serve its intended purpose.
	The bank abandoned the case on March 5, 2008.

THE UNITED KINGDOM

"Kayla" aka Ryan Ackroyd

"Kayla" is the handle of Ryan Ackroyd, one of the core members of LulzSec involved in a series of cyber attacks, from May 6 to June 26, 2011, dubbed 50 Days of Lulz. Kayla was responsible for hacking into multiple military and government websites, as well as the networks of Gawker in December 2010, HBGary in 2011, PBS, Sony, Infragard Atlanta, Fox Entertainment, and more.

ITEM	NOTES
Case name:	*R v Cleary, Davis, Al-Bassam and Ackroyd*
Citation:	Southwark Crown Court (May 16 and 24, 2013)
Jurisdiction:	United Kingdom, Southwark Crown Court in London
Main URL:	Free Anons, "Interview: Ryan Ackroyd AKA Kayla of LulzSec" (April 15, 2014) https://freeanons.org/interview-ryan-ackroyd-aka-kayla-lulzsec/.
	S. Storm, "London court: LulzSec hackers called 'latter day pirates' at 'cutting-edge' of cybercrime," *Computer World*, May 15, 2013, available at https://www.computerworld.com/article/2475432/cybercrime-hacking/london-court--lulzsec-hackers-called--latter-day-pirates--at--cutting-edge--of-cy.html.

Charged with:	Implied to be offences under Computer Misuse Act 1990 (with which others arrested in similar circumstances were charged)
Legislative provisions:	Computer Misuse Act 1990 section 3—unauthorized act to impair the operation of a computer
Main target:	Military and government, as well as large multinational companies
Motivation:	It has been suggested that LulzSec sought to achieve international notoriety and publicity (see Storm)
Convicted of:	April 9, 2013: Pled not guilty to DDoS attacks that were carried out under the LulzSec banner during its AntiSec campaign (discussed below). However, Ackroyd did plead guilty to violating the Computer Misuse Act (unauthorized act to impair the operation of a computer).
Sentence:	In 2013, Ackroyd was sentenced to a thirty-month prison sentence in England, but was released on a "home detention curfew" after serving ten months. He was on probation until 2015 and under a "serious crime prevention order," which prevented him from using encryption that allows hidden volumes, virtual machines, or from deleting his web history.
Additional important information:	In the case, Cleary and the other defendants (Davis, Al-Bassam, Ackroyd) all pled guilty to two counts of conspiracy to commit unauthorized act with the intent to impair the operation of a computer and unauthorized access and modification to websites. Ryan Ackroyd is now an associate lecturer at Sheffield Hallam University.

R v Weatherhead, Rhodes, Gibson and Birchall

Christopher Weatherhead ("Nerdo")—had a leading role in plotting the attacks.

Ashley Rhodes ("Nikonelite")—was the most "hands-on" of the four men and the only one with DDoS software on his computer.

Peter Gibson—played a lesser role in the attacks.

Jake Birchall ("Fennic")—conspired to impair the operation of computers during the attacks. Birchall was said to have a "great deal or organisational control" over "AnonOps." His sentence was handed down at a later date, once he turned eighteen.

The four men were each convicted of attacking anti-piracy and financial companies between August 2010 and January 2011. The assaults on PayPal, Visa, and MasterCard were in retaliation for those companies cutting ties with the whistle-blowing website WikiLeaks following its release of secret diplomatic cables.

ITEM	NOTES
Case name:	*R v Christopher Weatherhead, Ashley Rhodes, Peter Gibson, and Jake Birchall*
Citation:	Southwark Crown Court (January 24, 2013)
Jurisdiction:	United Kingdom, Southwark Crown Court in London
Main URL:	J. Halliday, "Anonymous Teenager Hacker Spared Jail over Cyber Attacks," *Guardian*, February 1, 2013, available at http://www.guardian.co.uk/technology/2013/feb/01/anonymous-teenage-hacker
Charged with:	DDoS on Paypal, Visa, and Mastercard in December 2010
Legislative provisions:	Computer Misuse Act 1990, section 3—unauthorized acts with intent to impair; conspiring to impair the operation of computers
Main target:	PayPal, Visa, MasterCard
Motivation:	In retaliation for companies cutting ties with the whistle-blowing website WikiLeaks following its release of secret US diplomatic cables
Convicted of:	Attacking anti-piracy and financial companies via DDoS attacks between August 2010 and January 2011. Weatherhead, Rhodes, and Gibson were convicted of one count each of conspiracy to impair the operation of computers (Rhodes and Gibson pled guilty).
Sentence:	Christopher Weatherhead: eighteen months in prison. Ashley Rhodes: seven months in prison. Peter Gibson: six month suspended sentence. Jake Birchall: eighteen-month youth rehabilitation order and a sixty-hours unpaid work.
Additional important information:	PayPal was repeatedly attacked in December 2010 after the website decided not to process payments made to the Wau Holland Foundation (an organization involved in raising funds for WikiLeaks). During trial, prosecutors said the attack had cost PayPal $5.5 million in loss of trading as well as in software and hardware updates to fend off similar attacks. Birchall was told he would have been imprisoned had he not been sixteen at time of the offence

R v Glenn Mangham

Glenn Mangham impersonated an employee of the social-networking site Facebook while on holiday and hacked into three of its servers. Using the code name "Gamma Ray" he stole the secret computer code "that gives Facebook its value" and downloaded it to his home computer's hard drive. Mangham claimed that his work was "ethical hacking" and he breached the security so that he could identify vulnerabilities within the site, which the developers could then strengthen.

ITEM	NOTES
Case name:	R v Glenn Steven Mangham. Court of Appeal: R v Glenn Steven Mangham
Citation:	Southwark Crown Court (February 17, 2012) Court of Appeal [2012] EWCA Crim 973 (April 4, 2012)
Jurisdiction:	United Kingdom, Southwark Crown Court in London; England and Wales Court of Appeal (Criminal Division)
Main URL:	E. Protalinski, "British student jailed for hacking into Facebook," Zdnet, February 18, 2012, available at http://www.zdnet.com/blog/facebook/british-student-jailed-for-hacking-into-facebook/9244 (last accessed December 21, 2016). M. Mangham, "The Facebook Hack: What Really Happened" on GMangham Blog (April 23, 2012), available at http://gmangham.blogspot.co.uk/2012/04/facebook-hack-what-really-happened.html (last accessed December 21, 2016). Case (Court of Appeal), http://www.bailii.org/ew/cases/EWCA/Crim/2012/973.html.
Charged with:	Three counts of unauthorized access and modification of a computer but he was convicted of two counts under the Computer Misuse Act 1990
Legislative provisions:	Computer Misuse Act 1990, sections 1 (unauthorized access), 3 (unauthorized acts with intent to impair a protected computer), and 3A (making, supplying or obtaining articles for use in offences under sections 1or 3)
Main target:	Facebook
Motivation:	Ethical hacking to identify site vulnerabilities

Convicted of:	Mangham pleaded guilty to four counts: counts one to three, securing unauthorized access to computer material with intent (contrary to the Computer Misuse Act 1990, section 1) and count four, the unauthorized modification of computer material, contrary to section 3 of that act
Sentence:	Was initially sentenced to eight months' imprisonment and was handed a "serious crime prevention" order, which restricted his access to the internet and forfeiture of computer. Later, the appeal was allowed and the sentence was reduced to four months' imprisonment, with the order quashed.
Additional important information:	The presiding judge told Mangham: "This was not just a bit of harmless experimentation—you accessed the very heart of the system of an international business of massive size." Mangham claimed he was an ethical hacker who had previously helped Yahoo improve its security and had wanted to do the same for Facebook.

AUSTRALIA

Matthew George

Matthew George was an Australian member of Anonymous who participated in what the group called Operation Titstorm. He was charged with inciting others to attack government websites and the magistrate likened his activities to cyber terrorism.

ITEM	NOTES
Case name:	Court case unreported online. Case details retrieved from news articles.
Citation:	Court case unreported online. Case details retrieved from news articles.
Jurisdiction:	Australia, Newcastle Local Court
Main URL:	S. Whyte. "Meet the Hacktivist Who Tried to Take Down the Government," *Sydney Morning Herald*, March 14, 2011, available at https://www.smh.com.au/technology/meet-the-hacktivist-who-tried-to-take-down-the-government-20110314-1btkt.html (last accessed November 7, 2011).
Charged with:	Unauthorized impairment of electronic communication to or from a Commonwealth computer
Legislative provisions:	Criminal Code Act 1995 section 477.3—unauthorized impairment of electronic communication

ETHICAL HACKING

Main target:	Denial-of-service attack against the websites of the prime minister and a cabinet minister in protest of proposed Internet filtering and the presence of certain URLs on a proposed blacklist
Motivation:	Protest Internet filtering
Convicted of:	Unauthorized impairment of electronic communication to or from a Commonwealth computer
Sentence:	$550 fine
Additional important information:	Another Anonymous member involved in the attack was Steve Slayo, who faced a good behaviour bond for the offence—the magistrate did not record a conviction for his offence.

Justin Michael Soyke

Australian teenage member of Anonymous, Justin Michael Soyke, aka "Juzzy" and "Absantos," received a three-year sentence for attempting to hack government and company servers. He was able to gain system and website administrator privileges, hence, accessing private information. The Commonwealth Director of Public Prosecutions claimed that it was likely that Soyke engaged with other hackers to perform the attack.

ITEM	NOTES
Case name:	Initial court case unreported online Criminal appeal case reported online: *Soyke v R*
Citation:	[2016] NSWCCA 112 (June 10, 2016)
Jurisdiction:	Australia, New South Wales Court
Main URL:	J. Saarinen, "Aussie Anon sentenced to three years' prison," IT News, November 19, 2015, available at https://www.itnews.com.au/news/aussie-anon-sentenced-to-three-years-prison-411978.
Charged with:	One count of unauthorized modification of computer data, in violation of Criminal Code Act 1995 section 477.2(1), one count of attempt to cause unauthorized modification of computer data, in violation of sections 477.2(1) and 11.1, and two counts of unauthorized access to data with intent to commit serious offence, in violation of section 466.1(1)(a)(i). Each carry a maximum penalty of ten years' imprisonment.

	Another seventeen offences of attempt to cause unauthorized access to restricted data under sections 478.1(1) and 11.1(1) of the code, which each carry maximum penalties of two years' imprisonment, were also taken into account.
Legislative provisions:	Criminal Code Act 1995 sections 477, 478.1(1), and 11.1(1)
Main target:	Government and company servers
Motivation:	Unknown, but believed to be in connection with Anonymous efforts to make information about corporations and governments publicly available
Convicted of:	One count of unauthorized modification of computer data, in violation of Criminal Code Act 1995 section 477.2(1); one count of attempt to cause unauthorized modification of computer data, in violation of sections 477.2(1) and 11.1; and two counts of unauthorized access to data with intent to commit serious offence, in violation of section 466.1(1)(a)(i). A further seventeen offences of attempt to cause unauthorized access to restricted data in violation of sections 478.1(1) and 11.1(1) were also taken into account.
Sentence:	October 15, 2015: Soyke was sentenced on twenty-one charges of computer hacking, with three years' imprisonment and an order that he be released on recognizance of $5,000 to be of good behaviour after serving twelve months. June 10, 2016: Soyke's appeal was dismissed.
Additional important information:	Soyke is linked to other hackers associated with Anonymous such as UK citizen Lauri Love, and two other Australians, Mathew Hutchison (aka "Rax") and Adam John Bennett (aka "Lorax"). Love, Hutchison, and Bennett have also faced legal consequences because of their involvement with Anonymous.

Anonymous Indonesia and BlackSinChan

In retaliation to the spying scandal conducted by the Australian government against Indonesian officials, including former Indonesian Prime Minister Susilo Bambag Yudhoyono, various Indonesian hacking groups targeted Australian law-enforcement websites. The attacks also targeted groups that were not involved with the spying scandal, including the Reserve Bank of Australia (RBA)—sparking threats from Anonymous Australia. At the time, concerns developed around the potential of cyberwarfare emerging between Anonymous Australia and Anonymous Indonesia.

ITEM	NOTES
Case name:	Unable to retrieve the case. Facts taken from news articles
Citation:	Unknown—unable to retrieve case
Jurisdiction:	Difficult to determine as both countries claim sovereignty. However, since the crime was conducted against Australia, this would be a federal offence
Main URL:	A. Coyne, "How the AFP nabbed an Aussie Anonymous hacker," It News, March 20, 2017, available at https://www.itnews.com.au/news/how-the-afp-nabbed-an-aussie-anonymous-hacker-455142. M. Ross, "Anonymous Indonesia hacker says RBA, AFP attacks were retaliation for spying scandal," ABC News, November 21, 2013, available at http://www.abc.net.au/news/2013-11-21/hacker-says-rba-afp-attacks-were-retaliation-for-spying-scandal/5108220. P. Smith, "Indonesian claims responsibility for RBA and AFP attack," *Australian Financial Review*, November 21, 2013, available at http://www.afr.com/p/technology/indonesian_claims_responsibility_Y8kgaLtlfixvXGV5V6FH3I. W. Ockenden, "Crime Stoppers website hacked, police email addresses published in spying scandal 'payback,'" ABC News, November 27, 2013, available at http://www.abc.net.au/news/2013-11-26/crime-stoppers-site-targeted-by-indonesian-hackers/5116856.
Charged with:	Again, the constraints concerning the cooperation between Australia and Indonesia hindered the ability for law enforcement to charge individuals of a crime. Furthermore, it is difficult to charge a collective with a crime when not all its members were responsible for the hacks.
Legislative provisions:	Criminal Code Act 1995—Part 10.7 Computer Offences
Main target:	Over 150 Australian websites, including those of the RBA, AFP, ASIS, and Crime Stoppers. Targeted websites were mainly law-enforcement sites, which Anonymous Indonesia deemed as "important" to Australia.
Motivation:	Retaliation to Australian spying scandal of Indonesian officials. Revenge and deterrence.
Convicted of:	It is unknown what legal action was taken in response to Anonymous Indonesia and Anonymous Australia, but some Australian hackers were convicted and sentenced for their attacks against Australian websites.

	Australian hacker, Justin Michael Soyke (aka "Juzzy and Absantos") was charged with sixty out of an alleged 300 offences related to the attack on government websites. Soyke pled guilty to twenty-one charges of computer hacking. Another two Australian hackers, Adam John Bennett (aka "Lorax") and Michael John Hutchison (aka "Rax"), were also charged. Bennett was convicted of six charges including aiding another person to cause the unauthorized impairment of electronic communications. Hutchison pled guilty to inciting others to commit an offence and to possessing a prohibited weapon.
Sentence:	Again, it is unknown what legal action was taken in response to Anonymous Indonesia and Anonymous Australia, but the three Australian hackers were sentenced. In October 2015, Soyke was sentenced to one year in jail and a three-year recognizance. In March 2016, Bennett was sentenced to two years' suspended imprisonment, 200 hours of community service, and an intensive supervision order. Hutchison entered guilty pleas for inciting others to commit an offence and to possessing a prohibited weapon.
Additional important information:	Many of the government groups that were targeted, such as the RBA, had nothing to do with the spying scandal. At the time, Anonymous Australia threatened to retaliate against Anonymous Indonesia if another hack against an innocent site were to be conducted.

CANADA

Rehtaeh Parsons Rape Case

Canadian teenager Rehtaeh Parsons was gang raped when she was fifteen. The rapists circulated a digital image of the rape, which was shared on the Internet. Parsons committed suicide after facing years of constant torment and related bullying. The Royal Canadian Mounted Police (RCMP) investigated the for a year but said it did not have sufficient evidence to lay charges. This outraged people all over the Internet, including Anonymous. Anonymous vowed to expose the identities of the rapists online. Anonymous confirmed the identities of two of the four alleged rapists.

In the group's statement, it claims to have seen what it calls a confession from one of the young men who allegedly admitted he raped Parsons and named three other boys who had gang raped her as well though the police only brought charges against two of the boys responsible of taking the photo and this circulating it.

ITEM	NOTES
Case name:	Rehtaeh Parsons rape case—Anonymous's attempt to identify the rapists via hacktivism
Citation:	No reported case found online—most likely due to the offenders being minors when committing the crime. Case information retrieved from news articles
Jurisdiction:	Nova Scotia, Canada
Main URL:	*Huffington Post*, "Anonymous Claims Suspect Confessed To Rehtaeh Parsons' Rape," April 12, 2013, available at http://www.huffingtonpost.com/2013/04/12/anonymous-suspect-confession-rehtaeh-parsons-rape_n_3070615.html.
	D. Bates, "Anonymous threaten to unmask boys who 'drove 17-year-old girl to hang herself after they gang raped her and put photo on web'," *Daily Mail*, April 11, 2013, available at http://www.dailymail.co.uk/news/article-2307266/Rehtaeh-Parsons-gang-rape-Anonymous-threaten-unmask-boys-drove-girl-hang-herself.html.
Charged with:	In 2014 and 2015, police reopened the case and laid child-pornography-related charges against two teenage males, one eighteen and the other nineteen, for taking and sharing indecent images of a child.
	The identities of the accused are shielded by Canada's Youth Criminal Justice Act because they were under the age of eighteen at the time of the alleged offences.
Legislative provisions:	Following the death of Rehtaeh Parsons, Canada passed a Cyber-Safety Act, an anti-cyberbulling law.
Main target:	Rehtaeh Parsons's rapists
Motivation:	To expose the identities of four rapists after what Anonymous viewed as police inactivity in relation to the case
Convicted of:	Members of Anonymous were not convicted in relation to this case

Sentence:	Members of Anonymous were not sentenced in relation to this case.
	The two teenage males who were charged in relation to child-pornography charges were sentenced to probation. One of the charged received a conditional discharge (conviction will not show on his criminal record unless he violates probation). The other male's conviction will be removed from his criminal record after five years.
Additional important information:	"Once Anonymous made their rage and intent clear, they were flooded with witness testimony, and from there built the case of the RCMP's incompetence on three points: that dozens of teens and adults had heard the rapists brag about taking part in the gang rape, that the photo taken of the rape was reportedly so widely circulated it's unlikely the authorities ever bothered to try and find it so they might look at the EXIF data, and that Parsons' school did nothing, despite the fact that child pornography was going viral in their hallways." (Waugh, "Rehtaeh Parsons Rape Case Solved by Anonymous.")
	In August 2013, Nova Scotia enacted a law allowing victims of cyberbullying to seek protection, including help in identifying anonymous perpetrators, and to sue the individuals or the parents in the case of minors. The law was passed in response to Parsons's suicide. However, the law was struck down to be redrafted after it was found to violate the Canadian Charter of Rights and Freedoms.

ISRAEL

State of Israel v Anat Kamm

The defendant secretly copied thousands of classified (many confidential) military files during her military service, which she leaked, giving the files to a *Haaretz* journalist.

ITEM	NOTES
Case name:	*State of Israel v Anat Kamm* (2010). *Anat Kamm v State of Israel* [2012]
Citation:	Case 17959-01-10
Jurisdiction:	Israel, District Court of Tel Aviv Jaffa Israel Supreme Court

Main URL:	Wikipedia, *Anat Kamm-Uri Blau Affair* (October 20, 2018) http://en.wikipedia.org/wiki/Anat_Kamm-Uri_Blau_affair
	Case, http://www.maannews.net/eng/ViewDetails. aspx?ID=275114
Charged with:	Aggravated espionage with intent to harm the security of the state (Penal Law (1977) cl 13b) Leaking secret information with the intention to harm the security of the state (cl 113c)
Legislative provisions:	Penal Law (1977) cl 13b and 113c
Main target:	Israel Defence Forces (IDF)
Motivation:	Kamm wanted to release some details of the IDF's operational procedures in the West Bank as she felt that they should be in the public domain. There was information in the leak that suggested that the military went against a ruling made by an Israeli court against the assassination of wanted militants who could have otherwise been arrested safely.
Convicted of:	Leaking classified materials
Sentence:	February 6, 2011: Kamm pled guilty in a plea bargain to leaking more than 2,000 secret military documents.
	October 30, 2011: Sentenced to four-and-a-half years' imprisonment (down from a maximum of fifteen years) and eighteen months' probation.
	December 31, 2012: The Supreme Court granted her appeal and shortened her sentence to three-and-a-half years in a majority decision, noting her cooperation in the investigation.
Additional important information:	Kamm was released in January 2014 after serving over two years in prison.

INDONESIA

Wildan Yani Ashari

Internet café worker Wildan Yani Ashari was arrested by police after he replaced the home page of then-Indonesian President Susilo Bambang Yudhoyono with the message: "This is a PayBack From Jember Hacker Team." This was believed to be in protest at growing corruption and wealth inequality in the country.

ITEM	NOTES
Case name:	Unable to retrieve case. Case facts taken from news articles
Citation:	Unknown—unable to retrieve case
Jurisdiction:	Indonesia
Main URL:	J. Goldman, "Indonesian Government Sites Hacked Following Hacker's Arrest," *eSecurity Planet*, January 31, 2013, available at http://www.esecurityplanet.com/hackers/indonesian-government-sites-hacked-following-hackers-arrest.html
Charged with:	Charged under the Information and Electronic Transaction Law (2008)
Legislative provisions:	Information and Electronic Transaction Law (2008)
Main target:	Indonesian president's website homepage
Motivation:	Increased anger over the current administration
Convicted of:	Unknown due to not being able to retrieve case. Presumably, sentencing would have been under the Information and Electronic Transaction Law.
Sentence:	Facing a maximum sentence of twelve years' imprisonment and a maximum fine of IDR 12 billion (US$1.2 million)
Additional important information:	Goldman referenced the *Jakarta Globe*, which reported: "In what were reportedly acts of solidarity for Wildan, Anonymous hackers hacked at least seven sites, including those of the Justice and Human Rights Ministry, the Social Affairs Ministry, the Tourism and Creative Economy Ministry, the Central Statistics Agency (BPS), the Business Competition Supervisory Commission (KPPU) and the Indonesian Embassy in Taskhent." Goldman referenced Voice of America's Kate Lamb, who reported: "Instead of the official pages, web users were greeted by a cloaked figure alongside the catchphrase: 'No Army Can Stop an Idea.'" Indonesia's then communications minister, Tifatul Sembiring, said there were 36.6 million incidents of hacking against the government in 2012.

JAPAN

Yusuke Katayama

Japanese police on Sunday arrested a man, Yusuke Katayama (aka "Demon Killer"), suspected of being behind a computer-hacking campaign following an exhaustive hunt that at one stage had authorities tracking down a cat for clues, according to reports.

ITEM	NOTES
Case name:	Unable to retrieve case. Case facts taken from news articles.
Citation:	Unknown—unable to retrieve case
Jurisdiction:	Japan, Tokyo District Court
Main URL:	*Sydney Morning Herald*, "Man Arrested Over Bizarre Hacking Campaign Involving Cat," February 11, 2013, available at http://www.smh.com.au/technology/technology-news/man-arrested-over-bizarre-hacking-campaign-involving-cat-20130211-2e77o.html
Charged with:	He was accused of five charges, including intimidation, business obstruction, using a remote computer, sending a mass-killing threat, and framing innocent people
Legislative provisions:	Unknown—unable to retrieve case and details regarding legislative provisions
Main target:	Several events around Japan
Motivation:	Grudge against authorities
Convicted of:	Unknown—unable to retrieve case and details regarding legislative provisions
Sentence:	Eight years' imprisonment
Additional important information:	According to the *Sydney Morning Herald*, Katayama created a set of riddles and messages going out to media outlets and investigators. He claimed that the details of a computer virus used to dispatch the threats were strapped to a cat living on an island near Tokyo.
	After authorities solved a set of riddles, they found the cat that led to the arrest of Katayama in February 2013. There was a digital memory card around the cat's collar saying "a past experience in a criminal case" had caused the hacker to act.

SINGAPORE

James Raj Arokiasamy AKA "The Messiah"

Anonymous member James Raj Arokiasamy (aka "The Messiah") hacked into the official Ang Mo Kio town council website to, he claimed, highlight the website's vulnerability. He also hacked into at least seven organizations' websites.

ITEM	NOTES
Case name:	*James Raj Arokiasamy v Public Prosecutor*
Citation:	[2014] 2 SLR 307 ("James Raj")
Jurisdiction:	Singapore, States Courts
Main URL:	Banyan, "Messiah complicated," *Economist*, December 7, 2013, available at http://www.economist.com/blogs/banyan/2013/12/hacking-singapore. Banyan, "Two steps back," *Economist*, February 25, 2014, available at http://www.economist.com/blogs/banyan/2013/06/regulating-singapores-internet. I. Poh, "Hacker who called himself 'The Messiah' jailed 4 years and 8 months," *Straits Times*, January 30, 2015, available at https://www.straitstimes.com/singapore/courts-crime/hacker-who-called-himself-the-messiah-jailed-4-years-and-8-months.
Charged with:	November 12, 2013: Charged under the Computer Misuse and Cybersecurity Act with carrying out unauthorized modifications to websites
Legislative provisions:	Computer Misuse and Cybersecurity Act Ch 50A (Rev Ed 2007)
Main target:	Various government, organization, and church websites
Motivation:	Retaliation against Singapore's new "Internet-licensing" regime
Convicted of:	Pled guilty in January 2015 to thirty-nine computer misuse offences and one count of drug consumption
Sentence:	Sentenced to four years and eight months in jail
Additional important information:	Denied bail—previously jumped bail and fled to Malaysia after facing drug-consumption charges in 2011. Organizations affected by the hack spent about $1.36 million assessing, repairing, and restoring affected computer systems.

	Expecting physical protests, instead the Singaporean government faced a plethora of hacks in protesting the licensing policy after the arrest of Arokiasamy, including the defacement of thirteen school websites on November 22, 2013.

GERMANY

Andreas-Thomas Vogel

Andreas-Thomas Vogel launched a denial-of-service attack against the website of German airline Lufthansa in protest of the company's treatment of asylum seekers. Vogel was angered with Lufthansa for making profit from deporting illegal immigrants and he wanted to publicize these grievances. He planned a denial-of-service attack June 20, 2001, and programmed a software, which protesters could download to enable a large number of page views. Vogel posted a call to action on the website libertad.de.

ITEM	NOTES
Case name:	*Libertad.de* (2006)
Citation:	File reference 1 Ss 319/05, March 22, 2006
Jurisdiction:	Germany, Higher Regional Court, Frankfurt am Main
Main URL:	J. Libbenga, "German court to examine Lufthansa attack," *The Register*, April 1, 2005, available at https://www.theregister.co.uk/2005/04/01/lufthansa_ddos_attack/. R. Bendrath, "Frankfurt Appellate Court Says Online Demonstration is Not Coercion," EDRi, June 7, 2006, available at https://edri.org/edrigramnumber4-11 demonstration/.
Charged with:	Coercion and incitement of alteration of data
Legislative provisions:	German Criminal Code sections 240 (coercion), 111 (public incitement to crime), and 303a (data tampering)
Main target:	Lufthansa
Motivation:	To protest Lufthansa's stance on asylum seekers and achieve publicity
Convicted of:	Vogel was indicted and convicted of coercion in the Frankfurt court. The Frankfurt Appellate Court reversed the decision, stating that the DDoS attack was a legitimate exercise of free speech.

Sentence:	Initially, Vogel was sentenced to pay a financial penalty or serve ninety days in jail. However, in his appeal, he was acquitted by the Higher Regional Court of Frankfurt.
Additional important information:	The demonstration had 13,614 participants with different IP addresses and encompassed 1,126,200 page views. The damages were about €5,500 for personal costs and €42,000 for further impairments.

Note

1. *United States of America v. Ford.*

CHAPTER V

Select Ethical-Hacking Incidences: Anonymous

One of the most well-known ethical-hacking "groups" is Anonymous. The word group here is arguably used incorrectly as Anonymous is more like an umbrella name or a movement for a plethora of smaller groups and operations. In addition to performing denial-of-service attacks, members of some of the smaller groups participate in more sophisticated forms of hacktivism that require a higher range of computer skills. Instances of these more sophisticated attacks include the release of names and details of the Mexican drug cartel, Los Zetas, the names and details of individuals who use child-pornography sites, and the capturing of secret documents held by governments around the world—some of these documents are then given and released by WikiLeaks.

Hacktivism is not limited to attacking information systems and retrieving documents. It also extends to finding technical solutions to mobilize people. At the height of the Egyptian e-revolution the major Internet-service providers and mobile-phone companies, under government direction, shut down the Internet, flipping the so-called Internet kill switch, preventing people from using the Internet and mobile phones. This, in turn, affected people's ability to mobilize. Anonymous worked around the clock to ensure that images from the revolution were still sent to international media.

This chapter takes selected notable ethical-hacking incidences from the quantitative work in chapter 3 and breaks down incident by group, target, date, source, motivation, type of attack, whether any other groups have claimed responsibility, damage caused, and additional important information. This chapter will only explore incidences by Anonymous. The following chapter addresses select incidences for CCC, CyberBerkut, LulzSec, and others. Again, some of the incidences from the last chapter, this chapter, and the proceeding chapter will be explored in great detail from technical, political, criminological, and policy perspectives based on their classification in chapters 7 through 9.

ANONYMOUS

Anonymous—Operation Titstorm

ITEM	NOTES
Target:	Australian Government/Kevin Rudd
Date:	February 10, 2010
Source:	P. Martin, "Australian Government Website Hacked in Protest," *Technorati*, February 10, 2010, available at http://technorati.com/politics/article/australian-government-website-hacked-in-protest/ (last accessed February 11, 2010).
	"Operation Titstorm—Anonymous Wants Their Small Boobs" (February 12, 2010), available at http://www.youtube.com/watch?v=FdPmbiK4JGY.
	"Anonymous Message to the Australian Government" (February 14, 2010), available at http://www.youtube.com/watch?v=yK1nsGFsvbo.
Motivation:	Protest Internet filtering
Type of attack:	Unauthorized access, modification of data, defacement
Any other groups claiming responsibility:	No
Damage caused:	Kevin Rudd's website defaced with the words "Operation Titstorm" for an unspecified period of time
Additional important information:	N/A

Anonymous—ACS:Law

ITEM	NOTES
Target:	ACS
Date:	September 21, 2010
Source:	Wecanchangetheworld, "4Chan Hacks Anti Piracy Lawfirm, Leaks Porn Downloaders' Names," *Buzzfeed*, November 29, 2010, available at http://www.buzzfeed.com/wecanchangetheworld/4chan-hacks-anti-piracy-lawfirm-leaks-porn-downlo-1q36 (last accessed November 21, 2011).
	Enigmax, "New 4chan DDoS Targets Hated Anti-Piracy Law Firm," *Torrent Freak*, September 22, 2010, available at https://torrentfreak.com/new-4chan-ddos-targets-hated-anti-piracy-law-firm-100922/.
Motivation:	Operation: Payback- Protesting anti-piracy actions by large corporate entities
Type of attack:	DDoS, unauthorized access, data leak
Any other groups claiming responsibility:	No
Damage caused:	Published company emails and 5,300 names of people accused of illegally downloading "pr0n"
Additional important information:	N/A

Anonymous—PayPal

ITEM	NOTES
Target:	PayPal
Date:	December 6–9, 2010
Source:	J. Leyden, "Anonymous attacks PayPal in 'Operation Avenge Assange,'" *The Register*, December 6, 2010, available at http://www.theregister.co.uk/2010/12/06/anonymous_launches_pro_wikileaks_campaign/.
	M. Raman, "FBI Cracks Down on 'Anonymous' Over PayPal Hacking, Arrests 14," *International Business Times*, July 20, 2011, available at https://www.ibtimes.com/fbi-cracks-down-anonymous-over-paypal-hacking-arrests-14-300225 (last accessed July 21, 2011).

	US Department of Justice, Office of Public Affairs, "Sixteen Individuals Arrested in the United States for Alleged Roles in Cyber Attacks" (press release, July 19, 2011), available at http://www.fbi.gov/news/pressrel/press-releases/sixteen-individuals-arrested-in-the-united-states-for-alleged-roles-in-cyber-attacks (last accessed November 10, 2011).
	"Anonymous—Antisec—OP PayPal" (July 27, 2011), available at http://www.youtube.com/watch?v=aa-h0HHp908.
Motivation:	Operation Avenge Assange—retaliation for blocking WikiLeaks donations
Type of attack:	DDoS
Any other groups claiming responsibility:	No
Damage caused:	It was reported that the attack lasted about eight hours and resulted in numerous disruptions. Little is known of what these disruptions entailed.
Additional important information:	Fourteen alleged members of Anonymous charged for intentional damage to protected computers, which carries a maximum penalty of ten years' (five for conspiracy) imprisonment and a $250,000 fine.
	The individuals named in the San Jose indictment are: Christopher Wayne Cooper, aka "Anthrophobic"; Joshua John Covelli, aka "Absolem" and "Toxic"; Keith Wilson Downey; Mercedes Renee Haefer, aka "No" and "MMMM"; Donald Husband, aka "Ananon"; Vincent Charles Kershaw, aka "Trivette," "Triv" and "Reaper"; Ethan Miles; James C. Murphy; Drew Alan Phillips, aka "Drew010"; Jeffrey Puglisi, aka "Jeffer," "Jefferp" and "Ji"; Daniel Sullivan; Tracy Ann Valenzuela; and Christopher Quang Vo. One individual's name was withheld by the court.

Anonymous—WikiLeaks revenge

ITEM	NOTES
Target:	MasterCard, Visa, Swedish prosecutor's office, Sara Palin's website
Date:	December 8–9, 2010
Source:	*The Australian*, "Wikileaks Complaint Against Visa" (July 5, 2011) https://www.theaustralian.com.au/news/world/wikileaks-complainst-against-visa/news-story/e5f38c1f5317f64cf0e73ca21921fa1c

	"Anonymous attack on MasterCard, discussed on 4 News" (December 8, 2010), available at http://www.youtube.com/watch?v=i4HKk5yB8fU.
Motivation:	Retaliation for blocking funding to WikiLeaks—Operation Avenge Assange
Type of attack:	DDoS
Any other groups claiming responsibility:	No
Damage caused:	• MasterCard's main site was down for seven hours on December 8. • Visa's site was down for two hours on December 9. • Sara Palin's site was down for six minutes; additionally, her and her husband's bank accounts were disrupted. • Swedish prosecutor's office website was taken off-line for an unspecified period of time.
Additional important information:	Wikileaks lodged a complaint with the European Commission regarding the actions of Visa and Master Card for banning payment to Julian Assange's legal fund (The Australian)

Anonymous—Sony (PS3)

ITEM	NOTES
Target:	Sony
Date:	April 4, 2011
Source:	J. Mick, "Anonymous Engages in Sony DDoS Attacks Over GeoHot PS3 Lawsuit," *Daily Tech*, April 4, 2011, available at http://www.dailytech.com/Anonymous+Engages+in+Sony+DDoS+Attacks+Over+GeoHot+PS3+Lawsuit/article21282.htm. M. Raman, "FBI Cracks Down on 'Anonymous' Over PayPal Hacking, Arrests 14," *International Business Times*, July 20, 2011, available at https://www.ibtimes.com/fbi-cracks-down-anonymous-over-paypal-hacking-arrests-14-300225 (last accessed July 21, 2011). "We are Anonymous—Sony hacked" (April 28, 2011), available at http://www.youtube.com/watch?v=370bq3VS5WU.

Motivation:	Retaliation for Sony taking legal action against George Hotz, a coder who wrote a tool that, Raman reported, "allows *homebrew* software to run on the PlayStation 3 (PS3)." The tool allows for the use of third-party software on the consoles.
Type of attack:	DDoS, data theft, unauthorized access.
Any other groups claiming responsibility:	LulzSec
Damage caused:	PS3 online capabilities were disrupted for almost a month.
Additional important information:	Compromised personal data of 77 million users worldwide; it is considered the largest breach of its kind to date.

Anonymous—Westboro Baptist Church

ITEM	NOTES
Target:	Westboro Baptist Church—church/organization
Date:	February, 2011
Source:	E-Li, "Anti-Gay Website Hacked by Anonymous," *lezbelib.over-blog.com*, June 4, 2011, available at http://lezbelib.over-blog.com/article-anti-gay-website-hacked-by-anonymous-75636306.html (last accessed June 5, 2011).
	"Anonymous v. Westboro Baptists" (February 22, 2011), available at http://www.youtube.com/watch?v=jUcW_8Ya32Q.
	"Anonymous Hacks Westboro Baptist Church During LIVE" (February 24, 2011), available at http://www.youtube.com/watch?v=OZJwSjor4hM.
	"Anonymous Members Allegedly Unmasked, Involved in Westboro Baptist Church Hacking Incident" (June 21, 2011), available at http://www.youtube.com/watch?v=QBExfh1oZCs.
Motivation:	Protesting homophobia; to retaliate for publicity church garnered in claiming prior Anonymous threats, which Anonymous denied
Type of attack:	Unspecified. Likely DDoS
Any other groups claiming responsibility:	No

Damage caused:	Took down a number of anti-gay websites for an unspecified period of time.
Additional important information:	The Westboro Baptist Church is the headquarters of campaign called "God Hates Fags," blaming the death of US soldiers on an acceptance of homosexuality by the United States, for example. Li reported that, in acknowledging the hack, Anonymous sent a message to the church that ended with "God hates fags: Assumption. Anonymous hates leeches: Fact."

Anonymous—Interpol attack

ITEM	NOTES
Target:	Interpol
Date:	28/3/12
Source:	B. Quinn, "Interpol Website Suffers 'Anonymous Cyber-Attack,'" *Guardian*, March 29, 2012, available at http://www.guardian.co.uk/technology/2012/feb/29/interpol-website-cyber-attack
Motivation:	Anonymous brought done a number of websites including the Interpol website in retaliation for arrest of twenty-five suspected members of Anonymous during Operation Unmask. Operation Unmask was part of a police operation where members of Anonymous were arrested for planned coordinated attacks against Columbia's defense ministry and presidential website.
Type of attack:	DDoS (suspected)
Any other groups claiming responsibility:	No
Damage caused:	Website off-line for a brief period
Additional important information:	N/A

Anonymous—Combined Systems (Bahraini contractor)

ITEM	NOTES
Target:	Combined Systems and Bahraini Government Website
Date:	February 14, 2012
Source:	D. Rushe, "Anonymous Sends Unhappy Valentine's Day Greetings," *Guardian*, February 14, 2012, available at http://www.guardian.co.uk/world/us-news-blog/2012/feb/14/anonymous-hacking-valentines-day-nasdaq
Motivation:	Response to alleged weapons sales of Combined Systems to the Bahraini Government, used in the suppression of anti-government protests
Type of attack:	DDoS (suspected)
Any other groups claiming responsibility:	Unknown
Damage caused:	Combined Systems and Bahraini Government Websites taken off-line
Additional important information:	Demonstrates (at least a segment of) Anonymous support for the Bahraini Uprising/Arab Spring

Anonymous—Nasdaq OMX—"Operation Digital Tornado"

ITEM	NOTES
Target:	Nasdaq OMX
Date:	February 14, 2012
Source:	D. Rushe, "Anonymous Sends Unhappy Valentine's Day Greetings," *Guardian*, February 14, 2012, available at http://www.guardian.co.uk/world/us-news-blog/2012/feb/14/anonymous-hacking-valentines-day-nasdaq.
Motivation:	"We are the 99%" protest against perceived corporate greed
Type of attack:	DDoS (suspected)
Any other groups claiming responsibility:	Handle "L0NGwave99"; may or may not be a member of Anonymous
Damage caused:	"Intermittent Service Disruption" to Nasdaq OMX website
Additional important information:	N/A

Anonymous—Puckett & Faraj law firm

ITEM	NOTES
Target:	Puckett & Faraj law firm (US Marine Frank Wuterich's defence lawyers)
Date:	February 6, 2012
Source:	D. Rushe, "Anonymous Publishes Trove of Emails from Haditha Marine Law Firm," *Guardian*, February 7, 2012, available at http://www.guardian.co.uk/technology/2012/feb/06/anonymous-haditha-killings
Motivation:	Protest against the firm defending Wuterich, a US Marine who pled guilty to a "dereliction of duty," but served no jail time, relative to the massacre of twenty-four unarmed Iraqi civilians by Marines in Haditha
Type of attack:	Unauthorized access—black-hat hacking
Any other groups claiming responsibility:	No
Damage caused:	"Trove" of emails leaked onto "The Pirate Bay" website. Excerpts ere also posted on Pastebin, the anonymous Internet posting site.
Additional important information:	Interesting that Anonymous attacked a law firm, and, seemingly too, notions of the innocence until proven guilty and defendants' rights. "In other emails released by Anonymous, members of the firm appear to worry that hack may 'completely destroy the Law Firm'" (Rushe).

Anonymous—London Metropolitan Police/FBI

ITEM	NOTES
Target:	London Metropolitan Police/FBI
Date:	Late January/early February 2012
Source:	J. Halliday, and C. Arthur, "Anonymous' Release of Met and FBI Call Puts Hacker Group Back Centre Stage," *Guardian*, February 3, 2012, available at http://www.guardian.co.uk/technology/2012/feb/03/anonymous-hack-met-fbi-call
Motivation:	Proof of ability to infiltrate two country's top investigative bodies. Also protest over arrest of LulzSec members.
Type of attack:	Unauthorized access

Any other groups claiming responsibility:	No
Damage caused:	Eighteen-minute inter-agency conference call from January 17, 2012, leaked in late January/early February 2012
Additional important information:	"The call reveals British police and the FBI discussing the delay of court proceedings against two alleged members of the LulzSec hacking group, which attacked a number of sites in 2011 including the US Congress and UK Serious Organised Crime Agency" (Halliday and Arthur).

Anonymous—MasterCard

ITEM	NOTES
Target:	MasterCard
Date:	June 28, 2011
Source:	J. Bergen, "Anonymous hacktivists take down MasterCard.com again in support of WikiLeaks," *Geek*, June 28, 2011, available at http://www.geek.com/articles/news/anonymous-hacktivists-take-down-mastercard-com-again-in-support-of-wikileaks-20110628/ (last accessed June 29, 2011). C. Fernandez, "Second WikiLeaks payback vs. MasterCard: LulzSec or Anonymous?," *International Business Times*, June 29, 2011, available at http://www.ibtimes.com.au/second-wikileaks-payback-vs-mastercard-lulzsec-or-anonymous-1283014 (last accessed June 30, 2011).
Motivation:	Protest WikiLeaks defunding
Type of attack:	DDoS
Any other groups claiming responsibility:	LulzSec—alluded to in reports, not formally claimed
Damage caused:	The MasterCard site was reportedly down for two hours
Additional important information:	N/A

Anonymous—Turkish Internet filter

ITEM	NOTES
Target:	Turkish government
Date:	July 2011
Source:	C. Zakalwe, "Turkish Government Websites Hacked in Protest at Internet Censorship" *Stop Turkey—BlogSpot* (July 7, 2011), available at http://stopturkey.blogspot.com/2011/07/turkish-government-websites-hacked-in.html
Motivation:	Protest Internet filtering
Type of attack:	Unauthorized access, data theft, data leak, defacement
Any other groups claiming responsibility:	No
Damage caused:	Anonymous claimed to have stolen data from over a hundred Turkish websites and defaced seventy-four government websites for an unspecified period of time. Unspecified what was done with the stolen data.
Additional important information:	N/A

Anonymous—Operation AntiSec

ITEM	NOTES
Target:	Law enforcement, Intelligence Agencies and Government Departments Globally—Eg. Scotland, United Kingdom, Arizona, California. ...
Date:	August 1, 2011
Source:	L. Constantin, "AntiSec Hackers Hit 77 Law Enforcement Websites," *Softpedia*, August 1, 2011, available at http://news.softpedia.com/news/AntiSec-Hackers-Hit-77-Law-Enforcement-Websites-214555.shtml "Operation AntiSec" (June 2011-September 2012) available at https://everipedia.org/wiki/lang_en/Operation_AntiSec/
Motivation:	Retaliation for law-enforcement personnel's actions against protesters and arrests relating to the PayPal hack
Type of attack:	Unauthorized access, data theft, data modification, and data leak.

Any other groups claiming responsibility:	As the operation involved multiple hacking incidences, several groups participated including LulzSec, Anonymous, AntiSec NL, LulzSec Brazil, RedHack and other individual handler names
Damage caused:	Claim to have stolen 5–10 GB of data, including personal info on 7,000 officers.
Additional important information:	Anonymous also claimed to have stolen inmate info from prison services, which they are redacting. They threatened to publicize informant information—the publication of such information would be problematic. There were over 30 hacking incidences all under the banner of AntiSec involving retrieval of confidential information, the shutdown of websites but mostly the publication of information, many of which was protected by privacy laws.

Anonymous—Neo-Nazi websites

ITEM	NOTES
Target:	Neo-Nazi websites
Date:	August 8, 2011
Source:	M. Kumar, "Anonymous Hackers hack neo-Nazis websites & leak personal info of 16,000 Finns," *Hacker News*, November 8, 2011, available at http://thehackernews.com/2011/11/anonymous-hackers-hack-neo-nazis.html
Motivation:	As per *Hacker News*, "an apparent desire to shame the Finnish government into improving data security"
Type of attack:	Unauthorized access, defacement, data leak
Any other groups claiming responsibility:	No
Damage caused:	Released user information on 16,000 members
Additional important information:	N/A

Anonymous—Operation Free Condor

ITEM	NOTES
Target:	Quayaquil City Homepage (Ecuador)
Date:	August 8, 2011
Source:	T. Lara, "Hackers Attack Government Website in Ecuador to Protest President's Policies Against Freedom of Expression" on Knight Center for Journalism in the Americas, *Journalism in the Americas Blog* (August 10, 2011), available at http://knightcenter.utexas.edu/blog/hackers-attack-news-website-ecuador
Motivation:	Protest government measures against freedom of expression
Type of attack:	Sabotage and defacement. Site down for unspecified length of time
Any other groups claiming responsibility:	No
Damage caused:	Details of 45,000 police officers published, government threatened
Additional important information:	YouTube video was originally posted at this link (no longer available), http://www.youtube.com/watch?feature=player_embedded&v=ieC3gM5d_JM
	Another website (link unknown) attacked during same operation. Website based in Francisco de Orellana in eastern Ecuador.

Anonymous—BART

ITEM	NOTES
Target:	San Francisco's Bay Area Rapid Transit (BART)
Date:	August 15, 2011
Source:	L. Romney, "Bart drafts new policy on disruption of cellphone service," *LA Times*, October 19, 2011, available at http://latimesblogs.latimes.com/lanow/2011/10/bart-outlines-cell-phone-service-disruption-policy.html (last accessed October 20, 2011).
	E. Limer, "Anonymous follows through on BART hack, organizes protest," *Geekosystems*, August 15, 2011, available at http://www.geekosystem.com/anon-hacks-bart/.

	X. Jardin, "Anonymous hacks BART after wireless shutdown; protests planned for Monday," *Boing Boing*, August 14, 2011, available at http://boingboing. net/2011/08/14/anonymous-hacks-bart-after-wireless-shutdown-protests-planned-for-monday.html. "Website for BART customers hacked by Anonymous" (ABC News [US], August 15, 2011), available at http://www.youtube.com/watch?v=DjFSq-aTMm8&feature=related.
Motivation:	Perceived breach of first amendment rights—restricting freedom of speech by disabling telecommunications services
Type of attack:	Unauthorized access, modification of data, website defaced, release of personal information
Any other groups claiming responsibility:	No
Damage caused:	Defaced myBART website, leaked info on myBART user database which also included non-BART employees. Also "assured" non-BART employees that "the only information that will be abused from this database is that of BART employees."
Additional important information:	Undifferentiated/disorganized release of information. Though they claimed only BART employees would be abused, Anonymous made no distinction which employees may or may not have even been involved in cellphone disruption. Circumstances would include the alleged "destruction of district property."

Anonymous—OpIndependencia

ITEM	NOTES
Target:	Mexican government
Date:	September 15, 2011
Source:	E. Comley, "Hackers target Mexico government websites," Reuters, September 15, 2011, available at http://www.reuters.com/article/2011/09/15/us-mexico-hackers-idUSTRE78E7AC20110915 (last accessed September 18, 2011).

	M. Kumar, "Operation OpIndependencia: Anonymous hit Mexican government official websites," *Hacker News*, September 16, 2011, available at http://thehackernews.com/2011/09/operation-opindependencia-anonymous-hit.html (last accessed September 30, 2011).
Motivation:	Unknown
Type of attack:	DDoS
Any other groups claiming responsibility:	No
Damage caused:	Government websites off-line for a number of hours.
Additional important information:	N/A

Anonymous—RevoluSec

ITEM	NOTES
Target:	Syrian government websites
Date:	September 26, 2011
Source:	*Jerusalem Post*, "Online activists hack into Syrian government websites," September 26, 2011, available at https://www.jpost.com/Middle-East/Online-activists-hack-into-Syrian-government-websites (last accessed September 27, 2011).
	Anonymous—Operation Syria (September 12, 2011), available at http://www.youtube.com/watch?v=MGfF1ixk7S0.
	"Activists deface Syrian official websites" (Al Jazeera English, September 26, 2011), available at http://www.youtube.com/watch?v=qX30M6gakQ4.
Motivation:	Protesting level of government monitoring and injuries/deaths of protesters
Type of attack:	Unauthorized access, modification of data, defacement
Any other groups claiming responsibility:	No

Damage caused:	Caricatures of President Bashar Assaad were posted on defaced websites, as were protest messages, along with an interactive map of those reportedly killed during protests. Sites remained defaced for an unspecified period of time.
Additional important information:	N/A

Anonymous—New York Stock Exchange, Operation Icarus

ITEM	NOTES
Target:	New York Stock Exchange
Date:	October 4–10, 2011
Source:	D. Grant, "NYSE Hacked! Is The Anonymous Infrastructure Crumbling?," *New York Observer*, October 10, 2011, available at http://www.observer.com/2011/10/nyse-remains-unhacked-is-the-anonymous-infrastructure-crumbling-video/ (last accessed October 10, 2011). P. Chiaramonte and J. Winter, "Hacker Group Anonymous Threatens to Attack Stock Exchange," Fox News, October 4, 2011, available at http://www.foxnews.com/scitech/2011/10/04/hacker-group-anonymous-threatens-to-attack-stock-exchange/ (last accessed October 4, 2011). "Operation Invade Wall Street—A Message to the Media" (October 2, 2011), available at http://www.youtube.com/watch?v=lsLuYnEyFLw.
Motivation:	Occupy Wall Street protest
Type of attack:	DDoS
Any other groups claiming responsibility:	No
Damage caused:	New York Stock Exchange off-line for two minutes
Additional important information:	Conflicting information over whether the attack was successful or whether it occurred at all. Anonymous claims that they did not perform this protest, and that it was a clever plot by law enforcement to accuse the group. There is too much conflicting information to know one way or another.

Anonymous/TeaMp0isoN

ITEM	NOTES
Target:	Oakland City Police
Date:	October 28, 2011
Source:	K. Fogarty, "Hackers come out of shadows to attack police, support Occupy protests," *IT World*, October 28, 2011, available at http://www.itworld.com/security/217561/hackers-come-out-shadows-attack-police-support-occupy-protests. "Anonymous Message to the Oakland Police Department and City of Oakland" (January 31, 2012), available at http://www.youtube.com/watch?v=SzDuSaf55ek.
Motivation:	Retaliation against police injuring a protester
Type of attack:	DDoS, SQL injection, unauthorized access, modification of data, website defaced, release of personal information
Any other groups claiming responsibility:	TeaMp0isoN—did not claim responsibility, but engaged in aspects of the protests
Damage caused:	Anonymous took the main Oakland Police Department website off-line for a number of hours, infiltrated a local government security server, and posted personal information of officers and information on the structure of the servers. TeaMp0isoN released a list of police-department websites vulnerable to MS-Access SQL injections, along with encouragements to participate in protest.
Additional important information:	No indication of collaboration between Anonymous and TeaMp0isoN

Anonymous—Operation Darknet

ITEM	NOTES
Target:	Those in possession of child pornography and child-pornography websites on the Dark Net
Date:	November 3, 2011
Source:	M. Liebowitz, "Anonymous releases IP addresses of alleged child porn viewers," NBC News, November 3, 2011, available at http://www.nbcnews.com/id/45147364/ns/technology_and_sciencesecurity/t/anonymous-releases-ip-addresses-alleged-child-porn-viewers/#.XAAS7S1L1PM (last accessed November 4, 2011).

	RT, "Anonymous busts Internet pedophiles," November 3, 2011, available at http://rt.com/usa/news/anonymous-child-tor-porn-513/ (last accessed November 15, 2011). QMI Agency, "Hacktivist group shuts down child porn sites," *Canoe Technology*, October 24, 2011, available at http://technology.canoe.ca/2011/10/24/18871656.html (last accessed October 25, 2011).
Motivation:	Expose those who are "ruining Tor for the majority of legitimate users." Lay ground work for investigations into child pornography.
Type of attack:	Spyware, brute-force attack, social engineering/phishing, release of identifying information of active child-pornography site visitors and those in possession of child pornography, and unauthorized access.
Any other groups claiming responsibility:	No
Damage caused:	No reported damage. Reputational damage to those identifiable; however, it is up to law enforcement to identify alleged paedophiles.
Additional important information:	Those identified as having child pornography claim that an add-on was accidentally created with Mozilla's permission through a browser update such that the child pornography was uploaded by someone else. This is seemingly unsubstantiated. No differentiation between those who have child pornography on their computer and whether this is known to users.

Anonymous—Operation Rainbow Dark

ITEM	NOTES
Target:	Rainbow Medical Associates, Dr. Carlo Musso
Date:	November 4, 2011
Source:	S. Seltzer, "For-Profit Company Oversaw Davis's Execution, Had Prompted Complaint for Illegal Purchase of Lethal Injection Drugs," *Alternet*, August 22, 2011, available at http://www.alternet.org/newsandviews/article/670237/for-profit_company_oversaw_davis%27s_execution,_had_prompted_complaint_for_illegal_purchase_of_lethal_injection_drugs/.

	AnonNews, "Operation Rainbow Dark," previously available at http://anonnews.org/?p=press&a=item&i=1162 (last accessed January 5, 2012).
Motivation:	Retaliation for execution of Troy Davis and the alleged use of illegally imported drugs for execution
Type of attack:	Possible unauthorized access, modification of data, website defacement, release of personal information
Any other groups claiming responsibility:	No
Damage caused:	Operation is unsubstantiated
Additional important information:	Same Anonymous post that something would be done pasted into various blogs and Anonymous-related sites. No indication that they followed through with threat.

Anonymous—OpCartel

ITEM	NOTES
Target:	Alleged associates of Los Zetas drug cartel in Mexico—corrupt law enforcement, those involved in managing and participating in Los Zetas operations
Date:	November 5, 2011
Source:	N. Mandell, "Anonymous hacker group threatens Mexican drug cartel Zetas in online video," *New York Daily News*, October 31, 2011, available at http://www.nydailynews.com/news/world/anonymous-hacker-group-threatens-mexican-drug-cartel-zetas-online-video-article-1.969859#ixzz1d4sAfvE6 (last accessed November 1, 2011)
Motivation:	Retaliation for alleged kidnapping of an Anonymous activist. General threat posed by criminal organizations.
Type of attack:	DDoS attack. Unauthorized access to communications. Threatened release of personal information of those involved in cartel operations.
Any other groups claiming responsibility:	No
Damage caused:	If information is released (or even if not released), more likely to pose a threat to Anonymous members depending on the nature and importance the Zetas cartel places on the information. The cartel may retaliate on the basis of publicity alone.

Additional important information:	Current reports indicate conflicting rumours whether "Opcartel" will go ahead. Little belief that Anonymous has the ability to do any kind of damage. Interesting note—"Anonymous likely won't be able to turn up more information than the U.S. government already has, but they are able to publicize more information than the U.S. government can." Stratfor, *Dispatch: Anonymous' Online Tactics Against Mexican Cartels* (November 1, 2011), available at https://worldview.stratfor.com/article/dispatch-anonymous-online-tactics-against-mexican-cartels#ixzz1cj0LSuso. UPDATE—No attack occurred: Pastebin, *OPCartel Proceeds* (November 3, 2011), available at http://pastebin.com/XZRpjUZq.

Anonymous—Israeli Government

ITEM	NOTES
Target:	Israel government, security-services websites
Date:	November 5, 2011
Source:	A. Pfeffer, and O. Yaron, "Israel government, security services websites down in suspected cyber-attack," *Haaretz*, November 6, 2011, available at http://www.haaretz.com/news/diplomacy-defense/israel-government-security-services-websites-down-in-suspected-cyber-attack-1.394042 (last accessed November 7, 2011). "An open letter from Anonymous to the Government of Israel" (November 4, 2011), available at http://www.youtube.com/watch?v=QNxi2lV0UM0.
Motivation:	Retaliation for intercepted Gaza flotilla
Type of attack:	DDoS
Any other groups claiming responsibility:	No
Damage caused:	Websites off-line for an unspecified amount of time, including that of the Israel Defence Force, Mossad, and the Shin Bet security services, in addition to a number of government portals and ministries.
Additional important information:	N/A

Anonymous—Operation #TMX

ITEM	NOTES
Target:	Toronto Stock Exchange
Date:	November 7, 2011
Source:	J. Errett, "Expecting Anonymous at #TMX" *Now Toronto*, November 7, 2011, available at http://www.nowtoronto.com/news/webjam.cfm?content=183319 (last accessed November 8, 2011)
Motivation:	Part of the Occupy movement; economy disparity, social inequality
Type of attack:	None—likely attempted DDoS
Any other groups claiming responsibility:	No
Damage caused:	None
Additional important information:	No confirmed reports of an attack

Anonymous—Operation Brotherhood Shutdown

ITEM	NOTES
Target:	Muslim Brotherhood websites
Date:	November 11, 2011
Source:	M. Kumar, "Operation Brotherhood Shutdown: Multiple Sites taken down by Anonymous Hackers," *Hacker News*, November 12, 2011, available at http://thehackernews.com/2011/11/operation-brotherhood-shutdown-by.html (last accessed November 13, 2011). "Anonymous—Operation Brotherhood Shutdown" (November 7, 2011), available at http://www.youtube.com/watch?v=ZnPTBLbazAo. "Anonymous—The Aftermath of Operation Brotherhood Shutdown" (November 12, 2011), available at http://www.youtube.com/watch?v=bBe9co3l9wI&feature=related.
Motivation:	"The Muslim Brotherhood has become a threat to the revolution Egyptians had fought for"
Type of attack:	DDoS

Any other groups claiming responsibility:	No
Damage caused:	Four websites were temporarily taken down by an attack of approximately 380,000 hits per second. Down time unspecified.
Additional important information:	N/A

Anonymous (Finland)—Operation Green Rights

ITEM	NOTES
Target:	Talvivaara
Date:	November 12, 2011
Source:	E. Kovacs, "Anonymous Turns Green and Goes After Polluters," *Softpedia*, November 15, 2011, available at http://news.softpedia.com/news/Anonymous-Turns-Green-and-Goes-After-Polluters-234681.shtml
Motivation:	Environmental destruction from waste water resulting in contamination of surrounding flora and fauna
Type of attack:	Unknown; most likely a series of DDoS attacks
Any other groups claiming responsibility:	No
Damage caused:	None as of yet
Additional important information:	N/A

Anonymous vs. Anonymous?

ITEM	NOTES
Target:	Anon Ops
Date:	November 16, 2011
Source:	E. Kovacs, "Anonymous Attacks Anonymous for Being Trolls," *Softpedia*, November 16, 2011, available at http://news.softpedia.com/news/Anonymous-Attacks-Anonymous-For-Being-Trolls-234949.shtml (last accessed November 18, 2011)

Motivation:	"Anonymous claims that those behind AnonOps are blind with power and instead of fighting corruption and internet censorship by welcoming newcomers, they treat them with disrespect and arrogance"
Type of attack:	Zero-day attack
Any other groups claiming responsibility:	No
Damage caused:	Shut down servers used by AnonOps
Additional important information:	Example of infighting and disunity inside Anonymous

Anonymous—Venezuelan Government Hacks

ITEM	NOTES
Target:	Venezuelan Government websites
Date:	Various, 2011
Source:	J. Wyss, "Political hackers are one of Latin America's newest headaches," *Miami Herald*, November 3, 2011, available at http://www.miamiherald.com/2011/10/31/2481360/political-hackers-are-one-of-latin.html
Motivation:	Anti-government protests
Type of attack:	Website hack
Any other groups claiming responsibility:	Reportedly affiliated with Anonymous
Damage caused:	Government websites defaced
Additional important information:	Two hundred attacks in 2011, a large number considering the country's "slow internet connections." Interesting to note the attack on a leftist government, in contrast with the centrist/centre-right governments of other attacks.

Anonymous—US Congress

ITEM	NOTES
Target:	US Congress
Date:	November 17, 2011
Source:	E. Kovacs, "Anonymous Threatens Congress Over SOPA," *Softpedia*, November 17, 2011, available at http://news.softpedia.com/news/Anonymous-Threatens-Congress-Over-SOPA-235201.shtml.

"Anonymous—A Message to Congress on SOPA you will not infringe on our rights" (November 18, 2011), available at http://www.youtube.com/watch?v=9rbyk0h3yeg. |
| Motivation: | Opposition to the proposed Stop Online Piracy Act; claims the proposed legislation would represent a breach of constitutional rights.

Fear that the act may have wider implications than what the title indicates. |
Type of attack:	None yet. Probably DDoS.
Any other groups claiming responsibility:	No
Damage caused:	None
Additional important information:	N/A

Anonymous—Operation Weeks Payment (Brazilian banks)

ITEM	NOTES
Target:	Brazilian banks
Date:	January 2012
Source:	F. Bajak, "Anonymous Hackers Claim They Were Infiltrated," *Bellingham Herald*, February 29, 2012, available at http://bellinghamherald.com/2012/02/29/2415830/anonymous-hackers-claim-they-were.html.

S. McCaskill, "Anonymous Targets Vatican Website," *Tech Week Europe*, March 8, 2012, available at http://www.techweekeurope.co.uk/news/anonymous-targets-vatican-website-65797. |
| Motivation: | Protest against "widespread inequality" |

Type of attack:	DDoS attacks
Any other groups claiming responsibility:	No
Damage caused:	Websites crashed, defaced
Additional important information:	Nine Brazilian banks were targeted

Anonymous—Polish Government

ITEM	NOTES
Target:	Polish government websites
Date:	January 21–22, 2012
Source:	T. Jowitt, "Anonymous Attacks Polish Websites for ACTA Support," *Tech Week Europe*, January 26, 2012, available at http://www.techweekeurope.co.uk/news/anonymous-attacks-polish-websites-for-acta-support-56450
Motivation:	In response to Poland's support for the proposed multinational Anti-Counterfeiting Trade Agreement (ACTA; not in force)
Type of attack:	DDoS
Any other groups claiming responsibility:	@AnonymousWiki (possibly linked to Anonymous)
Damage caused:	Polish government websites taken off-line
Additional important information:	ACTA protests follow earlier Stop Online Piracy Act (a controversial law proposed in the United States) protests.

Anonymous—Panda Security

ITEM	NOTES
Target:	Panda Security
Date:	March 6, 2012
Source:	M. Smolaks, "Anonymous Hits Back Over LulzSec Arrests," *Tech Week Europe*, March 7, 2012, available at http://www.techweekeurope.co.uk/news/anonymous-hits-back-over-lulzsec-arrests-65265

Motivation:	Retaliation for arrest of five LulzSec members and the ousting of LulzSec former leader Sabu
Type of attack:	Defaced website, gained access to staff details and shared the information online
Any other groups claiming responsibility:	No
Damage caused:	Thirty-sex defaced websites and the email details of Panda security staff were posted online
Additional important information:	Demonstrates Anonymous and LulzSec interconnection

Anonymous—Vatican (two occasions)

ITEM	NOTES
Target:	Vatican website, Vatican Radio website
Date:	First: March 7, 2012, Second: March 14, 2012
Source:	First: S. McCaskill, "Anonymous Targets Vatican Website," *Tech Week Europe*, March 8, 2012, available at http://www.techweekeurope.co.uk/news/anonymous-targets-vatican-website-65797. Second: M. Kumar, "Vatican Radio Hacked by Anonymous Hackers," *Hacker News*, March 14, 2012, available at http://thehackernews.com/2012/03/vatican-radio-hacked-by-anonymous.html.
Motivation:	First: Protest, "revenge for the 'corruption' of the Roman Catholic Church over the course of its history" (McCaskill). Second: "Anonymous justified its attack by claiming that Vatican Radio is responsible for high cancer rates in a neighborhood near the broadcaster's main transmission facility" (Kumar).
Type of attack:	First: Suspected DDoS Second: Website data compromised
Any other groups claiming responsibility:	No
Damage caused:	First: Vatican website inaccessible Second: Personal data of Vatican Radio journalists, Vatican website hacked

Additional important information:	Second: "The attack is part of the organization's recent declaration of war against religion" (Kumar).

Anonymous—Megaupload protest

ITEM	NOTES
Target:	US Department of Justice, Universal Music, Motion Picture Association of America
Date:	Early/mid-January 2012
Source:	J. Halliday and C. Arthur, "Anonymous' Release of Met and FBI Call Puts Hacker Group Back Centre Stage," *Guardian*, February 3, 2012, available at http://www.guardian.co.uk/technology/2012/feb/03/anonymous-hack-met-fbi-call
Motivation:	Protest over the closure on criminal charges of the Megaupload file-sharing website
Type of attack:	DDoS (suspected)
Any other groups claiming responsibility:	No
Damage caused:	Websites off-line temporarily
Additional important information:	Part of the growing rift between Hollywood and the online pirating community

Anonymous—Leader of NPD Germany

ITEM	NOTES
Target:	Website of NPD Germany party leader
Date:	Early January 2012
Source:	J. Halliday and C. Arthur, "Anonymous's Release of Met and FBI Call Puts Hacker Group Back Centre Stage," *Guardian*, February 3, 2012, available at http://www.guardian.co.uk/technology/2012/feb/03/anonymous-hack-met-fbi-call
Motivation:	Political protest
Type of attack:	DDoS (suspected)
Any other groups claiming responsibility:	No

Damage caused:	Unauthorized access, website off-line temporarily
Additional important information:	N/A

Anonymous—Chinese Government Websites

ITEM	NOTES
Target:	Hundreds of Chinese government websites, including governmental agencies and business enterprises.
Date:	March 30, 2012—April 6, 2012
Source:	J. Burt, "Anonymous Defaces Many Chinese Government Websites," *Tech Week Europe*, April 6, 2012, available at http://www.techweekeurope.co.uk/news/anonymous-defaces-chinese-websites-71791
Motivation:	Response to Chinese government "cracking down on dozens of Websites in the country." Also, pro-democracy social protest.
Type of attack:	DDoS, website defacing
Any other groups claiming responsibility:	No
Damage caused:	Hundreds of government websites defaced, at all levels (local, regional, national)
Additional important information:	Pro-democracy Pastebin message: "All these years, the Chinese Government has subjected their people to unfair laws and unhealthy processes," the message reads. "People, each of you suffers from tyranny of that regime. Fight for justice, fight for freedom, fight for democracy!..." (See E. Protalinski, "Anonymous Hacks Hundreds of Chinese Government Sites" ZDnet, April 4, 2012, available at https://www.zdnet.com/article/anonymous-hacks-hundreds-of-chinese-government-sites/.)

Anonymous—Operation Trial at Home (UK)—UK Home Office Website

ITEM	NOTES
Target:	UK Home Office website
Date:	April 7, 2012
Source:	M. Broersma, "Anonymous Claims Home Office Website Takedown," *Tech Week Europe*, April 8, 2012, available at http://www.techweekeurope.co.uk/news/anonymous-home-office-ddos-71886

Motivation:	"Intended to protest 'draconian surveillance proposals'" (Broersma)
Type of attack:	DDoS
Any other groups claiming responsibility:	No
Damage caused:	Website off-line for a brief period
Additional important information:	Promises of more attacks to come. The start of "Operation Trial at Home"

Anonymous—Operation Last Resort

ITEM	NOTES
Target:	US Sentencing Commission's website
Date:	January 25, 2013
Source:	V. Blue, "Feds Stumbling After Anonymous Launches Operation Last Resort," *ZDNet*, January 30, 2013, available at http://www.zdnet.com/feds-stumbling-after-anonymous-launches-operation-last-resort-7000010541/. V. Blue, "Anonymous Hacks US Sentencing Commission and Distributes Files," *ZDNet*, January 26, 2013, available at http://www.zdnet.com/anonymous-hacks-us-sentencing-commission-distributes-files-7000010369/.
Motivation:	To protest the "harsh treatment" by government prosecutors of Internet activist Aaron Swartz. As Blue reported, to call attention to "the federal sentencing guidelines which enable prosecutors to cheat citizens of their constitutionally-guaranteed right to a fair trial."
Type of attack:	Warheads, back door, and defacing
Any other groups claiming responsibility:	No
Damage caused:	Replaced the site's content with a video denouncing the government and praising Swartz. Transformed the ".gov" site into an interactive video game of *Asteroids*. Threatened that de-encryption keys would be publicly released (thus releasing information held on the stolen files) if the US government did not comply with Anonymous's demands for legal reform.

	Left a back door and made it editable in such a way that encourages other hackers to shell the server. In the defacement text, Anonymous also said it placed "multiple warheads" on "compromised systems" on various unnamed websites, and encouraged members to download the encrypted files from ussc. gov that are "primed, armed and quietly distributed to numerous mirrors."
Additional important information:	Commandeered federal websites, threatened to release government information, distributed files, and demanded legal reform. "Anonymous Operation Last Resort Video" (January 26, 2013), available at http://www.youtube.com/watch?v= WaPni5O2YyI.

Anonymous—Operation Trial at Home (UK)—10 Downing Street and Ministry of Justice

ITEM	NOTES
Target:	UK government websites, including 10 Downing Street (official residence of the prime minister) and the Ministry of Justice
Date:	April 7—April 10, 2012
Source:	T. Brewster, "Anonymous Strikes Downing Street and Ministry of Justice," *Tech Week Europe*, April 10, 2012, available at http://www.techweekeurope.co.uk/news/ anonymous-government-downing-street-moj-71979
Motivation:	Mixed motivations—protest over UK government's web-surveillance plans, protest over UK's extradition treaty with the United States
Type of attack:	DDoS
Any other groups claiming responsibility:	No
Damage caused:	Three government websites taken down temporarily: 10 Downing Street, Home Office, and Ministry of Justice websites
Additional important information:	Anonymous claimed that they would also attack Government Communications Headquarters (GCHQ)

Anonymous—Operation Ferguson

ITEM	NOTES
Target:	Ferguson Police Department, Ferguson, Missouri Jon Belmar, St. Louis County Police Chief
Date:	August 2014
Source:	D. Hunn, "How computer hackers changed the Ferguson protests', *St. Louis Post-Dispatch*, August 13, 2014, available at http://www.stltoday.com/news/local/crime-and-courts/how-computer-hackers-changed-the-ferguson-protests/article_d81a1da4-ae04-5261-9064-e4c255111c94.html
Motivation:	Police misconduct and its consequences. A doxing attack followed after Anonymous posted a video warning to the Ferguson police, admonishing them for fatally shooting Mike Brown, an unarmed African-American teenager, and vowing revenge if any protesters demonstrating against the police were harmed. Two reasons for the attack: 1) Because Jon Belmar refused to release the name of the officer who shot Mike Brown, and 2) Because Belmar challenged Anonymous, calling their threats hollow.
Type of attack:	Document tracing (doxing)—publishing personally identifiable information. DDoS on the Ferguson Police Department website.
Any other groups claiming responsibility:	No
Damage caused:	Information about Belmar's home address, phone number, and family members and their accounts on social media were all exposed and made public by Anonymous. Photos of Belmar's family members were also made public.
Additional important information:	Anonymous made threats to Belmar that his daughter's personal details, phone number, and home address would be made public in an hour if the name of the officer who shot Mike Brown was not released. However, Anonymous did not disclose the daughter's information, tweeting: "We will save the rest of our energy for the true perpetrator."

Anonymous member, Deric Lostutter—Steubenville High School rape case

ITEM	NOTES
Target:	Steubenville, Ohio
Date:	2012–2013
Source:	K. Baker, "Anonymous outs members of alleged Steubenville High School 'Rape Crew,'" *Jezebel*, December 24, 2012, available at http://jezebel.com/5970975/anonymous-outs-members-of-alleged-steubenville-high-school-rape-crew
Motivation:	Two male sixteen-year-old Steubenville High football players raped a sixteen-year-old girl from West Virginia at a party in Steubenville. The case received national coverage, in part because of the criticism placed upon media outlets, especially on CNN, for their biased coverage of the case, lack of focus on the victim, and sympathy for the rapists.
	Following the national coverage of the case, Anonymous threatened to reveal the names of other unindicted alleged participants.
	In December 2012, KnightSec, an offshoot of Anonymous, hacked an unaffiliated website, posting a demand for an apology by school officials and local authorities, who had allegedly covered up the incident in order to protect the athletes and the school's football program.
Type of attack:	Doxing. Lostutter hacked a list of school-board members, cell-phone numbers, and home addresses, and received damning files—internal emails, expense reports, and other incriminating records about the district—which he disseminated online, alleging that more people were involved in the incident.
Any other groups claiming responsibility:	KnightSec, an offshoot of Anonymous
Damage caused:	Personal information made public
Additional important information:	Questionable whether this is ethical hacking or online vigilantism.
	Lostutter was later indicted under the federal Computer Fraud and Abuse Act. Lostutter's home was raided by the FBI with a warrant targeting his hacking involvement, even though another person acknowledged responsibility for the hack.

Anonymous/WikiLeaks—Stratfor

ITEM	NOTES
Target:	Stratfor (US-based intelligence-gathering firm)
Date:	December 2011–February 2012
Source:	J. Ball, "WikiLeaks Publishes Stratfor Emails Linked to Anonymous Attack," *Guardian*, February 27, 2012, available at http://www.guardian.co.uk/media/2012/feb/27/wikileaks-publishes-stratfor-emails-anonymous
Motivation:	Exposing US military and geopolitical secrets
Type of attack:	Data theft/unauthorized access
Any other groups claiming responsibility:	Collaboration between Anonymous and WikiLeaks
Damage caused:	Personal information and login criteria stolen from user base (300,000 subscribers). Five and a half million emails were accessed, a limited number of which were published online.
Additional important information:	Hacking attack by Anonymous rather than a whistle-blower. WikiLeaks was merely the vehicle in which information was disseminated and promoted. Single-handedly took down the credibility of the otherwise reputable organization.

Anonymous—UK Ministry for Justice and Home Office

ITEM	NOTES
Target:	UK government; websites affected include the Ministry of Justice and the Home Office.
Date:	August 21, 2012
Country:	England
Source:	BBC News, "Anonymous hits UK government websites in Assange protest," August 21, 2012, available at http://www.bbc.com/news/technology-19330592
Motivation:	In retaliation of the United Kingdom's handling of the Julian Assange case
Type of attack:	Anonymous claimed responsibility on Twitter for the denial-of-service attacks that flooded UK government websites, causing disruption and access issues

Damage caused:	Access to websites was denied in brief intervals, no sensitive information was stolen.
Additional important information:	N/A

Anonymous—Scotland Yard

ITEM	NOTES
Target:	Scotland Yard
Date:	October 24, 2012
Country:	England
Source:	BBC News, "Anonymous hacking group target police web forum," October 24, 2012, available at http://www.bbc.com/news/uk-20072981
Motivation:	Retaliation against the police and armed forces for the injustice of the legal system
Type of attack:	Stole identity information, and an attack was undertaken which redirected readers from other police forums to a page showing a video approved by the collective
Damage caused:	Data compromised
Additional important information:	An Internet forum used by police to exchange information and discuss policing issues was "compromised" by hackers from Anonymous. Anonymous obtained the private email addresses of a number of serving and retired officers. Former and current police personnel received in their private email accounts an email containing the subject line "A message to the police and armed forces." It read: "Hello members of our UK police and armed forces, stand with us, not against us. We are not against you, only against the evil system that you defend, and we appeal to your consciences to stop protecting the traitors and banksters, and protect us from them instead."

Anonymous (and LulzSec)—UK GCHQ (Government Communications Headquarters)

ITEM	NOTES
Target:	Hacktivist groups Anonymous and LulzSec
Date:	February 5, 2014
Country:	England
Source:	L. Constantin, "U.K. spy agency attacked hacktivist groups," *Computer World*, February 5, 2014, available at http://www.computerworld.com/article/2487354/cybercrime-hacking/u-k--spy-agency-attacked-hacktivist-groups.html
Motivation:	In retaliation of hacktivist attacks on websites of various companies, organizations and governments
Type of attack:	Denial-of-service and other techniques to disrupt hacktivist groups' online activities and disrupted the hacktivists' communication channels
Damage caused:	Revealed identities of Anonymous and LulzSec hackers
Additional important information:	A unit of the GCHQ, the Joint Threat Research Intelligence Group (JTRIG) collected information on hacktivists and shared it with law-enforcement agencies, such as the US National Security Agency. JTRIG used human-intelligence techniques to gather information about members of Anonymous and LulzSec. JTRIG intelligence-gathering specifically targeted two hackers using the online handles "GZero" and "p0ke." JTRIG used undercover agents in IRC logs to gather the information on the identification of the hacktivists.

Anonymous—Operation DeathEaters

ITEM	NOTES
Target:	UK high-profile paedophilic ring
Date:	November 27, 2014
Source:	K. Baker, "Hacking group Anonymous to target paedophiles using the 'dark web' to carry out child abuse," *Daily Mail*, January 25, 2015, available at http://www.dailymail.co.uk/news/article-2924864/Hacking-group-Anonymous-target-paedophiles.html.

	L. Eleftheriou-Smith, "Anonymous calls for activists to help expose international paedophile networks with 'Operation DeathEaters,'" *Independent*, January 23, 2015, available at http://www.independent.co.uk/news/uk/home-news/anonymous-calls-for-activists-to-help-expose-international-paedophile-networks-with-operation-deatheaters-9998350.html.
Motivation:	Operation Death Eaters is an independent "tribunal" of hackers that have allegedly identified an elite club of paedophiles, including politicians, religious figures, royals, and celebrities, involved in the torture and murder of children
Type of attack:	Unknown
Any other groups claiming responsibility:	No
Damage caused:	Compromising data
Additional important information:	Anonymous released a video and tweeted, urging people to take to the streets of London to protest against the cover up of a "nightmarish" paedophile ring. They made reference to a number of high-profile cases in the United Kingdom, including those of Jimmy Savile, the Elm Guest House, and MP Cyril Smith, and are collecting further data toward proof of similar international rings. This will involve the group setting up a complex database, mapping connections between cases, and presenting it on social media.

Anonymous—#OpHK (Operation Hong Kong)

ITEM	NOTES
Target:	Chinese government websites
Date:	October 7, 2014
Source:	D. Grover, "Anonymous Hackers Threaten Web War Against Hong Kong Police and Government," *International Business Times*, October 2, 2014, available at http://www.ibtimes.co.uk/anonymous-hackers-threaten-web-war-against-hong-kong-police-government-1468220.
	A. K. Jha, "#OpHK aka Operation Hong Kong: Anonymous hacks Chinese Government website," *Tech Worm*, 2014, available at http://www.techworm.net/2014/10/operation-hong-kong-anonymous-hacks-chinese-government-website.html.

Motivation:	Support for pro-democracy protesters in Hong Kong.
	While pro-democracy protesters in Hong Kong were protesting on the ground, hacktivists from around the globe joined together online to support the protesters.
Type of attack:	Hacked and defaced Chinese government websites.
	DDoS
Any other groups claiming responsibility:	In addition to Anonymous, other groups took part in the operation dubbed #OpHK
	Report suggest that hundreds of Hong Kong–based websites were hacked and defaced under the Operation Hong Kong, while several hundred other were brought down via DDoS attacks by other hacker groups in support of the pro-democracy protests in Hong Kong.
	Major sites hacked and DDoS attacked include those of the Chinese Ministry of Justice, Ministry of Public Security, and the Hong Kong Police Force.
Damage caused:	A defaced webpage could not be accessed and displayed the message: "We are here to fight against Censorships, Corruptions, Government and against those things that obstruct humans rights. We encountered some problems and issues that we don't want the countries or world want. We are here to help you create a better world. People, we tell you that you are not alone!. This is Kyfx and I am one of the anonymous follower. Peace will not be silenced by fear We are here to expect more."
	Websites which were defaced, all on October 8, 2014, by Anonymous included:
	http://www.tielingws.gov.cn/, the website could not be accessed.
	http://www.bys.gov.cn/index.html, the webpage says "HACKED FUCK THE SYSTEM."
	http://www.tongcheng.jcy.gov.cn/Xnitro.html, the webpage says "Hacked by Xnitro ErTn and Hacked by Fallaga Team [Don't forget this name]."
	http://qxj.km.gov.cn/hector.html, the webpage says "Hacked—Cyber Freedom INCEF."
	The database of www.gyx.gov.cn was also leaked on Pastebin.

Additional important information:	Anonymous tweeted: "In the great tradition of civil disobedience, We, Anonymous, declared war on injustice a few years ago. Once again the Chinese government strikes hard at its own people. At this very moment Chinese police forces are hurting innocent citizens who cry for liberty. Since we are many and we do not fear ANY abusive government or institution in the globe, we also declared war against the Chinese Government, well known for its authoritarian posture. We are only targeting .gov.cn and .gov.hk .mil.cn in opposition to their oppressive ways. We emphatically condemn those attacks against non governmental or non military targets. We stand in solidarity with the citizens of Hong Kong, a Statement released by the Anonymous read."

Anonymous—Operation DestructiveSec/Lulzxmas

ITEM	NOTES
Target:	UK Banks, clothing retailer
Date:	December 2011
Source:	F. Rashid, "Anonymous Beards the Banks to Play Twisted Santa Claus," *Tech Week Europe*, December 21, 2011, available at http://www.techweekeurope.co.uk/news/anonymous-beards-the-banks-to-play-twisted-santa-claus-50922
Motivation:	Robin Hood mentality—rob from the rich, give to the poor
Type of attack:	SQL injection attack
Any other groups claiming responsibility:	Lulzxmas, Anonymous (potentially coordinated)
Damage caused:	About $75,000 stolen from UK Banks, $1.25M in virtual credit cards compromised
Additional important information:	

Anonymous—Operation Charlie Hebdo

ITEM	NOTES
Target:	Al-Qaeda, the Islamic State (ISIS), and terrorist organizations who impair freedom of speech. Threats also made to Turkey, Saudi Arabia, Qatar, and other countries supporting ISIS.
Date:	January 10, 2015
Source:	O. Solon, "Anonymous 'hacktivists' attack ISIS—strike down terrorist propaganda and recruitment sites," *Mirror,* February 9, 2015, available at http://www.mirror.co.uk/news/technology-science/technology/anonymous-hacktivists-attack-isis---5130966.
	L. Franceschi-Bicchierai, "Anonymous claims first victim in 'Operation Charlie Hebdo,'" *Mashable,* January 11, 2015, available at http://mashable.com/2015/01/10/anonymous-operation-charlie-hebdo/.
Motivation:	The *Charlie Hebdo* shootings in January 2015, and further terrorist attacks in Paris that February, which Anonymous called an attack on freedom of speech and democracy
Type of attack:	DDoS attacks
Any other groups claiming responsibility:	Unknown
Damage caused:	The French-language jihadist website ansar-alhaqq.net was down for more than an hour
Additional important information:	N/A

Anonymous—Support for Hong Kong protestors

ITEM	NOTES
Target:	Thirty Chinese local government websites
Date:	April 10, 2015
Source:	M. Russon, "Anonymous brings down 30 Chinese government websites to support Hong Kong protesters," *International Business Times,* April 13, 2015, available at http://www.ibtimes.co.uk/anonymous-brings-down-30-chinese-government-websites-support-hong-kong-protesters-1496069

Motivation:	To protest the arrest of five hacktivists in October 2014 who were accused of sending additional traffic to a Hong Kong government website during pro-democracy protests
Type of attack:	DDoS
Any other groups claiming responsibility:	No
Damage caused:	The attacked government websites went off-line
Additional important information:	N/A

Anonymous (James Jeffery)—BPAS

ITEM	NOTES
Target:	British Pregnancy Advisory Service (BPAS)
Date:	March 8, 2012
Source:	M. Broersma, "Hacker Pleads Guilty to Abortion Website Attack," *Tech Week Europe*, March 12, 2012, available at http://www.techweekeurope.co.uk/news/hacker-pleads-guilty-to-abortion-website-attack-66295.
	P. Gallagher, "Abortion Website Hacker Caught," *Guardian*, March 11, 2012, available at http://www.guardian.co.uk/world/2012/mar/11/abortion-website-hacker-caught.
Motivation:	Anti-abortion protest
Type of attack:	Twenty-six thousand attempts to attack BPAS servers during a six-hour period—most likely DDoS
Any other groups claiming responsibility:	Unknown
Damage caused:	Defacement with Anonymous logo and theft of BPAS database of information on those requesting BPAS services
Additional important information:	The normally left/liberal-leaning Anonymous (or one member, Jeffery) attacked a pro-abortion website. Suggests that Anonymous is far less homogeneous in its political stance than previously believed.
	Jeffery's defacement displayed conservative views on abortion.
	Jeffery goes by the pseudonym "Pablo Escobar" on Twitter.
	He was arrested and pled guilty to two offences under the Computer Misuse Act of 1990 (one relating to defacement, one to theft of personal information).

CHAPTER VI

Select Ethical-Hacking Incidences: Chaos Computer Club, CyberBerkut, LulzSec, Iranian Cyber Army, and Others

This chapter takes selected notable ethical-hacking incidences from the quantitative work in chapter 3 and breaks down each incident by: group, target, date, source, motivation, type of attack, whether any other groups claimed responsibility, damage caused, and additional important information. This chapter addresses select incidences for the Chaos Computer Club, CyberBerkut, LulzSec, and others. Again, some of the incidences from the last two chapters, this chapter, and the preceding chapter will be explored in detail from technical, political, criminological, and policy perspectives based on their classification in chapters 7 and 8.

CHAOS COMPUTER CLUB (CCC)

CCC—German Government

ITEM	NOTES
Target:	German government
Date:	October 26, 2011
Source:	Chaos Computer Club website, available at http://ccc.de/en/updates/2011/staatstrojaner.
	J. Leyden, "German states defend use of 'Federal Trojan'," *The Register*, October 12, 2011, available at http://www.theregister.co.uk/2011/10/12/bundestrojaner/.

	WikiLeaks, "Skype and the Bavarian Trojan in the middle," available at http://wikileaks.org/wiki/Skype_and_the_Bavarian_trojan_in_the_middle. "German hackers discover government spying" (Al Jazeera English, October 25, 2011), available at http://www.youtube.com/watch?v=lIwa_-jvbDQ.
Motivation:	Breach of rights by government and law enforcement, use of the Bundestrojaner (federal Trojan)
Type of attack:	Release of information, analysis of code. (Short critique available at http://web17.webbpro.de/index.php?page=analysis-of-german-bundestrojaner.)
Any other groups claiming responsibility:	No
Damage caused:	Reputation of government. This highlights issues of government-sanctioned malware use beyond the scope of what the courts and laws provide.
Additional important information:	Data encryption is non-existent or ineffective, can be accessed by almost anyone with an internet connection, which presents significant privacy issues outside of direct government involvement.

CCC—Hamburg attack

ITEM	NOTES
Target:	Hamburg bank, Bildschirmtext network
Date:	1985
Source:	J. Harrington, "Hacktivism: What is the Chaos Computer Club?," Suite101, September 8, 2011, previously available at http://joharrington.suite101.com/hacktivism-what-is-the-chaos-computer-club-a387917. WIKIPEDIA, "Chaos Computer Club," available at http://en.wikipedia.org/wiki/Chaos_Computer_Club.
Motivation:	To protest use of biometric data for personal documents
Type of attack:	Unauthorized access, modification of data, theft
Any other groups claiming responsibility:	No
Damage caused:	Some DM 135,000 from the bank was "donated" to the CCC

| Additional important information: | The funds were apparently returned the next day. Conflicting information regarding date of the hack. Some say 1984, others say 1985. Possibly closer to 1985, though unconfirmed. |

CCC—Quicken

ITEM	NOTES
Target:	Quicken database
Date:	1996
Source:	F. von Leitner, "Chaos Computer Club Clarifications," *Tasty Bits from the Technology Front*, February 17, 1997, available at http://tbtf.com/resource/felix.html. Wikipedia, "Chaos Computer Club," available at http://en.wikipedia.org/wiki/Chaos_Computer_Club.
Motivation:	To highlight system flaws
Type of attack:	Data modification, unauthorized access, fraud (though unlikely for personal gain)
Any other groups claiming responsibility:	No
Damage caused:	Changed personal data, cloned SIM cards, wrote ActiveX control, which, once executed, turns off Internet security
Additional important information:	

CCC—German government

ITEM	NOTES
Target:	German government, Minister of the Interior Wolfgang Schäuble
Date:	2008
Source:	S. Ragan, "CCC is at it again—hands out copies of German Interior Minister's fingerprint," *Tech Herald*, August 1, 2008, available at http://www.thetechherald.com/article.php/200814/581/
Motivation:	To protest use of biometric data for personal document authentication
Type of attack:	Unauthorized access.

Any other groups claiming responsibility:	No
Damage caused:	Duplicated the minister of interior's fingerprint (unknown whether the copy was obtained physically or digitally, i.e., from a database) and made it widely available. Fooled biometric scanners.
Additional important information:	Though biometric data is unique to individuals, databases containing such information can be compromised.

CYBERBERKUT

CyberBerkut—US vice-president

ITEM	NOTES
Target:	Joseph Biden's (then US vice-president) delegation officials
Date:	November 25, 2014
Source:	CyberBerkut, "CyberBerkut gained access to the documents of Joseph Biden's delegation officials," November 25, 2014, available at http://cyber-berkut.org/en/
Motivation:	CyberBerkut disagree with Washington's interference in Ukraine's internal affairs
Type of attack:	Unauthorized access of confidential files belonging to the US State Department via an official's mobile device.
Any other groups claiming responsibility:	No
Damage caused:	Publication of confidential government documents.
Additional important information:	CyberBerkut suggested the documents show that the Ukrainian army had become a branch of the US armed forces. They also detailed a high volume of financial support, some of which was credited to the personal accounts of Ukrainian military personnel.

CyberBerkut—German government

ITEM	NOTES
Target:	German government websites
Date:	January 7, 2015
Source:	D. Lynch, "Pro-Russian Hacker Group CyberBerkut Claims Attack On German Government Websites," *International Business Times*, January 7, 2015, available at http://www.ibtimes.com/pro-russian-hacker-group-cyberberkut-claims-attack-german-government-websites-1775874.

CyberBerkut, "CyberBerkut has blocked German Chancellor and the Bundestag's websites," January 7, 2015, available at http://cyber-berkut.org/en/. |
Motivation:	To urge the people and government of Germany to stop providing financial and political support to the political regime in Kiev, Ukraine's capital city. It accused the Ukrainian Prime Minister of using money from the European Union and International Monetary Fund to fund the war in eastern Ukraine.
Type of attack:	DDoS attack
Any other groups claiming responsibility:	No
Damage caused:	Several German government websites were brought down, including that of the German chancellor's government seat and the Bundestag.
Additional important information:	The attack was executed a day before the chancellor was to meet with the prime minister of Ukraine.

CyberBerkut—Ukrainian politician

ITEM	NOTES
Target:	Dmytro Yarosh (Ukrainian far-right politician)
Date:	February 1, 2015
Source:	RT, "Hacktivist leak alleges 'extortion & money laundering' by Ukraine's Right Sector leader," February 1, 2015, available at http://rt.com/news/228387-ukraine-hacktivists-leak-yarosh/

Motivation:	To disclose corruption and economic crimes in Ukraine. CyberBerkut said: "We are publishing documents that expose the criminal activities of the head of Ukrainian neo-Nazis, which confirm multiple incidences of extortion—the illegal and cynical seizure of properties and businesses belonging to Ukrainian citizens by Yarosh and his associates. The stolen money is then taken out of the country through fronts and deposited in offshore accounts."
Type of attack:	Unauthorized access and publication of documents allegedly obtained from the office of Dmytro Yarosh
Any other groups claiming responsibility:	No
Damage caused:	Publication of legal documents, Yarosh's passport and private documents, several contracts for the purchase and lease of property, allegedly signed under coercion, but which do not directly identify Yarosh.
Additional important information:	Yarosh was placed on Interpol's wanted list in 2015, at Russia's behest, for inciting terrorism (his name was removed in 2016). He has served in the Ukrainian parliament since November 2014. In 2014 Ukraine was named the most corrupt country in Europe by Transparency International. CyberBerkut is named after the previous, pro-Russian Ukrainian administration's unit responsible for public security, known for brutality; it has a reputation for targeting government figures and executing DDoS attacks.

ITEM	NOTES
Target:	Central Election Commission of Ukraine
Date:	May 21, 2014
Country:	Ukraine
Source:	A. K. Jha, "Pro-Russian Hackers leaks documents from Central Election Commission of Ukraine," *Tech Worm*, May 24, 2014, available at http://www.techworm. net/2014/05/pro-russian-hackers-leaks-documents.html. The hackers claimed responsibility for the attack in a statement released on their website, and said they would continue to make such information public on the following website: http://www.cyber-berkut.org/en/.
Motivation:	To protest the "legitimization of crimes"

Type of attack:	Destroyed the network and computing infrastructure of the Ukrainian election commission. Leaked information.
Damage caused:	As above
Additional important information:	Ethical-hacking protest. The leaks came just two days before presidential elections in Ukraine. Hackers also leaked a large archive of emails, as well as the technical documentation of the commission's system administrators. The hackers gave a "thank you" message to the commission of Ukraine, saying: "Our special thanks for a fascinating quest to wonderful administrators who were storing data on access to the network in text files on their desktops."

LULZSEC

LulzSec—Sony BMG Greece

ITEM	NOTES
Target:	Sony BMG—Greece
Date:	May 22, 2011
Source:	C. Wisniewski, "Sony BMG Greece the latest hacked Sony site," *Naked Security*, May 22, 2011, available at http://nakedsecurity.sophos.com/2011/05/22/sony-bmg-greece-the-latest-hacked-sony-site/. E. Mills, "Hackers taunt Sony with more data leaks, hacks," *CNET*, June 6, 2011, available at http://news.cnet.com/8301-27080_3-20069443-245/hackers-taunt-sony-with-more-data-leaks-hacks/.
Motivation:	Unspecified
Type of attack:	SQL injection, unauthorized access, data leak
Any other groups claiming responsibility:	No
Damage caused:	Release of usernames, identities, and email addresses of users registered on SonyMusic.gr. Release of internal network map.

Additional important information:	Large quantity of information reported to be incorrect. The hack emphasized that companies need to be more aware of the importance of performing penetration tests to ensure security.

LulzSec—FBI

ITEM	NOTES
Target:	Infragard (Atlanta)—FBI affiliate
Date:	June 3, 2011
Source:	R. Beschizza, "LulzSec claims FBI affiliate hacked, users and botnet are exposed," *Boing Boing*, June 3, 2011, available at http://boingboing.net/2011/06/03/lulzsec-claims-fbi-a.html. "LulzSec hacks Atlanta Infragard and challenges FBI" (June 3, 2011), available at http://www.youtube.com/watch?v=aROWwEIPgJA.
Motivation:	Unspecified
Type of attack:	Unauthorized access, data leak, modification of data, defacement
Any other groups claiming responsibility:	No
Damage caused:	Released personal information stored in the user database of 180 users, defaced http://infragardatlanta.org/, and caused reputational damage
Additional important information:	N/A

LulzSec—PBS

ITEM	NOTES
Target:	PBS
Date:	May 29–30, 2011
Source:	C. Wisniewski, "PBS.org hacked... LulzSec targets Sesame Street?," *Naked Security*, May 30, 2011, available at http://nakedsecurity.sophos.com/2011/05/30/pbs-org-hacked-lulzsec-targets-sesame-street/ (last accessed May 31, 2011).

	S. Ragan, "PBS: LulzSec attack an attempt to chill journalism," *Tech Herald*, May 30, 2011, available at http://www.thetechherald.com/article.php/201122/7215/PBS-LulzSec-attack-an-attempt-to-chill-journalism. "Happy Hour: Weinergate, PBS Hacked" (June 1, 2011) http://www.youtube.com/watch?v=BiGEIPT8XFQ.
Motivation:	According to Wisniewski, LulzSec "took offense to the portrayal of Bradley Manning in a segment on PBS's Frontline news magazine program"; pro-WikiLeaks attack
Type of attack:	As per Ragan, LulzSec claimed "they used a zero-day exploit in Movable Type 4 and were able to compromise Linux servers running outdated kernels."
Any other groups claiming responsibility:	No
Damage caused:	Released login credentials of database administrators/users and those of affiliates; defaced/injected their own website
Additional important information:	N/A

LulzSec—CIA

ITEM	NOTES
Target:	CIA
Date:	June 15, 2011
Source:	J. Davis, "LulzSec's CIA hack just one of many high-profile hackings," *International Business Times*, June 15, 2011, available at http://www.ibtimes.com/articles/163678/20110615/google-lulzsec-s-cia-hack-just-one-of-many-high-profile-hackings.htm (last accessed June 20, 2011). S. Schroeder, "LulzSec Hackers Take Down CIA Website," *Mashable*, June 16, 2011, available at http://mashable.com/2011/06/16/lulzsec-hackers-cia/. "LulzSec Hacks the CIA" (June 17, 2011), available at http://www.youtube.com/watch?v=QzQMBaIjo_w.
Motivation:	Unspecified
Type of attack:	DDoS

Any other groups claiming responsibility:	No
Damage caused:	CIA website was inaccessible for an unspecified period, though reported as "several hours."
Additional important information:	N/A

LulzSec—Lockheed Martin

ITEM	NOTES
Target:	Lockheed Martin
Date:	May 2011
Source:	Sky News, "Cyber-Warfare: The New Global Battlefield," October 31, 2011, available at https://news.sky.com/story/cyber-warfare-the-new-global-battlefield-10484457.
	"Chinese Regime Suspected in Lockheed Martin Hacking" (NTDTV, June 7, 2011), available at http://www.youtube.com/watch?v=1OXO0xgN1TU.
Motivation:	Unknown
Type of attack:	Unauthorized access
Any other groups claiming responsibility:	No
Damage caused:	Lockheed Martin claimed that no crucial data had been taken, though Sky News reported the company's "internal systems took a few days to fully recover."
Additional important information:	Many sources refer to Lockheed Martin being hacked and a recovery time of several days, though details are sparse.
	As per Sky, "Shortly after the breach, the UK government announced the formation of the National Cyber Security Programme, a special unit of the Ministry of Defence tasked with reducing the UK's vulnerability to cyber crime and attacks."

LulzSec—Russia

ITEM	NOTES
Target:	Sony Pictures Russia
Date:	June 6, 2011
Source:	E. Mills, "Hackers taunt Sony with more data leaks, hacks," *CNET*, June 6, 2011, available at http://news.cnet.com/8301-27080_3-20069443-245/hackers-taunt-sony-with-more-data-leaks-hacks/.
	L. Constantin, "Sony Pictures Russian Website Compromised," *Softpedia*, June 6, 2011, available at http://news.softpedia.com/news/Sony-Pictures-Russian-Website-Compromised-204563.shtml.
Motivation:	Unspecified
Type of attack:	SQL injection
Any other groups claiming responsibility:	No
Damage caused:	Site inaccessible for an unspecified amount of time (presumably down for maintenance).
	The hackers "published the structure of the database which appears to contain information about accounts registered on the content management solution (CMS) used by Sony Pictures, as well as the site's forum," Constantin reported.
Additional important information:	In announcing the hack on Postbin, they wrote "in Soviet Russia, SQL injects you..."

LulzSec—Brazil

ITEM	NOTES
Target:	Brazilian Government websites—website of the president, country's tax agency, Ministry of Sports, and political parties
	Brazilian Corporations—Petrobras Oil & Gas Company, Rede Globo television network
Date:	2011
Source:	P. Olson, "How Twitter Helped Brazil Become a Hotbed for Hacktivists," *Forbes*, February 27, 2012, available at http://www.forbes.com/sites/parmyolson/2012/02/27/how-twitter-helped-brazil-become-a-hotbed-for-hacktivists/

Motivation:	Unknown
Type of attack:	Data theft and publication
Any other groups claiming responsibility:	No
Damage caused:	Personal information of federal police agents and Petrobras employees was published.
Additional important information:	Associated with the broader LulzSec movement. Group noted for their use of Twitter.

LulzSec/Lance Moore—AT&T

ITEM	NOTES
Target:	AT&T
Date:	2011
Source:	FBI, "Sixteen Individuals Arrested in the United States for Alleged Roles in Cyber Attacks" (press release, July 19, 2011), available at http://www.fbi.gov/news/pressrel/press-releases/sixteen-individuals-arrested-in-the-united-states-for-alleged-roles-in-cyber-attacks (last accessed November 10, 2011). A. Martin, "How Two LulzSec Hackers Slipped Up," *The Atlantic*, July 20, 2011, available at https://www.the atlantic.com/technology/archive/2011/07/how-two-lulzsec-hackers-slipped/353089/.
Motivation:	Part of "50 Days of Lulz." "Just because we could."
Type of attack:	Unauthorized access/hack
Any other groups claiming responsibility:	LulzSec publicized that they had obtained and published the stolen information. Unclear whether Moore is a member of LulzSec or whether LulzSec published the information uploaded by Moore to file-sharing websites.
Damage caused:	Theft of confidential business information and publication via file-sharing websites
Additional important information:	Moore is a customer-support contractor and "exceeded his authorized access to AT&T servers" (i.e., a grey-hat hack). Moore is charged (there is no public record of the case having been resolved) with one count of accessing a protected computer without authorization.

	The charge of intentional damage to a protected computer carries a maximum penalty of ten years in prison and a $250,000 fine. Each count of conspiracy carries a maximum penalty of five years in prison and a $250,000 fine.

LulzSec—Jamaican Credit Union, school computers

ITEM	NOTES
Target:	Jamaican Credit Union and school computers
Date:	2012
Source:	J. Halliday and C. Arthur, "Anonymous' Release of Met and FBI Call Puts Hacker Group Back Centre Stage," *Guardian*, February 3, 2012, available at http://www.guardian.co.uk/technology/2012/feb/03/anonymous-hack-met-fbi-call
Motivation:	To release members of Anonymous who had been arrested and detained
Type of attack:	DDoS
Any other groups claiming responsibility:	No
Damage caused:	Jamaican Credit Union and several school computers hacked
Additional important information:	User arrested by joint operation between London Metropolitan Police and the FBI

LulzSec/Ryan Cleary—IFPI, BPI, SOCA

ITEM	NOTES
Target:	International Federation of the Phonograph Industry, British Phonographic Industry, Serious Organised Crime Agency
Date:	October–November 2010
Source:	V. Dodd and J. Halliday, "Teenager Ryan Cleary Charged Over LulzSec Hacking," *Guardian*, June 22, 2011, available at https://www.theguardian.com/technology/2011/jun/22/ryan-cleary-charged-lulzsec-hacking
Motivation:	To protest intellectual property laws
Type of attack:	DDoS, Botnet
Any other groups claiming responsibility:	Other Anonymous members were involved

Damage caused:	Cleary conspired to impair the operation of a computer
Additional important information:	In a statement, police said Cleary "did conspire with other person or persons unknown to conduct unauthorized modification of computers by constructing and distributing a computer program to form a network of computers (a botnet) modified and configured to conduct Distributed Denial of Service attacks." Cleary was charged with five offences stemming from the Criminal Law Act and the Computer Misuse Act; investigation by London Metropolitan Police's e-crime unit.

LulzSec—MilitarySingles.com

ITEM	NOTES
Target:	Dating site MilitarySingles.com
Date:	2011
Source:	C. Arthur, "Hacking Group Claiming to be LulzSec Targets US Military Dating Website," *Guardian*, March 28, 2012, available at http://www.guardian.co.uk/technology/2012/mar/28/hacking-group-lulzsec-dating-website
Motivation:	Unknown—potentially military protest or personal protest
Type of attack:	Unauthorized access
Any other groups claiming responsibility:	No
Damage caused:	Emails, passwords, and physical addresses of members leaked on Pastebin website
Additional important information:	

IRANIAN CYBER ARMY

Iranian Cyber Army—Twitter

ITEM	NOTES
Target:	Twitter
Date:	December 17, 2009
Source:	*Green Voice of Freedom*, "Who are the 'Iranian Cyber Army,'" December 15, 2010, previously available at http://en.irangreenvoice.com/article/2010/feb/19/1236 (last accessed December 16, 2010).

	"Twitter Hacked by Iranian Cyber Army (Poetry Reading)" (December 19, 2009), available at http://www.youtube.com/watch?v=rVHZ4MaCmmQ.
Motivation:	Appears to be retaliation for Western sanctions on Iran
Type of attack:	Unauthorized access, modification of data, re-directing communications, website defacement.
Any other groups claiming responsibility:	No
Damage caused:	Twitter and many sub-domains were inaccessible for an unspecified period. DNS redirection means that the site itself may not have been defaced; rather, that users were being sent to the wrong page.
Additional important information:	N/A

Iranian Cyber Army—Baidu

ITEM	NOTES
Target:	Baidu
Date:	January 11, 2010
Source:	BBC News, "Baidu hacked by 'Iranian cyber army.'" January 12, 2010, available at http://news.bbc.co.uk/2/hi/8453718.stm (last accessed January 13, 2010). *Green Voice of Freedom*, "Who are the 'Iranian Cyber Army,'" December 15, 2010, previously available at http://en.irangreenvoice.com/article/2010/feb/19/1236 (last accessed December 16, 2010).
Motivation:	Anti-democracy
Type of attack:	DNS cache poisoning, unauthorized access, modification of data, re-directing communications, website defacement
Any other groups claiming responsibility:	No
Damage caused:	Biadu website inaccessible for approximately four hours
Additional important information:	Unknown whether DNS records or the site itself was compromised. Interesting to note the attack of a Chinese tech giant—versus, say, Twitter in the United States—given Iran's good relations with China.

Iranian Cyber Army—VoA

ITEM	NOTES
Target:	Voice of America and related sites
Date:	February 22, 2011
Source:	S. Ragan, "Iranian Cyber Army defaces Voice of America and 93 other domains (Update)," *Tech Herald*, February 22, 2011, available at http://www.thetechherald.com/article.php/201108/6849/Iranian-Cyber-Army-defaces-Voice-of-America-and-93-other-domains. "VOICE of America News Website Hacked By Iranian Cyber Army" (February 22, 2011), available at http://www.youtube.com/watch?v=nDkVveI4G8Q.
Motivation:	To protest American interference with Islamic countries
Type of attack:	DNS cache poisoning, unauthorized access, modification of data, re-directing communications, website defacement
Any other groups claiming responsibility:	No
Damage caused:	Re-directed the Voice of America home site to one with a protest message. Claim to have hit ninety other sites with the same attack (most of them VOA-related). Sites inaccessible for an unspecified period
Additional important information:	N/A

Iranian Cyber Army—Tech Crunch

ITEM	NOTES
Target:	Tech Crunch
Date:	January 26, 2010
Source:	TechnoFriends, "TechCrunch Hacked? (yes, Techcrunch got hacked)," January 26, 2010, available at http://technofriends.in/2010/01/26/did-techcrunch-got-hacked/ (last accessed November 15, 2010). J. Kirk, "Iranian Cyber Army Moves Into Botnets," *PCWorld*, August 25, 2010, available at http://www.pcworld.com/businesscenter/article/208670/iranian_cyber_army_moves_into_botnets.html.
Motivation:	Unknown

Type of attack:	Potentially DNS cache poisoning, social engineering, and denial-of-service attack.
Any other groups claiming responsibility:	No
Damage caused:	Per Kirk, the group "installed a page on TechCrunch's site that redirected visitors to a server that bombarded their PCs with exploits in an attempt to install malicious software."
Additional important information:	N/A

OTHER GROUPS

Honker Union of China

ITEM	NOTES
Target:	US Military and government servers and sites
Date:	April 2001
Source:	J. Nazario, "Politically Motivated Denial of Service Attacks," available at http://www.ccdcoe.org/publications/virtualbattlefield/12_NAZARIO%20Politically%20Motivated%20DDoS.pdf.
	T. L. Thomas, "The Internet in China: Civilian and Military Uses," *Information & Security: An International Journal* 7 (2001), 159–173, available at http://fmso.leavenworth.army.mil/documents/china-internet.htm.
Motivation:	Retaliation for mid-air collision of a Chinese fighter jet and US spy plane, which killed the Chinese pilot
Type of attack:	DDOS, unauthorized access, modification of data, website defaced, defacement of websites
Any other groups claiming responsibility:	Not claiming responsibility but certainly participating were the Hacker Union of China and the China Eagle Union
Damage caused:	Defaced or crashed some hundred websites. Majority were .gov and .com domains. Defacements of US sites included the posting of pictures of the dead Chinese pilot and anti-US messages.
	Similar acts perpetrated by pro-US hackers on approximately 300 Chinese websites.

| Additional important information: | Some pro-Chinese hackers wiped several compromised servers. Generally considered bad form to do so. |

Unknown—Response to Chinese embassy bombing

ITEM	NOTES
Target:	US Energy and Interior Departments, National Park Service websites
Date:	May 9, 1999
Source:	CNN Tech, "Hackers attack US government Web sites in protest of Chinese embassy bombing," May 10, 1999, available at http://edition.cnn.com/TECH/computing/9905/10/hack.attack/ (last accessed November 10, 2011)
Motivation:	To protest NATO bombing of Chinese embassy in former Yugoslavia
Type of attack:	Unauthorized access, modification of data, defacement
Any other groups claiming responsibility:	No
Damage caused:	Websites were defaced for an unspecified period. One site was down for over twenty-four hours.
Additional important information:	White House website also went off-line, though this was claimed to be the result of equipment failure and not the work of hackers

Freedom Force Cyber Militia

ITEM	NOTES
Target:	Al-Jazeera—Qatar-based satellite TV network
Date:	March 25, 2003
Source:	Reuters, "War Hack Attacks Tit For Tat," Wired, March 28, 2003, available at http://www.wired.com/politics/law/news/2003/03/58275 (last accessed November 10, 2011)
Motivation:	To protest airing footage of British/American POWs and soldiers
Type of attack:	Unauthorized access, modification of data, and defacement
Any other groups claiming responsibility:	No

Damage caused:	Website defaced with pro-Western/US messages, Arabic-language version unavailable for twenty-four hours, English-language version unavailable for over five days.
Additional important information:	N/A

Operation Moonlight Maze

ITEM	NOTES
Target:	US Defense And Energy Departments, NASA, and US weapons labs
Date:	March 1998–1999
Source:	Bloomberg, "An Evolving Crisis," *Business Week*, April 10, 2008, available at https://www.bloomberg.com/news/articles/2008-04-09/an-evolving-crisis
Motivation:	Unknown
Type of attack:	Not specified
Any other groups claiming responsibility:	No
Damage caused:	Websites compromised
Additional important information:	Per a source quoted in the Bloomberg report: "At times, the end point [for the data] was inside Russia." The Russian Government denied responsibility.

Solar Sunrise (California and Israeli)

ITEM	NOTES
Target:	US Air Force and Navy computers
Date:	February 1998
Source:	Bloomberg, "An Evolving Crisis," *Business Week*, April 10, 2008, available at https://www.bloomberg.com/news/articles/2008-04-09/an-evolving-crisis
Motivation:	To protect Israel
Type of attack:	Malicious code
Any other groups claiming responsibility:	No

| Damage caused: | Malicious code infected |
| Additional important information: | Some attacks routed through United Arab Emirates.

The hackers were two teenagers from Cloverdale, California, and an Israeli accomplice who goes by the name of "Analyzer." |

Unknown—US nuclear sites

ITEM	NOTES
Target:	National Nuclear Security Administration (NNSA), US Department of Energy
Date:	March 20, 2012
Source:	A. Tarantola, "US Nuke Stockpile Control Systems Are 'Under Constant Attack,'" *Gizmodo*, March 21, 2012, available at http://gizmodo.com/5895033/us-nuke-stockpile-control-systems-are-under-constant-attack
Motivation:	Anti-US sentiment and pro-nuclear proliferation
Type of attack:	Ten million attacks per day, mostly via botnets
Any other groups claiming responsibility:	"Other countries' [governments], but we also get fairly sophisticated non-state actors as well," according to the NNSA's head (quoted in Tarantola).
Damage caused:	Security breach resulted in classified-data theft (from Oak Ridge National Laboratory in April 2011)
Additional important information:	These types of attacks are expected and managed well. By creating an "air gap" in their system to disconnect themselves from the Internet and run on smaller private networks, the scope for attacks on nuclear facilities is reduced, despite persistent threats. Perhaps this should be a model for other sensitive facilities. By focusing more in intranets and air gaps some cyber-security obstacles may be overcome, or at least better managed.

Unknown—US Thrift Savings Plan

ITEM	NOTES
Target:	US federal employees belonging to the Thrift Savings Plan
Date:	May 25, 2012
Source:	Fox News, "Cyberattack Targeted Personal Data of over 100,000 Federal Employees," May 26, 2012, available at https://www.foxnews.com/tech/cyberattack-targeted-personal-data-of-over-100k-federal-employees

Motivation:	Unknown
Type of attack:	Unknown
Any other groups claiming responsibility:	No
Damage caused:	Personal information on 100,000 federal employees seized, including detailed information on $133 billion worth of assets
Additional important information:	No funds were believed to be compromised

Hacker Prank—"Zombie" Attack

ITEM	NOTES
Target:	Two TV stations in Michigan and several in California, Montana, and New Mexico.
Date:	February 18, 2013
Source:	J. Finkle, "Zombie Attack Exposes Security Flaws, Experts Say," *Sydney Morning Herald*, February 15, 2013, available at http://www.smh.com.au/technology/technology-news/zombie-attack-exposes-security-flaws-experts-say-20130215-2egpw.html
Motivation:	Prank to expose security flaws
Type of attack:	The hackers used unchanged manufacturer's default passwords
Any other groups claiming responsibility:	No
Damage caused:	None, hackers just sent a bogus warning of a zombie apocalypse
Additional important information:	Per Finkle, "A male voice addressed viewers in a video posted on the internet of the bogus warning broadcast from KRTV, a CBS affiliate based in Great Falls, Montana: 'Civil authorities in your area have reported that the bodies of the dead are rising from the grave and attacking the living." The voice warned not "to approach or apprehend these bodies as they are extremely dangerous."' A fear is that perpetrators could prevent the government from sending out public warnings during an emergency or attackers could conduct a more damaging hoax than a warning of a zombie apocalypse.

TeaMp0isoN

ITEM	NOTES
Target:	UK police, RIM Blackberry
Date:	August 9, 2011
Source:	D. Neal, "Team Poison hacks Blackberry after riots," *Inquirer*, August 9, 2011, available at http://www. theinquirer.net/inquirer/news/2100557/team-poison-hacks-blackberry-riots.
Motivation:	Protest UK police tracking of looters and rioters after a man was fatally shot by police in London
Type of attack:	Unauthorized access and data theft
Any other groups claiming responsibility:	No
Damage caused:	None. Claimed to have access to RIM employee information and threatened to use it in a menacing way.
Additional important information:	Hacked LulzSec in early July 2011

TeaMp0isoN—London Metropolitan Police Anti-Terrorist Hotline

ITEM	NOTES
Target:	Metropolitan Police Anti-Terrorist Hotline
Date:	April 10, 2012
Source:	M. Smolaks, "Two Possible TeaMp0isoN Members Arrested," Tech Week Europe, April 13, 2012, available at http://www.techweekeurope.co.uk/news/teamp0ison-policeteampoison-arrested-72738
Motivation:	According to statements made by the hackers, the attack was a response to the recent events when London Metropolitan Police's Counter Terrorism Command and British courts extradited Babar Ahmad, Adel Abdel Bary, and other terrorism suspects to be tried in America
Type of attack:	Hotline hacked, prank calling, and computerized auto-dialling
Any other groups claiming responsibility:	No

Damage caused:	Service disabled and private conversations between anti-terrorist hotline staff posted online.
Additional important information:	Extradition was a key theme here

Bank of England

ITEM	NOTES
Target:	No target—this is a protective mechanism taken by the Bank of England regarding ethical hacking
Date:	April 23, 2014
Country:	England
Source:	D. Wilson, "Bank of England turns to 'ethical hackers' to fix financial security," *Tech Rader*, April 23, 2014, available at http://www.techradar.com/au/news/internet/web/bank-of-england-turns-to-ethical-hackers-to-fix-financial-sector-security-1244589
Motivation:	To fix financial-sector security
Type of attack:	This was not an attack
Damage caused:	N/A
Additional important information:	Bank of England hired white-hat (ethical) hackers to test and improve the resilience of networks behind twenty of the United Kingdom's biggest banks and financial-services firms. The bank oversees a programme of ethical hacking designed to improve computer security in the financial sector. Bank of England will hire specialists from approved companies with CREST (Council for Registered Ethical Security Testers) certification, who will perform penetration testing to look for vulnerabilities that might be exploited by unscrupulous cyber criminals. The Bank of England plans have been piloted and it is expected that major players like the Royal Bank of Scotland and London Stock Exchange will take part.

Gator League

ITEM	NOTES
Target:	British intelligence and surveillance agency Government Communications Headquarters (GCHQ)
Date:	December 23, 2014
Source:	G. C. Kharel, "Hactivist Group Gator League Brings Down British GCHQ Website, Takes Blame for N Korean Internet Outage," *International Business Times*, December 24, 2014, available at http://www.ibtimes.co.in/gator-league-brings-down-british-gchq-website-takes-blame-n-korean-internet-outage-618166. *The Anonymous Log*, Facebook (January 4, 2015), https://www.facebook.com/TheAnonymousLog. RT, "Hacktivist group 'takes down' GCHQ website, claims N. Korean blackout," December 24, 2014, available at http://rt.com/news/217211-gchq-website-down-hackers/. AnonWatcher, "GCHQ Hacked. North Korea Claimed," *AnonHQ*, January 3, 2015, available at http://anonhq.com/gchq-hacked-north-korea-claimed/.
Motivation:	GCHQ is an UK intelligence branch in conflict with Anonymous and LulzSec, hacktivists responsible for DDoS attacks. Gator League and Anonymous are allies and this attack was the Gator League's Christmas attack.
Type of attack:	DDoS
Any other groups claiming responsibility:	No
Damage caused:	Website down for more than an hour
Additional important information:	The GCHQ is an UK intelligence branch made up of specialist hackers tasked with using DDoS attacks against hackers themselves and revealing the identities of these hackers. A motivation for the hacktivists lies in the power that the GCHQ has, as it is not bound by international law and regulation.

Decocidio

ITEM	NOTES
Target:	European Climate Exchange
Date:	July 23, 2010
Source:	L. Leyden, "EU climate exchange website hit by green-hat hacker," *The Register*, July 26, 2010, available at http://www.theregister.co.uk/2010/07/26/climate_exchange_website_hack/ (last accessed July 27, 2010). Takver, "European Climate Exchange website hacked," *Independent Media Centre Australia*, July 25, 2010, available at http://indymedia.org.au/2010/07/24/european-climate-exchange-website-hacked (last accessed July 29, 2010).
Motivation:	Political protest related to carbon credits
Type of attack:	Unauthorized access, modification of data, website defaced
Any other groups claiming responsibility:	No
Damage caused:	Site was defaced for a weekend. Highlighted the group's opposition to carbon trading as a means of tackling climate change.
Additional important information:	Superficial solution when it may still be more profitable for a corporation to pay fines for environmental damage than to effectively minimize such damage. Cited links to the "Climategate" scandal in 2009, though information is sketchy. Leaked communications pertaining to manipulation of climate-change data by researchers. This was never found to be the work of hackers.

DAX stock index

ITEM	NOTES
Target:	German stock index DAX (or may have actually targeted French rugby team fan site)
Date:	October 2011
Source:	J. Leyden, "Hackers mistake French rugby site for German stock exchange," *The Register*, November 4, 2011, available at http://www.theregister.co.uk/2011/11/04/french_rugby_site_hacktivist_maul/.
Motivation:	Likely an Occupy Wall Street–style protest against the DAX website

Type of attack:	DDoS
Any other groups claiming responsibility:	No
Damage caused:	Accidently took down a French rugby team's fan site (allezdax.com) for two weeks.
Additional important information:	Not known who was responsible for the attack. Since no one has come forward, it can be assumed that the team website was not the intended target, though inconclusive. Seemed to have been reported only after the website was back up and running. Time of attack could possibly be mid-October.

Unknown—Union for a Popular Movement, France

ITEM	NOTES
Target:	Union for a Popular Movement (UMP), French political party
Date:	November 10, 2011
Source:	The Wrong Guy, "Activists hack French ruling party's phone numbers," *WhyWeProtest*, November 10, 2011, available at http://forums.whyweprotest.net/threads/activists-hack-french-ruling-partys-phone-numbers.96206/
Motivation:	Protesting apparent oppression of party members and treatment of protesters
Type of attack:	Unauthorized access and data leak
Any other groups claiming responsibility:	No
Damage caused:	Published personal details including phone numbers of senior members of right-wing French President Nicolas Sarkozy's UMP party
Additional important information:	N/A

French G20 conference files

ITEM	NOTES
Target:	G20 conference files from the French Finance Ministry
Date:	February 2011
Source:	S. Curtis, "China Implicated in Hack of French G20 Files," *Tech Week Europe*, March 7, 2011, available at https://www.silicon.co.uk/workspace/china-implicated-in-hack-of-french-g20-files-23062.
Motivation:	Protest in relation to Chinese government's treatment at the G20 (Chinese government resisted calls at the summit to target exchange-rate valuations, currency reserves, and economic surpluses)
Type of attack:	Most likely targeted Trojans embedded in legitimate government PDF files and other attachments
Any other groups claiming responsibility:	No
Damage caused:	Theft of G20 conference files and infection of up to 150 government computers
Additional important information:	No evidence of Chinese government involvement. However, according to an anonymous official, a "certain amount of the information was redirected to Chinese sites" (quoted in Curtis). "Although the Chinese connection has not been proved, there are hacker groups in China specialising in this sort of attack and claiming to be funded—directly or indirectly—by the military and/or government" (see Curtis).

RedHack

ITEM	NOTES
Target:	A number of organizations, including the cities of Kars and Amasya, the gas-distribution authority of Sakarya, the Ministry of Education.
Date:	February 10, 2014
Country:	Turkey

Source:	E. Kovacs, "RedHack begins hack attacks in protest against Turkey's New Internet Law," Softpedia, February 10, 2014, available at http://news.softpedia.com/news/RedHack-Begins-Hack-Attacks-in-Protest-Against-Turkey-s-New-Internet-Law-425418.shtml
Motivation:	To protest a new Internet law in Turkey, which is seen as a serious limit on freedom of speech
Type of attack:	Website defacement, copy of information, leak of information
Damage caused:	Defaced websites and leaked information
Additional important information:	RedHack leaked the phone numbers of "murderer police chiefs and superintendents."
	The hacktivists then defaced the website of the Kars municipality (kars.bel.tr), posting a message opposing the new Internet law.
	Another website targeted by RedHack was the gas-distribution authority of Sakarya, on which they posted a message saying that gas should be free because the government is "stealing enough from the people."
	The website of the city of Amasya was targeted, from which the hacktivists leaked AKP (Justice and Development Party) membership applications.
	The Ministry of Education was also attacked, whereby invoices and school expenditures were published online, on JustPaste.it. The hackers wrote on Twitter: "Ministry of Education—There are some astronomical expenditures which clearly shows there is degree of corruption, especially on water bills."
	The controversial Internet-censorship law has been criticized not only by Turkish citizens, but also by the EU. Peter Stano, spokesperson for European Commissioner for Enlargement Stefan Füle, said, "The Turkish public deserves more information and more transparency, not more restrictions. The law needs to be revised in line with European standards."

RedHack

ITEM	NOTES
Target:	Turkish Telecommunications Directorate (Telekomünikasyon İletişim Başkanlığı, or Tib)
Date:	March 28, 2014
Country:	Turkey
Source:	E. Kovacs, "RedHack Begins Hack Attacks in Protest Against Turkey's New Internet Law," *Tech Worm*, March 28, 2014, available at http://www.techworm.net/2014/03/redhack-ddoses-turkish.html
Motivation:	Done in protest of the government's banning of Twitter and YouTube across the country.
Type of attack:	DDoS
Damage caused:	Unknown
Additional important information:	TIB had blocked YouTube hours after an audio recording leaked, allegedly featuring the voices of Turkey's foreign minister, intelligence chief, and a top army general discussing the developments in neighbouring war-torn Syria was uploaded on YouTube. This ban came one week after TIB blocked Twitter in a move seen as a response to leaked audio recordings posted on site that appear to implicate Prime Minister Recep Tayyip Erodgan in the banning measure.

In response to the banning of Twitter and YouTube, RedHack took down the website of the Presidency of Telecommunication and Communication of Turkey.

The TIB website was attacked on a Thursday night and was restored on the Friday morning, but with an additional "tr" in the URL.

The original URL listed on Google is still not available. Typing in the original URL, one is automatically redirected to the new URL.

After the attack, RedHack posted this message on its Twitter account: "You forgot the coordinator of everything while calculating things. The ban is meant to be banned." |

RedHack

ITEM	NOTES
Target:	Turkish Cooperation and Coordination Agency
Date:	May 18, 2014
Country:	Turkey
Source:	A. K. Jha, "RedHack leaks email id's and password from Turkish Cooperation and Coordination Agency (TIKA)," *Tech Worm*, May 18, 2014, available at http://www.techworm.net/2014/05/redhack-leaks-email-ids-and-password.html
Motivation:	Corruption of the government
Type of attack:	Email usernames and passwords of agency personnel were leaked
Damage caused:	Email usernames and passwords made public online, including via Twitter
Additional important information:	The leak was done to protest government corruption. The leak was announced on RedHack's Twitter account. The leak also served to shame the email users with claims that users had accessed adult dating sites.

Shaltai Boltai

ITEM	NOTES
Target:	Russian Prime Minister Dmitry Medvedev
Date:	August 14, 2014
Country:	Russia
Source:	A. K. Jha, "Russian Prime Minister's Twitter account hacked," *Tech Work*, August 14, 2014, available at http://www.techworm.net/2014/08/russian-prime-ministers-twitter-account.html
Motivation:	To criticize the Russian government and President Putin
Type of attack:	Twitter account hacked
Damage caused:	Russian prime minister's Twitter account hacked
Additional important information:	Medvedev's official Twitter account had more than 2.52 million followers and was hacked, the hackers posting tweets through the account, such as: "I am resigning. Ashamed of the actions of the government. I'm sorry, Forgive me."

The hackers also managed to retweet several anti-Russian government and anti-Putin messages from several Russian anti-Putin journalists and democracy activists.

The tweets were removed after about forty minutes and a spokesperson for the Russian government later acknowledged the hack.

Hacker group Shaltai Boltai took responsibility for the hack. The group claimed it had obtained access to several of Medvedev's email accounts and data from three of his iPhones.

Shaltai Boltai claimed they represent disgruntled Russian government officials upset at Putin's recent hardline turn and aggressive policy toward Ukraine.

Unknown—HKEx

ITEM	NOTES
Target:	Hong Kong Stock Exchange (HKEx)
Date:	August 10, 2011
Source:	C. Wisniewski, "Hong Kong stock exchange (HKEx) website hacked, impacts trades," *Naked Security*, August 10, 2011, available at http://nakedsecurity.sophos.com/2011/08/10/hong-kong-stock-exchange-hkex-website-hacked-impacts-trades/.
	C. Wisniewski, "Hong Kong stock exchange attacked for second day in a row," *Naked Security*, August 12, 2011, available at http://nakedsecurity.sophos.com/2011/08/12/hong-kong-stock-exchange-attacked-for-second-day-in-a-row/.
Motivation:	Possibly to accompany occupy movements
Type of attack:	DDoS
Any other groups claiming responsibility:	Unknown
Damage caused:	Unspecified
Additional important information:	Possibly perpetrated by Anonymous

Unknown—Activism by mail

ITEM	NOTES
Target:	Chinese government
Date:	February 1, 2001
Source:	M. Farley, "Dissidents Hack Holes in China's New Wall," *Los Angeles Times*, January 4, 1999, available at http://articles.latimes.com/1999/jan/04/news/mn-60340
Motivation:	Freedom of speech, pro-democracy
Type of attack:	Subversion of security measures and mail/email
Any other groups claiming responsibility:	Multiple groups, including Bronc Buster, Cult of the Dead Cow, and the Hong Kong Blondes
Damage caused:	No apparent damage. Subversion of security protocols by using private email to distribute pro-democracy literature. Such literature was also sent to many Chinese government officials.
Additional important information:	N/A

Unknown—Hong Kong Civil Referendum Website

ITEM	NOTES
Target:	Hong Kong Civil Referendum Website
Date:	March 23, 2012
Source:	Reuters HK, "Hackers 'disable' Hong Kong Civil Referendum Website," *Guardian*, March 23, 2012, available at http://www.guardian.co.uk/world/2012/mar/23/hackers-hong-kong-civil-referendum
Motivation:	Unknown
Type of attack:	DDoS (suspected)
Any other groups claiming responsibility:	No
Damage caused:	Website disabled and servers "crippled"
Additional important information:	Website offered a mock civil referendum, launched to see how people would vote if given a choice. Completely non-binding and arguably not influential.

Unknown—GreatFire

ITEM	NOTES
Target:	GreatFire, a Chinese activist group that monitors and challenges Internet censorship in China.
Date:	March 19, 2015
Source:	A. Elise, A., "China Hacktivists GreatFire Hit with DDoS Attack Costing Up to $30,000 Per Day," *International Business Times*, March 21, 2015, available at http://www.ibtimes.com/china-hacktivists-greatfire-hit-ddos-attack-costing-30000-day-1854692.
Motivation:	Speculated to be in retaliation over an article in the *Wall Street Journal* describing escalating tension between free-speech activists and Internet censors, and outlining the effectiveness of GreatFire in delivering uncensored content into China
Type of attack:	DDoS
Any other groups claiming responsibility:	No
Damage caused:	GreatFire.org went off-line and the group had to upgrade to faster servers to manage the request load (the site offers censorship-defeating Internet tools). The growing data requests costs up to $30,000 per day.
Additional important information:	N/A

ISIS hacktivists—China's Tsinghua University

ITEM	NOTES
Target:	Tsinghua University
Date:	January 18, 2016
Source:	W. Ashford, "Chinese university targeted by Islamic State hacktivist," *Computer Weekly*, January 18, 2016, available at http://www.computerweekly.com/news/4500271103/Chinese-university-targeted-by-Islamic-State-hacktivist
Motivation:	Recruit students to join the Islamic State (ISIS)
Type of attack:	Unknown
Any other groups claiming responsibility:	No

| Damage caused: | University website pages were replaced with images of masked militants beneath the ISIS flag |
| Additional important information: | China was declared one of eighteen enemy states by ISIS in 2015; the Chinese government has blamed ISIS-affiliated militants for a series of armed attacks in the country's Xinjiang region. |

Unknown—Japanese government

ITEM	NOTES
Target:	Japanese government
Date:	January 25, 2001
Source:	ABC News, "Japanese Web Sites Hacked," January 25, 2001, available at http://abcnews.go.com/Technology/story?id=99306&page=1 (last accessed November 14, 2011)
Motivation:	To criticize the Japanese government's refusal to acknowledge the 1937 Nanjing Massacre in China
Type of attack:	Unauthorized access, modification of data, defacement
Any other groups claiming responsibility:	No
Damage caused:	Website defaced for an unspecified period. The Japan Science and Technology Agency's home page redirected to an adult website.
Additional important information:	First-ever hacking of the Japanese government computer system. A posted message read: "The Chinese people must speak up to protest the Japanese government for refusing to acknowledge the historical misdeed of the 1937 Nanjing Massacre."

Unknown—Japanese websites

ITEM	NOTES
Target:	Japanese government websites (including the Defence and the Internal Affairs and Communications Ministries) as well as the Supreme Court and Tokyo Institute of Technology. The websites of banks, utilities, and other private companies were also hit.
Date:	September 21, 2012

Source:	P. Muncaster, "Chinese hacktivists launch cyber attack on Japan," *The Register*, September 21, 2012, available at http://www.theregister.co.uk/2012/09/21/japan_china_attack_sites_senkaku/
Motivation:	China-Japan dispute over the Diaoyu/Senkaku islands. To deface websites with pictures of the Chinese flag.
Type of attack:	DDoS and vandalism
Any other groups claiming responsibility:	No
Damage caused:	Government websites were off-line for a number of hours. The Tokyo Institute of Technology site was defaced and the names and telephone numbers of over 1,000 staff members were leaked.
Additional important information:	Three hundred Japanese websites were short-listed for attack on a message board of the Chinese hacktivist group Honker Union, while around 4,000 individuals had posted messages about planned attacks on Chinese chat site YY Chat.

Alexploiter

ITEM	NOTES
Target:	Yemen customs
Date:	May 8, 2011
Source:	M. Kumar, "Customs Authority of Yemen Hacked for Protests against Government," *Hacker News*, August 5, 2011, available at http://thehackernews.com/2011/08/customs-authority-of-yemen-hacked-for.html
Motivation:	Protesting Yemeni government
Type of attack:	Unauthorized access, modification of data, defacement
Any other groups claiming responsibility:	No
Damage caused:	Customs website defaced for an unspecified period
Additional important information:	N/A

Kaotik Team

ITEM	NOTES
Target:	Indonesian government
Date:	August 1, 1998
Source:	C. Nuttall, "Chinese protesters attack Indonesia through Net," BBC News, August 19, 1998, available at http://connections-qj.org/article/internet-china-civilian-and-military-uses
Motivation:	To protest government oppression and occupation of East Timor
Type of attack:	Unauthorized access, modification of data, and defacement
Any other groups claiming responsibility:	No
Damage caused:	Forty-five Indonesian government sites reportedly defaced for an unspecified period. The home page of a site at www.bkkbn.go.id was replaced with a message saying "Warning from Chinese...This page is hacked for your national day. Please keep this page for 48 hours and punish the murderers in May immediately."
Additional important information:	N/A

China (suspected)—Vietnam

ITEM	NOTES
Target:	Vietnamese government
Date:	Early June 2010
Source:	BBC News, "Vietname and China Hackers Escalate Spratley Island Row" June 9, 2011 available at https://www.bbc.com/news/world-asia-pacific-13707921
Motivation:	Response to Spratly Islands dispute between China and Vietnam
Type of attack:	Website defacement
Any other groups claiming responsibility:	Attacked websites did not have high security. Could have been anyone with an IP address from China, or one redirected to China

Damage caused:	Two hundred Vietnamese websites hacked, including the Ministry of Agriculture and Rural Development.
	Hackers changed the attacked sites' homepage interface and left messages in Chinese or English, together with the images of the Chinese flag, according to BBC, adding that the attack methods were not sophisticated and seemed spontaneous.
Additional important information:	Seems like a crude hacking attempt from independent/ rogue hackers rather than the Chinese state. Chinese-state hacks do not typically feature the basic hacking/defacing features seen in this case.
	Demonstrates the use of hacking as a precursory method to actual physical conflict between nations. Perhaps cybercrime is used to fight virtual wars before the need for physical conflict.

Gator League

ITEM	NOTES
Target:	Democratic People's Republic of Korea (North Korea)
Date:	December 23, 2014
Source:	RT, "Eye for eye? N. Korea internet restored after 9.5hr blackout," December 23, 2014, available at http://rt.com/news/216887-north-korea-internet-blackout/.
	R. Satter and E. Sullivan, "North Korea outage a case study in online uncertainties," *The Sydney Morning Herald*, December 25, 2014, available at http://www.smh.com.au/digital-life/digital-life-news/north-korea-outage-a-case-study-in-online-uncertainties-20141224-12dltr.html.
Motivation:	Potentially a retaliation for the Sony attack; North Korea blamed the US government. However, hacktivist group Gator League claimed responsibility
Type of attack:	DDoS Attack
Any other groups claiming responsibility:	Lizard Squad
Damage caused:	A nearly ten-hour Internet-service outage in North Korea

Additional important information:	On Sunday, December 20, 2014, Gator League posted the tweet "#NorthKorea is about to be invaded by alligators…" The next day, Internet service in North Korea was down for almost ten hours. On December 24, Anonymous posted the tweet "#BREAKING: CONFIRMED: HACKING GROUP @GatorLeague TOOK NORTH KOREA OFF OF THE INTERNET DECEMBER 21st-22nd. #NorthKorea."

Joint attack by 3xplr3_./split0 & N3roB]—(Bangladesh)

ITEM	NOTES
Target:	Subordinate courts of Bangladesh
Date:	November 2011
Source:	Hackers Media, "Subordinate Court of Bangladesh Hacked," previously available at http://www.hackersmedia.com/2011/11/subordinate-courts-of-bangladesh-hacked.html
Motivation:	To inform government websites of their vulnerability
Type of attack:	Unauthorized Access Deface
Any other groups claiming responsibility:	Unknown
Damage caused:	Website defaced
Additional important information:	N/A

3xp1r3 Cyber Army

ITEM	NOTES
Target:	Bangladesh Supreme Court website
Date:	November 10, 2011
Source:	M. Kumar, "Bangladesh Supreme Court website hacked," Hacker News, November 11, 2011, available at http://thehackernews.com/2011/11/bangladesh-supreme-court-website-hacked.html (last accessed November 12, 2011)
Motivation:	Apparently, to make website administrators aware of insecure site
Type of attack:	Unauthorized access and defacement

Any other groups claiming responsibility:	No
Damage caused:	Website defaced for unspecified period. No data leaked or deleted.
Additional important information:	N/A

TeaMp0isoN

ITEM	NOTES
Target:	Foreign governments, and also included the armynet.mod.uk and aph.gov.au sites
Date:	November 7, 2011
Source:	M. Kumar, "International Foreign Government E-Mails Hacked by TeaMp0isoN," *Hacker News*, November 7, 2011, available at http://thehackernews.com/2011/11/international-foreign-government-e.html
Motivation:	Generic dislike of government
Type of attack:	Unauthorized access and release of data
Any other groups claiming responsibility:	No
Damage caused:	Released personal information/email username/passwords of over 200 government officials
Additional important information:	N/A

The UnderTakers—AmEn, Swan, Bondbey, DanqeoN

ITEM	NOTES
Target:	Sony Music Brazil
Date:	June 4, 2011
Source:	M. Kumar, "Sony Music Brazil Gets Defaced!," *Hacker News*, June 5, 2011, available at http://thehackernews.com/2011/06/sony-music-brazil-gets-defaced.html (last accessed June 6, 2011)
Motivation:	Unknown—defacement alludes to an opposition to war

Type of attack:	SQL injection, unauthorized access, defacement
Any other groups claiming responsibility:	No
Damage caused:	Website down/defaced for over twelve hours
Additional important information:	Group unaffiliated with LulzSec. Unknown whether affiliated with other Brazilian hackers.

3xp1r3 Cyber Army (Bangladesh)

ITEM	NOTES
Target:	Indian websites
Date:	February 2012
Source:	"H4Ck3D By 3xp1r3 Cyber Army," Pastebin (February 12, 2012), available at http://pastebin.com/GRAmd7qq
Motivation:	Protesting the brutal treatment of Bangladeshi at the Indian borders.
Type of attack:	Website defaced
Any other groups claiming responsibility:	No
Damage caused:	Unknown
Additional important information:	Seven hundred Indian and Indian-linked websites attacked (see http://pastebin.com/GRAmd7qq)

Milw0rm

ITEM	NOTES
Target:	India's Bhabha Atomic Research Centre
Date:	May 1998
Source:	A. Penenberg, "Hacking Bhabha," Forbes, November 16, 1998, available at http://www.forbes.com/1998/11/16/feat.html (last accessed November 11, 2011)
Motivation:	To protest nuclear tests
Type of attack:	Unauthorized access, modification of data, data theft, data leaks
Any other groups claiming responsibility:	T3k-9—child

| Damage caused: | Unspecified. Facility's servers were reportedly breached. |
| Additional important information: | Milw0rm is now defunct |

NaijaCyberHacktivists

ITEM	NOTES
Target:	Niger Delta Development Commission's website
Date:	May 26, 2011 (estimate)
Source:	N. Jidenma, "Naija Cyber Hactivists Hack EFCC website to protest proposed internet censor in Nigeria," *Next Web,* September 28, 2011, available at http://thenextweb.com/africa/2011/05/26/nigerian-government-agency-website-hacked-by-cyberhacktivists/
Motivation:	Displeased with presidential inauguration budget of N$1 billion
Type of attack:	Unauthorized access, modification of data, and defacement
Any other groups claiming responsibility:	No
Damage caused:	Website defaced for an unspecified period
Additional important information:	N/A

Colombian government hacks

ITEM	NOTES
Target:	Colombian Ministry of Education, Colombian Senate, Colombian president, and government webpages. National communication system and other state infrastructure also targeted
Date:	2011
Source:	J. Wyss, "Political hackers are one of Latin America's newest headaches," *Miami Herald*, November 3 2011, available at http://www.miamiherald.com/2011/10/31/2481360/political-hackers-are-one-of-latin.html
Motivation:	Anti-government protesting
Type of attack:	Website hack

Any other groups claiming responsibility:	Reportedly affiliated with Anonymous
Damage caused:	Website defacing
Additional important information:	There were 480 hacks of Colombian Government websites in 2011, up from 250 in 2010. Colombian police officers' contact information published.

Ecuadorian government hacks

ITEM	NOTES
Target:	Ecuadorian government websites
Date:	2011
Source:	J. Wyss, "Political hackers are one of Latin America's newest headaches," *Miami Herald*, November 3, 2011, available at http://www.miamiherald.com/2011/10/31/2481360/political-hackers-are-one-of-latin.html
Motivation:	Anti-government protest
Type of attack:	Website hack
Any other groups claiming responsibility:	Reportedly affiliated with Anonymous
Damage caused:	Government websites defaced
Additional important information:	Two hundred and thirty attacks in 2011.

Latin Hack Team—Ecuador presidential website

ITEM	NOTES
Target:	Rafael Correa, Ecuador government
Date:	June 20, 2011
Source:	ElUniverso, "Website of the Presidency of Ecuador suffered cyber attacks," June 20, 2011, available at http://www.eluniverso.com/2011/06/20/1/1355/pagina-internet-presidencia-ecuatoriana-sufrio-ataque-informatico.html?p=1354&m=638 (last accessed June 21, 2011)
Motivation:	To protest alleged political corruption
Type of attack:	DDoS

Any other groups claiming responsibility:	Possibly Anonymous
Damage caused:	Presidential website out of commission for over two hours, elciudadano.com (government e-newspaper) down for an hour.
Additional important information:	Conflicting information on the group responsible. Some report that the so-called Latin Hack Team is a part of Anonymous.

N33—Venezuelan Pro-Government Hacks

ITEM	NOTES
Target:	Journalists, artists, opposition politicians
Date:	July 2011
Source:	J. Wyss, "Political hackers are one of Latin America's newest headaches," *Miami Herald*, November 3, 2011, available at http://www.miamiherald.com/2011/10/31/2481360/political-hackers-are-one-of-latin.html
Motivation:	Pro-government protest
Type of attack:	Twitter hacking
Any other groups claiming responsibility:	N33
Damage caused:	Twitter accounts hacked
Additional important information:	"N33's calling card is the image of a red beret — one of President Chávez's symbols." This and targeted hacking alludes to a pro-Chavez stance.

DonR4ul

ITEM	NOTES
Target:	Brazilian presidency blog
Date:	October 13, 2011
Source:	Xinhua, "Brazilian presidency's blog hacked in protest of corruption," October 14, 2011, *China Daily*, previously available at http://www.chinadaily.com.cn/xinhua/2011-10-14/content_4060557.html
Motivation:	Corruption in government departments and high fuel prices

Type of attack:	Unauthorized access, modification of data, and website defaced
Any other groups claiming responsibility:	No groups. Alleged to be the work of one hacker, "@DonR4UL."
Damage caused:	Defaced blog website for a number of hours.
Additional important information:	N/A

Raise Your Voice (Lebanese Hacktivists)

ITEM	NOTES
Target:	Lebanese government websites, Lebanese Energy and Water Department, MTV Lebanon
Date:	April 17, 2012
Source:	J, Karia, "Lebanese Hacktivists Take Down 15 Government Websites," *Tech Week Europe*, available at http://www.tech weekeurope.co.uk/news/lebanese-hacktivists-15-government-websites-73313
Motivation:	Social protest—living conditions
Type of attack:	DDoS
Any other groups claiming responsibility:	No
Damage caused:	Up to fifteen government websites taken off-line
Additional important information:	Social protest of living standards and conditions. Draws parallels to Tel Aviv's tent-city protests of 2011. Interesting that Lebanese youth adopt hacktivism to promote daily living concerns.

Khosrow Zare Farid—Central Bank of Iran

ITEM	NOTES
Target:	Central Bank of Iran, Iranian banking customers
Date:	April 2011 (reported April 19, 2012)
Source:	J. Kahria, "Hacker exposes Three Million Iranian Bank Account Details," *Tech Week Europe*, available at http://www.techweekeurope.co.uk/news/hacker-three-million-iranian-bank-accounts-73161

Motivation:	To increase awareness about data security in Iran, provoke a reaction from Iranian banks
Type of attack:	Accessed and published data on three million credit-card details obtained from more than twenty Iranian banks.
Any other groups claiming responsibility:	No
Damage caused:	Data from three million customers' accounts compromised
Additional important information:	Khosrow Zare Farid, identified by Kabir News, was a manager at a payments-services company that had several national banks as clients. "Around one year ago I found a critical bug in the system," said Zare Farid, according to Kabir News. "Then I wrote and sent a formal report to all the CEO of banks in Iran but none of them replied to me." Zare Farid then published a thousand, and later, three million, card details on his blog.

Cyber Warriors Team (Iran)—NASA hack

ITEM	NOTES
Target:	National Aeronautics and Space Administration (NASA)
Date:	May 16, 2012
Source:	M. Liebowitz, "Iranian 'Cyber Warriors Team' takes credit for NASA hack," NBC News, May 22, 2012, available at http://www.nbcnews.com/id/47522497/ns/technology_and_sciencesecurity/t/iranian-cyber-warriors-team-takes-credit-nasa-hack/#.XADd5y1L1PM
Motivation:	Geopolitical conflict
Type of attack:	SSL vulnerability exploited
Any other groups claiming responsibility:	No
Damage caused:	Personal information of thousands of NASA employees stolen
Additional important information:	"How to" video of hack posted online

CabinCr3w

ITEM	NOTES
Target:	Citigroup CEO, Vikram Pandit
Date:	October 18, 2011
Source:	A. Couts, "Hackers leak Citigroup CEO's personal data after Occupy Wall Street arrests," *Digital Trends*, August 18, 2011, available at http://www.digitaltrends.com/computing/hackers-leak-citigroup-ceos-personal-data-after-occupy-wall-street-arrests/
Motivation:	Apparently in response to arrests of protesters at a Citibank branch
Type of attack:	Unauthorized access and release of personal information
Any other groups claiming responsibility:	No
Damage caused:	Mobile and office phone numbers, an email address, two home addresses, legal and financial information, and information about Pandit's family posted online
Additional important information:	N/A

realloc()

ITEM	NOTES
Target:	The SCO group website (http://www.sco.com)
Date:	November 29, 2004
Source:	R. Millman, "SCO hit by hacker protest," *SC Magazine*, November 29, 2004, available at http://www.scmagazineus.com/sco-hit-by-hacker-protest/article/31510/
Motivation:	"Apparent protest over the ongoing legal proceedings the company is waging against Linux"
Type of attack:	Unauthorized access, modification of data, defacement
Any other groups claiming responsibility:	No
Damage caused:	Website defaced for unspecified period
Additional important information:	N/A

Herbless—HSBC

ITEM	NOTES
Target:	HSBC UK, Greek and Spanish websites, and British Arab Commercial Bank
Date:	September 20, 2000
Source:	J. Ticehurst, "HSBC internet sites hacked," *V3*, September 20, 2000, available at http://www.v3.co.uk/v3-uk/news/2007500/hsbc-internet-sites-hacked
Motivation:	Support to fuel protests in the United Kingdom
Type of attack:	Unauthorized access and potentially SQL injection
Any other groups claiming responsibility:	No
Damage caused:	UK site and three international sites were unavailable for an unspecified period
Additional important information:	Hacker claimed that personal information was neither accessed nor sought

Comment Group—Brian Milburn

ITEM	NOTES
Target:	Solid Oak Software Inc.—Milburn's family-owned firm in California
Date:	June 24, 2009–early 2012 (months after a February 2012 settlement)
Source:	M. Riley,"China Mafia-Style Attack Drives California Firm to Brink," *Bloomberg*, November 28, 2012, available at http://www.bloomberg.com/news/2012-11-27/china-mafia-style-hack-attack-drives-california-firm-to-brink.html. P. Muncaster, "US software firm hacked for years after suing China," *The Register*, November 29, 2012, available at https://www.theregister.co.uk/2012/11/29/solid_oak_china_hacked_three_years/.
Motivation:	Reaction to Milburn's accusation that China appropriated his company's parental filtering software, CYBERsitter, for an Internet-censoring project.

Type of attack:	Spear phishing.
	The malware had downloaded software that burrowed into the company's Microsoft operating system, automatically uploading more tools the hackers could use to control the network remotely.
Any other groups claiming responsibility:	No
Damage caused:	Assailed Solid Oak's computer systems; repeatedly shut down web and e-mail servers; spied on an employee with her webcam; gained access to sensitive files in a battle that caused company revenues to collapse; and sabotaged online sales by causing timeouts during payment.
Additional important information:	Milburn told Bloomberg, "If they [the Chinese hackers] could just put the company out of business, the lawsuit goes away."
	A forensic analysis of the malware by Joe Stewart, a threat expert at Atlanta-based Dell SecureWorks, identified the intruders who rifled Solid Oak's networks as a team of Shanghai-based hackers involved in a string of sensitive national-security-related breaches going back years. Commercial hacker hunters—who refer to the team as the Comment Group for the hidden program code they use known as "comments"—tie it to a multitude of victims that include the president of the European Union Council, major defence contractors, and even Barack Obama's 2008 presidential campaign. According to leaked classified cables, the group has been linked to the People's Liberation Army and China's military.
	Milburn settled a $2.2 billion lawsuit against the Chinese government and a string of computer companies.

Charles Tendell, ethical hacker

ITEM	NOTES
Target:	Baby monitors
Date:	January 28, 2015
Source:	J. Allen, "Ethical hacker points out security concerns with using home baby monitors," 7News Denver, January 28, 2015, available at http://www.thedenverchannel.com/news/local-news/ethical-hacker-points-out-security-concerns-with-using-home-baby-monitors01282015

Motivation:	Security awareness
Type of attack:	No attack—a cyber-security expert based out of Monument, Colorado, showed a news reporter how easy it is to hack into thousands of baby-monitor video feeds.
Any other groups claiming responsibility:	N/A
Damage caused:	N/A
Additional important information:	N/A

Laxman Muthiyah, ethical hacker

ITEM	NOTES
Target:	Facebook
Date:	February 10, 2015
Source:	M. Desjardin, "How a White Hat Hacker Saved Your Facebook Photos," *Reviewed*, February 19, 2015, available at https://www.reviewed.com/cameras/news/how-a-hacker-saved-your-facebook-photos. L. Muthiyah, "Deleting Any Album—How I Hacked Your Facebook Photos," *Zero Hack*, November 8, 2015, available at https://thezerohack.com/how-i-hacked-your-facebook-photos#articlescroll.
Motivation:	Laxman Muthiyah discovered a means for anyone with some hacking knowledge to delete people's photo albums from Facebook
Type of attack:	This was not an attack; Muthiyah notified Facebook of the security risk and was awarded a bounty of $12,500 by the company
Any other groups claiming responsibility:	N/A
Damage caused:	N/A

Additional important information:	Muthiyah exploited vulnerabilities in Facebook's Graph API, which would allow a hacker to use access tokens to delete entire photo albums of other users.
	The access tokens that would enable this were available through the Facebook application for Android devices.
	The hacking process would involve each hacker generating a basic script to generate the sequential photo album IDs and test their vulnerability automatically. This security risk presented a real risk that could have been easily executed.

Unknown—Susan G. Komen Foundation for the Cure

ITEM	NOTES
Target:	Susan G. Komen Foundation for the Cure
Date:	February 2, 2012
Source:	A. Abad-Santos, "Susan G. Komen Foundation was Hacked Last Night," *Atlantic Wire*, February 2, 2012, available at http://www.theatlanticwire.com/national/2012/02/susan-g-komen-foundation-website-was-hacked-last-night/48192/
Motivation:	To protest the foundation's decision to pull funding from Planned Parenthood
Type of attack:	Unauthorized access and modification of data
Any other groups claiming responsibility:	No
Damage caused:	Website defaced for a period of time
Additional important information:	N/A

N33—Twitter

ITEM	NOTES
Target:	Hugo Chavez opponents
Date:	September 1, 2011

Source:	F. Sanchez, "Hackers hijack Twitter accounts of Chavez critics," *NBC News*, September 27, 2011, available at http://www.nbcnews.com/id/44689342/ns/technology_and_sciencesecurity/t/hackers-hijack-twitter-accounts-chavez-critics/
Motivation:	Political opposition, "improper use of Twitter"
Type of attack:	Phishing, unauthorized access, modification of data.
Any other groups claiming responsibility:	No
Damage caused:	Hacked the Twitter accounts of several political opponents, reputational damage, and release of personal information/communications/photos
Additional important information:	N/A

Électricité de France (EDF)

ITEM	NOTES
Target:	Greenpeace
Date:	2004–2006
Source:	E. Kovacs, "French Nuke Company Fined After Hacking Greenpeace," *Softpedia*, November 16, 2011, available at http://news.softpedia.com/news/French-Nuke-Company-Fined-After-Hacking-Greenpeace-234900.shtml. "EDF Hacking into Greenpeace" (November 10, 2011), available at http://www.youtube.com/watch?v=-70sjmTJlsQ.
Motivation:	To stop an operation against one of their plants
Type of attack:	Unauthorized access and data theft
Any other groups claiming responsibility:	No
Damage caused:	Fourteen hundred documents stolen from a campaign manager
Additional important information:	EDF was fined $2 million and some EDF staff received jail sentences. Illustrates how hacking can also be used in attempts to prevent non-technological activism.

Turkish hackers

ITEM	NOTES
Target:	Anonymous, AnonPlus
Date:	July 2011
Source:	J. Leyden, "Anonymous hackers hacked by Young Turks," *The Register*, July 22, 2011, available at http://www.theregister.co.uk/2011/07/22/anonplus_hacked/ (last accessed July 23, 2011).
	G. Cluley, "AnonPlus, Anonymous's social network, is hacked," *Naked Security*, July 22, 2011, available at https://nakedsecurity.sophos.com/2011/07/22/anonplus-anonymouss-social-network-is-hacked/.
Motivation:	Possibly to highlight Anonymous's poor password security, or perhaps in retaliation for Anonymous' Operation Turkey in June 2011
Type of attack:	Unauthorized access, modification of data, defacement
Any other groups claiming responsibility:	Unknown
Damage caused:	Anonymous members' Google+ account/group site hacked and defaced for an unspecified period of time.
Additional important information:	May have been accessed due to poor password security, which is what Anonymous criticizes others for.

Hacking for Girlies (HFG)—New York Times

ITEM	NOTES
Target:	*New York Times*
Date:	September 13, 1998
Source:	A. Penenberg, "Hacking Bhabha," *Forbes*, November 16, 1998, available at http://www.forbes.com/1998/11/16/feat.html (last accessed November 11, 2011).
	BBC News, "A-Z Hack Attack," February 11, 2000, available at http://news.bbc.co.uk/2/hi/uk_news/639248.stm.
Motivation:	"Reportedly a retaliation against a book written about super-hacker Kevin Mitnick by a Times reporter"— BBC News
Type of attack:	Website defacement

Any other groups claiming responsibility:	Unknown
Damage caused:	Pornographic images defaced the *New York Times* website
Additional important information:	N/A

Rafay Baloch

ITEM	NOTES
Target:	Pre 4.4 versions of Android
Date:	September 2, 2014
Source:	R. Baloch, "Android Browser Same Origin Policy Bypass < 4.4—CVE-2014-6041," Rafay Hacking Articles: http://www.rafayhackingarticles.net/2014/08/android-browser-same-origin-policy.html.
	Other media: D. Fisher, "Flaw in Android Browser Allows Same Origin Policy Bypass," *Threat Post*, September 15, 2014, available at http://threatpost.com/flaw-in-android-browser-allows-same-origina-policy-bypass/108265#comment-317786.
	D. Pauli, "THREE QUARTERS of Android mobiles open to web page spy bug," *The Register*, September 16, 2014, available at http://www.theregister.co.uk/2014/09/16/three_quarters_of_droid_phones_open_to_web_page_spy_bug/.
	BUILDER, "Metasploit: Major Android Bug is a Privacy Disaster (CVE-2014-6041)," *LinusTechTips*, September 15, 2014, available at http://linustechtips.com/main/topic/216087-metasploit-major-android-bug-is-a-privacy-disaster-cve-2014-6041/.
	P. Ducklin, "'Shocking' Android browser bug could be a "privacy disaster": here's how to fix it," *Naked Security*, September 16, 2014, available at http://nakedsecurity.sophos.com/2014/09/16/shocking-android-browser-bug-could-be-a-privacy-disaster-heres-how-to-fix-it/.
	T. Brewster, "Widespread Android Vulnerability 'A Privacy Disaster,' Claim Researchers," *Forbes*, September 16, 2014, available at http://www.forbes.com/sites/thomasbrewster/2014/09/16/widespread-android-vulnerability-a-privacy-disaster-claim-researchers/.

E. Kovacs, "Dangerous 'Same Origin Policy' Bypass Flaw Found in Android Browser," *Security Week*, September 16, 2014, available at http://www.securityweek.com/dangerous-same-origin-policy-bypass-flaw-found-android-browser.

L. Constantin, "Many Android devices vulnerable to session hijacking through the default browser," *Computer World*, September 16, 2014, available at http://www.computerworld.com/article/2684059/many-android-devices-vulnerable-to-session-hijacking-through-the-default-browser.html.

NDTV Correspondent, "Android Browser Security Hole Affects Millions of Users, Says Expert," *Gadgets360*, September 16, 2014, available at http://gadgets.ndtv.com/mobiles/news/android-browser-security-hole-affects-millions-of-users-says-expert-592578.

H. Bray, "Rapid7 of Boston warns of Android flaw," *Boston Globe*, September 15, 2014, available at http://www.bostonglobe.com/business/2014/09/15/rapid-boston-finds-android-flaw/JJ9iHJB6YTcs10a7O9TjpN/story.html.

S. Malhotra, "Android security flaw affects millions of users," *digit*, September 16, 2014, available at http://www.digit.in/mobile-phones/android-security-flaw-affects-millions-of-users-23921.html.

A. Friedman, "Android bug called a 'privacy disaster,'" *Phone Arena*, September 16, 2014, available at http://www.phonearena.com/news/New-Android-bug-called-a-privacy-disaster_id60750.

D. Walker, "Android bug allowing SOP bypass a 'privacy disaster,' researcher warns," *SC Magazine*, September 16, 2014, available at http://www.scmagazine.com/android-bug-allowing-sop-bypass-a-privacy-disaster-researcher-warns/article/371917/.

P. Bright, "Android Browser flaw a 'privacy disaster' for half of Android users," *Ars Technica*, September 17, 2014, available at http://arstechnica.com/security/2014/09/android-browser-flaw-a-privacy-disaster-for-half-of-android-users/.

M. Kumar, "New Android Browser Vulnerability Is a 'Privacy Disaster' for 70% Of Android Users," *Hacker News*, September 16, 2014, available at http://thehackernews.com/2014/09/new-android-browser-vulnerability-is.html.

	A. Alizar, "AOSP Browser SOP," *Xakep*, September 18, 2014, available at http://xakep.ru/news/aosp-browser-sop/.
	S. Huang, "Same Origin Policy Bypass Vulnerability Has Wider Reach Than Thought on TREND MICRO," *Security Intelligence Blog* (September 29, 2014), available at http://blog.trendmicro.com/trendlabs-security-intelligence/same-origin-policy-bypass-vulnerability-has-wider-reach-than-thought/.
	Urdu Point, September 17, 2014, available at http://daily.urdupoint.com/livenews/2014-09-17/news-303641.html.
	Daily Pakistan, September 17, 2014, available at http://dailypakistan.com.pk/daily-bites/17-Sep-2014/144263.
	F. Baloch, "Online Security: Pakistani helps Google avoid privacy disaster," *The Express Tribune*, September 20, 2014, available at http://tribune.com.pk/story/764713/online-security-pakistani-helps-google-avoid-privacy-disaster/.
	DAWN, "Pakistani researcher reveals privacy flaw in Android browsers," *Dawn*, September 20, 2014, available at http://www.dawn.com/news/1133178/pakistani-researcher-reveals-privacy-flaw-in-android-browsers.
	Express Tribune, "Credit to our white-hats," *Express Tribune*, September 21, 2014, available at http://tribune.com.pk/story/764925/credit-to-our-white-hats/.
	S. Talal, "Pakistani Researcher Helps Google in Preventing a Massive Security Disaster, *ProPakistani*, 2014, available at http://propakistani.pk/2014/09/23/pakistani-researcher-helps-google-preventing-massive-security-disaster/.
	M. Hughes, "This Android Browser Bug Will Make You Upgrade To KitKat," *Make Use Of*, September 25, 2014, available at http://www.makeuseof.com/tag/this-android-browser-bug-will-make-you-upgrade-to-kitkat/.
Motivation:	Security-flaw exposure and to fix security flaw
Type of attack:	Baloch identified a security flaw in pre-4.4 versions of Android and wrote the code to fix it
Any other groups claiming responsibility:	N/A
Damage caused:	No damage. Baloch identified and developed a correction.

| Additional important information: | The security flaw would have allowed hackers to gain access to personal data, including online banking details.

As Android does not have vulnerability rewards program in place, Baloch was unrewarded for his efforts. |

Jonathan Hall, ethical hacker

ITEM	NOTES
Target:	Yahoo and WinZip
Date:	September 24, 2014
Source:	S. Gallagher, "White hat claims Yahoo and WinZip hacked by 'shellshock' exploiters," *Ars Technica*, October 7, 2014, available at http://arstechnica.com/security/2014/10/white-hat-claims-yahoo-and-winzip-hacked-by-shellshock-exploiters/. F. Rashid, "Hackers Compromised Yahoo Servers Using Shellshock Bug," *Security Week*, October 6, 2014, available at http://www.securityweek.com/hackers-compromised-yahoo-servers-using-shellshock-bug.
Motivation:	Hall said that disclosure of the "bash vulnerability" made him curious to explore these security threats. He was motivated to make his findings public as he felt that companies like Yahoo were ignoring the problem, which he considered as negligent and almost criminal.
Type of attack:	Identification of security threat, the "shellshock vulnerability"
Any other groups claiming responsibility:	No
Damage caused:	This vulnerability would allow a hacker to use the vulnerable scripts to send commands to local operating systems, and possibly gain remote access and control of the server. It had the potential to affect every consumer.
Additional important information:	N/A

Microsoft and Symantec—Botnet

ITEM	NOTES
Target:	Internet users
Date:	February 7, 2013
Source:	C. Arthur, "Microsoft and Symantec Take Out Botnet Responsible for More Than $1m of Fraud," *Guardian*, February 7, 2013, available at http://www.guardian.co.uk/technology/2013/feb/07/microsoft-symantec-botnet-fraud-pcs
Motivation:	Monetary fraud counterattack
Type of attack:	The criminals behind the scheme took advantage of search advert pricing, which could be as small as four-hundredths of a cent, meaning that they had to build up a large botnet that remained undetected by infected users and hijack huge amounts of traffic in order to profit. The process by which clicks were rerouted via "traffic brokers" to paying advertisers was so complex, said Symantec, that in some cases it went through ten hops before reaching the actual advertiser.
Any other groups claiming responsibility:	No
Damage caused:	N/A
Additional important information:	Microsoft and Symantec disabled a two-year-old network of remotely controlled PCs, a botnet, that was responsible for at least $1 million dollars in "click fraud" every year—and possibly substantially more—and which may have controlled as many 1.8 million PCs.
	The ringleaders are believed to be spread globally, in Britain, Russia, Romania, the United States, and Australia. They used false names and stolen credit-card details to register a string of domains and hire server space in a number of locations. They have never been formally identified or arrested.
	The Bamital botnet, set up in late 2009, took over PCs and would silently click on specific adverts in search results—hijacking an average of three million clicks per day, and exposed the PCs' owners to the risk of more infection as they were taken to other sites that could carry further malware.

CHAPTER VII

Online Civil Disobedience

Online civil disobedience is the use of any technology that connects to a network in pursuit of a cause or a political or social end. There are many forms of online civil disobedience. A person or groups of individuals may block access to a website, redirect web traffic to a spoof website, deface a website, or flash messages on screen. The off-line equivalents would be a sit-in blocking access to a building, a protest that prevents people from using a street such that they are redirected, protesting with signs and images, or handing out flyers or placing flyers in mailboxes. Some of these off-line activities are illegal while others are not. As will be seen, some of the equivalent off-line acts are legal while the online equivalent is ambiguous at best, and at worst will attract civil liability or criminal sanction.

It is important to reiterate the difference between online civil disobedience and hacktivism. Because hacktivism (as discussed in ch. 5) involves the unauthorized access and/or use of and/or interference with data or computer or network, it always falls within the purview of a crime. This is because the so-called Budapest Convention—the only institutional arrangement for international cooperation on cybercrime—makes unauthorized access, use, or interference of data, a network, or a computer illegal. There are no exceptions for security research or public interest found in the convention. Many countries, including Canada, Australia, and those of the Europe Union, are signatories to the convention and, as such, have adopted compatible legal frameworks. By and large, there are few exemptions from criminal and civil liability. The few existing exemptions are specific to jurisdiction, as will be explored further throughout the book. Often hacktivism involves a further crime after unauthorized access, such as credit-card theft or the copying and public posting of private information. Nonetheless, the boundaries between online civil disobedience and hacktivism may be thin at times.

7.1 Online Civil Disobedience in Context

Online civil disobedience incorporates a variety of techniques such as SQL injection,[1] DNS hijacking,[2] adware/spyware,[3] phishing,[4] ransomware,[5] DDoS attack,[6] botnet,[7] cloud,[8] and IoT.[9] These terms were explained in detail in chapter 2 but the most important terms are explained again below for your conenience. The terms are important, as are the specifics of the techniques used to carry out an act of civil disobedience. Why? Because using one method to, for example, perform a DDoS attack may require unauthorized access to data or a network, which is captured by criminal law, while another technical method to perform DDoS does not involve unauthorized access or use, and is therefore less likely to be captured by the law. As will be further demonstrated, there is insufficient case law to fully appreciate how many of these activities would be interpreted by the courts.

One of the most common forms of online civil disobedience is a DDoS attack. I will discuss the different methods of performing DDoS, then I will look at three separate DDoS events. The first involves unauthorized access of data and computer in Anonymous's Operation Titstorm, where criminal law was used to prosecute one of the participants in Australia. The second example looks at a DDoS incident in Germany, where the courts refused to convict the organizer of a DDoS protest. The last incident looks at the Canadian example of a quasi-DDoS as regards a Twitter campaign protesting a Canadian public-safety minister's surveillance proposals, which was clearly an act of legal protest.

There are many ways to launch a DDoS protest, but the most common method is through what is known as a botnet. Recall that a botnet is typically a collection of compromised computers that are remotely controlled by a bot master. Botnets can be made, hired/rented, and purchased. Botnets, however, can also exist with non-compromised systems where the individual authorizes their computer to become part of a botnet as is the case with LOIC and similar services. These are re-explained further below as the method used is relevant to the legal implications of the protest participant.

Make a Botnet. A person could physically make a botnet, though through painstaking hours of labour since it would entail compromising several hundred if not thousands of computers. This type of botnet would require the botnet master to have a high level of computer skills. Typically, the botnet master installs software onto a third-party system without their authorization, and these computers become compromised and part of the botnet. The compromised machines are then used to launch a DDoS attack/protest.

Hire/Rent a Botnet. A second type is whereby the person merely hires someone to execute a denial-of-service attack. This requires no computer skills but for the ability to use Google. Bot-agent design and bot delivery have become a commoditized service industry.[10] A small botnet is sufficient to launch an effective denial-of-service attack causing much damage, and costs as little as US$200 for a twenty-four-hour attack.[11] A person does not require any special computer skills to use a botnet to commit a crime. Figure 10 is a sample of the commercialization of denial-of-service attacks with a botnet. The customer would merely specify the targeted website to attack,

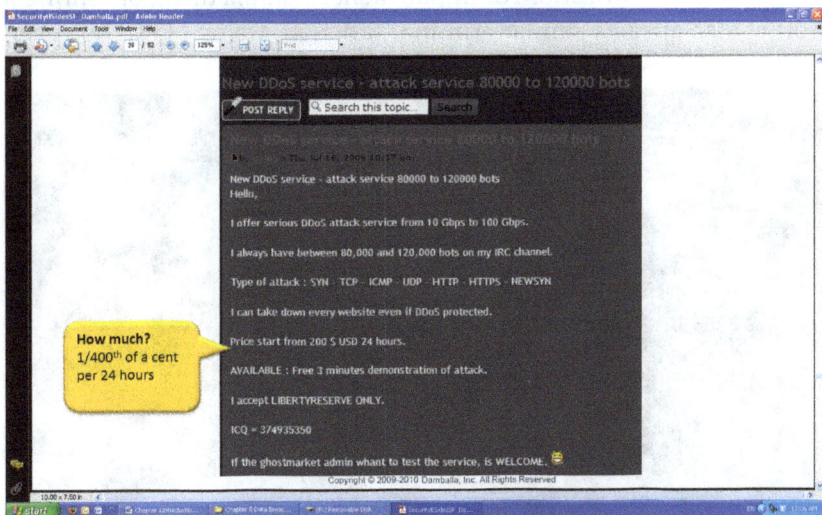

Figure 10. Denial-of-Service Attack as Commercial Service.[12]

pay a nominal fee of US$200, and a denial-of-service attack would be launched for twenty-four hours against the website.

Purchase Crimeware Kit with Botnet. Commercialization is also occurring within another context known as crime kits. In this instance, a person is able to purchase a copy of the botnet code in the form of a crime kit. The kit comes with a licence to use the botnet, and instructions. ZeuS, for example, is a popular crimeware kit that may be purchased for US$700.[13] Expert computer skills are not required for botnet usage. A criminal may elect to purchase a crimeware kit with simple instructions on how to execute an attack.

LOIC or Similar Software. The last botnet involves the free LOIC software program. LOIC is used for most of the denial-of-service attacks performed by members of Anonymous. Figure 11 captures an image of LOIC executing a denial-of-service attack against PayPal. Use of LOIC requires minimal computer skills. One googles LOIC, downloads the software with a click, types in the URL (e.g., www.paypal.com), and presses start. The denial-of-service attack then commences and people join in from all over the world using LOIC.

Differentiating between these types of botnets has legal implications. In the instance of making a botnet, the botnet master would have had to acquire control over a user's computer without their authorization, thereby attracting cybercrime liability for unauthorized access, modification, or impairment to data. Hiring or renting a botnet also attracts similar criminal sanction. Using LOIC, however,

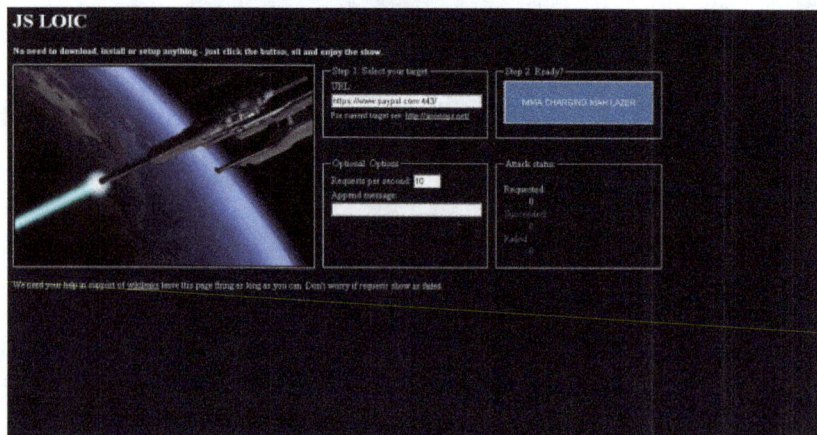

Figure 11. LOIC DDoS Attack Against PayPal.[14]

would not necessarily attract criminal sanction for unauthorized access. This is because users of computers connected to LOIC are doing so voluntarily. The issue of whether an attack involves unauthorized access as opposed to a form of legitimate civil disobedience is contentious, as will be illustrated in the case studies below.

Amplified Junk. To complicate matters further there is speculation that DDoS performed through services that merely amplify "junk" mail would not violate criminal law. Ragebooter is an example of this. In 2012, Ragebooter, a DDoS "testing service" came to surface. The company offered customers the ability to test how robust their systems were in relation to DDoS attacks. The service operates by taking the existing junk mail sent to the server then duplicating it, and then sending significantly more junk mail to the server. In this respect, the junk mail is merely amplified to the point where the server cannot handle the requests and returns an HTTP 503 error page. Essentially, the site's bandwidth is flooded so that it no longer functions properly.

Bandwidths may be flooded in many ways. For example, some web scrapers, such as Google, when retrieving information from websites may scrape too much too quickly, resulting in the overuse of bandwidth, rendering the site unavailable. In another example, when Australia did its first online census, in 2016, they did not anticipate that most people would log-on to complete the census within a narrow band of time; thus, the server's bandwidth was flooded, causing the system to crash. Systems like Ragebooter, however, are set up to deliberately crash a server or system.

In 2013, the journalist Brian Krebs investigated the legality of the Ragebooter service being offered by the site's creator, Justine Poland, uncovering some interesting findings. One of which was that Poland had links with the FBI.

> They allow me to continue this business and have full access. The FBI also use the site so that they can moniter [sic] the activitys [sic] of online users. They even added a nice IP logger that logs the users IP when they login.[15]

Ragebooter proclaimed itself as a "legal testing service," but an investigation by Krebs revealed that the site was being used to launch DDoS attacks outside of legal testing. It is unknown if the site has been used for ethical-hacking purposes, but it remains a strong possibility, especially if you consider that Poland has gone on record as saying "I also work for the FBI on Tuesdays at 1pm in Memphis."[16] Poland did in fact work one day per week for the FBI, and allowed the FBI to use the site to monitor users' online activities. Ragebooter is one of several similar so-called stress-testing services. Others include Vastresser.ru and Asylumstresser.com. The legality of the service is questionable. From a purely technical perspective, there might not be unauthorized access—junk mail already sent to the server is merely amplified. One would be inclined to think, however, that the intent behind the amplification of junk mail would be a factor in deciding to prosecute. How successful a prosecution might be remains to be seen.

There are also many services that mitigate DDoS events. Cloudflare, for example, is a content-distribution network that protects sites against DDoS attacks. Cloudflare is also used by sites such as Ragebooter and Asylumstresser to shield DDoS attacks. Curiously, the site could be used for ethical-hacking websites or other sites that promote human rights, or that encourage civil disobedience or dissident groups. As will be seen in the case study on a hacktivist and hackback event involving Anonymous, Julian Assange, and MasterCard, Cloudflare was used successfully by Anonymous to thwart counter-DDoS attacks (ch. 8 and 10).

7.2 Timeline

A timeline of selected incidences from chapters 4 to 6 (which provides information about global incidences of online civil disobedience) is shown in figure 12. As you can see, issues of denial-of-service attacks and website defacements have been reported in North America, Europe, China, Russia, and the Middle East. As you will see, you may question how some of these incidences would be deemed "ethical." In fact, many of these incidences could conceivably fall within the parameters of vigilantism, such as the defacement of the *New York Times* website, reportedly related to a book about hackers by a *Times* reporter. Other incidences are clearly within the online protest space.

Chinese Protesters Deface 45 Indonesian Government Websites — **Aug 1998**

Sept 1998 — New York Times Website Defaced in Retaliation for Book About Hacker

First Hack of Japanese Government Defaces and Redirects Websites — **Jan 2001**

Mar 2003 — Al-Jazeera's Website Defaced With Pro Western Messages

SCO Group Website Hacked to Protest IP Claim Over Linux Code — **Nov 2004**

Feb 2010 — Operation Titstorm Takes Down Australian PM's Site

Carbon Credit Protest Through European Climate Exchange Website Defacement — **Jul 2010**

Dec 2010 — Operation Avenge Assange Disrupts PayPal, Visa, and Mastercard

U.S. Anti-Gay Westboro Baptist Church Website Defaced — **Jun 2011**

Feb 2012 — U.S. Non-Profit's Website Defaced After Pulling Funds From Planned Parenthood

Takedown of Bahrani Government and Weapons Contractor Websites (Anniversary of Arab Spring) — **Feb 2012**

Aug 2012 — Takeover of Russian Prime Minister's Twitter Account

Chinese Government Websites Defaced by Pro Democracy Hackers — **Oct 2014**

Jan 2016 — U.S. State of Michican' Website is Brought Down by Anonymous In Relatiation of Its Treatment of the Residents of Flint Michigan in the Wake of the Water Poisoning Crisis

Operation Opicarus Enters 5th Phase of Targeting Worldwide Websites and Services Related to the Global Financial System Using DDOS Attacks and Defacement — **Jun 2017**

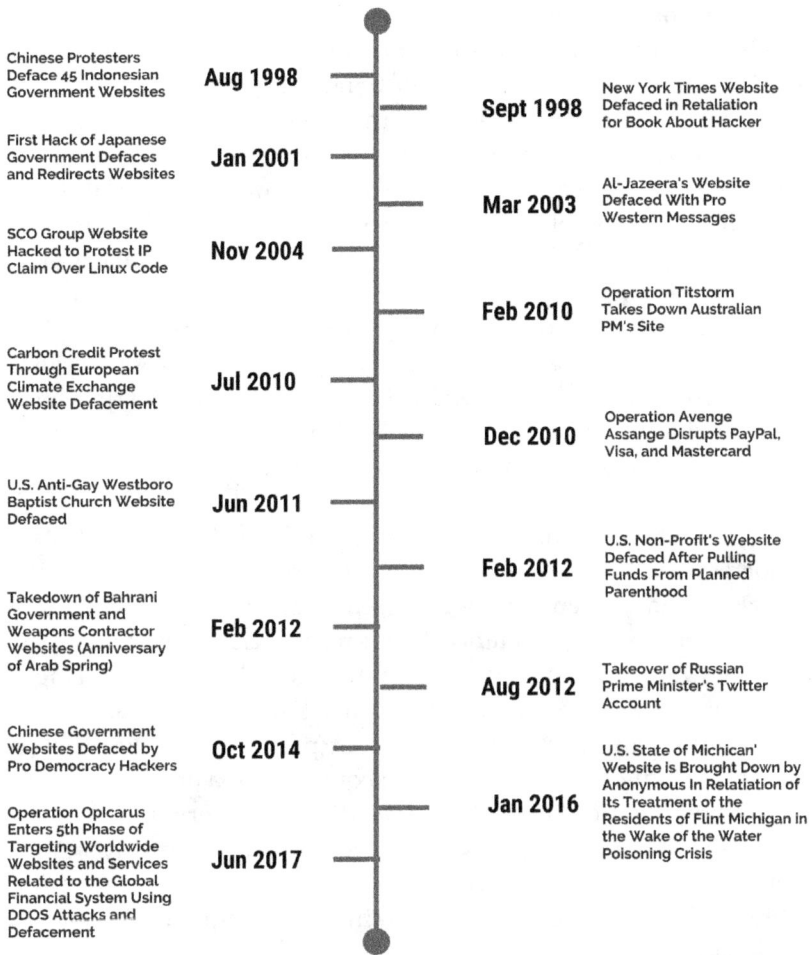

Figure 12. Online Civil Disobedience Timeline.

7.3   Case Studies

Three case studies using DDoS are explored and contrasted below. They have been specifically selected because they highlight different methods of protest, which, in turn, produced different legal outcomes. These three case studies are Anonymous's Operation Titstorm, in Australia; the German Lufthansa online protest; and the Canadian Twitter campaign #Vikileaks.

7.3.1 Anonymous, Operation Titstorm

In 2010, the Australian government sought to introduce a mandatory internet filter. This was unofficially referred to as a "clean feed" proposal. Internet filtering in this context would mean requiring Internet-service providers (ISPs) such as Optus, Telstra, and iiNet to implement technical means to filter out a set list of illegal websites, most notably websites with images of child abuse and child pornography, but also, potentially, websites about abortion or pornographic images. Internet-filtering techniques are commonly used in authoritarian regimes such as China and Iran, as well as in Western democracies such as Canada, the United Kingdom, France, and Sweden. Although Australia would not have been the first country, authoritarian or democratic, to implement internet filtering, the proposed filtering system has many unique features, separating it from other jurisdictions.

For instance, Australia would have been the first Western democracy to mandate internet filtering through formal legislation. ISPs would have been legally required to block "unwanted" material. In countries such as France, Belgium, and Germany, courts have mandated ISPs to block hate speech and illegal P2P file sharing of copyright-protected materials. In countries such as Canada and the United Kingdom, informal government pressure led to voluntary internet-filtering frameworks by the countries' major ISPs.

There was no Australian legislation on internet filtering at the time (2010), just the proposal; therefore, the prospective consequences were vague. The criteria for the evaluation of websites to be blocked remained equally uncertain and ambiguous. As it stood, the clean-feed proposal had two tiers. The first tier—blacklist filtering—was not controversial. The second tier—content filtering—was.

1. *Blacklist Filtering:* The first tier was an Australian Communications and Media Authority (ACMA)–issued blacklist of "child pornography" websites and "other prohibited" materials to be blocked by ISPs at the URL level. The scope of "other prohibited" materials was unknown. This would be mandatory for all Australians with no ability to opt out of the scheme. Circumvention of the blacklist would have been illegal. The blacklist would only block those URLs found on the ACMA blacklist. It would not have blocked

websites with child pornography and other prohibited content as found on:

- P2P systems (e.g., BitTorrent, Winnie),
- encrypted channels,
- chatrooms,
- Microsoft's MSN messaging service,
- mobile phones, and
- other websites, as it was unknown whether a blocked URL would block every website operating on a domain name or merely the specific offending material (e.g., www.youtube.com versus a specific video on YouTube).

2. *Content Filtering:* The second tier was intended to block types of materials which were legal but potentially unwanted. The scope of such material had not been delineated, but examples would likely have included adult pornography and other "R"-rated material—material inappropriate for children but clearly legal for adults. The advocacy group Australian Christian Lobby indicated that they wanted many forms of pornography filtered, regardless of whether they were legal or not. What types of filtering techniques to used was undetermined. Potentially, these could have included URL blacklists, deep packet inspection, P2P content inspection, and URL- and http-content inspection. Users would have been able to opt out of content filtering, as well as legally circumvent this type of filtering.

There were a number of off-line, marching protests in response to the Australian government's decision to introduce a mandatory filter, with protest signs in Canberra and online acts of protest. Many websites and ISPs participated in "Black Australia," wherein they blackened their websites as a form of protest against censorship.[17] One of these online protests was the online defacement and DDoS attack of the Australian parliamentary website, in 2010.

The Anonymous operation was dubbed Operation Titstorm (see fig. 13). The operation saw the parliamentary website taken down and images of penises and breasts were splashed on the parliamentary landing page for the website. Australia has a long history of both censorship and opposition to censorship. Unlike Canada, the United

Figure 13. Advertisement, Operation Titstorm.

States, and many parts of Europe, in Australia human rights are not constitutionally protected.[18] The courts in Australia have less ground to strike down legislation that infringes civil liberties. Emphasis is, therefore, placed on protesting policy proposals and bills before they become acts of parliament.

Figure 13 reproduces the global advertisement of the protest. Communications about the event could be found on IRC channels, on websites, and on social media. Dedicated websites were listed, whereby people could participate in DDoS in a variety of ways, such as using their own botnet, hiring a botnet, or sending individual requests to the parliamentary website server, but most popular was the use of LOIC to participate in the attack.

As evidenced in the figure, participation was not limited to Australians. The campaign sought participation from anywhere.

Matthew George was an Australian member of Anonymous who participated in Operation Titstorm by using the LOIC software. He was charged and convicted of incitement. A magistrate stated that George had incited others to attack government websites, and went so far as to liken his activities to cyber terrorism—a claim that is truly outrageous given the context of the protest. George was given a $550 fine. George was not a ringleader but merely a participant, using LOIC software. Furthermore, he did not deface the government websites; he merely participated in a coordinated DDoS protest against the government. As George told the *Sydney Morning Herald*,

> We hoped to achieve a bit of media attention to why internet censorship was wrong...

> I didn't think that I would ever get caught. I was actually downloading connections from other computers in America, so I didn't think the Australian government would be able to track me down.

> I had no idea that what I was doing was illegal. I had no idea that there was incitement and it was illegal to instruct others to commit a legal [sic] act.[19]

The above represents an underlying theme, whereby many DDoS protest participants do not realize that they are participating in an illegal activity. This can be clearly contrasted, as will be seen in chapter 5, to participants in hacktivism when they know that they are breaking the law but continue to do so as a form of activism. In other words, hacktivists know that what they are doing is illegal and they continue to do so for ethical reasons. With online civil disobedience, the line of legality is not clear, and participants do not always realize that they are engaging in illegal activities. They assume that a virtual sit-in or denial-of-service attack is a legitimate form of protest, similar to picketing, barricading, and physical sit-ins.

Meanwhile, many users of the LOIC software are unaware that the software provides no anonymity, even when they are participating in an act under the umbrella movement Anonymous. Many of the arrests of members of Anonymous who participated in other operations, as was seen in chapter 5, were LOIC users, but they often went further in their protest, such as in defacing a website. Hacktivism as defined in this book typically requires proficient computer skills and involves more than the ability to use LOIC.

7.3.2 German Lufthansa Protest

In 2001, two civil-rights activist groups, Libertad and Kein Mensch ist illegal (No One Is Illegal), had called for protests against Lufthansa for their policy of helping to identify and deport asylum seekers. There was an off-line protest at the Lufthansa shareholders' meeting.

This was met with an online protest. The online protest consisted of a DDoS attack where over 13,000 people participated, shutting down Lufthansa's server for two hours (this is pre-LOIC).[20]

One of the protest organizers, Andreas-Thomas Vogel, was convicted of coercion by a German regional court. On appeal, a higher court found that there was no coercion under section 240 of the German criminal law. They reasoned that there was no violence or threatening behavior. Further, the court reasoned there needs to be a permanent and substantial modification of data to be deemed guilty of an incitement of alteration of data. The court viewed the DDoS attack as a modern form of non-violent blockade, one fully within the right to freedom of expression. In Australia, a similar attack attracted comments from the court as falling within terrorist activity, with no mention of freedom of expression or freedom of assembly.

7.3.3 Twitter #TellVicEverything Campaign

In 2012, the Canadian government introduced a lawful-access bill, known as Bill C-30, that would require ISPs to monitor and store a range of communications data about its users. Canadians took to both off- and online means to protest the surveillance bill, which the government called the Protecting Children from Internet Predators Act, including signatures to the "Stop Spying" petition, letters to Members of Parliaments, and a unique Twitter campaign. The minister of public safety, and the person responsible for introducing Bill C-30, Vic Toews, had been publicly vocal about standing with the government against child pornographers, and was actively using Twitter. Canadians responded with the hashtag #TellVicEverything, whereby hundreds of thousands of Canadians sent tweets to Toews's account, telling the minister about all sorts of mundane events in their life, such as "I flushed the toilet," "my dog barked," "I had cereal for breakfast," and so forth; it was a rather humorous protest.[21] While there were record-breaking Canadian-based Twitter peaks for the campaign, no server was crashed. This was not a DDoS. However, had the same traffic been amplified to the Canadian Parliament's website, or to Toews's email, these services would likely have been overloaded. Sending tweets is a legal form of online protest. Sending requests directed at a server, even if in protest, is a DDoS attack. This is illogical and, as will be seen in chapter 10, likely a contravention to the Canadian Charter of Human Rights and Freedoms.

7.4 Observations

Online civil-disobedience participants are motivated by the same reasons as participants in traditional off-line acts of civil disobedience. For example, a sit-in may have similarities with virtual sit-ins. Barricades with denial-of-service attacks and website redirection. Political graffiti may be aligned with website defacements. Wildcat strikes might also be similar to denial-of-service attacks and website redirection. Site parodies, blogs, social-media protest posts are similar to underground presses. Petitions exist both off- and online.

The motivation is derived from a strong desire to protest that which is seen to be immoral, corrupt, undemocratic, and, above all, to send a strong message to ensure transparent governance. There is a strong link between the protection of civil liberties and online civil-disobedience activity.

The main targets are often the websites and databases of governments and organizations linked to government, including departments of defence, intelligence agencies, and law enforcement. The other main target is organizations that are viewed as corrupt.

The main relation between motivation and targets is perception of the target behaving immorally. In many instances "immoral" means infringing civil liberties, whether this be freedom of the press, freedom of expression, or privacy. Police brutality is another common link between target and motivation. There are many videos of police brutality that are shown in Anonymous, LulzSecm and CabinCr3w Twitter feeds. For instance, there is a video on CabinCr3w's Twitter, from January 3, 2012, showing the beating of a fifteen-year-old boy by Harris County police in Texas after the accused had turned himself in.[22] The video can no longer be found on Twitter or any other messages on Twitter by CabinCr3w. This may have something to do with the subpoenas to Twitter to ascertain the identities of members of CabinCr3w who were arrested and jailed. The Texas court later blocked the viewing of the video but community activist Quanell X legally acquired access to the video which was later aired on television channel ABC. In other instances, "immoral" is a combination of violation of civil liberties as well as more severe instances, where perceived "tyrant" governments stand in the way of democracy.

With the case of Operation Titstorm, the convicted Matthew George stated that it was his first and last experience with online protests. Arrests of LulzSec members in the United States and the

United Kingdom has had the opposite effect. Other members of the group, as seen in chapters 5 and 8, have met the arrests with counterattacks on law-enforcement databases and any organization which they see as having aided in the arrest of these individuals. It is important to note that companies such as Twitter have fought court orders to reveal account details and other information about their clients. Twitter has been taken to court on many occasions to assist with the revealing of identities behind accounts, such as those of WikiLeaks supporters.[23] Further, academics from around the United States appeared in a US Senate hearing in January 2012 to give evidence of the acute lack of transparency in the American regulation of Internet matters, where they expressed their concerns about a growing surveillance state.

The issues with online civil disobedience are in many ways the same issues with off-line civil disobedience. One commenter asks, "If a building is blockaded by protestors, is it civil disobedience or infringement on freedom of assembly? Is a book burning activism or censorship? Are causes more important than rights?"[24] There have been a paucity of cases addressing the issue; therefore, the issues are very much open for debate. Critical mass is important as to which causes get taken up. Which causes are taken up by a critical mass remain unpredictable, but perhaps not for long. Social-media data and data on the surface Web are routinely used to feed into big-data algorithms that allow governments or corporations to use machine learning to perform predictive analytics—such predictive analytics could in theory predict which events or incidences are likely to attract activism.

Notes

1. SQL: Defacing a website involves the insertion of images or text into a website. This is often done via a SQL injection. A SQL injection is an attack in which computer code is inserted into strings that are later passed to a database (see Security Spotlight 2010). A SQL injection can allow someone to target a database giving them access to the website. This allows the person to deface the website with whatever images or text they wish.
2. DNS hijacking allows a person to redirect web traffic to a rogue domain name server (Security Spotlight 2010). The rogue server runs a substitute IP address to a legitimate domain name. For example,

www.alanna.com's true IP address could be 197.653.3.1 but the user would be directed to 845.843.4.1 when they look for www.alanna.com. This is another way of redirecting traffic to a political message or image.

3. Adware refers to any software program in which advertising banners are displayed as a result of the software's operation. This may be in the form of a pop-up or as advertisements displayed on the side of a website such as Google or Facebook.

4. Phishing refers to the dishonest attempt to obtain information through electronic means by appearing to be a trustworthy entity.

5. Ransomware is a type of malicious software that prevents the user from accessing or using their data (often through encrypting the data) where a fee must be paid or service performed before the user's data is decrypted).

6. DDoS is the most common form of online civil protest. A denial-of-service attack is distributed when multiple systems flood a channel's bandwidth and/or flood a host's capacity (e.g., overflowing the buffers). This technique renders a website inaccessible.

7. A botnet is a collection of compromised computers that are remotely controlled by a bot master.

8. The cloud is a term for web-based applications and data-storage solutions. Companies such as Google, Microsoft, Yahoo, and Amazon are among the many companies that offer cloud computing services for individuals, corporations, and governments to store and access their data online, on the cloud (Soghoian 2009).

9. The IoT refers to "the network of physical devices, vehicles, home appliances, and other items embedded with electronics, software, sensors, actuators, and connectivity which enables these things to connect, collect and exchange data" (Wikipedia, "Internet of Things"). IoT sees traditionally non-Internet-connected devices or objects becoming connected to Internet-connected devices in a network, thereby rendering such devices or objects monitorable and controllable.

10. Ollmann 2010.

11. Ollmann 2010.

12. Image from Ollmann 2010.

13. See Trend MICRO 2010.

14. Image from Poulsen 2013.

15. Krebs 2016.

16. Krebs 2016.

17. Moses 2010.

18. Cook et al. 2011.

19. Whyte 2011.

20. Bendrath 2006.

21. CBC News 2012.

22. See http://twitter.com/#!/search?q=%23CabinCr3w. This link has been removed from Twitter. The video of the beating can now be found on news websites such as https://www.youtube.com/watch?v=Doh_gGIzuHQ (February, 2011).
23. Shane and Burns 2011.
24. Thomas 2001.

CHAPTER VIII

Hacktivism

8.1 Hacktivism in Context

Hacktivism was defined as the clever use of technology that involves unauthorized access to data or a computer system in pursuit of a cause or political end. Hacktivism is more than the online equivalent of sit-ins and protesting, acts of online civil disobedience. Hacktivism involves hacking for a cause, often political; however, hacktivism takes that one step further, such as in the collection and disclosure of personal emails, or even of extortion or blackmail for a political cause.

Common forms of hacktivism include information theft (e.g., copying emails, account information, government documents, credit-card information; hacking the viewing habits of Internet users—especially if criminal, e.g., child pornography), virtual sabotage (SQL injection whereby content on the website is replaced with the content of the attacker), insertion of a back door, or manipulation of software development.

It is often assumed that incidents of hacktivism and online civil disobedience are done in order to attract media attention to a cause. While that is true in many incidents, there is also a growing movement of silent activists who view the current political landscape as a long-term information war.[1] When security vulnerabilities are found in government and corporate databases, the information is kept secret. They are not looking for media attention, but wish to ensure that there continue to be back doors available toward accessing information. In some instances, software or hardware is purposefully developed with a back door included in its coding. In this instance, the software company and contractor are not aware of the default in the product (e.g., surveillance software used by governments and corporations). This type of insertion of a deliberate vulnerability is performed by security experts working in the field. Their active participation in hacktivism is not publicized. They do not seek media attention and there is no media reportage on their activities. Their goal is to fly under the radar. They possess the highest level of computer skills. This type of hacktivism has a particular focus on information related to democracy—censorship, surveillance, and military action.

Software development is another critical form of hacktivism. The technologies used in WikiLeaks, for example, ensure the integrity of the document and the anonymity of the informant. Additionally, WikiLeaks has developed technology that allows people in non-democratic jurisdictions such as China a way to access their otherwise filtered content. Other hacktivism technologies include anonymizers such as the Tor which allow people to view online content anonymously, and browser extensions, such as DoNotTrackMe and TrackMeNot, that block Internet trackers as well as data mining.

8.2 Timelines

Figures 14 to 17 present four timelines which capture select incidences of hacktivism, along with the evolution of Anonymous, the CCC, as well as other hacking groups.

Former Israeli Solider Anat Kamm Gives CD with Over 2000 IDF Classified Files to Journalist Uri Blau

Jun 2008

Feb 2010 Chelsea Manning Sends Iraq War Logs (400,000 documents) to Wikileaks

Names and Addresses of Sky Broadband Users that Had Illegally Shared Porn on P2P Networks Released on 4Chan After ACS: Law Hack

Sep 2010

Jun 2011 Brazillian Federal Police and Petrobras Oil Company Employees' Personal Information Published after Websites are Hacked

Citigroup CEO Vikram Pandit has his Family Structure, Home Address, and Personal Financial Details Published Online in Retaliation for Arrest of Occupy Protesters

Oct 2011

Nov 2011 Anonymous' Operation Darknet Uses Spyware to Track Downloaders of Child Abuse Material on Tor Network; Almost 200 Alleged Paedophiles have IP Addresses Published

Puckett & Faraj Law Firm is Hacked and Firm Emails are Released on The Pirate Bay in Retaliation for Representing U.S. Marine Frank Wuterich who Pled Guilty to Killing 24 Unarmed Iraqi Civilians

Feb 2012

Feb 2012 U.S.-Based Intelligence Firm StratFor is Hacked and Over 5 Million Emails are Published Over Next 2 Years

Anonymous Attacks the Ferguson, Missouri Police Department Computer Servers and Releases Name of Police Officer Purportedly Involved in the Shooting of Unarmed Man

Aug 2014

Oct 2016 Russian-Linked Fancy Bear Group Hacks World Anti-Doping Agency (WADA)and Releases Athlete's Therapeutic Use Exemptions Data; WADA Claims Data Has Been Manipulated

The Shadow Brokers Publish Second Set of Hacking Tools Atributed to the U.S. National Security Agency Including Tools That Target the SWIFT Financial System

Apr 2017

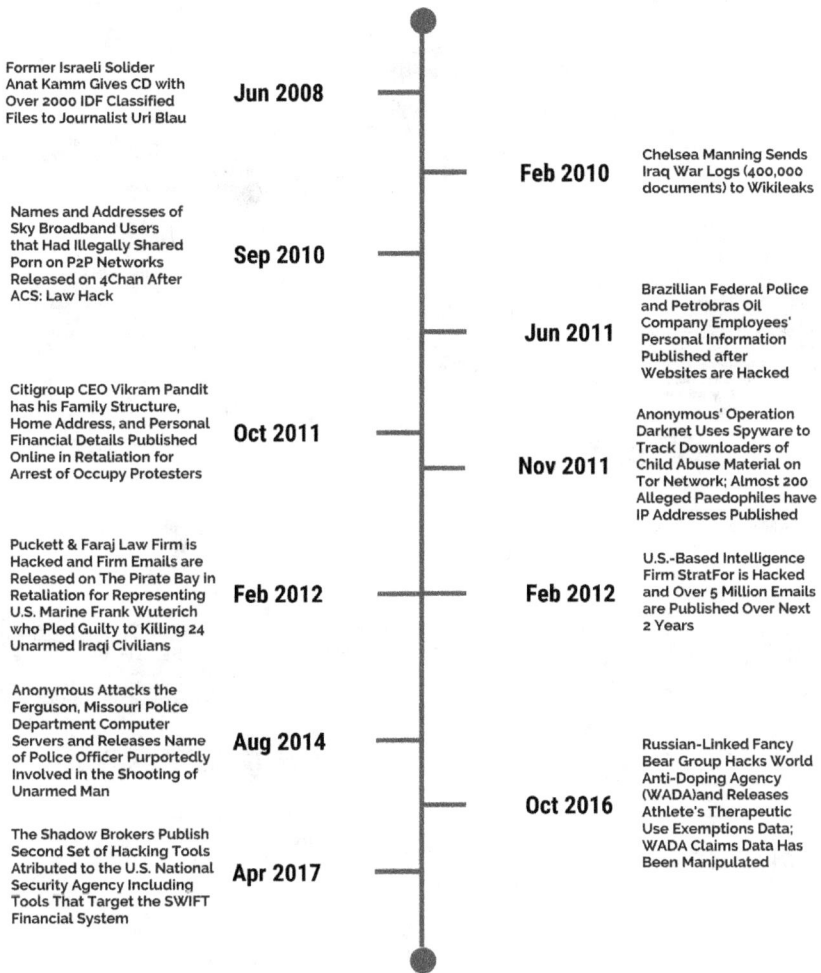

Figure 14. Hacktivism.

Anonymous Begins as a Group of Participants on the 4chan Image Board; They Get Their Name from the Default Name of Posters on the Board and They Initiate Actions for the Lulz (for Fun)

Jun 2005

Jul 2005

Anonymous Continues to Create Mischief on the Internet by Hacking into User Accounts and Defacing Pages on Popular Platforms Such as Myspace

Anonymous Creates a Raid (a Concerted Group Effort) to Annoy Finish Children Playing the Online Game Habbo Hotel; They Create Identical Avatars and Block Other Players from Going to the Virtual Pool in the Game; Thus, Spawning the 'Pool's Closed' Meme

Jul 2006

Jan 2008

Anonymous Begins its First Hacktivist Campaign with Project Chanology; During the Campaign, Anonymous Launches DDOS Attacks on Sites Owned by The Church of Scientology in Retaliation for IP Infringement Claims it Made against YouTube and other Internet Sites that Hosted Leaked Scientology Videos

Anonymous Launches Operation Avenge Assange and Disrupts PayPal, Visa, and Mastercard in Retaliation of the Payment Processors Prevention of Donations to WikiLeaks

Dec 2010

Jan 2011

Anonymous Supports the Arab Spring Movement in Tunisia by Taking Down Tunisian Government Websites with DDOS Attacks, Helping Propagate Videos of the Protests and Government Reactions Online, and Helping Disseminate Anonymizing Software to Dissidents.

Anonymous Launches a DDOS Attack on the New York Stock Exchange and Temporarily Shuts Down Trading as a Sign of Supporting the Occupy Movement

Oct 2011

Anonymous' Operation Darknet Uses Spyware to Track Downloaders of Child Abuse Material on Tor Network; Almost 200 Alleged Paedophiles have IP Addresses Published

Nov 2011

Nov 2011

Anonymous Uses a Zero Day Hack Against an Anonymous Faction Called AnonOps and Brings Down Their Servers Because AnonOps is "Blind with Power"

Anonymous Launches Attack Against the U.S. Dept. of Justice, Universal Pictures, and the Motion Picture Association of America to Protest the Closure of the Filesharing Site Megaupload

Jan 2012

Jan 2012

Anonymous Hacks into a Conference Call Between the U.S. Federal Bureau of Investigations and the U.K. Metropolitan Police While They are Discussing a Related Hacking Group; Audio from the Call is Posted Online

Feb 2012

Anonymous Attacks U.S.-Based Intelligence Firm StratFor and Over 5 Million Emails are Published Over Next 2 Years

Anonymous Defaces the U.S. Sentencing Commission's Site to Protest Federal Sentencing Guidelines and the Treatment of Internet Pioneer Aaron Swartz After His Suicide

Jan 2013

Jan 2015

Anonymous Launches Attacks Against Islamic State Sites in Retaliation to the Murder of Journalists at the Office of French Magazine Charlie Hebdo

Anonymous-Linked Group Takes Down Over 10,000 Darknet Websites Hosted by Fredoom Hosting II on Tor In Retaliation for Hosting Child Abuse Materials

Feb 2017

Aug 2018

Anonymous Temporarily Takes Down Government Websites in Spain Including the Constitutional Court in Rsponse to Spain's Treatment of Catolonia

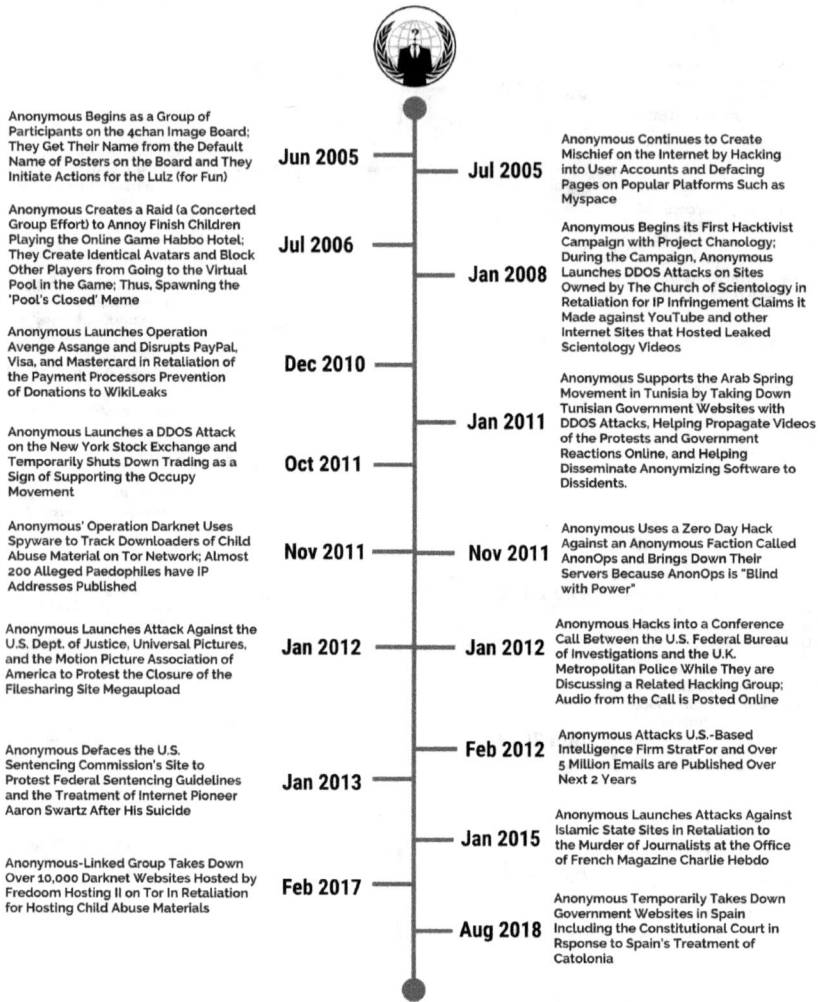

Figure 15. Anonymous.

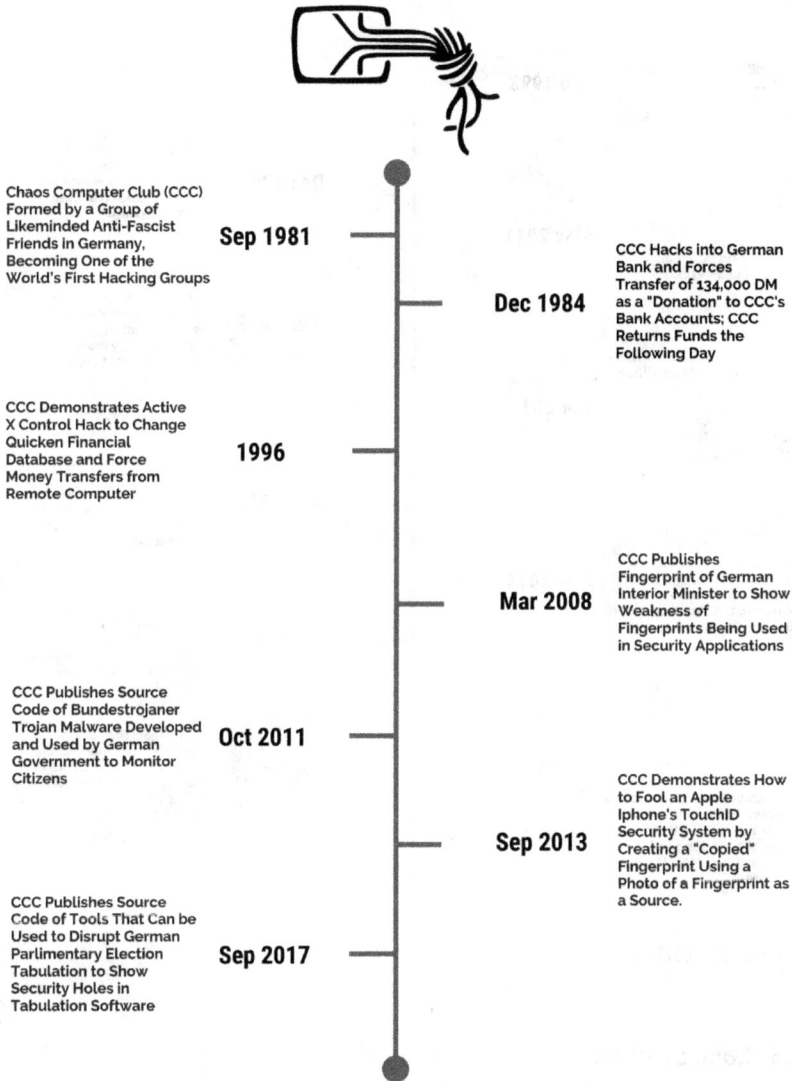

Sep 1981 — Chaos Computer Club (CCC) Formed by a Group of Likeminded Anti-Fascist Friends in Germany, Becoming One of the World's First Hacking Groups

Dec 1984 — CCC Hacks into German Bank and Forces Transfer of 134,000 DM as a "Donation" to CCC's Bank Accounts; CCC Returns Funds the Following Day

1996 — CCC Demonstrates Active X Control Hack to Change Quicken Financial Database and Force Money Transfers from Remote Computer

Mar 2008 — CCC Publishes Fingerprint of German Interior Minister to Show Weakness of Fingerprints Being Used in Security Applications

Oct 2011 — CCC Publishes Source Code of Bundestrojaner Trojan Malware Developed and Used by German Government to Monitor Citizens

Sep 2013 — CCC Demonstrates How to Fool an Apple Iphone's TouchID Security System by Creating a "Copied" Fingerprint Using a Photo of a Fingerprint as a Source.

Sep 2017 — CCC Publishes Source Code of Tools That Can be Used to Disrupt German Parlimentary Election Tabulation to Show Security Holes in Tabulation Software

Figure 16. Chaos Computer Club.

Two California Teens and an Israeli Accomplice Hack Computer Systems at Multiple U.S. Navy and Air Force Bases

Feb 1998

Dec 2009
The Iranian Cyber Army Hacks DNS Records of Twitter and Causes Site Redirection to a Message Warning about U.S.-Led Iranian Embargo

LulzSec Defaces the Website of U.S. Broadcaster PBS and Releases Login Credentials after the Network Airs "Unflattering" Story about Chelsea Manning

May 2011

Feb 2012
3xp1r3 Cyber Army Defaces Over 700 Indian Websites in Retaliation for Treatment of Bangladeshi by Indian Border Security Force

TeaMp0isoN Hacks into Phone Network of U.K. Metropolitan Police Service's Anti-Terrorist Hotline and Posts Conversations Online in Relaliation for Treatment of Muslims in U.S. and U.K.

Apr 2012

Feb 2014
RedHack Defaces Multiple Turkish Government Websites and Releases Phone Numbers of Officials in Reponses to Turkey's New Internet Censorship Laws

CyberBerkut Hacks the Mobile Device of an Official Traveling with U.S. Vice President Joe Biden on a Delegation to Kiev and Publishes Documents Related to U.S. Funding of the Ukrainian Government

Nov 2014

Dec 2014
Gator League Brings Down U.K. Intelligence and Surveillance Agency GCHQ's Website Through a DDOS Attack in Retaliation for Pursuit of Anonymous and Lulzsec

Hackers Associated with Islamic State Deface Pages of Chin's Tsinghua University Ostensibly to Help Recruit Students

Jan 2016

Sep 2016
Azerbaijani Based Group, Anti-Armenia Team, Claims Responsibility for Leaks of Foreign Visitors' Passport Details and Other Govrnment Data

Over 200,000 Worldwide Router Switches, Most in Russia and Iran, Are Hacked With An ASCII Grapic of a U.S. Flag and the Message "Don't Mess With Our Elections ..."

Apr 2018

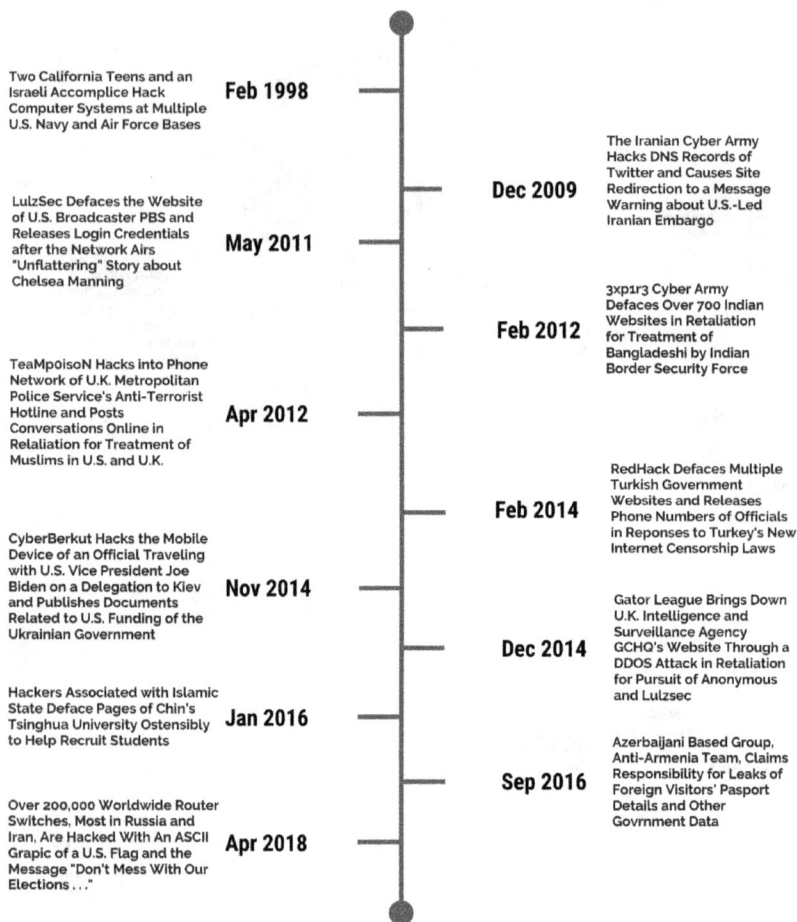

Figure 17. Other.

8.3 Case Studies

There are many instances of online civil disobedience spilling into hacktivism.

There are thousands of incidences, as was seen in chapters 3–6. Three of the most interesting examples, however, are the Christmas charity donation drive by Anonymous and the exposure of key officials linked to the neo-Nazi movement in Europe.

8.3.1 Anonymous, Post-Christmas Charity Donations

The 2011 post-Christmas Anonymous attack targeted credit-card information of the clients of US-based security think tank Stratfor. In this instance, members of Anonymous were able to access and steal credit-card numbers of Stratfor clients. Clients included members of intelligence agencies, law enforcement, and Fox News journalists. The credit-card numbers were later used to give money, as Christmas donations, to charities such as the Red Cross, Care, and Save the Children.[2]

According to Anonymous postings, the personal information, credit-card details, and emails of Stratfor were not encrypted. This echoes a reoccurring theme of poor and sub-par security practices of large corporations, governments, and even security-minded think tanks entrusted with sensitive data.

8.3.2 Neo-Nazi Website

Anonymous claimed responsibility for an attack on a neo-Nazi website in Finland. Website members had their information stolen and publicly released. The list of members included a parliamentary aide who later resigned from her post. It was later reported that Anonymous had issued a statement, which read, in part,

> We have no tolerance for any group based on racial, sexual and religion discrimination as well as for all the people belonging to them and sharing their ideologies, which is the reason why we decided to carry out last Monday's attack.

Similar types of attacks have been launched to reveal membership of paedophilia groups and organized-crime cartels.

8.3.3 WikiLeaks, Operation Payback

WikiLeaks founder Julian Assange was arrested in London in connection to charges of sexual assault under Swedish law, which sought his extradition. Many viewed this as a false arrest and an indirect way of incarcerating Assange for the release of secret US cables to WikiLeaks. A legal defence fund was quickly established where people could make donations via MasterCard or PayPal. However, MasterCard and PayPal disallowed payments to the Assange defence fund, causing an international uproar, in particular within hacktivism communities.

Members of LulzSec launched a denial-of-service attack against MasterCard and PayPal, which took down their capabilities in December 2010 and then again in June 2011. As will later be seen in chapter 10, there was a denial and counter-denial-of-service attack showdown, which might best be seen as gunfire between warring factions, with evidence that the US government contracted security firms to perform attacks against WikiLeaks and other journalists. Protest/attack was met with counterattack.

The story becomes much more complicated, and is the type that attracts conspiracy theories and movie scripts. Hacktivist Jeremy Hammond leaked millions of emails by Stratfor to WikiLeaks. The emails revealed disturbing evidence of the corruption in Stratfor, including insider-trading techniques, coercive methods, and off-shore share structures. Revealed emails showed Stratfor's web of informers, pay-off structure, payment-laundering techniques, and psychological methods. Also, the emails revealed its confidential and corrupt connections with large corporations such as Dow Chemical, Lockheed Martin, Northrop Grumman, Raytheon, and governmental agencies including the US department for Homeland Security, the US Marines, and the US Defence Intelligence Agency. One example included emails that revealed secret cash bribes. and Hammond, from Chicago, did what he did to unmask unlawful surveillance and intelligence-gathering efforts—a controversial topic, certainly, but a trend in most countries across the world.

Hammond's motivation is clearly what he perceives to be ethical:

> I felt I had an obligation to use my skills to expose and confront injustice—and to bring the truth to light.... I have tried everything from voting petitions to peaceful protest and have found that those in power do not want the truth exposed.... We are confronting a power structure that does not respect its own systems of checks and balances, never mind the rights of its own citizens or the international community.[3]

Hammond was arrested and charged with conspiracy to violate the Computer Fraud and Abuse Act, in violation of 18 U.S.C. section 1030(b), for a cyber attack in June 2011 on computer systems used by Arizona Department of Public Safety.[4] Hammond pleaded guilty but was quick to refer to claims that the US government, through the FBI, directed his attacks on foreign websites.[5] The leaked emails included emails from the case judge's husband to Stratfor. Further, Hammond has stated that "The government celebrates my conviction and imprisonment, hoping that it will close the door on the full story. I took responsibility for my actions, by pleading guilty, but when will the government be made to answer for its crimes?"[6]

8.4 Observations

There is no singular motivation at the heart of hacktivism. The motivation of such players may often not be well articulated, if articulated at all. There are, however, some reoccurring themes among many hacktivism activities. At the heart of all hacktivism is a sense of some sort of moral wrongdoing that either needs to be exposed and/or needs to be punished, and a wider sense of public loss of confidence in their institutions.[7] Many hacktivism activities expose corruption and/or humiliate the establishment.

Some hacktivists are motivated to expose the insecure practices of corporations and governments handling personal information, as seen in the Sony and Stratfor incidences.

Most hacktivism, however, is related to a political cause. For example, many hacktivists are motivated by exposing censorship and surveillance of individuals by governments and corporations. WikiLeaks, for example, has posted documents outlining the surveillance activities of governments around the world. Secret filtering blacklists of websites blocked by ISPs on behalf of governments frequently find their way to the Internet. Other hacktivists target oppressive governments and enable the free flow of information in and out of areas where media coverage and access to local and foreign press is restricted. These include areas in Iran, China, Egypt, Syria, Libya, and include more local venues in recent Occupy movements around the world. Other hacktivism efforts target child-pornography websites and both the ISPs that host such repugnant content and the customers of this material. Religions such as Scientology have also been targeted with claims that such groups disseminate misinformation and have a corrupt hand in the lobbying efforts of US governments.

Hacktivism and online civil disobedience are linked to empowerment and the strongest desire to find an effective public voice. This also applies equally to social-media movements, including online petitions. The motivation of much hacktivism is closely linked to whistle-blowing. Generally, critical mass is important in determining which causes get taken up. In this sense, it is very democratic. Hacktivism is not anarchy nor does it have a top-down leadership which steers its course. Critical mass is required, and generally speaking, the stronger the cause, the more likely hacktivism activity will be seen as ethical. Equally important, however, is predictability. Suelette Dreyfus, who is a researcher in both hacking, hacktivism, and whistle-blowing, indicates that hacktivism targets are not predictable. Which causes are taken up by a critical mass remain unpredictable.

As is the case with online civil disobedience, the main targets are the websites and databases of governments and organizations linked to government (e.g., Stratfor), as well as organizations that are viewed as corrupt or who are linked to corrupt organizations.

The main relation between motivation and targets is similar to online civil activism perception of the target behaving immorally. In many instances "immoral" means infringing civil liberties, whether this be freedom of the press, freedom of expression, or privacy. Surveillance, intelligence gathering and contracting security firms to discredit hacktivist groups is currently a strong motive. In other instances, "immoral" is a combination of violation of civil liberties as well as more severe instances where tyrant governments stand in the way of democracy.

Many operations by LulzSec, however, are difficult to qualify as ethical hacking when the release of innocent third-party personal information is disclosed on the Internet, and no motive other than "just for the laughs" is apparent in many LulzSec attacks.

Principles in hacktivism parallel those in online civil disobedience. When Anonymous member Barrett Brown (former journalist and founder of Project PM, an online collective investigating the world of intelligence agencies) was asked to comment on television whether the activities of Anonymous were ethical, he encouraged the public to make a comparison chart. Chart what is good versus what is bad about each Anonymous Operation, then compare it with the issue that Anonymous sought to bring attention to. In other words, compare it with the actions of the traditional institution. For example, the actions of hacktivists must be compared with Arabic states' governments trying to "turn off" the Internet and to control social media; the treatment of WikiLeaks after publishing controversial information and continuing to assert its right of free speech; the heavy-handed crackdown on the non-violent worldwide Occupy movement by various local and national governments; and the lack of law around the shutting off of critical payment services, as in the case of MasterCard and PayPal. Conversely, many hacktivism activities run the risk of being perceived as immoral, especially when the personal information of innocent parties is released online.

Transgressive forms of hacking may be viewed as illegal yet ethical. It remains to be seen whether in ten years' time these same forms of transgressive hacking will become a legal part of the civil-disobedience landscape.

Unlike many people who participate in online civil disobedience, participants in hacktivism are well aware that their actions are not legal and take precautions to ensure their anonymity online. As has been seen with online civil-disobedience groups, many participants are unaware that using software such as LOIC to take part in a denial-of-service attack is illegal; they assume that such is a lawful form of protest. When hacktivists hack, copy, view, and disclose the personal information of others they are clearly aware that their actions are illegal and they have taken a calculated risk, despite the threat of criminal sanction.

Historical evidence shows that some hackers who are caught and later convicted of conspiracy or unauthorized use will either give up such activities or use their talents in a legitimate matter, such as working as a security expert or in some form of technology field. This is well documented in Dreyfus and Assange's interviews with hackers in *Underground*. Raol Chiesa's work in *Profiling Hackers* also notes that the law offers deterrence to younger hackers (script kiddies) but not to other levels of hacking. Both studies, however, reveal that the law offers no deterrence to future generations of hackers; the deterrence value is only individualized and is limited to the person who has been charged with a crime. Criminal prosecutions and convictions fuel the underworld of hackers, have the sole effect of driving the hacking world further underground, and have led to the development of many obfuscation technologies that make traceback to the source of an attack difficult (see ch. 12). As Dreyfus and Assange note, prosecutions and convictions have not sent a message of "don't hack" but, rather, of "don't get caught."

Many of the studies that have been done to date, however, have been about hacking in general and not about ethical hacking. It is not known whether the prosecution and conviction of ethical hackers will act as a deterrent, sending the message "ethical hacking is wrong," or whether such prosecutions will act as a catalyst to even more ethical hacking as a sign of protest. When members of Anonymous were arrested in the United States, there were a series of attacks of law enforcement, news channels (Fox News), and university websites as a form of public protest. Similar attacks were performed on security firms who contract with governments and corporations to attack Anonymous, LulzSec, and WikiLeaks. This is explored further in chapter 10.

At the heart of all hacktivism is a sense of some sort of moral wrongdoing that either needs to be exposed and/or needs to be punished, and a wider sense of public loss of confidence in their institutions—even if the actions of LulzSec are poorly articulated, if at all (the membership of this group seems to be confined to young males, unlike the membership of Anonymous, with participants of all ages and walks of life).

Hacktivism and online civil disobedience are linked to empowerment and the strongest desire to find an effective public voice. This equally applies to social-media movements such as online petitions.

The motivation of much hacktivism is closely linked to whistle-blowing, which is discussed further in chapter 13.

Notes

1. As do WikiLeaks members; see, e.g., Pilger 2011.
2. R. Adhikari, "Anonymous Implicated in 'Robin Hood' Hack on Christmas Day," *Tech News World*, December 27, 2011, available at https://www.technewsworld.com/story/Anonymous-Implicated-in-Robin-Hood-Hack-on-Christmas-Day-74058.html.
3. Video released by Jeremy Hammond in November 2013 on YouTube. It has since been removed and is no longer retrievable via search engines Bing and Google, for example. But there are countless news article and blogs that have quoted Jeremy's speech.
4. *United States of America v. Jeremy Hammond.*
5. Pilkington 2013.
6. Pilkington 2013.
7. Interviews with Dreyfus and Samuel. Dreyfuss interivew, December 2010, Sydney Australia. Samuel, phone interview, December 2010. See also Chiesa, Ducci, and Ciappi 2009.

CHAPTER IX

Penetration/Intrusion Testing and Vulnerability Disclosure

This chapter looks at penetration/intrusion testing and security-vulnerability disclosure, which, for the purpose of this book, is separated from counterattack/hackback and security activism. The reality, however, is that a response to a security threat may involve aspects of all the above. The differentiation, therefore, serves a point of utility for the structure of the book.

9.1 Penetration Testing and Vulnerability Disclosure in Context

Recall that penetration/intrusion testing is a type of information-systems security testing on behalf of the system's owners, also known in the computer-security world as ethical hacking. There is some argument, however, as to whether penetration testing must be done with permission from a system's owner or whether benevolent intentions suffice. Whether permission is obtained or not does not change the common cause, which is improving security.

Most penetration or intrusion testing occurs when a security expert is hired to test the security of an organization's network. In this sense, the security expert has permission to hack into the organization's network such that the law will view this as authorized, thereby not inviting criminal sanction.

In the past few years a mature vulnerability-disclosure and bug-bounty market has come to fruition, though predominantly in the United States. Vulnerability discovery is the process of finding weaknesses and ways in a network, device, or within the organization themselves that are capable of being exploited by others (sometimes for nefarious reasons). Vulnerability discovery is often done with the authorization of the owner/operator of a network or device, but not always. A bug-bounty market is a program or online platform that pays a monetary sum or benefit (e.g., frequent-flyer points) for information about a systems weaknesses, often in what is known as a software bug.

The legal ambiguity arises when these security experts find security vulnerabilities and actively investigate further without permission or authorization from the system's owner, and then go on to disclose the vulnerability. In this situation, the act would be considered as legally and morally ambiguous, thus qualifying as ethical hacking.

Security activism is similar to penetration/intrusion testing in that the motivation is to improve security. Security activism goes beyond mere testing of security—it works to gather intelligence on crackers and to launch offensive attacks to disrupt criminal online enterprises. This type of reaction is known as counterattack or hackback and will be explored in chapter 10. A good example of security activism involves botnet tracking and takedown, as will be seen in chapter 11.

When people think of ethical hacking it often conjures images of Anonymous, notable for their use of Guy Fawkes masks. As we saw in previous chapters, movements like Anonymous and the CCC have evolved over the years, garnering a great deal of media attention. The timelines below look at the evolution of some of the protests hacks of Anonymous and the CCC.

Less known are the thousands of other ethical-hacking incidences that occur every day, outside the limelight. One of the most fascinating developments in cyber security has been vulnerability disclosure, bug bounties, and the rise of the marketplace for both. Cyber-security experts are paid to perform penetration testing on networks for various organizations. They also, in their spare time, hunt for vulnerabilities and bugs even in the absence of financial incentive. This has been documented in general of the cyber industry, starting with the open-source-code movement. In 1999, Eric Raymond's *The Cathedral and the Bazaar: Musings on Linux and Open Source by an Accidental Revolutionary* was published. In the book, he describes with exacting precision the culture of computer scientists working together to improve algorithms and the prominent role of reputation in the industry. Penetration testers also shared (and still do in many respects) this ethos. This ethos and the industry as a whole has evolved.

Penetration testers used to predominantly work with a computer emergency response team (CERT) to report vulnerabilities about systems, or they would dialogue directly with affected companies. As will be seen below, this has not always been met with open arms, despite the effort, cost, and diligence expended to find and report the vulnerability or bug. Instead, many researchers have been met with civil suits, threats to prosecute, and, in some instances, prosecution and jail sentences. As a response to the landscape, companies such as Vupen emerged, from which law enforcement and intelligence agencies could purchase licenses to learn about the latest zero-day vulnerabilities. Penetration testers would sell software vulnerabilities to Vupen for financial reward, becoming vendors to the company. After ethical concerns about Vupen began to mount, a different kind of market emerged, whereby the pen tester would submit the bug or vulnerability to a third party—such as HackerOne or Bugcrowd—whereupon such entity would act as an intermediary between the organization and the pen tester. However, as will be seen in the next section, some of the case studies show that such was not always met with appreciation and gratitude.

9.2 Timeline

Figure 18 presents a timeline of key vulnerability disclosures.

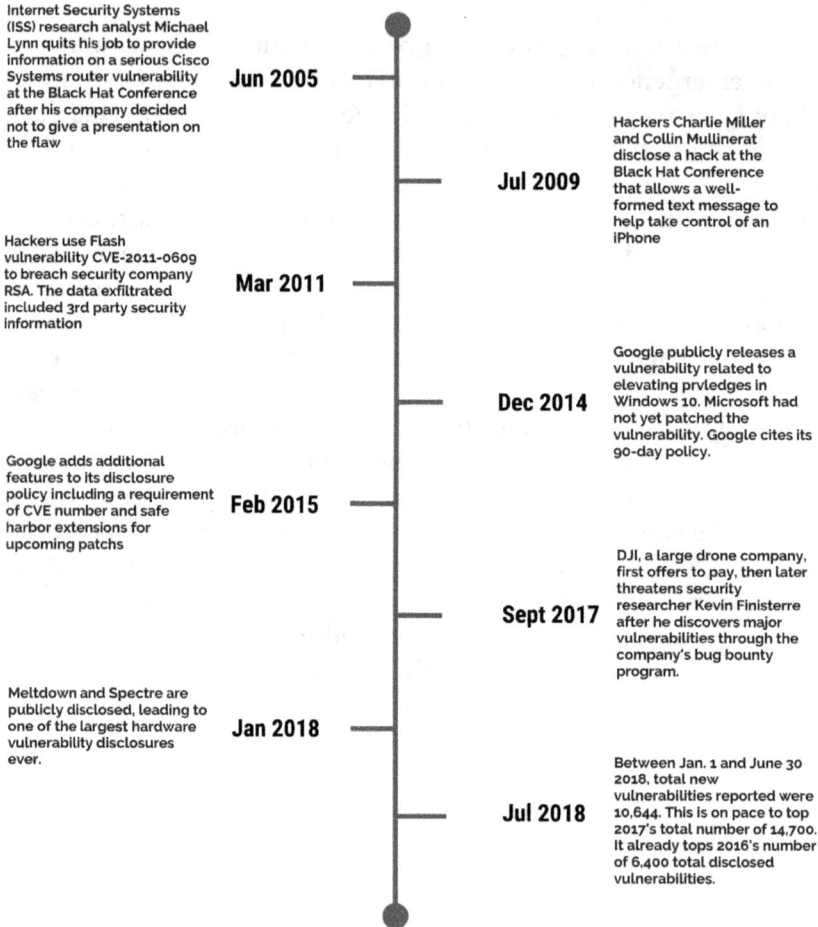

Internet Security Systems (ISS) research analyst Michael Lynn quits his job to provide information on a serious Cisco Systems router vulnerability at the Black Hat Conference after his company decided not to give a presentation on the flaw — **Jun 2005**

Jul 2009 — Hackers Charlie Miller and Collin Mullinerat disclose a hack at the Black Hat Conference that allows a well-formed text message to help take control of an iPhone

Hackers use Flash vulnerability CVE-2011-0609 to breach security company RSA. The data exfiltrated included 3rd party security information — **Mar 2011**

Dec 2014 — Google publicly releases a vulnerability related to elevating prvledges in Windows 10. Microsoft had not yet patched the vulnerability. Google cites its 90-day policy.

Google adds additional features to its disclosure policy including a requirement of CVE number and safe harbor extensions for upcoming patchs — **Feb 2015**

Sept 2017 — DJI, a large drone company, first offers to pay, then later threatens security researcher Kevin Finisterre after he discovers major vulnerabilities through the company's bug bounty program.

Meltdown and Spectre are publicly disclosed, leading to one of the largest hardware vulnerability disclosures ever. — **Jan 2018**

Jul 2018 — Between Jan. 1 and June 30 2018, total new vulnerabilities reported were 10,644. This is on pace to top 2017's total number of 14,700. It already tops 2016's number of 6,400 total disclosed vulnerabilities.

Figure 18. Vulnerabilities.

9.3 Case Studies

The case studies for penetration/intrusion testing and vulnerability disclosure are difficult to distinguish as they are closely related.

9.3.1 Australian Security Expert Patrick Webster

Patrick Webster, a white-hat security expert in Australia, was threatened with legal action and criminal charges for disclosing a serious security flaw in an Australian superannuation fund, the not-for-profit First State Super (FFS).[1] When Webster went to log into FFS's system to check on his pension he noticed that the URL contained his individual identity information linking to his superannuation account. He found this odd and investigated further. Patrick ran a simple for loop script to check for other anomalies. The script started with the scan of one account number then continued to scan by incremented numbers. In the time that it took to initialize the script and make tea, the script revealed hundreds of megabytes of account numbers. Upon seeing this, Patrick ascertained that potentially every account was exposed to the Internet. He quit running the program. In the scanning time, the script automatically saved the details of the first 500 accounts.[2]

Alarmed at this security flaw, Webster notified FSS. Some IT personnel sent him emails, thanking him.[3] However, the chief information officer at the fund reacted differently, alleging that by accessing not just his own account but the accounts of others, Webster had committed a crime. Webster was served with legal papers and told that he may face charges, having personally discovered a security flaw that should have been picked up through basic security compliance checks. As a result of the flaw, over 770,000 FSS accounts were vulnerable, as well as the details of another 1.2 million accounts from other companies who outsourced their data storage to Pillar Administration, Australia's largest superannuation administrator. The alarming rate of corporations having their data compromised has sparked data-breach notification laws around the globe. Yet corporations and organizations still have not implemented many basic security mechanisms. At the time, in 2011, FFS was reviewing its data storage contract with Pillar, as well as its own personal handling of personal information.

It has become standard industry practice to thank and often reward those individuals who alert companies to security flaws. Corporations such as Facebook and Google have offered rewards.

Anti-virus and anti-spyware companies also pay money for zero-day vulnerabilities. In this instance, however, FSS's reaction was to threaten Patrick Webster with civil and criminal proceedings if he did not turn his computer over to the IT personnel at FSS for them to verify that he had deleted the information from those 500 accounts.[4] In the end, Webster was not charged and was cleared of any wrong-doing by the Australian privacy commissioner. However, the incident set off alarm bells for security researchers in Australia and elsewhere.

In the words of Webster:

> I am genuinely disappointed the government legislation will not provide safeguards for security researchers, though I am not the least bit surprised.

> I've encountered clients who are actively being attacked by a compromised legitimate website and considered counter attack-ing in self defence to protect my client and the comprised orga-nization.... I haven't, but it would be nice if we could.

> My only hope is that my incident with First State Superannuation sets a precedent for future researchers. Obviously not in Australian law as the NSW [New South Wales] Police stated that no laws were broken and I was providing a civil duty, and Minter Ellison [FSS's law firm] halted proceedings, but with any luck the media attention will convince corporations that not everybody is acting with malicious intent. If it helps just one researcher in the future I'll be happy.[5]

The incident is a timely reminder of the lack of legitimate exemptions for security research. After the breaking news of Webster's vulnerability discovery the privacy commission opened an investigation and found that FSS's data security at the time was inadequate.[6]

9.3.2 Cisco Router

There are many renowned international computer-security and hack-ing conferences, such as Black Hat, DefCon, Hack in the Box, and the CCC. These conferences are unique in that they bring together hack-ers, crackers (those for criminal gain), white-hat security researchers and experts, as well as law enforcement, and corporate and security vendors. Many of these conferences have competitions where hackers earn money, reputation, and future clients by identifying security vulnerabilities. Typically the winner will accept the cash prize then hand over their method of exploiting a vulnerability to the vendor. In this sense, the disclosure is limited to the vendor (and perhaps others present at the conference), and allows the vendor the opportunity to patch the vulnerability. In this situation, there is no unauthorized access or use, so threat of civil liability and criminal sanction is very low. Not all conference presentations where vulnerabilities are disclosed, however, have the same happy ending, especially when the vendor has not elicited information about a vulnerability.

The most famous security-vulnerability disclosure occurred during the 2005 Black Hat conference in Las Vegas, where Michael Lynn gave a controversial presentation on vulnerabilities found in a Cisco router. The incident may be the best case study for examining ethical and legal issues surrounding vulnerability disclosure. Most of the Internet's infrastructure relies on Cisco routers. Basically, routers are network devices that forward packets from one network to another. Security researchers have found flaws in Cisco's router software in the past, but typically such flaws were minor, resulting only in a denial-of-service attack. Lynn, then a security researcher with Internet Security Systems (ISS), discovered what is believed to be the first known vulnerability of buffer overflow against a Cisco router. This significant vulnerability would allow an attacker to take over a network. The vulnerability has been described as a potential Pearl Harbour of vulnerabilities.[7]

Lynn's employer, ISS, was in discussion with Cisco about this vulnerability. Cisco was notified that ISS was to present on the router vulnerability at the 2005 Black Hat conference. Cisco's response was to threaten ISS with a lawsuit and demand that the Black Hat organizers remove the presentation from the conference. At this point Cisco had neither fixed the vulnerability (though known to them) nor notified their clients of this potentially serious vulnerability.[8] No patch was available at this time. Instead of backing down, Lynn quit ISS, told the Black Hat organizers that he would present a different talk. But, part way into his presentation, Lynn began to discuss the flaw in Cisco's router. While Lynn did not publish his findings nor display the full vulnerability on screen, the partial descriptions and titbits of code displayed allowed a room full of hackers to fully ascertain and share among themselves the shell code by the end of the presentation.[9]

Cisco filed lawsuits against Lynn and the conference organizers, claiming infringement of intellectual property. There is a research exemption and reverse-engineering right under fair-use (copyright in the United States) and fair-dealings doctrine (in Commonwealth countries), but any publication of the vulnerability afterward may attract copyright sanctions. Copyright infringement can be filed both against the person who publishes (oral presentations included) as well as the distributors—in this case, the conference organizers. The legal suits were dropped against Black Hat and Lynn on the condition that they restrain from future discussion about the vulnerability and the incident in general.

Code that exploits Cisco vulnerabilities often has a substantial market value. Experts have estimated that Lynn could have sold the vulnerability to Cisco at a market value of $250,000.[10] As such, Cisco vulnerabilities are generally not disclosed, even in conferences. Lynn decided to present on this highly important vulnerability due to inaction (some might classify it as a gross lack of action) on Cisco's part to fix the vulnerability once they were notified. Lynn had notified them on several occasions of the vulnerability and had been urging Cisco to fix the problem. Months passed and there was still no action. At this point, Lynn sought to expose the vulnerability to encourage better security practices.

9.3.3 LulzSec Hacking to Incentivize Sony to Fix Known Software Bugs

Arizona college student Cody Kretsinger, allegedly a member of LulzSec, was arrested and charged in the United States with multiple counts of conspiracy and unauthorized impairment of a protected computer for allegedly hacking Sony Pictures Entertainment. The hacking is said to be that of Sony's computer system, which was compromised in May and June 2011. LulzSec, unlike Anonymous, performs hacks both for political reasons and "for laughs" ("lulz" is computer slang for laughs). LulzSec has not formally announced any political reason for the hack. Interesting, however, are the many media comments and blog responses that sympathize with LulzSec, many of which resent the lapse security measures of corporations. As one blogger writes:

> The main offender here is Sony. They were fully aware of the vulnerability of their current system. They were just too lazy to fix it. All it took was a Google search and some script kiddies

entered in one SQL line and broke into the system. This wasn't a "zero day attack," it was a well known vulnerability to their system that was public. It's like having a stack of money just behind a gate with no lock. All it takes is one simple well known action and you are in. Why do you think class action lawsuits were charged against Sony if it wasn't their fault?[11]

Other members of LulzSec have been arrested and detained in Italy, Switzerland, and the United States for hacking websites. It is much more difficult to see any public benefit or ethical conduct in many of LulzSec's operations, other than the media coverage exposing the poor security habits of corporations and governments. Security experts have been urging companies and governments to improve their outdated and insecure protection of their systems for decades. During the last decade, however, many corporations still do not use basic encryption to protect personal information of their customers, nor do they adequately protect their own assets. The LulzSec attacks may act as a catalyst for corporate improvement to security.

9.3.4 Guardians of Peace, North Korea, and the Sony Pictures Hack

Since Sony's outing of using hidden rootkits, the corporation has been a favourite destination of attack by hackers since 2006. In 2014, a hacking group calling itself the "Guardians of Peace" released personal and confidential emails from employees of the Sony Pictures film studio. This is referred to as the Sony Pictures hack, as the attack was allegedly in response to the release of the movie *The Interview*, a parody of North Korea's leader Kim Jong-un, perceived in North Korea as disrespectful, even as a threat. This incident could be a case of state-sponsored hacking, which would not fall under our definition of ethical hacking. Nonetheless, I have given it a charitable view. Security experts have stated that the group had been accessing a back door for at least a year prior in Sony's system (it is thought that the back door was used, in addition to a listening implant, proxy tool, destructive cleaning tool, and destructive hard-drive tool).[12]

9.3.5 Vulnerability Hunter Glenn Mangham

The only criminal-law decision that clearly addresses the role of ethical hacking and security-vulnerability disclosure is the United Kingdom 2012 decision against Glenn Mangham. In *R v Mangham*,[13] Mangham was charged with three counts of unauthorized access and modification of a computer but was convicted of two counts under the Computer Misuse Act 1990. He was sentenced initially to eight months' imprisonment by the Southwark Crown Court. Later the Court of Appeal (Criminal Division) reduced the sentence from eight to four months due to a lack of malicious intent.[14] Mangham, a university student, took advantage of a vulnerability to penetrate Facebook's firewall. Once Mangham discovered the vulnerability in Facebook's network system, he continued to probe deeper into Facebook's network and, at one point, had downloaded a copy of Facebook's source code. Prosecutor Sandip Patel stated that Mangham, "acted with determination, undoubted ingenuity and it was sophisticated, it was calculating," that he stole "invaluable" intellectual property, and that the attack "represents the most extensive and grave incident of social media hacking to be brought before the British courts."[15] Mangham issued a lengthy public statement regarding the affair, wherein he describes himself as an ethical hacker who had previously been awarded a fee for finding security vulnerabilities within Yahoo.[16] While Mangham takes responsibility for his actions in his statement, he made a number of claims which he felt should have been taken into account. In the past, companies such as Yahoo had paid Mangham for security vulnerability discovery. Mangham had a history of ethical security-vulnerability disclosure. He did not use proxies or anonymizers to shield his identity when discovering vulnerabilities, as his intention was never to use the information for commercial gain. In fact, Mangham had a history of rejecting fees for vulnerability discovery.

This case is potentially interesting for those who disclose security vulnerabilities on a number of grounds. The first is that had Mangham used an anonymizer and proxy server, he could have sold the vulnerability to a security-vulnerability company with impunity. There is no legal requirement for security-vulnerability companies such as Zerodium to verify if a vulnerability has been discovered by breaking the law—most forms of hacking do.

The study of such criminal sanctions for the use of exploits is not central to this chapter but does form part of the legal context in which considerations regarding regulation may occur given that the potential end use may have significant consequences.

9.3.6 Da Jiang Innovation

Da Jiang Innovation (DJI) is a Chinese company that produces the majority of drones worldwide.[17] They announced a bug-bounty program on their website in 2017, offering money for threat identification, and in particular to identify threats relating to users' privacy and vulnerabilities that reveal proprietary source codes of back doors that circumvent safety settings. The specific wording at the time was:

> Rewards for qualifying bugs will range from $100 to $30,000, depending on the potential impact of the threat. DJI is developing a website with full program terms and a standardized form for reporting potential threats related to DJI's servers, apps or hardware. Starting today, bug reports can be sent to bugbounty@dji.com for review by technical experts.[18]

Most other bug-bounty programs contain specific information related to the scope of permissible threat hunting, along with clarification that the company will not pursue civil or criminal suits against the researcher. A researcher by the name of Finisterre was on the open-code platform GitHub, where he found a set of API keys for Amazon Web Services, Amazon's cloud-computing unit, for the DJI source code. API keys are unique identifiers used for authentication. Finisterre used the API keys to access DJI accounts with Amazon Web Services, where he was able to find a series of vulnerabilities. DJI responded with threat of civil suit for going outside of the scope of the bug-bounty program. In the end, a settlement was reached after much negotiation.

9.4 Observations

Most people who perform penetration testing and who hunt for vulnerabilities and bugs provide professional services, or they aspire to become recognized as a cyber-security professional. They are motivated predominantly for professional reasons, which include legitimate financial gain, improved employment prospects, and reputation. In my capacity as providing legal information to many cyber-security experts, I would say that they are, by and large, driven to reducing, if not eliminating, security threats, that they enjoy helping others to learn more about cyber security, and, in general, improving the overall cyber ecosystem to make it more secure.

For many cyber-security professionals, in particular penetration testers, it is not enough to be paid to find vulnerabilities and lapse security practices for an organization. They are committed to ensuring that the organization takes action to fix the vulnerabilities. When organizations repeatedly practice lapse security and where they do nothing to fix vulnerabilities where innocent people may be affected, cyber-security professionals become frustrated to the point where they feel an ethical duty to disclose such poor practices. This is similar to many acts of hacktivism where the goal is to assist with the process of reprimanding individuals or groups engaged in harmful activity, such as those who trade in child pornography or are part of criminal gangs, where law enforcement is seen as being ineffective or under resourced. It is a slippery slope, with some forms of ethical hacking becoming acts of vigilantism.

As we will see in the next chapter, actions that "fight fire with fire" may be perceived in many different ways, ranging from acceptable forms of ethical hacking to acts of self-defence, to acts of vigilantism from, as some call them, "cyber-security cowboys."

Notes

1. Moses 2011.
2. Email correspondence with Patrick Webster 2011.
3. Grey 2011.
4. Grey 2011.
5. Email correspondence with Patrick Webster, 2011.
6. IT Security Training, "First State Super in Breach of Privacy Act' June 7, 2012, available at https://www.itsecuritytraining.com.au/articles/first-state-super-breach-privacy-act. The link to the privacy commission's report has gone dead. See https://www.oaic.gov.au/publications/reports.html
7. Lemos 2005.
8. Zetter 2005.
9. Discussion with a computer-security analyst who was present at the presentation.
10. Lemos 2005.
11. Herpderp1189, *Huffington Post*, January 5, 2012.
12. Lennon 2016.
13. The decision was given in the Southwark Crown Court on February 17, 2012. The decision itself is not reported. Information was obtained through media stories. See BBC News, "York Facebook hacking student Glenn Mangham jailed."

14. *R v Glenn Steven Mangham.*
15. Protalinski 2012.
16. Mangham 2012.
17. With thanks to PhD candidate Rob Hamper for providing me the reference to the DJI case.
18. Da Jian Innovation, "DJI To Offer 'Bug Bounty' Rewards."

CHAPTER X

Counterattack/Hackback

Many forms of ethical hacking are rooted in ensuring the security of networks. This has taken shape in four main ways. The first is through intrusion or penetration testing, where experts are invited to expose any security vulnerabilities of an organization's network. The second is somewhat more controversial as it involves hackers who, without authorization, illegally access a network, software, or hardware to expose security vulnerabilities. Sometimes these hackers will go so far as to fix the vulnerability or, more likely, will report it to the system's owner. Third, many security experts are forming self-organized security communities to actively engage in intelligence gathering and counterattacks, here called security activism. Last, there is a growing concern that many organizations, including corporations and governments, are engaging in counterattack efforts to deter attacks to their systems. This is known as hackback or counterattack. Increasingly, attacks have moved into the corporate world, where organizations are moving from defensive protection against cyber threat to responding with similar measures.

As will also be seen through an examination of emerging events, many corporations and organizations are engaged in some form of counterattack/hackback. Intrusion-detection software not only detects denial-of-service attacks but also automatically initiates counter-denial-of-service attacks. There are no legal exemptions for these types of counterattacks. The problem of corporate hackback, while still controversial, is increasingly being recognized as an issue that requires new law and policy. Both governments and corporations are moving from a defensive cyber-threat posture to one of mitigation of threat, and often moving to the offensive or active cyber-security posture. The legal ambiguity arises when these security experts find security vulnerabilities, then actively investigate further without permission or authorization from the system's owner, and then go on to disclose the vulnerability. Or, security researchers may sell the vulnerability to be used to hackback as a method of offensive cyber security.

This chapter has the modest aim at looking at hackback, drawing from recent case studies, including deliberate corporate hackback with plausible deniability, the use of hackback by third-party providers contracted by intelligence units (also with plausible deniability), and automated methods to counter denial of service. The chapter then examines recently proposed legislation in the United States to legalize hackback. The conclusion looks at appropriate legal and policy frameworks relative to emerging issues in ethical hackback.

10.1 Counterattack/Hackback in Context

As noted, counterattack is also referred to as hackback or strikeback. Counterattack is when an individual or organization which is subject to an attack of their data, network, or computer takes similar measures to attack back at the hacker/cracker.

Counterattack also refers to a self-help measure used in response to a computer offence. In criminal law, this is expressed as self-defence. In most instances, computer offences refers to an act that is or has already occurred, such as a cyber attack (e.g., deliberate actions to alter, disrupt, or destroy computer systems; unauthorized access or modification to data or computer system, e.g., this may merely mean accessing a computer system), installing malware onto a computer system, or launching a denial-of-service attack.

Consider the example of a denial-of-service attack launched against a corporation's website. A botnet has been used to launch the attack. The corporation would have several options to pursue:

- Implement passive measures to strengthen its defensive posture (e.g., upgrade security software, firewalls, and training to staff).

- Report the cyber attack to law-enforcement authorities and leave it to them to take appropriate action. If the denial-of-service attack has been done for blackmailing purposes, the corporation may elect to pay the sum.
- Do nothing and wait for the attack to be over. Purchase insurance against cyber attack to mitigate against future attacks.
- Contact a third party specializing in cyber attacks to assist in the matter (e.g., AusCERT, SANS Institute, National Cyber-Forensics and Training Alliance).
- Take self-help measures to gather information and investigate the source of the attack toward mitigation of damage and traceback to the source.
- Take actions to actively neutralize the incoming attack through forms of counter-strike, such as a counter of denial-of-service attack

Often an organization will use a combination of options in dealing with the matter. Mitigation of damages is the key priority of most corporations under cyber attack.[1] The most important component in mitigating against damage is protecting assets not already compromised. This could mean protecting data that has not yet been stolen. It could also mean stopping the denial-of-service attack as soon as possible through various means—technical measures, paying a ransom, or launching a counter-denial-of-service attack. Damage control may also mean limiting media attention to the matter in order to keep stock prices from falling, say. Corporations and organizations are taking self-help measures such as counterattack.

Hackback is controversial. There are no shortage of academics and experts writing on the topic. Indeed, many academics—such as Messerschmidt,[2] Rosenzweig,[3] Kallberg,[4] Kesan,[5] and Halberstam,[6] generally take a negative view of hackback where it is unlawful, but additionally have grave concerns about the legalization of hackback as well. These authors look at a wide range of hackback, listed in table 2.

Table 2. Parties and Lawfulness of Hackback

Parties involved in Hackback	Lawfulness of Action
State-to-state counterattack	The Tallinn Manual 2.0 is a NATO initiative to address possible rules around cyberwarfare. Generally, the policy document outlines that states may engage in cyber attacks during times of war and armed conflict.
	In theory, international laws govern this area, but in practice there is no international agreement by states. China and Russia, for example, take a guarded view of the manual, and of many other international laws. They have been vocally opposed to many of the Tallinn provisions.
State sponsored (hire a private entity) for counterattack of private organization	Not lawful under international law or Tallinn. State-sponsored attacks by private entities are considered state-to-state attacks.
Law-enforcement counterattack on a private entity	Lawful in some countries, but under very strict frameworks.
	The Computer Crimes Act in the Netherlands, for example, gives law-enforcement investigators the right to hack into private computers and install spyware, or to disable access to files. Law-enforcement investigators are permitted to do so if there is a serious offence and a special warrant. There are several other technical restrictions.
Law-enforcement or government entity hiring or working with a private entity to engage in counterattack of a private entity	Unlawful.
	But there seems to be some toleration for this type of activity, as will be explored in this paper.
	This scenario is not contemplated by most authors writing on hackback as these incidents are kept secret and rarely make the news. They are generally dealt with in a way so as to have plausible deniability. These scenarios typically only come to light through whistle-blowers and on websites such as WikiLeaks or on the Dark Net.

Parties involved in Hackback	Lawfulness of Action
	Or in the case where cryptocurrency is involved, the only way to recover these funds typically involves a form of hacking though not necessarily hackback. Cryptocurrency hacks typically involve the theft of "coins." These types of cryptocurrency recovery instances typically involve private organization counter-hack to recover the coins. One cannot use traditional legal frameworks for recovery of stolen assets or money-laundering leaving counterattack as the only means possible of recovering stolen goods and money.
Hiring a private entity to perform counterattack on a private entity	Unlawful in most jurisdictions as the notion of "self-defence" is currently unrecognized in the cyber context. There is a bill in the United States (the so-called Hackback Bill), however, that could make hackback legal under certain conditions. More precisely, the bill—the Active Cyber Defense Certainty Act (amended Computer Fraud and Abuse Act 1986)—would provide a defence to persons who are prosecuted for performing hackback if it was to defend themselves or property. There are many other proposed restrictions.
Private organization counterattack of another private entity	Unlawful in most jurisdictions as "self-defence" is currently unrecognized in the cyber context. The proposed Active Cyber Defense Certainty Act (the Hackback Bill) may have an effect, as noted above.
Private entity counterattack of a law-enforcement or state entity (or private entities engaged by a state or law enforcement)	Unlawful

10.2 Case Studies

There are some interesting hackback scenarios that what could only be described as potential movie material. One such incident is the hack and hackback exchange between LulzSec, MasterCard, PayPal, and Aaron Barr, CEO of the computer-security firm HBGary Federal. Other incidences, however, involve everyday corporate network activities as will be seen below.

10.2.1 LulzSec, MasterCard and PayPal, and Barr

WikiLeaks founder Julian Assange was arrested in London on charges of sexual crimes under Swedish law. Many viewed this as a false arrest and an indirect way of incarcerating Assange for the release of secret US cables to WikiLeaks. A legal defence fund was quickly established wherein people could make donations via MasterCard or PayPal. But MasterCard and PayPal soon disallowed payments to be made to the Assange defence fund, causing an international uproar, particularly within hacktivism communities. Members of LulzSec launched a denial-of-service attack against MasterCard and PayPal, which took down their capabilities in December 2010, and then again in June 2011.

The LulzSec DDoS attacks against MasterCard and PayPal were motivated by the treatment of the companies' refusals to accept online donations for the WikiLeaks situation. Someone (perhaps members of the MasterCard and PayPal team, or perhaps other security researchers upset with WikiLeaks) launched a counter-denial-of-service attack against the LulzSec website. One DDoS attack was met with a counterattack.

Additionally, law enforcement was on the hunt for the members of LulzSec who had launched the attacks against MasterCard and PayPal. During this time, HBGary Federal CEO Aaron Barr was investigating the matter and claimed that he had identified the members who had performed the attacks, claiming he had proof. Barr's emails on the matter were leaked to the Internet and may be found on a number of websites.[7] According to the leaked emails, Barr used IRC to obtain the handle names of those members involved in the attack. He then used social media, such as Facebook and LinkedIn, to allegedly look at friends and family of the hacker group. He then made inferences to the point where he claimed he had identified members who launched the attack. Members of LulzSec retaliated, claiming he had put many innocent individuals in danger. If Barr had indeed used social media to retrieve this information, his methodology remains unclear. Most people are unable to view one's Facebook account unless they befriend them. There are, however, methods to hack into a Facebook account without authorization.[8] It is likely that Barr had indeed accessed this information without authorization. Members of LulzSec responded to Barr's claims by allegedly copying 40,000 emails from HBGary Federal and making it available on the Pirate Bay file-sharing site, launching a denial-of-service attack to his company's website, and posting: "now the Anonymous hand is bitch-slapping you in the face."

According to the *Guardian*, the exposed emails from HBGary revealed that they, along with security firms Palantir and Berico, "were discovered to have conspired to hire out their information war capabilities to corporations which hoped to strike back at perceived enemies, including US activist groups, WikiLeaks and journalist Glenn Greenwald."[9] My interview with Dreyfus (December 2010, Sydney, Australia) revealed a similar theme of corporations and governments engaging "cowboy security firms" to perform attacks either directly on hacktivism websites and other targets. Dreyfus also revealed that there were several recent attacks performed by cowboy security firms who had made it look as though such attacks came from Anonymous. This, of course, cannot be verified as having occurred for certain. The contracting out of intelligence services, "for hire cyber-attack services" by governments to security firms was also exposed in the Canadian television program *The Agenda*.[10] Identifying attack sources is a difficult proposition.

There are ongoing investigations and arrests had been made against two members of LulzSec for participation in the MasterCard and PayPal attacks. There has been no public investigation or charges laid against those responsible for the counter-DDoS attack against the LulzSec website. Furthermore, there has not been a public investigation made or charges laid in relation to how Barr obtained his supposed information of members of LulzSec through social media. There have not been any arrests made for those members of LulzSec/Anonymous responsible for releasing Barr's personal email and for the DDoS attack of his website. It would appear that investigations and charges are highly, and perhaps unfairly, discretionary.

10.2.2 Illegal Streaming Link Sites

Watching professional sporting events is expensive in many parts of the world. Sometimes coverage of the sport is only offered through one service provider, and a subscription can be beyond the means of most people. The only legal way to view the big match is to purchase a ticket to be physically present in the stadium, pay the price for the subscription to the provider carrying the event, or go to a bar or venue showing the event. This means that many devoted fans are not able to legally watch sporting events from the comfort of their homes. Whether it is soccer/football, cricket, rugby, badminton, tennis, football, or ice skating, fans will always find ways to watch, whether it is by legal or illegal means. Some popular methods are to watch through illegal streaming sites or through P2P channels. Google can be used to find a single site streaming the event, but more often than not, a sports fan will use a torrent index site to see where and how the big game can be watched. These indexing sites do not host the content, nor do they stream the content; they merely provide an index to sites and torrents that will show the content.

Some of these linking indexes include Wiziwig, FirstRowSports, MyP2P.eu, and Rojadirecta. These indexing sites have been treated differently in courts around the world. In 2009, for example, a Spanish district court declared Rojadirecta did not violate copyright law as they only provided links to the materials in question.[11] Such indexes are lawful in many parts of the world. Even in jurisdictions where the indexes do violate copyright law, and are therefore unlawful, there is little that a company can do to take down the foreign-based infringing indexes. A website simply has to register in a jurisdiction with copyright-friendly laws and it becomes out of legal reach.

Since 2013, sporting index sites have suffered ongoing denial-of-service attacks which temporarily take down the sites.[12] This is particularly common right before or during a high-profile sporting event. While no one has openly claimed responsibility for these attacks, there are two prevalent theories. The first is that a competing sporting index is DDoS-ing the competition. In fact, they could be routinely DDoS-ing one another. The second, and more likely, is that the entities with exclusive rights to a sporting event have engaged a private entity to DDoS these indexing sites. Of course, neither of these activities is lawful in a jurisdiction with hacking provisions. They both clearly violate the hacking provisions in most countries in the world, but not in all countries. The DDoS could have been performed in a country with no cybercrime law, or in a country where enforcement is unlikely and there are no extradition treaties between that country and the United States or Europe Union, or, lastly, the DDoS could have been performed on a vessel strategically located in "non-jurisdiction" international waters.

10.2.3 Automated Counter-DDoS
The ironic reality is that hackback occurs hundreds of thousands of times per day around the globe without anyone deliberately setting

out to perform a counterattack. This is because many cyber-security software and systems have several technical features to minimize the damage caused from a DDoS attack and to thwart a DDoS altogether. Many of these systems automatically perform counter-DDoS as a means of reducing and blocking the threat. There is an assumption that these systems are perfectly legal, when of course, they are not; the law does not allow for unauthorized access or modification of any system. There are no exemptions to these "hacking" provisions.

10.3 The Legalization of Hackback

The legalization of hackback has been gaining momentum in the United States. It is important to recognize that hackback involving state actors is governed under international law and is not considered within the scope of ethical hacking in this book. For example, the International Court of Justice upholds state-to-state counterattacks where four criteria are met.[13] First, the counterattack must have been directed at whomever performed the original cyber attack. Second, the attacker must have been asked to cease the attack. Third, the counterattack must be proportionate to the original act and reversible. Fourth, the counterattack must induce the attacker to comply with international standards.

Law enforcement's use of hackback has become legal in some jurisdictions. The Netherlands permits law-enforcement agencies to perform counterattack. Under the country's Computer Crime Act, investigative officers have the right to hack into private computers to install spyware (this allows attribution) and to destroy or disable access to files. Law enforcement must first obtain permission from prosecutorial services, after which it may proceed in court to obtain written authorization. The authorization is limited to a serious offence and must meet many technical requirements.

The United States is considering the legalization of hackback outside of law-enforcement and state-to-state contexts, specifically corporate hackback. The Active Cyber Defense Certainty Act, a bill proposed by US Senator Tom Graves in 2017, addresses "active cyber defence," which is a disputed term. Task force and cyber-security expert Bob Chesney describes the term as:

> "Active defense" is a phrase of contested scope, but the general idea is that when someone has hacked into your system, there

are steps the victim might take (or might hire someone to take) that help identify or even disrupt that unauthorized access (including, perhaps, steps that take place outside your system, giving rise to the phrase "hacking back").[14]

Under the proposed bill—dubbed the Hackback Bill in the press—a person prosecuted under computer-crime provisions may raise active defences in response to a cyber intrusion. The general framework of self-defence is fraught with ambiguities and uncertainty as to how it would be applied to "cyber." The point of the bill is to recognize a range of activities that are permissible in response to a cyber intrusion. An organization may engage a third party to perform work outside of their own network to disrupt, monitor, and react to a cyber intrusion on their network system.

The two glaringly obvious problems with any form of hackback are attribution and damage to innocent third-party systems. The Hackback Bill provides many limitations. The first is the limited definition of "victim" to only include an entity that has suffered from a *persistent* unauthorized *intrusion* of the entity's computer or network. Figure 19 below looks at a typical life cycle of a cyber intrusion.

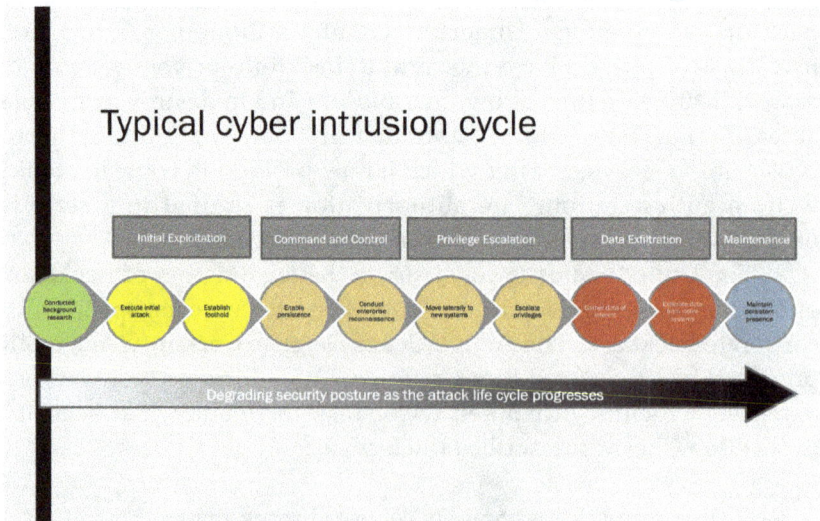

Figure 19. Life cycle of a Cyber Intrusion.[15]

In the above instance, there is an escalation of the initial exploitation, leading to privileged escalation and later data exfiltration. The
Hackback Bill only requires that there is an intrusion that is done
more than once and does not suddenly stop—it must be continuous.
Intrusion in this life cycle and proposed in the bill is something more
significant than a denial-of-service attack.

As the bill would require that the attack be persistent and
intrusive, this precludes denial-of-service attacks. By not including
denial-of-service threats, it stands to reason that the act also would
not legalize a counter-denial-of-service attack.

Other requirements under the proposed act include the duty
of the entity performing active defence to notify the FBI National
Cyber Investigative Joint Task Force prior to engaging in activity.
The counterattack must be proportionate. Active defence measures
are described as:

- undertaken by, or at the direction of, a victim; and
- consisting of accessing without authorization the computer
  of the attacker to the victim's own network to gather information in order to establish attribution of criminal activity; to
  share with law enforcement or to disrupt continued unauthorized activity against the victim's own network.

There are a few parts to the permissible activities above that
require further speculation. The first is that attribution is assumed
possible. Second is that attribution intelligence when shared with
the FBI will lead to establishing that the attribution is in fact correct.
Third, and more important, is that the active measures will disrupt
the attack.[16] While all the above is noble in theory, it assumes that
attribution is possible, and that an active measure would be directly
against the person/entity responsible for the initial attack. A distinct
problem with this line of reasoning is that attackers hardly ever use
one system, let alone their own, to perform an attack. Third-party
devices are nearly almost always used to perform cyber intrusion.
These third-party devices are rarely, if ever, aware that they are part
of the attack. They are obfuscated.

Because attribution is inherently difficult and attackers nearly
always use multiple third-party devices, innocent parties will most
likely be affected by any active defence mechanism. It is one thing to
say that the active defence may be liable for damages, but the reality

is that the innocent parties will never know if they have been used to commit an attack, or why active defence measures are being taken against their systems. The incoming data traffic will only read as an attack. Also, there is no obligation under the bill to notify third-party systems of active defence measures. In other words, if damage is caused by the active defence measures, they would not know who to sue for damages. Even more problematic is that innocent third-party devices are likely scattered across the globe—jurisdiction for any of this mess would be a nightmare for legal recourse.

The Hackback Bill states that the defence is no longer valid if the measure destroys information on the other system, there is physical injury, or a threat to public safety or health.

If the active defence is later found to be excessive, the entity who performed active defence can be liable for damage caused, and the defence will no longer apply. This means that the entity could be charged with a computer-crime offence. The reality is that Senator Graves' proposal is likely to remain just that for now, a proposal that will not lead to legislation. However, the questions the bill raises remain essential. Appropriate responses to cyber-security threats are few and far between. Finding a way forward in this discussion is a nearly insurmountable task.

10.4 Observations

Counterattacks are launched as a form of self-defence or as a means of retribution. The LulzSec and PayPal examples certainly highlight the retribution motive. However, most organizations perform acts of counterattack as a form of self-defence. In 2001, researchers surveyed 528 IT managers in Western Australia and Victoria to obtain their views on counterattack. Those surveyed were asked a variety of questions, including whether strikeback should be allowed if their organization was subject to an attack (65 per cent replied "yes," 30 per cent "no," and 5 per cent were undecided).[17] This question was then broken down into specific types of attacks, such as attempt at network access and attempt to destroy or alter data, which resulted in increased "yes" response rates to ranges between 70 per cent and 93 per cent. The survey was done in 2001. The author is unaware of any more current surveys on hackback.

The main targets are the IP addresses (often of websites or computers) that initialize the attack. Information may also be gathered and collected, where possible, of those individuals who perform the attack, though this can be difficult to trace.

Again, the motivation is either to defend or retaliate against the origin of the attack. The target is normally a website and does not typically involve the individual per se behind the attack (because identification is often difficult).

There are a variety of ethical and moral issues at play with counterattack. One principle could be seen as defending one's property against attack. The other main principle is retribution. There appears to be an additional principle of hacking to discredit an organization, typically by deliberately launching an attack to make it look as though it has come from another organization. Plausible deniability is endless with hacking and hackback.

There is no consensus as to whether corporations and organizations engaged in counterattack are aware of the illegality of their activity. Some security software will automatically initialize a counterattack, whereby the organization may or may not be aware. It may be the case that those individuals running the security of the organization are aware of the illegality of the action, but that the board of directors are kept in the dark. There is also evidence that many organizations employ former black-hat hackers under strict control and surveillance, yet this type of arrangement is rarely publicized.[18]

Self-defence may apply to some forms of counterattack. There are no cases that deal with defending oneself against an online attack. There is likewise little literature on the topic in most jurisdictions other than the United States, where there is an emerging discussion but no advancement in terms of a clear policy or legislative reform. Indeed, the Hackback Bill has no sufficient support from Congress or the Senate. Curiously, Australia's Model Criminal Code (MCC) provides guidance as to the scope of self-defence in such situations. The MCC discussed at length the growing trend in the United States for corporations' use of computer software with counter-strike abilities. The MCC committee stated that:

> It is possible that the defence of self-defence in chapter 2, s.10.4 of the Model Criminal Code might extend to some instances of computerised counterattack against cybernet intruders. Self-defence includes conduct which is undertaken "to protect property from unlawful appropriation, destruction, damage or interference". It is possible that a strikeback response to the

hacker's attack could be characterised in this way. In practice, counterattack involves serious risk since hackers are likely to adopt precautions which divert the counterattack to innocent third parties. It is apparent that principles of self-defence of persons, which extend without undue strain to include protection of tangible property, are inadequate for the purpose of regulating computerised counterattack against hackers. The familiar concepts of necessity and reasonable response, which excuse or justify counterattack against physical threats, are next to useless as guides in this field.[19]

The MCC committee concluded that "legislative intervention would be 'premature.'" They further noted that corporations who resorted to self-help/hackback "would be left to the uncertain promise of a merciful exercise of prosecutorial discretion."[20] The concluding sentence provides even more ambiguity to the MCC, where it is stated:

The familiar criteria of necessity and proportionality which govern self-defence in other applications have no obvious application here. Reliance on a test of what is or is not reasonable in the way of counterattack against hackers would place an inappropriate legislative burden on courts to determine issues of telecommunications policy.[21]

The conclusion seems to echo a recurring theme of "This is a tough one so let's wait and see." The MCC committee declared that legislation was premature and that courts should not be the ones to determine issues of telecommunications policy. So who should make these determinations? The reality is that individuals and corporations are making these determinations as a matter of internal policy. The actions and reactions of corporations are simply non-transparent at the moment. In the United States, however, Senator Graves's bill recognizes that corporate hackback is occurring and that appropriate measures need to be taken to form not only sound policy, but a certain legislative framework.

There has been much criticism of hackback as it is seen by many as a form of cyber vigilantism. Common concerns include the risk of launching a counterattack on an innocent third party. There are many obfuscation methods used in hacking, such as routing traffic through third-party devices and networks.[22] A counterattack would almost definitely affect these third-party systems. Even if an organization believes that it will not affect innocent third-party systems, the risk of misidentifying the source/person responsible is inherently challenging. Attribution remains a significant hurdle. Others question whether hackback would have a deterrent effect or whether it would merely provoke an escalation of hacking and counter-hacking. The notion of what is proportionate as a response to a hack is also a challenging area. It is further contended that legalizing hackback with insufficient oversight by a public body could result in deteriorating trust in the international system and could even go so far as to undermine cyber norms.

Is there a way forward? Perhaps. There used to be a time where security-vulnerability disclosure was highly contentious and fraught with legal uncertainties with constant legal threats to researchers who exposed significant vulnerabilities in corporate and government systems. The US Department of Justice worked to develop policy around vulnerability disclosure, authorized vulnerability, and bug-bounty platforms, such as HackerOne and Bugcrowd, and has openly discouraged legal action against cyber-security researchers. The result is that many corporations are openly publishing vulnerability and bug-bounty programs that limit legal recourse and pay researchers for finding vulnerabilities and bugs in the code, albeit the money paid out being a small amount in comparison with the time, effort, and number of coders working to find such.

Hackback is clearly different from cyber-security vulnerabilities and bug bounties, but the aims are similar: to discourage and disrupt cyber-security threats through soft policy and change in corporate attitudes toward novel programs. Hackback requires soft policy that has been negotiated between government, relevant authorities such as CERTs, and with private corporations. This could start with a pilot project in one jurisdiction to see how this would work in practice. Perhaps attribution and third-party damage is more problematic than anticipated, or perhaps it is not. This would make for an interesting case study that could lead to policy at the national level, and, later, at the international level, if the pilot projects are successful.

Of course, diplomacy in parts of the world where cyber threats are clearly attributed is also an option, especially when coupled with an international agreement. Intellectual property and counterfeit goods by way of example have been the subject of intense international negotiations, trade retaliation, and soft measures. This has led to some effective programs in jurisdictions with known IP issues, such as China. While not a perfect solution, there has been progress. However, corporate hackback is only at the beginning phase as a topic of limited conversation, one lacking a global audience.

Notes

1. Email correspondence with Ron Plescoe, director of the National Cyber-Forensics and Training Alliance (NCFTA) 2009 as part of PhD Thesis MAURUSHAT, A. 2011. Notes from the interview have been kept on file by the author.
2. Messerschmidt 2013.
3. Rosenzweig 2013.
4. Kallberg 2015.
5. Kesan and Hayes 2012.
6. Halberstam 2013.
7. For a link to the emails, see *The Old Computer* in references.
8. AusCERT 2011 presentation by Christian Heindrick.
9. B. Brown 2013.
10. *The Agenda,* "Attack of the Hacktivists."
11. Ernesto, 2010.
12. Andy, 2013.
13. Chesney 2017.
14. Chesney 2017.
15. Figure provided with permission by cyber-security firm Gridware.
16. Centre for Homeland Security, George Washington University 2016.
17. Hutchinson and Warren 2001.
18. For example, former botnet master Owen Walker is now employed by Telstra; see Maurushat 2011.
19. Model Criminal Code, p. 108.
20. Model Criminal Code, p. 109.
21. Model Criminal Code, p. 109.
22. Dupont 2017.

CHAPTER XI

Security Activism

Security activism is similar to penetration/intrusion testing in that the effort is to improve security. Security activism goes beyond mere testing of security, however, to gathering intelligence on crackers and to launch offensive attacks to disrupt online criminal enterprises. This type of reaction could also be perceived as a form of counterattack or hackback. One example, as will be explored in this chapter, is the activist community involved in taking down a botnet.

11.1 Security Activism in Context

Security activism is a curious beast. I often ask people how they would feel about the off-line equivalent, looking at escalating scenarios. First, I ask how they feel about someone walking about the perimeter of their house, on public land, and letting the owner know of open windows, unsecure doors, and other aspects that lend a house less secure. I ask the same question about someone doing this walking on their property to take notes. Things then escalate to someone stepping inside of the house without authorization, through an open door, to observe security defects, then reporting to the owner. Lastly, I cite someone entering the house without permission through an open window, and once inside fixing the security flaws as an act of kindness before exiting. In many ways the above scenarios reflect the work of how many ethical hackers view cyber security: they are passionate about exposing risks, and protecting and defending systems.

11.2 Case Studies

The case studies look at early security activism against spammers and then move to botnet removal communities. Finally, a case study that looks at how some ethical hackers exposed security flaws and fixed these flaws without authorization is considered.

11.2.1 Spamhaus Project

The Spamhaus Project, a global organization of volunteer guardians in the computer industry, composes blacklists of some of the worst spam propagators, this to aid ISPs and businesses to better filter spam. The company E360insight.com sued the Spamhaus Project in a US district court in Illinois, alleging it was a legally operating a direct-marketing company and should not be blacklisted as a spam provider. Spamhaus did not file a response and did not appear before the court. As such, the arguments presented before the court were unilateral, such that the court issued a default judgment.[1] The court ordered Spamhaus to pay US$11.7 million, to post a notice that E360 was not a spammer, and ordered that the Spamhaus Internet address be removed from the Internet Corporation for Assigned Names and Numbers (ICANN). Spamhaus ignored the ruling, did not pay the money, and did not post a notice on its website that E360 was not a spammer, nor did ICANN remove the Spamhaus website from its root server. In a similar situation, the anti-virus and anti-spyware company Symantec was taken to court in California by a firm that it defines and reports as a spyware company. Hotbar.com claims that the classification of its software as spyware is in violation of trade libel laws and constitutes interference with contract. The suit was reported as settled, with Symantec agreeing to classify Hotbar as "low risk."[2]

11.2.2 Spam Fighter

The US court decision of *Sierra v. Ritz*[3] involved unauthorized use of a DNS zone transfer. Zone transfers are, generally speaking, open-access public information. They provide data about all of the machines within a domain. Without zone transfer, you would literally have to type in an IP (internet protocol) address every time you went to a website—it is one factor contributing to the convenience of the Internet. The information may be retrieved by the use of "host command" with the "l" option. Zone transfers contain public information to varying degrees, depending on the protocols used by an organization. Zone transfers may be disabled to the greater public with only trusted machines and senior administrators having access on a "need to know" basis. This is a form of limited authorized public access. In Sierra's case, the zone transfer was more widely available in the sense that the system allowed zone transfers to everyone, thereby publicizing potentially private data. There would be no way for a person accessing the zone transfer in the latter context to know whether Sierra was truly allowing shared access or whether it was merely a misconfiguration. From a technical perspective, this is a situation of authorized access to the information found in the zone transfer. From a legal perspective, the judge ruled that access was unauthorized, with emphasis placed on the defendant's intention to obtain and divulge information found in the zone transfer.[4] David Ritz is a well-known anti-spammer. There has been debate as to whether Sierra has facilitated spam in the past. Neither of these two issues appeared to weigh into the decision. While *Sierra v. Ritz* is a civil suit, Ritz was criminally charged with unauthorized access to a computer in North Dakota. Although the charges were later dropped, Ritz lost the civil suit and the court reasoned that "Ritz's behaviour in conducting a zone transfer was unauthorized within the meaning of the North Dakota Computer Crime Law."

The case illustrates how the terms "unauthorized" and "access" do not produce a similar set of shared assumptions in the technical, legal, or ethical fields. A technical researcher may falsely assume that they are operating within safe legal parameters only to discover that such parameters do not translate across fields. The technical researcher would likely assume that he/she is authorized to perform an act where technical protocols and programming convention allow for it. From a legal standpoint, authorization and consent involve a number of factors, including intention, damage, and the bargaining position of affected parties. One commentator on the decision noted that it is the equivalent of, "Mommy, *can* I have a cookie? Sure you can have a cookie, but you *may* not."[5] The case foregrounds a recurring theme: if a user interacts with a server in a way that the protocol does not prohibit but is upsetting to the server's operator, should this be construed as "unauthorized access" as a matter of law?[6] The scope of unauthorized access in computer-fraud statutes is an old question.[7] Whether or not this would constitute a "hack" is one question, and if it is a "hack," then surely the motives appear to be somewhat ethical.

11.2.3 Botnet Removal Communities

There exists a number of undocumented independent research communities that were (or still are) actively involved with botnet-harm mitigation, interdiction, counterattack, and takedown. This may include attempts by the C&C source to program and reprogram its bots, altering payloads of malicious applications delivered on botnets, and launching a denial-of-service attack on C&C servers.[8] The Offense-in-Depth Initiative (OID) was launched in 2008 as a group-targeted approach to fighting cybercrime. OID is comprised of volunteers who work within smaller subset groups dedicated to botnet countermeasures. Each subgroup specializes in one particular botnet. So, for example, there were the OID-Kraken and OID-Torpig small working groups targeting the Kraken and Torpig botnets. The main goal of the OID teams is to erode the profit model of specific major cybercriminals, while obtaining intelligence for use by law enforcement.[9] Each specialist subgroup divides their roles into reverse-engineer operations specialist, coder, social-engineer linguist, and information warrior. In some instances the same person could fulfil multiple roles, and in other instances the roles are somewhat superficial.

The group's aim was to form small working groups, singling out one botnet or criminal operation, with the purpose of long-term disruption (OID has since disbanded). Other small independent research groups have performed countermeasures for a few weeks or a month, then the countermeasures stop, allowing the criminal operation a chance to regroup and get back to "business as usual."[10] OID's focus was on long-term countermeasures aimed at disrupting the profitability of the botnet operations. Whether a cybercriminal continues operating depends on many factors. OID has singled out three major factors: complexity of the operation, risk of getting caught, and reward/profit of the crime.[11] OID uses methods aimed to increase the complexity of the criminal's organization, forcing them to spend more time, effort, and money into maintaining their criminal operations. For instance, techniques include subverting the C&C or by either increasing or decreasing the size of the botnet. There has been some research done on optimal botnet size for certain types of activities.[12] Compromised machines can be remediated so that they are no longer part of a botnet. If you remediate enough machines, the size of the botnet becomes untenable for criminal operations. Likewise, if you grow a botnet from 100,000 to 10,000,000 it becomes difficult to effectively manage the botnet without constantly writing new instructions for the C&C. The botnet master ends up spending extraordinary amounts of time and effort to control the bots. Just as one person may only successfully tend to a set amount of sheep or cattle within a set amount of land, an increase in the size of the herd requires more land, water, and labour. Similar to caring for livestock, taking care of botnets is often referred to as "herding" bots.

When a botnet's operations are interrupted, it may create the need for more complex operations in order to adapt to the new environment. In the case of botnets, if the complexity becomes too great for the criminal, more expertise may be needed in the form of hiring a programmer to develop new encryption methods or programs. It is believed that, in turn, this forces the cost of business to rise. It is hoped that if the disruption is continuous and that costs of doing business rise so that profitability will be reduced, then this will correspond with a lower level of criminal activity. There is no evidence to suggest that this has worked to date. Botnet activity remains a growth industry. Nonetheless, this is, or was, the belief of groups such as OID. As stated in the OID mission, it is about long-term disruption. It may be too early to ascertain whether such countermeasures are effective.

OID tactics were decided by looking at effectiveness, stealth, ethics, and ability to avoid collateral damage to third parties. Such an approach to tactics is not an official code but represents a rough understanding between members of the group.[13] Ultimately what tactics are used depends on the decisions of the specialist group. While the operations of the OID groups were not openly discussed, many of its operations had involved working with select individuals who worked for computer-security companies. Such companies, unlike OID, often make information on botnet infiltration and countermeasures taken against a botnet available to the public. This was the case with the Kraken botnet, which OID members infiltrated and took down in December of 2008. OID members have not publicly discussed how the botnet was taken down. Researchers with the security corporation TippingPoint, however, have provided publicly available information about the Kraken botnet and the infiltration process available from their security blog.[14]

Researchers at TippingPoint infiltrated Kraken by starting with a sample of the code provided by the company Offensive Security. The various protocols of the botnet were noted. The C&C instructions were encrypted. Researchers had to reverse engineer the computer code, which entailed decrypting the encryption routes. TippingPoint created a fake server (often referred to as a sinkhole) to redirect Kraken traffic. TippingPoint played a somewhat passive role in that they did not rewrite instructions and send alternative instructions via the C&C. In their words, "we are not talking back to any of the Kraken zombies that are phoning home to us. We are simply listening passively, decrypting the request and recording statistics."[15] As such, they were able to then redirect traffic to their server. Researchers at TippingPoint recorded the list of all uniquely infected IP addresses and applied a reverse DNS lookup to ascertain what types of computers and locations of IP addresses were part of the botnet. The majority of the compromised computers were home broadband users, with compromised devices predominantly based in the United States, Spain, United Kingdom, Colombia, Mexico, Peru, and Chile.[16]

TippingPoint wrote an update code capable of cleaning up the compromised computers of Kraken. They have even provided a video demonstrating their capability of removing the Kraken botnet altogether. TippingPoint researchers have not cleaned up the botnet for ethical and legal reasons, chief being that there is no security-research exemption in criminal law.

11.2.4 Cyber-Security Researcher Y

The identity of this cyber-security ethical hacker remains anonymous. He wants his story to be shared, but not his identity. He discovered a serious critical vulnerability in an organization's system. He identified and developed a correction for the security vulnerability. Instead of notifying the organization of the vulnerability, or asking for money for the information, he chose simply to patch the vulnerability as an act of benevolence. The vulnerability would have otherwise allowed hackers to gain unauthorized access to a variety of data. Curiously, this researcher was in the habit of quietly fixing the vulnerabilities of other's systems. After seeing other researchers charged with criminal offences for the mere discovery of security vulnerabilities, researcher Y decided to give up such activism. While I cannot say how prevalent this type of security activism is, I can say that I have heard of many hackers who have performed similar deeds.

11.3 Observations

Self-organized security communities recognize that there is great need for action to alleviate the inept legal and regulatory systems in an attempt to reduce cybercrime. When viewed in this light, the work of self-organized communities may be seen by those involved with these communities as "doing justice" where justice has otherwise proven to be non-functioning.

The motto To Do Justice[17] is potentially applicable to both self-help security communities and botnet communities. There is, for example, mounting evidence that eastern European communities have likened Internet crime such as fraud to a legitimate activity—Robin Hood stealing from rich Western countries to give to poor developing ones. Many types of malware and botnets for hire are now distributed with end-user license agreements, and some have even been registered for copyright protection. Conversely, anti-botnet communities have justified breaking the law where required to achieve justice. The motto To Do Justice parallels the actions of many self-organized security communities who are "fighting malware and botnets" under the motto of Doing Justice in the absence of effective regulatory responses to the problems. In fact, regulation may never effectively deal with botnets. The point is, rather, that the perception of the absence of regulation or the presence of ineffective regulation motivates people to take matters into their own hands.

Main targets vary for security activists. In some instances, the target might be simply to gather intelligence in a honeypot. A honeypot is a network that is set up to detect and collect network traffic. A honeypot is often set up to lure cyber attackers, detect malicious software, and may even deflect and protect against such attacks. In other instances, the target may involve actively taking down a botnet, or removing malware from infected websites, or sending information to companies whose security has been compromised, to collecting information and handing it over to law enforcement.

Targets are either performing illegal criminal functions (running a botnet, stealing credit-card information) or they are organizations whose security practices are poor (and often not fully compliant with security standards). The underlying link between target and motivation is inept security and the ability to exploit vulnerabilities.

Security activists almost always have excellent computer skills. There is no one set of hacker ethos that applies to all hackers, though anecdotal evidence and the opinion of Dreyfus highlights that expert security activists share a common set of ethics that can be best described as responsible engagement.[18] This does not, however, imply that all actions are within the law. Security activism and research is a grey, murky area of the law.

It is difficult to qualify or quantify perceptions without empirical research. Nonetheless, my observations from my research and with interviews of cyber-security experts is that they are highly skilled individuals who are acutely aware that what they are doing is illegal in many jurisdictions, but that they view their activities as necessary and ethical. For example, university researchers investigating the Torpig botnet invaded the privacy of those individuals whose computers had been compromised in order to gain intelligence about the botnet propagation trends. They did so without consent of the computer owners and in clear violation of the law. Law enforcement was notified of these violations but did not press charges. If anything, they condoned the actions.[19]

As a general proposition, security activists are not deterred by the law; frequently, the law turns a blind eye and thus encourages ethical hacking for these purposes. Security researchers are imperative in any initiative to combat cybercrime. For example, there has yet to be a single takedown of a botnet that did not involve cooperation from a number of entities, including security researchers from specialized security-software companies and universities, ISPs, DNS providers, and often law enforcement—these parties are routinely located in different parts of the world.

There have been few incidents where security activists have been the target of criminal investigations, though there have been many security researchers who have been threatened with criminal sanctions. There have, however, been several instances of civil lawsuits against security activists. Two of these civil (quasi-criminal) cases are discussed below.

Exemption from liability and criminal prosecution has been argued for application to security researchers and for acts that threaten to cross technical and accepted protocols. A resounding question underlies the debate: do the ends justify the means?

Examples might include the recording industry's proposal to hack into users' computers to find infringing material, and cyber-activists placing "Trojan horse" software on child-pornography sites, embedded within digital images, to track and record the contents of offenders' hard drives for evidential purposes. These examples go to the question of intent as well as whether an act may be justified as a social utility for the good of the public, similar to how public-interest exemptions work for the admissibility or otherwise inadmissibility of evidence in court.

For example, if one argues that David Ritz had indeed accessed the zone transfer without authorization, inevitably one must question his motive, intent, and whether such activities were performed in the public interest. Peering into the zone transfer to document illegal spamming activity may indeed be in the public interest. If one successfully concludes that no unauthorized access was performed due to the public nature of the zone transfer and DNS, it seems equally perverse to not consider motive and intent. By way of analogy, if I have equipment to make fake passports, along with a stack of 200 UK passport shells, the trajectory toward the commission of a crime is called into question. Accessing information in the zone transfer for illicit purposes should attract attention, if not a penalty. The implication, however, of criminalizing an act of accessing publicly available information without illicit intent calls into question the utility of "unauthorized access" provisions. The inconsistency of the courts' interpretation of "unauthorized access" makes the use of the provision unpredictable as well as malleable to prosecutorial will. The scope of "unauthorized access" is ripe for reconsideration and debate.

There is no public-interest exemption for computer offences. A public-interest exemption refers to unauthorized access, modification, or impairment where it is in the public interest to break the law. Typically, this might relate to security research, but there are other instances that go beyond mere research which may justify the law being broken. There are reasons to allow for a public-interest exemption, though these reasons are not sufficiently compelling at this point in time as to open up the exemption beyond security research. The idea of a public-interest exemption, however, should be given further consideration by governments.

Notes

1. *E360 Insight, LLC et al v. The Spamhaus Project.*
2. Messmer 2006.
3. The judgment is unreported. A copy of the decision is accessible from private listservs as well as from the webpages of SpamSuite.com. See *Sierra Corporate Design Inc. v. David Ritz.*
4. A detailed analysis of the case can be found on SpamSuite.com available at http://www.spamsuite.com/node/351.
5. Rash 2008.
6. Original idea expressed by Paul Ohm in the CyberProf listserv.
7. Kerr 2003.
8. Smith, B. 2005.
9. Observations from email correspondence with members of the OID Initiative. From 2009–2010.
10. Internet Security Operations and Intelligence (ISOI) is one such group. Members complained of the unfocused, ad hoc short-term approach of ISOI.
11. Observations from founder of OID in listserv correspondence.
12. Li et al. 2009.
13. Observations from Listserv correspondence.
14. TippingPoint 2008.
15. TippingPoint 2008.
16. TippingPoint 2008.
17. Tamanaha 2001.
18. Interview with Dreyfus, December 2010, Sydney, Australia. Chiesa, Ducci, and Ciappi 2009.
19. TrustDefender, "In-Depth Analysis."

CHAPTER XII

Ethical-Hacking Challenges in Legal Frameworks, Investigation, Prosecution, and Sentencing

There is often a false belief among law makers that if the right legislation is enacted, and if enough resources are allocated to the task, that the law can rise to the challenge and overcome a myriad of obstacles to combat cyber security and cybercrime. Cybercrime investigations, whether it be for online-identity theft, selling counterfeit products via spam, or hacking (unauthorized access, modification of or impairment/interference with data or data systems), involve unique challenges. The challenges involve difficulty with the harmonization of laws, jurisdictional issues, resource implications, lack of training, ambiguity in terms of how a criminal provision will be interpreted alongside human-rights protections, and, above all, a host of technical hurdles that makes tracing back to the "offender" difficult. In spite of advances in machine learning, big-data techniques, and artificial intelligence, attribution remains a formidable challenge. If these hurdles are overcome, there remain issues with inconsistency in sentencing and, where relevant, in determining appropriate damages. These challenges are the same for ethical hacking

The following chapter addresses hurdles to the investigation and prosecution of an ethical hacker. In some contexts—where ethical hacking moves toward vigilantism—where prosecution is desirable as a deterrent to escalating acts. But there are also good arguments, as previously discussed, for exemptions to apply to many ethical-hacking incidents, especially in situations where the online activity corresponds with legal off-line activity.

12.1 Criminal Landscape: Convention on Cybercrime and the Canadian Criminal Framework

The Convention on Cybercrime, an agreement between member nations of the European Union, is the only international agreement in the area of cybercrime. It is unique in that it is open for signature by non-EU states. The United States, Canada, and Japan have all signed the convention, with the United States also ratifying it.

The convention may be divided into three key divisions: substantive law, procedural requirements, and international cooperation. All signatories to the convention must criminalize certain activities.

The convention creates four main categories of substantive offences:

1. offences against the confidentiality, integrity, and availability of computer data and systems, comprising interference and misuse of devices;
2. computer-related offences, such as forgery and computer fraud;
3. content-related offences, in particular the production, dissemination, and possession of child pornography; and
4. offences related to copyright infringement.

Canada already criminalizes these four categories of conduct. One would presume that only the first category would be relevant to ethical hacking. Indeed, the computer offences are the most relevant area to ethical hacking, but some ethical-hacking incidences may also be relevant to areas such as copyright, child pornography, and fraud.

The convention also addresses the procedural aspects of cybercrime. The main categories here are:

1. expedited preservation of stored computer data,
2. expedited preservation and partial disclosure of traffic data,
3. production orders,
4. search and seizure of stored computer data,
5. real-time collection of traffic data, and
6. interception of content data.

Each of the procedural requirements is of some relevance to botnets and malware investigation.

Finally, the convention contains provisions relating to international cooperation. While some of these provisions are contentious, the convention allows a certain amount of flexibility in terms of how a nation might negotiate some of the issues. These may broadly be categorized as:

1. extradition,
2. mutual assistance, and
3. designation of a 24/7 network contact.

Each of these international-cooperation components of the convention exists to combat cybercrimes.

Table 3 lists the substantive provisions of the convention with the Canadian Criminal Code. While there are some minor differences between Canadian law and the substantive provisions found in the convention, there is significant overlap between them. An expanded version—table 4—is found at the end of this chapter.

Table 3. Comparison of Convention on Cybercrime and Canadian Criminal Framework

Convention on Cybercrime	Canada
Offences against the confidentiality and availability of computer data and systems	
Article 2—Illegal access	Section 342.1 of the Criminal Code
Article 3—Illegal interception	Section 342.1 of the Criminal Code
Article 4—Data interference	Section 430 (1.1) of the Criminal Code
Article 5—System interference	Section 430 (1.1) of the Criminal Code
Article 6—Misuse of devices	Section 326 (1)(b) of the Criminal Code Section 327 (1) of the Criminal Code
Forgery and online fraud	
Article 7	Section 366 of the Criminal Code
Article 8	Part X of the Criminal Code
Child sexual-exploitation materials	
Article 9	Section 163.1 of the Criminal Code
Copyright infringement	
Article 10	Section 42 of the Copyright Act Criminal Remedies

As has been demonstrated throughout this book, ethical hacking almost always involves a form of unauthorized access, modification, or interference with data, a network, a computer, or a device connected to a network. Both the convention and Canadian law cast the net wide, with broad provisions. Indeed, all jurisdictions who have ratified the convention cast a wide net, with no security research or public-research exceptions to the criminal provisions. Curiously, the exceptions only apply to copyright. For instance, in Canada there are exceptions to the infringement of copyright found in sections 29 through to 32 of the Copyright Act. The most relevant exceptions are Security (s. 30.63) and Encryption Research (s. 30.62). Where a person has consent/authorization to perform a range of cyber-security functions, such as assessing the vulnerability of a computer, the exception applies. This makes perfect sense given that criminal laws don't apply where hackers are authorized to "hack" a system. Under the Canadian Copyright Act, encryption research is exempted provided it is not practical to do the research without making a copy, the work has been lawfully obtained, and the copyright owner has been informed. Note, informed—this is a lower threshold than consent. Curiously, there is no exception for encryption research under the Criminal Code. So, if a researcher informed a copyright owner, and the other conditions were met but the copyright owner did not want the researcher to continue with the research, there would be an exemption for copying the code. However, the researcher could still foreseeably be charged with a computer offence under the Criminal Code, where there are no exemptions.

Less relevant to ethical hacking are the online-fraud and child-pornography provisions. In the examples where credit-card information was copied and then used to make donations to charity as an act of protest, the law has clearly been broken, with no exemptions in place. There should not be any exemptions for theft, even when done for a seemingly altruistic motive. Likewise, where ethical hackers work to expose people who engage with child pornography, or where ethical hackers take down Dark-Net forums dedicated to such, they will likely inadvertently have accessed child pornography. There are no exemptions for these acts either. Ethical hackers are always at the mercy of law enforcement, under prosecutorial guidelines, as to whether they will be charged with an offence. Though, as will be explored below, attributing an act to an individual and pressing charges with a successful prosecution are made difficult due to attribution, jurisdiction, and evidence collection, among other factors.

12.2 Attribution

Many different techniques exist to make attack traceback difficult. These technologies/techniques are tools of obfuscation, as they allow people to evade technological controls and legal sanction.[1] As discussed in chapter 2, commonplace obfuscation techniques include dynamic DNS, multihoming, fast flux DNS, distributed C&C (super botnet), encryption, proxy servers, TOR, virtual platforms, rootkits, cloud, IoT, and the use of P2P channels. These tactics allow people to hide behind a cloak of anonymity and lower the possibility of attack traceback.

Take the example of traceback to an IP address. Security researcher Guillaume Lovet describes the difficulty of traceback to the IP address of a botnet master in the following persuasive manner:

> To put it simply, when a stateful Internet connection (a.k.a. a TCP connection) is established between Alice and Bob, Alice sees Bob's IP address. Thus if Bob does bad things to Alice via this connection, his IP address can be reported. Now, if Cain connects to Bob, and from there, connects to Alice with bad intentions, Alice will still only see Bob's IP address. In other words, Cain has masked his IP address with Bob's. The component which allows Cain to use Bob as a relay is called a proxy (there are various types of proxies, though in cybercriminal schemes socks4 and socks5 proxies are mostly used). Such a component, of course, may have been installed on Bob's computer without his knowledge, by Cain. Or by Daniel, and Cain just rented or purchased access to it. As a matter of fact, most trojans and bots embed a proxy, and in any case, have the capability of loading one after prime infection. Given the prevalence of bot-infected machines (a.k.a. zombie computers), that makes a virtually endless resource of proxies for cybercriminals, all sitting on machines of innocent, unaware users. This is something cyber-criminals understand perfectly and exploit ruthlessly, sometimes on a large scale.[2]

When an obfuscation method such as a proxy or fast-flux is utilized, traceback will often only lead to the infected bots that form part of the botnet. Once the IP address is known for the bot, the individual who has registered the Internet connection from that computer to the ISP may be contacted. Of course, bots are devices of innocent third parties. An IP address of a bot does nothing to show you who is in control of the botnet. Even in the rare event that the botnet master is discovered, this won't necessarily tell you who launched the DDoS protest because someone could have rented out the botnet, or hired the botnet master to perform the protest.

As always, an IP address does not necessarily reveal who used a computer to perform a crime. If a computer is used by several people, identifying the botnet master will require additional evidence other than a mere IP address. The botnet master may only be targeted upon discovering where the C&C is occurring and tracing back through proxies to the original source. Discovering the C&C point where a botnet receives its instructions from, however, neither reveals the exact computer source nor the identity of the botnet master. Increasingly, cloud services and the IoT are used to connect to botnets. In the rare chance that the identity of a botnet master can be traced, the botnet master can always use Trojan-horse or bot defences, which may or may not prove successful (see below). Of course, whether it's a botnet or other, the botnet master may not even be the perpetrator of an act. They could have merely rented out their services on the Dark Net. This is common.

As noted in previous chapters, many online civil-disobedience participants do not have the computer skills required to use such obfuscation techniques. They are often limited to using open-source LOIC. That tool does not use measures to hide IP addresses. As was seen in the case of Matthew George, he did not use other anonymizers such as a VPN or TOR to connect to LOIC because he believed that he was participating in a lawful protest. Only those with limited technical skillsets are likely to be prosecuted for DDoS as a form of protest. Those with a modicum of technical savvy will either use a different technology or use LOIC with TOR and/or VPN. This then makes attribution difficult.

12.3 Jurisdiction

Computer crimes often involve parties located abroad. These crimes may involve people located in different jurisdictions, whether they are different states or provinces within a country or different countries altogether. Each jurisdiction may have its own laws dealing with an issue as well as its own unique set of evidence procedures in courts. Uniformity is a real problem. Successful prosecution often involves assistance and cooperation of authorities from an outside jurisdiction. For a variety of reasons, some jurisdictions may or may not be willing to cooperate. Such cooperation generally must proceed through the cogs of bureaucracy in cases where time and access to good digital evidence (unaltered) is of the essence. This often means applying for warrants in multiple jurisdictions, which may translate into a loss of valuable time, and perhaps a loss of obtainable evidence.

The greatest challenge, however, remains in identifying and determining the physical location of the computer, and then the actual individual(s) who used the computer/network to commit a crime. Police in Canada, for example, cannot obtain a warrant to wiretap someone in Mongolia, and they cannot compel an ISP in Papa New Guinea to provide data logs. This type of international policing requires the cooperation of law enforcement and courts in other jurisdictions. Law enforcement could contact authorities in the location of the hacker, but cooperation may not be forthcoming. First, inter-jurisdictional investigations rely on the offence being given similar priority in both jurisdictions. For truly repugnant cases, such as child pornography, jurisdictions tend to have similar strong mandates.[3] In the case of hacking (i.e., unauthorized access), the priorities are often disparate. This is especially true in jurisdictions without computer-misuse offenses. It is of no coincidence that WikiLeaks servers are located in protective jurisdictions. The LulzSec website is rumoured to be located in a protected cloud space.

The situation is somewhat reversed when subpoenas for data logs are sent to US-based communication services such as Google, Twitter, or Facebook. In this instance, the law of the server—where the server is physically located where possible—prevails. For example, if I am a Twitter user located in Australia, an American law-enforcement entity may issue an administrative subpoena without a warrant or transparent declaration of the scope of a criminal investigation to actively retrieve all data logs connected to a hashtag.

For example, one could request all communications, IP addresses, and subscriber information for everyone who communicated in the Occupy Wall Street movement, including those of people around the world. In this sense, the international criminal-justice system, by way of established treaties and data protection of citizens in foreign countries, is subverted. The law of the server (often in the United States) prevails. Where data is hosted on a cloud server, and the physical location is unknown, jurisdiction is even more difficult to ascertain.

The second challenge is related to the first in that police tend to use their resources to respond to local problems. Where there is no victim in the locale of a particular police force, priority there will not be given to an overseas investigation. Third, there is the "de minimus rule," whereby in order to justify valuable police resources, a certain threshold of damages must be met. The jurisdictional hurdles stem from practical considerations as well as a lack of criminalization of an act across jurisdictions.

IFW Global is a company that conducts private investigations of cybercrime and, in particular, criminal-fraud syndicates. In our work (recall that I am on the board of directors) we took down the international fraud group known as the Bristol Boys. The investigation lasted over two years and involved twenty-five separate jurisdictions with registered companies, physical locations of servers and offices, virtual offices, bank accounts, and more—see figure 20.

Figure 20. Jurisdictions Involved with the Bristol Boys Investigation.

Although the case involved online organized cyber fraud, the jurisdictional issues for ethical hacking are similar, especially when people from various points in the world anonymously participate in an ethical-hacking incident.

12.4 Evidence

One of the greatest challenges for ethical-hacking prosecutions is how evidence is obtained. If governments are outsourcing intelligence to security firms, it is likely that many of such firms will use hacking methods to obtain their information. There is no legal mechanism that allows such firms to perform such actions. There is furthermore no way to ensure the accountability of such firms at present. Nowhere was this more apparent than in the WikiLeaks Operation Payback, and the responses by LulzSec and Stratfor.

One assumes that evidence collected by law enforcement is done according to the law, but this too turns out to be a murky legal area. For example, in 2001 the US Federal Bureau of Investigation lured two Russian criminal hackers to Seattle under the guise of a job offer with an FBI-devised corporation, Invita. Alexey Ivanov and Vasily Gorshkov were arrested shortly after arriving to the US. What they thought would be a job interview quickly turned into an interrogation from law enforcement. The two had allegedly broke into the networks of banks and other companies. The FBI remotely installed keylogging Trojan horses on the suspects' computers and collected evidence, including the passwords to email accounts while the pair were at the ruse job interview, where they were asked to prove that they were competent hackers. Incriminating evidence from the suspects' computers and servers utilized for email were used to convict the two on charges under the Computer Fraud and Abuse Act, as well as on twenty counts of conspiring to commit fraud and a number of fraud counts.[4] The evidence was collected without a warrant, but a US court nonetheless deemed the evidence valid, rejecting motions for its suppression. The court ruled that the right against unreasonable search and seizure under the fourth amendment was not violated because the accused had no right to privacy when using computers at "Invita."

12.5 Integrity, Volatility of Evidence, and the Trojan-Horse Defence

Digital evidence suffers from volatility. Volatility refers to the ease by which one may alter or damage evidence, whether it is done accidentally or intentionally. This in turn makes it relatively easy to expunge volatile evidence and to create "reasonable doubt." For example, the mere making of a copy of a file and putting it onto a USB memory stick interferes with the integrity of the digital evidence. Another common example is when an employee with a company's technical division takes it upon herself to view a quick online tutorial then proceeds to install and use forensics software on the company's computer or server. When forensics software and equipment are used without proper training it is probable that the integrity of the evidence will be jeopardized. Forensics investigators, by way of example, use a device which makes tampering with evidence impossible and take a virtual snapshot of a computer or server (if possible), which can then be analyzed at a later date. Without such preventative measures, digital evidence is subject to being expunged from evidence.[5] Forensics investigators have these basic technologies which allow for proper collection and preservation of data. The concern, therefore, is not that such technologies are not widely available or that their cost is prohibitive. The concern is one of education and training. When proper forensics techniques are not used, the integrity of the evidence is lost.

Where technology is involved in a crime, the accused will often use the Trojan-horse or bot defence. In the case of the former, a party claims that they are not responsible for an action but, rather, a malicious software program such as a Trojan was unknowingly downloaded to their computer by a third party. In the bot defence, the argument is that the defendant's computer became a bot and was controlled by a malicious third party. Thus, software or a bot is to blame. In the case of a botnet, it may seem odd that a Trojan-horse defence would be tried when the criminal act is often the very installation of unauthorized software onto someone else's computer. This, however, is not necessarily the case. A botnet master, for example, could argue that his/her computer was being used as a proxy to make it look as though the botnet was installing Trojans. This argument could conceivably extend to the claim that C&Cs were orchestrated to come through his/her computer via malware, where the bots (software programs) were installed by a third party. Alternatively, a botnet master might claim to operate a botnet but could make the argument that a third party (another botnet master) took over his/her botnet through the issuance of an unauthorized bot (software code) to perform illegal acts.

An example of such successful defence is a judgement in the United Kingdom against Aaron Caffrey. Caffrey, aged nineteen, was charged with launching a DDoS attack on September 20, 2001, affecting computers serving the Port of Houston, Texas.[6] The attack caused major havoc with shipping logistics. The accused claimed that a malicious program had been installed on his computer, that he did not perform such acts. The jury acquitted in spite of the fact that upon examination, common hacker tools were found on the defendant's computer, the defendant was a known hacker who regularly participated in discussion of how to launch DDoS attacks and other types of malware, while possible forms of malware were absent on the defendant's computer.[7] The evidence was overwhelmingly in favour of a successful prosecution, but the technical evidence was presented in a confusing manner, which one journalist described as:

> Had the jurors been technology experts, or even computer-literate, I wonder if the ruling would have been the same. I spent most of the first week of the trial in the public gallery and found it didn't take long before the jury's eyes glazed over because the technical arguments sounded like a Russian version of Moby Dick that had been translated into English using Babelfish. By the third day, one of the jury members had to be discharged because of a severe migraine, which was indubitably brought on by the jargon.[8]

This case reinforces that while digital evidence is volatile, even sound evidence can be subject to a Trojan-horse or bot defence due to the inability of jurors and judges to understand the technical complexities of some cybercrime cases.[9] While the Caffrey case did not involve an ethical-hacking incidence, rather an act that is clearly criminal with no justifiable motive, it still portrays the difficulties of prosecution.

12.6 Damages

In theory, if there has been unauthorized access or modification or impairment of data, an investigation may be mounted and perpetrators prosecuted. In practice, often a victim must be able to prove that a certain amount of money was lost or damage was done in order to prompt an investigation.[10] The amount is often pure conjecture. Many jurisdictions have predetermined thresholds amounts in order for an investigation to be launched. Arguably, many forms of unauthorized access or a denial-of-service attack for two hours may not cause enough damage to attract investigation. These thresholds are determined by prosecutorial services. Not all law-enforcement agencies have minimal monetary amounts in order to commence an investigation. In some jurisdictions, a decision to launch an investigation in the case of computer-related cybercrimes is dependent on a wide range of factors, including whether the crime is serious or organized crime, and whether the investigation is within the capabilities of the local police.[11]

That said, when the target of an act of hacktivism or online civil disobedience involves a government website, defence website, or other entities connected to critical infrastructure such as water, electricity, banks, and hospitals, the mere target of the protest makes it a priority for law enforcement.

12.7 Sentencing and Dealing with Mental Disorders—Addiction and Autism Spectrum (with PhD candidate Hannah Rappaport)

Cybersecurity legal cases often involve young men who have autism, are addicted to computers, and sometimes are both autistic and addicted to computers. The medical conditions are first explained below, followed by why cyber security, and in particular hacking, might be appealing to people on the autism spectrum, and why these characteristics may make people on the spectrum particularly talented at cyber security.

Autism is a lifelong neurodevelopmental condition that occurs in approximately 1 per cent of the global population. The term "autism spectrum" is used to reflect the wide scope of abilities and difficulties found within the autism community. The most recent version of the Diagnostic and Statistical Manual of Mental Disorders defines autism-spectrum disorder as a deficit in social communication and social interaction, marked by restricted and repetitive behaviour, interests, or activities, with early onset. Unfortunately, this description focuses solely on the difficulties experienced by people on the autism spectrum and fails to acknowledge strengths that are often found in autistic individuals. A study investigating rates and types of savant skills in 137 autistic individuals found that thirty-nine individuals (28.5 per cent) met criteria for a savant or exceptional cognitive skill, although previous estimates have been lower. A postal survey of 5,400 parents of autistic children found that 531 (9.8 per cent) were reported to have savant abilities. Of this subset, the most common skills were music (53 per cent), memory (40 per cent), mathematical/calculation skills (25 per cent), and art (19 per cent).

A growing body of research suggests that autistic individuals who are considered high functioning (i.e., average or above average intelligence) outperform their neurologically typical counterparts in a variety of visual local perceptual processing tasks, such as finding shapes embedded in a complex background. Autistic individuals also perform better in Raven's matrices, a nonverbal fluid-intelligence test in which participants use analytical abilities to complete visual patterns. One study found that autistics were on average 40 per cent faster than neurotypicals in solving the matrices.

Capabilities in visual perception are invaluable to the cyber-security sector, where the ability to spot anomalies in large data sets is paramount. Indeed, there is a growing interest in the skills and talents that people on the autism spectrum can bring to the workplace. For example, in 2012 the Israel Defense Forces established an intelligence unit, called Ro'im Rachok ("seeing far"), which specifically recruits high-functioning autistic teenagers and young adults to analyze aerial reconnaissance photographs. The unit was founded by two former Mossad agents who recognized that certain individuals on the autism spectrum may be uniquely skilled in noticing anomalies in complex images. While software may one day replace the human decipherer, the leaders of the unit believe that this is not yet on the horizon. In addition to the military benefits, the Ro'im Rachok program facilitates social interaction, encourages independence, and helps participants to prepare for future careers.

The Israelis are not the only ones who have noticed the employment potential in the autism community. In March of 2017, the

Defence Academy of the United Kingdom hosted a collaborative industry event to discuss the skill sets of people on the autism spectrum and how these skills could fill gaps in the cyber sector.

A number of companies, including Microsoft and EY, are also beginning to recognize that people on the autism spectrum may provide invaluable skills to their workforce, and such companies are now dedicated to training and employing autistic adults. Burgeoning interest in recruiting autistic individuals is an exciting development, given that currently only 16 per cent of adults with autism are estimated to be in full-time employment. Autistic talent is often missed due to overreliance on the interview process in employment or to the lack of flexibility on the part of companies.

While some governments and organizations are looking to use the unique skillset of individuals on the spectrum, the unemployment rate remains very high among this group. It is of no surprise, then, that a higher than normal portion of "hackers," ethical or otherwise, are on the spectrum.

We have seen in previous chapters participation in ethical hacking by LulzSec member Ryan Cleary, activist Aaron Swartz, and hacker Adrian Lamo—all identified as being on the autism spectrum, having Asperger's syndrome. Recall that Cleary was involved in the highly controversial WikiLeaks MasterCard showdown with Stratfor.[12]

The nineteen-year-old Cleary was also arrested in Essex in the United Kingdom, where was charged under the Computer Misuse Act for his hacking effort of the UK's Serious Organised Crime Agency. He is alleged to have broken into many other law-enforcement agencies, both in the United Kingdom and the United States. Cleary is purportedly a member of LulzSec. He is said to suffer from agoraphobia and he has been diagnosed with Asperger's and attention-deficit disorder. Similar cases against hackers in the United Kingdom, Australia, and New Zealand in the last ten years have involved people addicted to computers, those who suffer from agoraphobia, and others on the spectrum disorder or have attention-deficit disorder. A hacker who went by the handle Wandii was acquitted on all counts of computer misuse in the United Kingdom due to a computer addiction. A nineteen-year-old New Zealand hacker, Owen Walker, was brought up on several charges of computer misuse. The first charge was under section 252(1) of the New Zealand Crimes Act 1961, accessing a computer system without authorization. The second charge related to interfering with a computer system under section 250(2)(c) of the act. The third charge was the use of a computer system for dishonest purpose under section 249(2)(a). He was additionally charged under section 251(a) and (b) of the act for possession of software for the purpose of committing a crime. Walker pleaded guilty to all charges. He could have been sentenced to up to sixteen years of imprisonment under the four offences, but was instead discharged without conviction and was ordered to pay NZD$9,526 in reparation, as well as to relinquish any assets acquired as a result of gains he achieved through the use of his botnet. The court noted that Walker committed the crimes over a two-year period when he was aged sixteen to eighteen. The court heard evidence of Walker's difficulty in socializing due to Asperger's syndrome. Walker now works in Melbourne, Australia, for Telstra (the largest telecoms and ISP in Australia). There has been no study that has looked at the link, if any, between agoraphobia, Asperger's, or attention-deficit disorder and hackers.

Aaron Swartz, a renowned computer-science genius and passionate human-rights advocate, was arrested by MIT campus police and a US Secret Service officer on break-and-enter charges in 2011. Swartz had been downloading the JSTOR repository[13] (JSTOR is a non-profit organization that compiles academic journal articles, many of which, held in its digital library, are protected by copyright laws), and it was suspected that Swartz intended to put the contents of the database online so that everyone—whether rich or poor, educated or not—could have open access to these articles.

The threat of thirteen separate counts of wire fraud and other serious computer offences, which could have seen him jailed for over thirty-five years and liable for US$1,0000,000 in fines, proved to be too much for Swartz, who committed suicide, aged twenty-six. Swartz had authorized access to several of MIT's databases, including JSTOR, and there is a good chance that he would not have been found guilty of the charges. Clearly an action for copyright infringement would have provided the most appropriate remedy if Swartz was liable, yet the government chose a different path, to prosecute.

It is alleged within internal hacking circles[14] that the real controversy was that Swartz was the source of many confidential leaks to WikiLeaks, and in particular certain congressional research reports, which may have been part of the **Guerrilla Open Access Manifesto**, a movement that Swartz had started. The congressional reports in question were not in the public domain; they are often used as a type of currency or bartered good among lobbyists and special-interest groups. There are many proponents to making these reports available to the public, including support from US Senator John McCain, the 2008 Republican presidential nominee (now deceased). It *might* also be the case that Aaron aided in the leak of the Manning materials, US military documents (mostly about the war in Iraq and Afghanistan) unlawfully released by US Private Bradley Manning to WikiLeaks. It is perhaps of no coincidence that Swartz's home was searched and computer equipment seized around the same time as the Manning material was published. It is also interesting to note that if you Google "the Manning materials" or "Manning materials" you will not be sent to WikiLeaks or other mirror sites. You will only find media coverage of the Bradley Manning trial and conviction. This is of no coincidence. These materials have been removed by companies such as Google by order of the United States government, though you will find no legal documents to support this removal as such requests are secret under national-security legislation.

The case of Lamo was perhaps the most curious. Adrian Lamo was convicted in 2003 for hacking into the network of the *New York Times*, among other targets and other hacks.[15] He too is identified as having Asperger's syndrome. The curious part, however, is that he was the FBI informant who handed over evidence that led to the discovery and arrest of Bradley Manning. How Lamo was linked to Manning remains surrounded with questions. What is particularly intriguing is the that you have three individuals involved with WikiLeaks in very different ways who are all on the autism spectrum.

Individuals on the autism spectrum charged with hacking offences have been treated differently depending on the jurisdiction. In New Zealand, a nineteen-year-old man charged with several counts of computer offences was given a suspended sentence, ordered to pay a modicum of damages for a DDoS attack against Carnegie Melon, then was recruited by Telstra and the New Zealand police to work for them.[16] Contrast this with the United States, where some individuals on the spectrum have been given twenty-five-year sentences.[17] Others have been given suspended sentences provided they become FBI informants and betray others, as has been the case with members of Anonymous who turned on other members.[18]

12.8 Observations

Ethical hacking is a messy area with no clear or obvious legal reso-
lution. There has been no research to date that examines how many
hackers and ethical hackers have Autism or common diagnoses. If
this eventual research reveals a connection, more thought will need
be given as to how to best deal with this.

A most problematic theme has emerged with hacktivism. Many
hacktivists seek to rebel against what they perceive to be unjust policies or measures that infringe against civil liberties. As a consequence
of the flurry of hacktivist activities, however, governments around
the globe are using more and more forms of surveillance, and civil
liberties are eroding further than in the pre-hacktivism era. At this
point, it is a vicious circle with laws being broken by both sides.

It would be interesting to see what degree of law-enforcement
resources are being allocated to hacktivist investigations compared
with resources allocated to the fight of online organized crime, such
as in mass fraud, identity theft, and corporate espionage. The other
aspect in this area that is rarely spoken about is the visibility of hacktivists. Hacktivists often perform acts that are deliberately public or
done in a matter to get media attention to a cause. Other malicious
entities sit silently on systems, performing far more nefarious acts.
But because they are stealthy there is less attention and certainly
less prosecution. A more detailed look at the legal provisions from
the Convention on Cybercrimes and the Canadian Criminal Code
is found in table 4.

Table 4. Comparison of Convention on Cybercrime and Canadian Criminal Framework (expanded)

Convention on Cybercrime	Canada
Offences against the confidentiality and availability of computer data and systems	
Article 2—Illegal access Each Party shall adopt such legislative and other measures as may be necessary to establish as criminal offences under its domestic law, when committed intentionally, the access to the whole or any part of a computer system without right. A Party may require that the offence be committed by infringing security measures, with the intent of obtaining computer data or other dishonest intent, or in relation to a computer system that is connected to another computer system.	**Section 342.1 of the Criminal Code** Unauthorized use of computer to commit an offence in relation to Section 430. Computer System = a device that, or a group of interconnected or related devices, one or more of which, (a) contains computer programs or other data, and (b) pursuant to computer programs, (i) performs logic and control, and (ii) may perform any other function Data = representations of information or of concepts that are being prepared or have been prepared in a form suitable for use in a computer system
Article 3—Illegal interception Each Party shall adopt such legislative and other measures as may be necessary to establish as criminal offences under its domestic law, when committed intentionally, the interception without right, made by technical means, of non-public transmissions of computer data to, from or within a computer system, including electromagnetic emissions from a computer system carrying such computer data. A Party may require that the offence be committed with dishonest intent, or in relation to a computer system that is connected to another computer system.	

Convention on Cybercrime	Canada
Article 4—Data interference 1. Each Party shall adopt such legislative and other measures as may be necessary to establish as criminal offences under its domestic law, when committed intentionally, the damaging, deletion, deterioration, alteration or suppression of computer data without right. 2. A Party may reserve the right to require that the conduct described in paragraph 1 result in serious harm.	**Section 430 (1.1) of the Criminal Code** Commits mischief which amounts to an indictable offence for the wilful destroying, altering or interferes with the lawful use of data
Article 5—System interference Each Party shall adopt such legislative and other measures as may be necessary to establish as criminal offences under its domestic law, when committed intentionally, the serious hindering without right of the functioning of a computer system by inputting, transmitting, damaging, deleting, deteriorating, altering or suppressing computer data.	

Article 6—Misuse of devices
1. Each Party shall adopt such legislative and other measures as may be necessary to establish as criminal offences under its domestic law, when committed intentionally and without right:
a) the production, sale, procurement for use, import, distribution or otherwise making available of:
  i) a device, including a computer program, designed or adapted primarily for the purpose of committing any of the offences established in accordance with Articles 2 through 5;
  ii) a computer password, access code, or similar data by which the whole or any part of a computer system is capable of being accessed, with intent that it be used for the purpose of committing any of the offences established in Articles 2 through 5; and
	Section 326 (1)(b) of the Criminal Code
	Commits theft who fraudulently, maliciously or without a colour of right uses any telecommunication facility or obtains any telecommunication services
	
	Section 327 (1) of the Criminal Code
	Without lawful excuse, the proof of which lies on him, manufactures, possesses, sells or offers for sale or distributes any instrument or device or any component thereof, the design of which renders it primarily useful for obtaining the use of any telecommunication facility or service, under circumstances that give rise to a reasonable inference that the device has been used or is or was intended to be used to obtain the use of

Convention on Cybercrime	Canada
b) the possession of an item referred to in paragraphs a.i or ii above, with intent that it be used for the purpose of committing any of the offences established in Articles 2 through 5. A Party may require by law that a number of such items be possessed before criminal liability attaches. 2. This article shall not be interpreted as imposing criminal liability where the production, sale, procurement for use, import, distribution or otherwise making available or possession referred to in paragraph 1 of this article is not for the purpose of committing an offence established in accordance with Articles 2 through 5 of this Convention, such as for the authorised testing or protection of a computer system. 3. Each Party may reserve the right not to apply paragraph 1 of this article, provided that the reservation does not concern the sale, distribution or otherwise making available of the items referred to in paragraph 1 a.ii of this article.	any telecommunication facility or service without payment of a lawful charge therefor, is guilty of an indictable offence.
Forgery and online fraud	
Article 7 Each Party shall adopt such legislative and other measures as may be necessary to establish as criminal offences under its domestic law, when committed intentionally and without right, the input, alteration, deletion, or suppression of computer data, resulting in inauthentic data with the intent that it be considered or acted upon for legal purposes as if it were authentic, regardless whether or not the data is directly readable and intelligible. A Party may require an intent to defraud, or similar dishonest intent, before criminal liability attaches.	**Section 366 of the Criminal Code** Deals largely with forgery and offences resembling forgery. However, there are no provisions for forgery committed by the way of alteration of computer data resulting in inauthentic data with intent to be considered or acted upon as if it were authentic.

Convention on Cybercrime	Canada
Article 8 Each Party shall adopt such legislative and other measures as may be necessary to establish as criminal offences under its domestic law, when committed intentionally and without right, the causing of a loss of property to another person by: a) any input, alteration, deletion or suppression of computer data, b) any interference with the functioning of a computer system, with fraudulent or dishonest intent of procuring, without right, an economic benefit for oneself or for another person.	**Part X of the Criminal Code** Deals largely with fraud and related fraudulent conduct. However, there are no provisions for fraud committed of computer data using a computer system.
Child sexual exploitation materials	
Article 9 1. Each Party shall adopt such legislative and other measures as may be necessary to establish as criminal offences under its domestic law, when committed intentionally and without right, the following conduct: a) producing child pornography for the purpose of its distribution through a computer system; b) offering or making available child pornography through a computer system; c) distributing or transmitting child pornography through a computer system; d) procuring child pornography through a computer system for oneself or for another person; e) possessing child pornography in a computer system or on a computer-data storage medium. 2. For the purpose of paragraph 1 above, the term "child pornography" shall include pornographic material that visually depicts: a) a minor engaged in sexually explicit conduct;	**Section 163.1 of the Criminal Code** Subsection 1—Definition Similar to Clause 2, 3 & 4 in corresponding Article Subsection 2—Making child pornography No indication of said offence depicting production of child pornography for the purpose of its distribution through a computer system. Subsection 3—Distribution Distribution of any child pornography guilty of an indictable offence punishable on summary convictions. No indication of said offence depicting offering or make available or distribute or transmit or procure of child pornography through a computer system. Subsection 4—Possession No indication of said offence depicting possession of child pornography in a computer system or on a computer-data storage medium.

Convention on Cybercrime	Canada
b) a person appearing to be a minor engaged in sexually explicit conduct; c) realistic images representing a minor engaged in sexually explicit conduct. 3. For the purpose of paragraph 2 above, the term "minor" shall include all persons under 18 years of age. A Party may, however, require a lower age-limit, which shall be not less than 16 years. 4. Each Party may reserve the right not to apply, in whole or in part, paragraphs 1, sub-paragraphs d. and e, and 2, sub-paragraphs b. and c.	*An Act respecting the mandatory reporting of Internet child pornography by persons who provide an Internet service, SC 2011, c 4.* Act that requires mandatory report of Internet child pornography activities by Internet providers. Corresponding Regulation: Internet Child Pornography Reporting Regulations, SOR/2011-292
Copyright infringement	

Article 10
1. Each Party shall adopt such legislative and other measures as may be necessary to establish as criminal offences under its domestic law the infringement of copyright, as defined under the law of that Party, pursuant to the obligations it has undertaken under the Paris Act of 24 July 1971 revising the Bern Convention for the Protection of Literary and Artistic Works, the Agreement on Trade-Related Aspects of Intellectual Property Rights and the WIPO Copyright Treaty, with the exception of any moral rights conferred by such conventions, where such acts are committed wilfully, on a commercial scale and by means of a computer system.
 	
2. Each Party shall adopt such legislative and other measures as may be necessary to establish as criminal offences under its domestic law the infringement of related rights, as defined under the law of that Party, pursuant to the obligations it has undertaken under the International Convention for the Protection of Performers, Producers of Phonograms and Broadcasting
	**Section 42 of the Copyright Act
	Criminal Remedies**
	
	Offences
	42 (1) Every person commits an offence who knowingly
	   (a) makes for sale or rental an infringing copy of a work or other subject-matter in which copyright subsists;
	   (b) sells or rents out, or by way of trade exposes or offers for sale or rental, an infringing copy of a work or other subject-matter in which copyright subsists;
	   (c) distributes infringing copies of a work or other subject-matter in which copyright subsists, either for the purpose of trade or to such an extent as to affect prejudicially the owner of the copyright;
	   (d) by way of trade exhibits in public an infringing copy of a work or other subject-matter in which copyright subsists;

Convention on Cybercrime	Canada
Organisations (Rome Convention), the Agreement on Trade-Related Aspects of Intellectual Property Rights and the WIPO Performances and Phonograms Treaty, with the exception of any moral rights conferred by such conventions, where such acts are committed wilfully, on a commercial scale and by means of a computer system. 3. A Party may reserve the right not to impose criminal liability under paragraphs 1 and 2 of this article in limited circumstances, provided that other effective remedies are available and that such reservation does not derogate from the Party's international obligations set forth in the international instruments referred to in paragraphs 1 and 2 of this article.	(e) possesses, for sale, rental, distribution for the purpose of trade or exhibition in public by way of trade, an infringing copy of a work or other subject-matter in which copyright subsists; (f) imports, for sale or rental, into Canada any infringing copy of a work or other subject-matter in which copyright subsists; or (g) exports or attempts to export, for sale or rental, an infringing copy5 of a work or other subject-matter in which copyright subsists. **Possession and performance offences** **(2)** Every person commits an offence who knowingly (a) makes or possesses any plate that is specifically designed or adapted for the purpose of making infringing copies of any work or other subject-matter in which copyright subsists; or (b) for private profit causes to be performed in public, without the consent of the owner of the copyright, any work or other subject-matter in which copyright subsists.

Convention on Cybercrime	Canada
	Punishment
	(2.1) Every person who commits an offence under subsection (1) or (2) is liable
	(a) on conviction on indictment, to a fine of not more than $1,000,000 or to imprisonment for a term of not more than five years or to both; or
	(b) on summary conviction, to a fine of not more than $25,000 or to imprisonment for a term of not more than six months or to both.

Notes

1. Lovet 2009.
2. Lovet 2009, p. 2.
3. Wall 2007.
4. *United States of America v. Gorshkov.*
5. Klein 2010.
6. The case is not reported in law databases but was covered by the British media and is mentioned by several cybercrime researchers. See BBC News, "Questions Cloud Cyber Crime Cases." The case is cited as *R v. Caffrey* (2006) in Clayton 2006.
7. Grabosky 2007.
8. Brenner, Carrier, and Henninger 2004.
9. Walden 2010.
10. de Villiers 2003.
11. Correspondence with Detective Van der Graf, head of the fraud squad, New South Wales Police.
12. Batty 2011.
13. Poulsen 2013.
14. This information has been given to me in confidence from a reliable source.
15. Poulsen 2010.
16. *Sydney Morning Herald*, "Telstra offshoot hires teen hacker 'Akill.'"
17. Ronson 2009; Poulsen 2010.
18. Bastone and Goldberg 2014.

CHAPTER XIII

Ethical Hacking, Whistle-Blowing, and Human Rights and Freedoms

If we accept Martin Luther King Jr.'s statement "injustice any-where is a threat to justice everywhere" as true—as I believe we must—we should be grateful that, in the twenty-first century, the Internet provides an effective medium to expose grave injustices perpetuated around the world. While it is not suggested that the Internet itself offers a solution to correct these problems, its exis-tence enables the facilitation of the first of King's four basic steps in a non-violent campaign: "[C]ollection of the facts to determine whether injustices are alive." While it is accepted that the quality of information provided might be affected by personal opinions and beliefs, or may be manipulated, it still enables the collection and discussion of injustices throughout the world. King's discussion of being "caught in an inescapable network of mutuality, tied in a single garment of destiny" reminds us of metaphors of the Internet as a net or a web. King's remarks portend the capability of the Internet to enable protest from anywhere about activities anywhere because of the Internet's proliferation, and because it is not tied down to a geographical location.

In my interview with hacker and hacktivism expert Dr. Dreyfus, she stated that there was usually a correlation between the number of participants in an online protest and the worthiness and morality of the cause.[1] While this finding suggests that the unnoticed pleas for support using social media are less meritorious in the eyes of the masses, this must be considered against King's assertion that "if repressed emotions do not come out in these nonviolent ways, they will come out in ominous expressions of violence." It is worth considering here a movement by Ronny Edry, an Israeli graphic designer, who posted an image on Facebook showing himself with his daughter along with the graphic: "Iranians, we will never bomb your country. We [heart] you." The image garnered such international support it became a catalyst for dialogue between the people of two nations on the brink of war.[2] The point of this is to illustrate the effectiveness of non-violent forms of protestation and really emphasize the values exposed by King. "I [heart] Iran," however, is very different from the acts of hacktivism and online civil disobedience covered in this book.

In many instances, it is not difficult for us to look at some of these hacking acts differing only with regard to intent. While we may agree, for instance, that hacking into the Sony database as an act to contest Sony's lapse security practices breaks the law, we might also agree that such hacktivists should not be prosecuted or punished in the same fashion as someone who hacked into the system for personal and financial gain (e.g., stole and then used third-party credit-card information). It becomes more difficult to see acts of denial of service or online defacements as criminal acts attracting harsh sentences of computer offences under the criminal law. Should DDoS attacks be seen more as acts of political barricades? Should online defacements be considered as a form of leafleting or picketing? What role does freedom of expression and freedom of peaceful association play in this equation?

13.1 The Canadian Charter of Human Rights and Freedoms

The Canadian Charter of Human Rights and Freedoms[3] is the constitutional framework in Canada that legally provides for rights and freedoms for not only Canadian citizens but for those physically in Canada. The Charter is used in this chapter as a way of engaging the content through the lens of human rights. The Charter is further considered one of the strongest protections of human rights of any legal framework in the world. Courts around the world look to decisions rendered under the Charter for guidance in their own jurisdictions.

Online civil-disobedience participants are motivated by the same reasons as participants in traditional off-line acts of civil disobedience. For example, consider the off-line and online acts of civil disobedience in table 5.

Table 5. Off-line and Online Comparison

Off-Line	Online
Sit-ins	Virtual sit-ins
Barricades	Denial-of-service attacks and website redirection
Political graffiti	Website defacements
Wildcat strikes	Denial-of-service attacks and website redirection
Underground presses	Site parodies, blogs, Facebook protests
Petitions	Web petitions (e.g., Facebook likes)
Whistle-blowing	Unauthorized taking of information (often via hacking) and leaking it to another organization or to the media

Table 6 presents some off-line acts and provides the relevant Charter protection as well as leading case law and legal principles.

Table 6. Leading Case Law and Legal Principles

Action	Charter Protection	Legal Principles	Leading Case Law
Picketing	• Freedom of Expression (s. 2b of the Canadian Charter and art. 3 Quebec Charter of Human Rights and Freedoms) • Freedom of Peaceful Assembly and Association (s. 2(c) of the Canadian Charter and art. 3 of the Quebec Charter)	• Picketing falls under freedom of expression. • It does not extend to acts of violence. • It does not extend to destruction of property, assault or other unlawful conduct. • Picketing may be restricted if it is inconsistent with the function of the place it takes place in. • Injunction is unlikely to be granted if the police can control the situation.	• *K Mart Canada Ltd v. United Food and Commercial Workers* • *R.W.D.S.U., Local 558 v. Pepsi-Cola Canada Beverages* • *Dolphin Delivery Ltd v. RWDSU* • *Chum Ltd v. NABET* • *Blackstone Industrial Products Ltd. v. Parsons (1979)* • *Ontario Public Service Employees Union v. Ontario (Attorney General)*

Action	Charter Protection	Legal Principles	Leading Case Law
Protesting	• Freedom of Expression (s. 2b of the Canadian Charter and s. X Quebec Charter) • Freedom of Peaceful Assembly and Association (s. 2(c) of the Canadian Charter and art. 3 of the Quebec Charter)	• Comes within freedom of expression because it is an effort to influence social/political decisions. • Comes within peaceful assembly because it allows assembly for the purposes of protesting state action. • Unlawful strikes are still protected as "expression." • However, not all government property can be used as a physical areas on which to protest. • Public streets can be. • As with picketing, it can be restricted if it is inconsistent with the function of the place it occurs in.	• *HEU & BCTF et al. v. HEABC & BCPSEA* • *Re General Motors*
Graffiti	• Freedom of Expression (s. 2b of the Canadian Charter and art. 3 Quebec Charter)	• Graffiti falls under freedom of expression because the forms of "expression" can be written and/or artistic. • If the graffiti contains political commentary and social expression, it is protected by the Charter.	• *Ontario (Attorney-General) v. Dieleman, 1994 CanLII 7509 (ON SC)* • *Cherneskey v. Armadale Publishers Ltd. (1978), 1978 CanLII 20 (SCC), 90 D.L.R. (3d) 321 at p 330*

Action	Charter Protection	Legal Principles	Leading Case Law
		• This protection also extends to pictures or photos. • Offensive or insulting graffiti is not reason enough to restrict it. • If the act involves violence it is not protected by the Charter. • Some suggestion that neither Canadian nor Quebec Charters protect property damage.	• *Irwin Toy Ltd. v. Quebec (Attorney-General), supra, at p 606-8* • *R. c. Quickfall, 1993 CanLII 3509 (QC CA)*

Let us use Anonymous's Operation Titstorm as an example for our discussion. Participating in a denial-of-service attack against a parliamentary website is a form of protest. In this case, it was to protest censorship in Australia. The DDoS attack could be considered similar to a barricade. In this instance, images of penises and breasts were also displayed on the parliamentary website. It is difficult to see this SQL injection as being different from a form of picketing or leafleting outside of a parliament with similar images, or similar to spraying graffiti, albeit distasteful. The intent is the same—protesting government censorship.

In the Canadian context, freedom is a constitutional right under subchapter 2(b) of the Charter.[4] It has never been an absolute right in Canada. Freedom of expression is rationalized under three main ways: it is essential to democracy, it is an instrument of truth, and it is an instrument of personal fulfilment.[5] The Supreme Court of Canada accepted these rationales in *Irwin Toy v. Quebec*.[6] In *Irwin Toy*, the province of Quebec had introduced legislation targeting commercial advertising to children under the age of thirteen. This meant, for example, that commercial advertisements for toys during morning television cartoon programs were not allowed. Irwin Toy company unsuccessfully challenged the Quebec legislation on the grounds that it was an unlawful restriction on freedom of expression.

A number of cases following *Irwin Toy* further articulated these freedom-of-expression rationales.[7]

The Supreme Court's decision in *Kmart*[8] held that consumer leafleting was to be distinguished from other forms of picketing, such as striking employees. In *Kmart*, the court found that statutory regulation of labour strikes could be justified, but that such acts differed substantially from acts such as consumer leafleting. Depending on the content of an SQL injection, one could easily see the act as a form of consumer leafleting or of a public protest—both acts are protected under the Charter. *Irwin Toy* gave a broad power of freedom of expression, while *Kmart* gave a limited power for, as per the Charter, "freedom of peaceful assembly."

In *Dolphin Delivery*,[9] the Supreme Court of Canada, as per Justice McIntyre, stated that:

> There is always an element of expression in picketing. The Union
> is making a statement to the general public that it is involved
> in a dispute. This freedom doesn't extend to threats of violence.
> It would not protect the destruction of property, or assaults, or
> other clearly unlawful conduct.

In the case of a DDoS protest to a government website, such as the parliamentary website, which acts as an online a directory of Members of Parliament, it is difficult to see how blocking access for a short period of time would constitute the destruction of property. Once the protest stops, the website commences functioning again exactly as it did pre-protest. Indeed, there is no physical damage or destruction of property.

In *Ontario Public Service Employees Union*,[10] strikers picketed in front of provincial courts, thereby blocking access to the courts. The Supreme Court held that while picketing falls within the ambit of freedom of expression, an injunction to limit the activity was considered reasonable as access to courts is seen as an integral part of the rule of law. The question then becomes whether blocking access to a website can be seen as interfering with the rule of law. Here there are two hurdles. The first is how does one impose an injunction restricting a DDoS attack? This may be very difficult as it requires knowledge of who is protesting, addresses to serve notice (usually information links back to an IP address or a device and not an individual), and can only be served (at least easily) to people participating in the attack in Canada. The second hurdle is one of rule-of-law threshold. Preventing people from accessing a court runs clearly in the face of impeding the law and rule-of-law principles. A DDoS attack against a website or portal for electronic submission of court documents might also be seen as impeding the rule of law. Impeding access, however, to information found on parliamentary websites strays far from principles of the rule of law. The Parliament of Australia website has information about senators and members, information on how the Senate and House of Representatives works, list of the various committees, current bills, and provides access to the Parliamentary Budget Office and Parliamentary Library.[11] The website provides information and is not the sole provider for such widely available public information. If the DDoS protest had occurred on a more specific government website preventing people from accessing health portals, social assistance, or immigration portals, then this becomes more about restricting access to essential services, which could be argued to limit sections 2(b) and 2(c) of the Charter. Not being able to access the parliamentary website, however, for a day or two neither impedes the rule of law or essential services. It is difficult to see how such activity should not be seen as a legitimate and protected protest.

Of course, online acts of civil disobedience and hacktivism have a unique feature—they are potentially more inclusive. There may be 100,000 people spread across North America who wish to protest army deployment or climate-change policy, but it is extremely difficult, and for some impossible, to meet up in person to protest on the ground. Online platforms by their very nature can enable people from disparate backgrounds and physical locations to join in solidarity for a cause.

As we saw in chapter 7, the #TellVicEverything Twitter campaign was lawful and fell outside of criminal-law provisions on unauthorized access and use of interference. However, we noted that if the same volume of traffic for the exact same purpose would have been directed at a website, causing it to crash, this would become a DDoS event, subjecting participants to the possibility of being prosecuted. Same method, same intent. Because one cannot "crash" or "DDoS" Twitter or a Twitter feed (or it would be extremely difficult), this is considered a legitimate form of protest. Using LOIC to launch a DDoS event at a website or server could trigger a response from prosecutors seeking to apply criminal-law legislation. It will be interesting to see how higher courts deal with similar online acts of protests in the years to come.

13.2 Whistle-Blowing and Ethical Hacking

Hacktivism, as we have seen, goes beyond mere barricades and political graffiti, escalating to acts more aligned with whistle-blowing, as systems are often broken into to retrieve data. There is either unauthorized access where the person did have authority to view or copy documents and/or there is an unauthorized use where the person may have had authority to access the documents but such authority was subject to restrictions on consequent uses.

Whistle-blowing is the disclosure of illegal, immoral, or illegitimate practices of an organization by a member or employee of the organization.[12] Disclosure could be to the media, to a regulatory authority, or to the public in general (such as via disclosure on a website). Whistle-blowing involves the disclosure of otherwise confidential information where it is a matter of "public interest." Many jurisdictions have enacted legislation that shields a whistle-blowing member or employee of a government, corporation, or organization from criminal sanction and legal liability, including copyright. As will be seen, this protection is not, however, absolute.

The concepts of external and internal whistle-blowing are somewhat confusing.[13] The terms "external" and "internal" refer to the recipients of the information and not to the person who exposes the information. An internal whistle-blower is a member or employee of an organization who sends leaked information to someone within the organization. External whistle-blowing occurs when the person chooses to share the information with someone external of the organization. In some jurisdictions, both internal and external whistle-blowers are protected under the law, while in other jurisdictions the recipient must be internal.

Whistle-blowers enjoy legal protection in many jurisdictions. The United States, the United Kingdom, Canada, and Australia all have whistle-blowing legislation. Depending on which jurisdiction, whistle-blowers are protected from criminal charges, civil liability, and being fired for disclosing information about corrupt, illegal, or immoral practices of governments and corporations.

When someone external to an organization exposes wrongdoing they are not considered a whistle-blower and they are not shielded from criminal sanction and legal liability. Third parties, therefore, are not protected by whistle-blower legislation. If an ethical hacker, for example, obtains a document by gaining unauthorized access to a computer, they are not considered a whistle-blower under legislation in the United States, the United Kingdom, Canada, and Australia. The primary goal of whistle-blowing legislation is to reduce—if not prevent—retaliation for exposure of malpractice or wrongdoing in the workplace. The goal of whistle-blowing has never been given a broad interpretation to cover third parties. Regardless of who blows the whistle and why someone blows the whistle, whether they be a government employee or an ethical hacker, the goal remains essentially the same—to expose wrongdoing.

Ethical hackers are often not afforded legal protection when they disclose corrupt, illegal, or immoral practices of governments and corporations, as they are third parties in the disclosure process. Whistle-blowing legislation only offers protection to employees or members of an organization, which does not extend to third parties. In a typical scenario, an ethical hacker will access a database without authorization to retrieve information on corrupt practices. This information will then be published to a website, given to a newspaper and/or submitted to a leak site. This unauthorized access of data, a database or computer will constitute a criminal offence in Australia, the United States, the United Kingdom, Canada, and in many other countries. Most jurisdictions have enacted computer-related offences, which are often referred to as unauthorized access, modification, or interference to data systems or electronic communications. Such criminal provisions generally address situations where any component of a computer (hard drive, software, network) is tampered with allowing for unauthorized access, modification, impairment, or interference to data or a data system. The very nature of hacking—whether it be to expose corrupt practices or out of mere curiosity—involves the exploration (and sometimes exploitation) of vulnerabilities which, at a minimum, involve unauthorized access to data. There are no public-interest exemptions to criminal-computer offences in any jurisdiction.[14]

13.3 Observations

"May you live in interesting times"… an expression that, as they say, can be a blessing or a curse. Never before has so much information been at the disposal of humankind. We have the ability to participate in online citizenship, to hide our identities behind encryption technologies, express our opinions no matter how misinformed or treacherous to anyone anywhere, to deliberately misinform others, to set trends, to share information, to manipulate data, and to participate in online protests in whatever form they may take. Our digital ecosystem and ways of communicating and thinking are changing due to technology.

Politicians and courts are often slow to adapt to the reality of the society in which they live. People, and younger generations in particular, have grown up in a digital world. People are so reliant on technology that it is a part of their everyday ecosystem to the point where the evolution of neurological connections in a human brain are adapting to technology exposure. It is not simply that people expect to do things online or through digital technologies; cognitively, the brain works differently now than it did twenty or thirty years ago by virtue of the fact that our neurological pathways change when we use technologies.[15] Neural pathways also change when we play or listen to music or make art.

Is it acceptable for one generation to curtail and insist upon set methods for online protests for younger generations? Is this the same as an entity requiring something to be handwritten, or typed on a typewriter as opposed to using a computer? Or insisting that people get to work by horse and buggy? Or that females may not drive a car? While these questions are somewhat sensationalized, they still get at the essence of the matter. To what extent is it permissible to insist on specific mediums of protest? Does this no longer make sense? As will be seen in the next chapter, I will advocate for changes to regulatory frameworks to better accommodate forms of hacking that fall within the range of ethical hacking.

Notes

1. Interview with Dreyfus, December 2010, Sydney, Australia.
2. Edry, "Israel and Iran."
3. Canadian Charter of Rights and Freedoms.
4. Canadian Charter of Rights and Freedoms.
5. See Moon 2000.
6. *Irwin Toy v. Quebec.*

7. *Edmonton Journal v. Alberta; R v. Keegstra; Dagenais v. Canadian Broadcasting Corp.; R. v. Sharpe;* and *R v. Zundel.*

8. *U.F.C.W., Local 1518 v. Kmart Canada Ltd.* This followed from the earlier Supreme Court decision in *R.W.D.S.U. v. Dolphin Delivery Ltd.*

9. *R.W.D.S.U. v. Dolphin Delivery Ltd.*

10. *Lavigne v. Ontario Public Service Employees Union.*

11. https://www.aph.gov.au.

12. A. J. Brown (n.d.). See also Gobert and Punch 2000.

13. Dworkin and Baucas 1998.

14. Maurushat, A. 2013.

15. Von Ooyen A. and Butz-Ostendorg M. *The Rewiring Brain.* Academic Press (an Imprint of Elsevier), 2017.

CHAPTER XIV

Toward an Ethical-Hacking Framework

14.1 Ethical Hacking in Context

Ethical hacking is a complex area. This book broke down ethical hacking into online civil disobedience, hacktivism, counterattack/hackback, penetration/intrusion testing and vulnerabilities, and security activism. We used a mixed-methods approach in chapter 3 to capture emerging ethical-hacking incidences as found in the media, blogs, law databases, and forums on the Dark Net. Chapters 4 through 6 looked at over 200 of the most interesting legal cases and incidences of ethical hacking across the globe. Chapters 7 through 11 used case studies to provide a deeper understanding around motivation, techniques, ethical issues, and other considerations.

The online civil-disobedience chapter compared online versus off-line protests, and argued that the characterization of online civil disobedience as criminal versus off-line protests as legitimate was inappropriate in the digital age. Likewise, the penalties for online civil disobedience were disproportionate with the form of protest. We saw that some people who participated in acts of online civil disobedience believed that their actions were lawful forms of protest. There were no legal exemptions for acts of online civil disobedience under most criminal-law frameworks.

Hacktivism was more controversial in that it was evident that drawing the line between lawful protest and criminal act was not as clear cut as in the case of online civil disobedience. Here some acts showed elements of vigilantism; specifically, acts that were extra-legal and, in some instances, extra-state. Here individuals had become so fed up with political or social processes that they no longer had faith in the government to deal with a problem in an ethical or just fashion. There are no legal exemptions for hacktivist actions under criminal-law frameworks. That said, the connection between protected human rights and supposed unlawful acts is a territory that courts will have to grapple with in the years to come.

Even security researchers encounter ethical and legal issues when performing penetration testing and vulnerability discovery. Again, the law does not provide security research or public-interest exemptions from the criminal framework. While copyright law in some jurisdictions provides a "fair dealing" framework, allowing security research and encryption research, these exemptions require several conditions to be met. These exemptions, however, only provide assurance from being prosecuted for copyright offences, they do not provide exemptions from being prosecuted for an offence in a criminal code or act.

As will was seen in the counterattack/hackback case studies, some organizations are engaged in some forms of counterattack/hackback, though this is not widely known and rarely spoken of publicly. Some intrusion-detection software for computer networks not only detects denial-of-service attacks but also automatically initiates counter-denial-of-service attacks. There are no legal exemptions for these types of counterattacks. The problem of corporate hackback, while still controversial, is increasingly being recognized as an issue that requires new law and policy. Both governments and corporations are moving from a defensive cyber-threat posture to one of mitigation of threat, and, even further, to the offensive or active cyber-security posture.

Security activism is likewise an area where professional security experts and researchers are faced with an abundance of ethical and legal issues. Many incidences were noted where security experts sat quietly in systems, performing actions to clean up cyber issues or fixing security vulnerabilities. Some may find this similar to a neighbour shovelling the snow from your driveway before you wake in the morning or cutting your grass—acts of kindness. The difference with security activism is that often the end user or organization is unaware that the random act of kindness has occurred. Again, there are no legal exemptions from relevant criminal-law frameworks for these actions. As with all instances of ethical hacking, there is only the discrepancy to prosecute or not to prosecute. Prosecution guidelines are rarely made public.

While most instances of ethical hacking are illegal, it is interesting to note that some methods used by law enforcement, and by security firms contracted to perform criminal-intelligence gathering, may also be illegal or, at best, highly controversial. Yet the legal framework is a blunt object which is rarely applied to certain acts, but remains deliberately broad to allow the prosecution of an individual when political appetites change. This, as has been seen throughout the book, makes working in cyber security—expert or not—an ever-changing field of play, where low risk today is high risk tomorrow

As was seen in the case studies, some individuals involved in hacking were considered to have an addiction in the same way that an individual may become addicted to gambling, video games, drugs, or alcohol. The role of hacking addiction in sentencing has been mentioned in a few key legal decisions, but there has been no detailed analysis of how a framework should be established to properly deal with technology addiction. Likewise, autism has featured in some of the ethical-hacking incidences, with some jurisdictions such as the United States not factoring this into sentencing young hackers. Whereas we have seen that, in Australia and New Zealand, having Asperger's has led courts to show leniency, to render suspended sentences on condition of community work, which, in one case, led a hacker to lawful employment in the cyber-security field.

There are no simple solutions to the issues that arise with ethical hacking. Below contains some recommendations which should be explored further through multi-party stakeholder processes, where stakeholders could include organizations, internet and cyber-security associations, human-rights groups, relevant CERTs, and government policy-makers, with input from hackers, psychologists, and autism groups.

14.2 Encourage Legitimate Space for Virtual Protests

What might a legitimate space for virtual protests look like? Many would argue that there are already legitimate spaces for virtual protests. These are online petitions, expressing opinions on social media, supporting online political advertisements and awareness campaigns, and sending communications, by paper or online, to legislative representatives. Yet none of these allows for the same online effect that a physical protest might have outside of a parliament.

Off-line protests are allowed if certain conditions are met. Depending on the jurisdiction that you are in, you may need a license for the protest. You may need to make certain that you do not block access to essential services. And you need to ensure that you do not damage property or cause violence, otherwise you clearly cross the line of potentially legal to illegal. DDoS is the closest thing at the moment to the equivalent in an online world. But what if there was a way to perform DDoS or achieve the same effect with similar off-line restrictions? In theory this could be done by allowing people the right to protest where posters and other could be displayed on visible parts of the website. This is not a DDoS, but the protest message is clearly visible on the landing page of the website. There is no physical damage to property, no one is injured, and essential online services are not blocked. This is merely one example of how a legitimate space might work for online civil protest. A multi-stakeholder group could develop other methods and policies.

14.3 Guidelines and Policy

The government should provide publicly available policies and guidelines for the different types of ethical hacking. These policies and guidelines will play two important roles. The first, is that people will know what is and is not legal, but, more importantly, make prosecution guidelines transparent. Such guidelines operate to say that, while an action may be caught within the broad scope of the criminal law, prosecution should only occur when certain conditions are met. These guidelines could further look at appropriate sentences for acts of ethical hacking.

The Netherlands was the first country to issue guidelines for responsible disclosure, in 2013.[1] Afterward, the US Department of Justice developed guidelines and policies for responsible vulnerability disclosure and bug-bounty programs. This is an excellent example of a government initiative to assist in clarifying exemptions to criminal and civil law when security activities are performed in ways deemed to be within an acceptable range. The cyber-security unit within the Computer Crime and Intellectual Property Section of the Criminal Division of the US Department of Justice issued

"A Framework for a Vulnerability Disclosure Program for Online Systems" in 2017.[2] The framework is a public document that clearly discusses acceptable and lawful methods of security-vulnerability disclosure. But it also does more than this; the framework sends a clear message that organizations should be viewing responsible disclosure as something positive. The framework likely would not work on its own without the complementary bug-bounty programs and platforms (such as HackerOne and Bugcrowd) that have emerged as third-party organizations that coordinate lawful security-vulnerability disclosure and payment for services between "hacker" and organization. These platforms also strongly encourage ethical conduct among their cyber-security researchers, as will be seen below.

14.4 Code of Conduct for Hackback

Codes of conducts and similar documents are emerging in the security-vulnerability space. For example, HackerOne has on its website landing page "Vulnerability Disclosure Philosophy,"[3] which outlines principles that should be respected, including:

Finders should...
- **Respect the rules.** Operate within the rules set forth by the Security Team, or speak up if in strong disagreement with the rules.
- **Respect privacy.** Make a good faith effort not to access or destroy another user's data.
- **Be patient.** Make a good faith effort to clarify and support their reports upon request.
- **Do no harm.** Act for the common good through the prompt reporting of all found vulnerabilities. Never wilfully exploit others without their permission.

Security Teams should...
- **Prioritize security.** Make a good faith effort to resolve reported security issues in a prompt and transparent manner.
- **Respect Finders.** Give finders public recognition for their contributions.
- **Reward research.** Financially incentivize security research when appropriate.

- **Do no harm.** Not take unreasonable punitive actions against finders, like making legal threats or referring matters to law enforcement.

This approach is interesting in that it does not refer to absolutes found in criminal law, such as authorized or unauthorized access. Here, one is expected to make "good faith" efforts to not perform certain acts. While this is not a binding legal document, having the guidelines up front allows some form of transparency in processes.

The question becomes whether there should be transparent guidelines and policies for hacktivism or hackback in the same way as there are for vulnerability finding and disclosure? There are clearly different ethical considerations and policy goals in hacktivism than there are for security-vulnerability disclosure. The latter has the benefit of incentivizing the finding and disclosure of security vulnerabilities. Whereas, hacktivists are incentivized by righting a wrong; disclosure of what they see as wrongful or unjust acts; or promoting a political cause or party. As with unlawful protests, participants accept that they may be arrested and detained for peaceful protest. Where an act of hacktivism is also peaceful, participants should also accept that they may be arrested and detained. There is a body of case law, however, for unlawful peaceful protest including a common understanding of when it might be appropriate to prosecute, what offences to use, and what sentences may or may not be appropriate. There is no equivalent for hacktivists. A white paper on hacktivism is highly desirable in order to start conversations around the limits of acceptable hacktivism and appropriate responses.

Hackback is both similar and different from hacktivism. Where hackback takes the form of retaliation for a prior act of hacktivism it is more readily associated with retribution and/or vigilantism. As seen in the WikiLeaks, MasterCard, and Stratfor debacle, where the initial hacktivist act quickly spiralled into an out-of-control retaliatory conflict involving all parties. Here, guidelines would be useful for not only hacktivists, but also considering guidelines for governments and law-enforcements agencies (or their hired third-party agents) on appropriate conduct. Where hackback moves into the area of protecting corporations and shielding assets, it begins to look more like self-defence. As was discussed, the United States is looking at legitimizing hackback. Again, there are many restrictions imposed and the Hackback Bill faces fierce opposition. However, the bill initiates a discussion on whether hackback might be appropriate under certain conditions. More work is needed at the global level to discuss possible rules around hackback and, in particular, what would constitute sufficient evidence of attribution.

14.5 Transparency of Government Engagement with Hackback

As previously mentioned, there needs to be more transparency when law enforcement, government agencies, and third-party contractors engage with hackback techniques. While there are clear rules for law-enforcement use of hackback, the use of third-party contractors for investigations and hackback functions is not readily discussed in the media, at conferences, or other forums. This activity deliberately remains in the shadows so that the actions of the third party remain at arm's length from law enforcement, intelligence agencies, and such. This is not well-documented in the area of cyber security outside the discussion of cyberwar. Cyberwar involves state-to-state measures, or state-to-state sponsored measures. Hackback, as discussed in this book, referred to at least one non-state party or non-state-sponsored party—there is little to no literature for corporate hackback. There needs to be more open discussion around corporate hackback.

14.6 Security Research Exemption and Public-Interest Consideration

Exemption from liability and criminal prosecution has been argued for application to security researchers. A resounding question underlies the debate: do the ends justify the means? Some examples might include the recording industry's proposal to hack into users' computers to find copyright-infringing material and cyber-activists placing Trojans on child pornography to track and record the contents of offenders hard drives for evidential purposes. These examples go to the question of intent as well as whether an act may be justified as a social utility, for the good of the public, similar to how public-interest exemptions work for the admissibility of evidence in court.

It is indeed curious that, in some jurisdictions, there are both security-vulnerability and encryption-research exemptions found in copyright legislation, but these exemptions are not defences to hacking offences in criminal codes and acts. If security research is considered a public benefit (and it is difficult to see how it is not), then a security- and encryption-research defence should be considered a vital requirement to any criminal code or act. That is not to say that the exemption should be automatic; indeed, there will need to be detailed regulations and guidelines in terms of who, how, and what would satisfy the requirements for a security-research exemption. But it is ludicrous that professional cyber-security researchers perform their work under the duress of the possibility of criminal charges and civil lawsuits.

14.7 Concluding Remarks

There is no shortage of work to be done in the field of cyber security and, within that field, ethical hacking. Working with cyber-security professionals and all shades of hackers over the past seventeen years has taught me that while many *claim* to understand the frameworks and limits of the law, I have yet to meet a hacker—ethical or otherwise—who *clearly* understood those laws and frameworks. Much work remains to be done on finding appropriate ways of responding to ethical hacking that protect civil liberties while providing proficient deterrence to some forms of hacking.

It is my firm opinion that the broad wording of computer offences, both within the Convention of Cybercrime and in domestic criminal law, desperately needs to be revisited. At the moment the legal framework is the same for any act, regardless of the motivation, lack of damage, or whether it was a form of ethical hacking. There is only prosecutorial discretion. Can you imagine if we charged someone with stealing a bag of chips to give to someone in need? If we did, the act would clearly be a misdemeanour. There are no misdemeanour equivalents in these computer offences. And to make matters worse, often those called upon to make prosecutorial decisions are not versed with a deep understanding of the technologies and techniques involved, and some could be described as cyber-illiterate. I will leave you with a recent news story that perhaps best sums up why revision is required to all cyber-security frameworks, law, and policies, and, within those, revisions to ethical hacking. Japan's newly appointed deputy minister responsible for cyber security openly admitted in parliament that he has not used a computer in forty-three years, and that he did not know what a USB stick was.[4] On the plus side, as one commentator ironically stated, "If a hacker targets this

Minister Sakurada, they wouldn't be able to steal any information. Indeed it might be the strongest kind of security!"

Notes

1.   National Cyber Security Centrum 2013.
2.   United States Department of Justice, "A Framework for a Vulnerability Disclosure Program for Online Systems."
3.   HackerOne 2018.
4.   Currie 2018.

Bibliography

Legislation and Treaties

California Business and Professions Code (United States).

Canada Act 1982 (UK) 1982, c 11.

Canadian Charter of Human Rights and Freedoms.

Canadian Criminal Code, R.S.C. 1985, c.46.

Computer Fraud and Abuse Act 1986 (United States).

Computer Misuse Act 1990 (United Kingdom).

Computer Misuse and Cybersecurity Act Ch 50A (Rev Ed 2007) (Singapore).

Convention to the International Covenant on Civil and Political Rights, 999 UNTS 302 (1967).

Council of Europe Convention on Cybercrime, 22296 UNTS 167 (2001).

Criminal Code Act 1995 (Australia).

Espionage Act (1917) (United States).

German Criminal Code (1914).

Information and Electronic Transaction Law (2008) (Indonesia).

Model Criminal Code (January 2001) (Australia).

Penal Law (1977) (Israel).

Stored Communications Act (1986) (United States).

Uniform Code of Military (United States).

Youth Criminal Justice Act S.C. 2002, c. 1 (Canada).

Case Law

1-800 Contacts v. WhenU.com (2005) 414 F.3d 400.

1-800 Solutions v. Zone Labs.

Alberta (Education) v Canadian Copyright Licensing Agency (Access Copyright) [2012] 2 SCR 345.

Anat Kamm v State of Israel [2012] Case 17959-01-10 (Israel Supreme Court).

Auernheimer v. United States of America, No. 13-1816 (United States, Third US Circuit Court of Appeals).

Ashdown v Telegraph Group Ltd [2001] EWCA Civ 1142.

Australian Broadcasting Corporation v Lenah Game Meats Pty Ltd (2001) 185 ALR 1.

Bank Julius Baer & Co. Ltd. v. WikiLeaks (2008) No. C 08-00824 JSW (February 29, 2008) (US District Court for the Northern District of California); see https://www.eff.org/files/filenode/baer_v_wikileaks/wikileaks102.pdf.

Cadbury Schweppes v FBI Foods [1999] 1 SCR 142.

Campbell v Acuff-Rose Music (1994) 510 U.S. 569.

Cassava (CasinoOnNet) v. Sunbelt Software.

CCH Canadian Ltd. v Law Society of Upper Canada [2004] 1 SCR.

Claria (Gator) v Internet Advertising Bureau.

Collier Constructions Pty Ltd v Foskett Pty Ltd (1991) 20 IPR 666.

Commonwealth v John Fairfax (1980) 147 CLR 39.

Corrs Pavey v Collector of Customs [1987] FCA 26.

Dagenais v. Canadian Broadcasting Corp. [1994] 3 S.C.R. 835.

E360 Insight and David Linhardt v. The Spamhaus Project (2007) 500 F. 3d 594 (United States Court of Appeals for the Seventh Circuit).

E360 Insight, LLC et al v. The Spamhaus Project (2006) Case No. 06 C 3958 (United States District Court, Northern District of Illinois, September 13, 2006). Access to default judgment at http://www.spamhaus.org/archive/legal/Kocoras_order_to_Spamhaus.pdf.

Edmonton Journal v. Alberta (A.G.) [1989] 2 S.C.R. (Canada).

Hyde Park Residence v Yelland, [2001] Ch. 143.

IceTV Limited v Nine Network Australia Pty Limited [2009] HCA 14.

IceTV Limited v Nine Network Australia Pty Limited [2008] HCATrans 358.

Imutran Ltd v Uncages Campaigns Ltd, [2001] CP Rep. 28.

In re § 2703(d) Order (2013) No. 11-5151 (US Court of Appeals Fourth Circuit) (January 25 2013).

See also Justia US Law, *In re 2703(d) Application*, No. 11-5151 (Fourth Cir. 2013), available at https://law.justia.com/cases/federal/appellate-courts/ca4/11-5151/11-5151-2013-01-25.html.

Legal documents also available at, Electronic Privacy Information Center, *In re Twitter Order Pursuant to 2703(d)*, available at https://www.epic.org/amicus/twitter/wikileaks/.

In re § 2703(d) Order (2011) 830 F. Supp. 2d 114 (US District Court, Eastern District of Virginia, Alexandria Division) (November 10, 2011).

Irwin Toy v. Quebec [1989] 1 S.C.R. 927 (Canada).

James Raj Arokiasamy v Public Prosecutor [2014] 2 SLR 307 ("James Raj") (Singapore, States Courts).

Lauri Love v. the Government of the United States of America [2018] EWHC 172, see https://freelauri.com/wp-content/uploads/2018/02/lauri-love-v-usa.pdf.

Libertad.de (2006) File reference 1 Ss 319/05, March 22, 2006 (Germany, Higher Regional Court, Frankfurt am Main).

Lion Laboratories v Evans, [1985] QB 526.

McAuliffe v The Queen [1995] 183 CLR 108.

McCabe v British American Tobacco Services Limited [2002] VSC 73.

Microsoft Corporation v. John Does 1027 (Feb. 22, 2010) United States District Court for the State of Victoria, Civil Action 1:10 cv 156 (LMB/JFA).

Microsoft Corporation v. Newport Internet Marketing Corporation Does 2-20 (2005) No. 03-2-12648-9 SEA (United States, King County Superior Court Seattle, Washington).

Lavigne v. Ontario Public Service Employees Union [1991] 2 S.C.R. 211.

Little Sisters Book and Art Emporium v. Canada (Minister of Justice) [2000] 2 S.C.R. 1120.

Paracha v. Obama (2011) No. 04-2022 (PLF) (April 29, 2011) (US District Court for the District of Columbia).
Case:
https://scholar.google.com.au/scholar_case?case=7165402973414950017&q=Paracha+wikileaks&hl=en&as_sdt=2006&as_vis=1#r[1].
Petitioner's (Paracha's) emergency application: https://fas.org/sgp/jud/par/042711-access.pdf.
Respondents' (Obama et al.'s) response: https://fas.org/sgp/jud/par/061511-response376.pdf.

Regan Gerard Gilmour v Director of Public Prosecutions (Commonwealth) [1996] NSWSC 55.

R v. Caffrey (2006).

R v Christopher Weatherhead, Ashley Rhodes, Peter Gibson, and Jake Birchall (January 24, 2013) (United Kingdom, Southwark Crown Court in London).

R v Cleary, Davis, Al-Bassam and Ackroyd (May 16 and 24, 2013) (United Kingdom Southwark Crown Court in London).

R v Glen Steven Mangham (February 17, 2012) (United Kingdom, Southwark Crown Court in London).

R v Glen Steven Mangham Court of Appeal [2012] EWCA Crim 973 (April 4, 2012) (England and Wales Court of Appeal (Criminal Division)), see http://www.bailii.org/ew/cases/EWCA/Crim/2012/973.html.

R v. Keegstra [1990] 3 S.C.R. 697.

R v National Post [2010] 1 SCR 477.

R v. Sharpe [2001] 1 S.C.R. 45.

R v Stevens [1999] NSWCCA 69.

R v Walker [2008] NZHC 1114.

R v. Zundel [1992] 2 S.C.R. 731.

Rocket v. Royal College of Dental Surgeons of Ontario [1990] 2 S.C.R. 232 (Canada).

R.W.D.S.U. v. Dolphin Delivery Ltd. [1986] 2. S.C.R. 573.

Salter v DPP [2008] NSWSC 1325.

Sierra Corporate Design Inc. v. David Ritz (2007) File No. op-05-C-01660 (United States, District Court, County of Cass, State of North Dakota). See www.spamsuite.com.com/node/351.

Society of Composers, Authors and Music Publishers of Canada v Bell Canada [2012] 2 SCR 326.

Sony Computer Entertainment, Inc. v. Connectix Corporation (2000) 203 F. 3d 596, Ninth Circuit.

Soyke v R [2016] NSWCCA 112 (June 10, 2016).

Specht v. Netscape Communications Corp. (2002) 306 F. 3d 17, Court of Appeals, Second Circuit.

State of Israel v. Anat Kamm (2010) Case 17959-01-10 (Israel, District Court of Tel Aviv Jaffa). See http://www.maannews.net/eng/ViewDetails.aspx?ID=275114.

Théberge v. Galerie d'Art du Petit Champlain [2002] 2 S.C.R. 336.

U.F.C.W., Local 1518 v. Kmart Canada Ltd. [1999] 2 S.C.R. 1083.

United States of America v. Aaron Swartz, 1:11-cr-10260 (US District Court for the District of Massachusetts).

United States of America v. Bradley Manning E., PFC (2013) (United States, Army Military District of Washington).

United States of America v. Daniel Spitler and Andrew Alan Escher Auernheimer, Mag. No. 11-4022 (CCC) (United States, District of New Jersey). Criminal Complaint, available at http://www.justice.gov/usao/nj/Press/files/pdffiles/2011/Spitler,%20Daniel%20et%20al.%20Complaint.pdf.

United States of America v. Dennis Collins, et al (2011), No. CR 11-00471 DLJ (United States District Court, Northern District of California, San Jose Division). For indictment, see http://ia600502.us.archive.org/24/items/gov.uscourts.cand.242989/gov.uscourts.cand.242989.1.0.pdf.

United States of America v. Ford, 765 F.2d 1088, 1090 (11th Cir.1985).

United States of America v. Gorshkov (2001) WL 1024026 (United States, Western District Washington).

United States of America v. Jarrett (2003) 338 F. 3d 339, No. 02-4953 (July 29, 2003) (United States, Court of Appeals, Fourth Circuit). See http://scholar.google.com.au/scholar_case?case=7704360326371177621.

United States of America v. Jeremy Hammond (2013) 12 Cr. 185 (LAP) (United States District Court of Southern District of New York).

Case, available at http://www.justice.gov/usao/nys/pressreleases/May13/
HammondJeremyPleaPR/U.S.%20v.%20Jeremy%20Hammond%20S2%20
Information.pdf.

Free Jeremy (website), legal documents: https://freejeremy.net/category/
legal/ including Sentencing Letter by Jeremy Hammond.

United States of America v Kevin George Poe (2011) CR 11 01166 (United States,
District Court for the Central District of California).

United States of America v. Kretsinger (2:11-cr-00848) (US Central District of
California (Los Angeles)).

United States of America v. Lauri Love (US District Court for the District
of New Jersey), see https://www.scribd.com/doc/179595899/Love-
Lauri-Indictment.

United States of America v. Raynaldo Rivera, CR No. 12-798-JAK (US District
Court for the Central District of California).
Plea agreement: https://freeanons.org/wp-content/uploads/court-
documents/Raynaldo-Rivera.pdf.

United States of America v. Steiger (2003) 318 F. 3d 1039, Nos. 01-15788, 01-16100
and 01-16269 (January 14, 2003) (United States, Court of Appeals
11th Circuit). See http://scholar.google.com.au/scholar_case?case=
5611821785646747519.

Zitierung: BVerfG, 1 BvR 370/07 vom 27.2.2008, Absatz-Nr. (1–333), see
http://www.bverfg.de/entscheidungen/rs20080227_1bvr037007.html.

Books

Aitchison, R. "DNS Records." In *Pro DNS and BIND,* Apress Publishers, 2003.

Anderson, R. *Security Engineering: A Guide to Building Dependable Distributed
Systems,* 2nd ed. Indianapolis: Wiley Publishing, 2008.

Athanasopoulos, E., Anagnostakis, K., and Markatos, E. "Misusing
Unstructured P2P Systems to Perform DoS attacks: The Network
that Never Forgets" Lecture Notes in Computer Science for *Applied
Cryptography and Network Security.* Springer Berlin, 2006. Available at
http://www.springerlink.com/content/xk82663475474857/.

Atkin, T. et al. *Information Security Management Handbook.* CRC Press, 2006.

Barlow, J. P. "Crime and Puzzlement," Appendix 1 in Ludlow, P. (ed.),
High Noon on the Electronic Frontier: Conceptual Issues in Cyberspace. MIT
Press, 1996.

Barton, P., and Yegneswaran, V. "An Inside Look at Botnets." In Somesh, J.,
Maughan, D., Song, D., and Wang, C. (eds.), *Malware Detection.* New York:
Springer, 2007.

Bentham, J. *Panopticon,* in Miran Bozovic (ed.), *The Panopticon Writings.*
London: Verso, 1995), 29-95.

Blount, S. *Electronic Contracts: Principles for the Common Law.* Australia: Reed
International Books, 2009.

Bowrey, K. *Law & Internet Cultures*. Cambridge University Press, 2005.

Brenner, S. W. *Law in an Era of "Smart" Technology*. Oxford University Press, 2007.

Brown, A. J. *Whistleblowing in the Australian Public Sector: Enhancing the theory and practice of internal witness management in public sector organisations*. ANU Press, Canberra. Available at http://epress.anu.edu.au/anzsog/whistleblowing/mobile_devices/index.html, accessed February 10, 2014.

Chan, J., Goggin, G., and Bruce, J. "Internet Technologies and Criminal Justice." In Jewkes, Y., and Yar, M., *Handbook of Internet Crime*. Willan Publishing, 2010.

Chiesa, R., Ducci, S., and Ciappi, S. *Profiling Hackers: The Science of Criminal Profiling as Applied to the World of Hacking*. UNICRI and CRC Press, 2009.

Clayton, R. "Failures in a Hybrid Content Blocking System." In Danezis, G., and Martin, D. (eds.), *Privacy Enhancing Technologies*. PET 2005. Lecture Notes in Computer Science, vol 3856. Springer, Berlin, Heidelberg, pp. 78–92. https://doi.org/10.1007/11767831_6.

Cohen, F. *A Short Course on Computer Viruses*, 2nd ed. Wiley, 1994.

Corones, S., and Clarke, P. *Consumer Protection and Product Liability Law*, 3rd ed. Thomson Lawbook, 2008.

Curcereau, D. *Aspects of Regulating Freedom of Expression on the Internet*. Intersentia, 2006.

Dreyfus, S., and Assange, J. *Underground*. Random House Australia, 2011.

Dunham, K., and Melnick, J. *Malicious Bots: An Inside Look into the Cyber-Criminal Underground of the Internet*. CRC Press, 2009.

Fitzgerald, B., Fitzgerald, A., Middleton, G., Lim, Y., and Beale, T. *Internet and E-Commerce Law: Technology, Law and Policy*. Thomson 2007.

Fleming, J. *The Law of Torts*, 8th ed. The Law Book Company, 1992.

Garfinkel, S., and Spafford, G. *Practical UNIX & Internet Security*, 2nd ed. California: O'Reilly, 1996.

Geist, M. (ed.). *The Copyright Pentalogy: How the Supreme Court of Canada Shook the Foundations of Canadian Copyright Law*. Ottawa: Ottawa University Press, 2013.

Godwin, M. "Some 'Property' Problems in a Computer Crime Prosecution." In Ludlow, P. (ed.), *High Noon on the Electronic Frontier: Conceptual Issues in Cyberspace*. MIT Press, 1996.

Grabosky, P. *Electronic Crime*. Prentice Hall, 2007.

Harris, S., Harper, A., Eagle, C., and Ness, J. *Grey Hat Hacking: The Ethical Hacker's Handbook*. McGraw Hill, 2008.

Himanen, P. *The Hacker Ethic: and the Spirit of the Information Age*. Random House, 2001.

Kerr, I., and Gilbert, D. "The Role of ISPs in the Investigation of Cybercrime." In MENDINA, T., and BRITZ, J. (eds.), *Information Ethics in an Electronic Age: Current Issues in Africa and the World*. McFarland Press, 2004.

Levy, S. *Hackers: Heroes of the Computer Revolution*. New York: Doubleday, 1984.

Levy, A. *Crypto: How the Code Rebels Beat the Government—Saving Privacy in the Digital Age.* Viking, 2001.

Libicki, M. *Conquest in Cyberspace: National Security and Information Warfare.* Cambridge, 2007.

Li, Z., Liao, Q., and Striegel, A. *Botnet Economics: Uncertainty Matters.* Springer, 2009.

Ludwig, M. *The Giant Black Book of Computer Viruses,* 2nd ed. American Eagle, 1998.

Lynch, A., and Williams, G. *What Price Security?* UNSW Press, 2006.

Malcom, J. *Multi-Stakeholder Governance and the Internet Governance Forum.* Termium Press, 2008.

Matswshyn, A. (ed.). *Harboring Data: Information Security, Law, and the Corporation.* Stanford University Press, 2009.

Maurushat, A. "Australia." In *Freedom on the Internet: A Global Assessment of Internet and Digital Media,* Cook S. (ed.). New York: Freedom House, 2011.

——. *Disclosure of Security Vulnerabilities.* Springer, 2013.

Moon, R. *The Constitutional Protection of Freedom of Expression.* University of Toronto Press, 2000.

Mueller, M. *Ruling the Root: Internet Governance and the Taming of Cyberspace.* Massachusetts Institute of Technology, 2002.

Oram, A. (ed.). *Peer-to-Peer: Harnessing the Power of Disruptive Technologies.* O'Reilly Media: Sebastopol, 2001.

Oxford Pocket Dictionary of Current English, 4th ed. Oxford University Press, 2009.

Pfleeger, C., and Pfleeger, S. *Security in Computing,* 4th ed. Prentice Hall, 2006.

Phair, N. *Cybercrime: The Reality of the Threat.* Privately published, 2007.

Poulsen, K. *Kingpin: The True Story of Max Butler, the Master Hacker Who Ran a Billion Dollar Cyber Crime Network.* Hachette, 2011.

Provos, N., and Holz, T. *Virtual Honeypots: From Botnet Tracking to Intrusion Detection.* Safari, 2008.

Raymond, E. *The Cathedral & the Bizaar: Musings on Linux and Open Source By an Accidental Revolutionary.* O'Reilly Media, 2001.

Reyes, A., O'Shea, K., Steele, J., Hansen, J., Jean, B., and Ralph, T. *Cyber Crime Investigations: Bridging the Gaps Between Security Professionals, Law Enforcement, and Prosecutors.* Syngress, 2007.

Rice, D. *Geekonomics: The Real Cost of Insecure Software.* Addison-Wesley, 2008.

Ross, S. *UNIX System Security Tools.* McGraw-Hill, 1999.

Saltzer, J., Reed, D., and Clark, D. "End-to-End Arguments in System Design." In Partridge, C. (ed.), *Innovations in Internetworking.* Artech House, 1988.

Samuel, A. "Hacktivism and the Future of Political Participation." PhD thesis, Harvard, 2004.

Schiller, C., Binkley, J., Harley, D., Evron, G., Bradley, T., Willems, C., and Cross, M., *Botnets: The Killer Web App.* Syngress, 2007.

Schneier, B. *Secrets and Lies.* Robert Ipsen, 2000.

Singh, S. The *Code Book: The Evolution of Secrecy from Mary, Queen of Scots to Quantum Cryptopgraphy.* Doubleday, 1999.

Smith, R., Grabosky, P., and Urbas, G. *Cyber Criminals on Trial.* Cambridge University Press, 2004.

Taylor, P. "Hacktivism: In Search of Lost Ethics?" In *Crime and the Internet.* London & New York: Routledge.

Taylor, R., Caeti, T., Loper, K., Fritsch, E., and J. R. Liederbach. *Digital Crime and Digital Terrorism.* Pearson, United Kingdom, 2005.

Thoreau, H. D. *Resistance to Civil Government* (original title, 1849; also known as *Civil Disobedience: On the Duty of Civil Disobedience).* In N. Rosenblum (Ed.), Thoreau: Political Writings(Cambridge Texts in the History of Political Thought, pp. 1-22). Cambridge: Cambridge University Press.

Tien, L. "Architectural Regulation and the Evolution of Social Norms." In Balkin, J., Grimmelmann, J., Katz, E., Kozlovski, N., Wagman, S., and Zarsky, T. (eds.), *Cybercrime: Digital Cops and Laws in a Networked Environment.* New York University Press, 2006.

Walden, I. "Computer Forensics and the Presentation of Evidence in Criminal Cases." In JEWKES, Y., and YAR, M., *Handbook of Internet Crime.* Willan Publishing, 2010.

Wall, D. *Cybercrime: Crime and Society Series.* Polity Press, 2007.

Yar, M. "The Private Policing of Internet Crime." In Jewkes, Y., and Yar, M. (eds.). *Handbook of Internet Crime.* Willan Publishing, 2010.

——. "Public Perception and Public Opinion about Internet Crime." In Jewkes, Y., and Yar, M., *Handbook of Internet Crime.* Willan Publishing, 2010), 104-120.

Yegneswaran, V., and Barford, P. "An Inside Look at Botnets." In Christodorescu, M., Jha, S., Maughan, D., Song, D., and Wang, C. (eds.), *Advances in Information Security: Malware Detection.* Springer, 2007.

Journal Articles

Bambauer, D., and Day, O., "The Hacker Aegis," 60 *Emory Law Journal* (2011).

Bond, C., "There's Nothing Worse Than a Muddle in all the World: Copyright Complexity and Law Reform in Australia," 34 *UNSWLJ* 1145 (2011).

——, "Commonwealth v Wikileaks: Fairfax Revisisted," 18 *M&ALR* 310 (2013).

Brenner, S. W., Carrier, B., and Henninger, J., "The Trojan Horse Defense in Cybercrime Cases," 21 *Santa Clara Computer and High Technology Law Journal* (2004).

Broadhurst, R., "Developments in the Global Law Enforcement of Cyber-Crime," 29(3) *Policing: An International Journal of Police Strategies and Management* 408, 418 (2006).

Chandler, J., "Security in Cyberspace: Combating Distributed Denial of Service Attacks," 1 *University of Ottawa Law & Technology Journal* 231 (2003–2004).

——, "Liability for Botnet Attacks," *Canadian Journal of Law and Technology* (2006).

Chandler, J., "Technological Self-Help and Equality in Cyberspace," 55 *McGill Law Journal* (2010).

Clarke, R., "Information Technology and Dataveillance," 31(5) *Communications of the ACM* 499 (1988).

Clarke, R., and Maurushat, A., "Who Will Bear the Cost of Insecure Devices," 18 *Journal of Law, Information and Science* 8 (2007).

——, "The Feasibility of Consumer Device Security," *UNSW Law Review Series* 5 (2009).

Cohen, F., "Computer Viruses: Theory and Experiments," 6(1) *Computers & Security* (1987).

Colangelo, A., and Maurushat, A., "Exploring the Limits of Computer Code as a Protected Form of Expression: A Suggested Approach to Encryption, Computer Viruses and Technological Protection Measures," 1 *McGill Law Journal* 51(2006).

Davis, N., "Presumed Assent: The Judicial Acceptance of Clickwrap," 22 *Berkeley Technology Law Journal* 577 (2007).

Demetriou, C., and Silke, A., "A Criminological Internet 'sting': Experimental Evidence of Illegal and Deviant Visits to a Website Trap," 43 *British Journal of Criminology* 213 (2003).

De Villiers, M., "Virus Ex Machine Res Ipsa Loquitor," *Stanford Technology Law Review* 1 (2003).

——, "Free Radicals in Cyberspace: Complex Liability Issues in Information Warfare," 4 *Northwestern Journal of Technology and Intellectual Property* 1 (2005).

——, "Distributed Denial of Service: Law, Technology & Policy," 39(3) *World Jurist Law/Technology Journal* (2006).

——, "Reasonable Foreseeability in Information Security Law: A Forensic Analysis" 30 *Hastings Communications and Entertainment Law Journal* (2008).

Dupont, B., "Bots, Cops, and Corporations: On the Limits of Enforcement and the Promise of Polycentric Regulation as a Way to Control Large-Scale Cybercrime," 67 *International Centre for Comparative Criminology* 103 (2017).

Dworkin, T. M., and Baucas, M., "Internal vs. External Whistleblowers: A Comparison of Whistleblowing Processes," 17(12) *Journal of Business Ethics* (1998).

Edwards, L. "Dawn of the death of Distributed Denial of Service: How to Kill Zombies," 24(1) *Cardozo Journal of Arts and Entertainment Law* 23 (2006).

Epstein, R., "The Theory and Practice of Self-Help," 1(1) *Journal of Law, Economics and Policy* 1 (2005).

Evron, G., "Battling Botnets and Online Mobs: Estonia's Defense Efforts During the Internet War," 9(1) *Georgetown Journal of International Affairs* (2008).

Fitri, N., "Democracy Discourses Through the Internet Communication: Understanding the Hacktivism for the Global Changing," 1 *Online Journal of Communication and Media Technologies* 2 (2011).

Freedman, J., "Protecting State Secrets as Intellectual Property: A Strategy for Prosecuting WikiLeaks," 48(1) *Stanford Journal of International Law* 185 (2012).

Geist, M., "Is There a There There: Toward Greater Certain for Internet Jurisdiction," *Berkeley Technology Law Journal* (Fall 2001).

Gervais, D., and Maurushat, A., "Fragmented Copyright, Fragmented Management: Proposals to Defrag Copyright Management," 2(1) *Canadian Journal of Law and Technology* (2003).

Gilbert, D., and Kerr, I., "The Medium and the Message: Personal Privacy and the Forced Marriage of Police and Telecommunications Providers," 51(4) *Criminal Law Quarterly* (2006).

Gobert, J., and Punch, M., "Whistleblowers, the Public Interest, and the Public Interest Disclosure Act 1998," 63(1) *The Modern Law Review* (2000).

Guzman, L., "Unleashing a Cure for the Botnet Zombie Plague," 59(2) *Catholic University Law Review* 527 (2010).

Halberstam, M., "Hacking Back: Reevaluating the Legality of Retaliatory Cyberattacks," 46 *George Washington International Law Review* 199 (2013).

Hardy, K., "Operation Titstorm: Hacktivism or Terrorist Act?," 16(1) *University of New South Wales Law Journal* (2010).

Hutchinson, W., and Warren, M., "Attitudes of Australian Information System Managers Against Online Attackers," 9(3) *Information Management & Computer Security* 106 (2001).

Jenkins, J. "Copyright Law and Political Theology: Censorship and the Forebear's Desire," 25(1) *Law and Literature* 165 (2013).

Johnston, L., "What is Vigilantism?," 26(2) *British Journal of Criminology* (1996).

Jordan, T., "Mapping Hacktivism," 4 *Computer Fraud and Security* (2001).

Kallberg, J., "A Right to Cybercounter Strikes: The Risks of Legalizing Hack Backs," 17(1) *IT Professional* 30 (2015).

Katyal, N., "Criminal Law in Cyberspace," 149 *University of Pennsylvania Law Review* 1004 (2001).

Kerr, O., "Cybercrime's Scope: Interpreting 'Access' and 'Authorization' in Computer Misuse Statutes," 78(53) *New York University Law Review* (2003).

——, "Virtual Crime, Virtual Deterrence: A Skeptical View of Self-Help, Architecture, and Civil Liability," 1 *Journal of Law, Economics and Policy* 197 (2005).

Kesan, J. P., and Hayes, C. M., "Mitigative Counterstriking: Self-Defense and Deterrence in Cyberspace," 25 *Harvard Journal of Law & Technology* 482 (2012).

Lessig, L., "Reading the Constitution in Cyberspace," 45 *Emory Law Journal* 1 (1997).

——, "The Law of the Horse: What Cyberlaw Might Teach," 113 *Harvard Law Review* 501 (1999).

Lin, P., "Anatomy of the Mega-D Takedown," 12 *Network Security* 4–7 (December 2009).

Maurushat, A., "Hong Kong Anti-Terrorism Ordinance and the Surveillance Society: Privacy and Free Expression Implications," 1(12/3) *Asia Pacific Media Educator* (2002).

——, "Data Breach Notification Law Across the World from California to Australia," *Privacy Law and Business International* (April 2009).

——, "Australia's Accession to the Cybercrime Convention: Is the Convention Still Relevant in the Era of Obfuscation Crime Tools," 16(1) *University of New South Wales Law Journal* (2010).

——, "Forced Transparency: Should We Keep Secrets in Times of Weak Law, and Should the Law do More?," 17(2) *Media and Arts Law Review* 239 (2012).

Maurushat, A., and Watt, R., "Australia's Internet Filtering Proposal in the International Context," 12(2) *Internet Law Bulletin* 18 (2009).

Messerschmidt, J. E., "Hackback: Permitting Retaliatory Hacking by Non-State Actors as Proportionate Countermeasures to Transboundary Cyberharm," 52 *Columbia Journal of Transnational Law* (2013).

Ohm, P., "The Rise and Fall of Invasive ISP Surveillance," *University of Illinois Law Review* (2008), available at http://ssrn.com/abstract=1261344 (last accessed April 15, 2009).

Oleson, K., and Darley, J., "Community Perceptions of Allowable Counterforce in Self-Defense and Defense of Property," 23(6) *Law and Human Behavior* (1999).

Posner, R., "Killing or Wounding to Protect a Property Interest," 14(1) *Journal of Law and Economics* 201 (1971).

Rychlicki, T., "Legal Issues of Criminal Acts Committed Via Botnets," 12(5) *Computer and Telecommunications Law Review* 163 (2006).

Rose, C., and Gordon, J., "Internet Security and the Tragedy of the Commons," 1 *Journal of Business and Economics Research* 11 (2003).

Salgado, R., "The Legal Ramifications of Operating a Honeypot," 1 *IEEE Magazine Security and Privacy* (2005).

Shock, J., and Hupp, J., "The 'Worm' Programs—Early Experience with a Distributed Computation," 25(3) *Communications of the ACM* (1982).

Smith, B., "Hacking, Poaching and Counterattacking: Digital Counterstrikes and the Contours of Self-Help," 1(1) *Journal of Law, Economics and Policy* 185 (2005).

Smith, H., "Self-help and the Nature of Property," 1(1) *Journal of Law, Economics and Policy* 69 (2005).

Soghoian, Christopher, "Caught in the Cloud: Privacy, Encryption, and Government Back Doors in the Web 2.0 Era," 8 *Journal on Telecommunications and High Technology Law*. 359 (August 17, 2009); Berkman Center Research Publication No. 2009-07, 361, available at https://ssrn.com/abstract=1421553.

Solove, D., "Privacy and Power: Computer Databases and Metaphors for Information Privacy," 53 *Stanford Law Review* 1393 (2001).

Steel, A., "The Meaning of Dishonesty in Theft," 38(2) *Common Law World Review* (2009).

Tamanaha, B., "Socio-Legal Positivism and a General Jurisprudence," 21(1) *Oxford Journal of Legal Studies* 21 (2001).

Thomas, J., "Ethics of Hacktivism," SANS Institute, 2000-2002, available at http://www.dvara.net/hk/Julie_Thomas_GSEC.pdf.

Thomas, T. L.,"The Internet in China: Civilian and Military Uses," (2001) 7 *Information & Security: An International Journal*, 159–173, available at http://fmso.leavenworth.army.mil/documents/china-internet.htm.

Trottier, D., "Digital Vigilantism as Weaponisation of Visibility" 30(1) *Philosophy & Technology* 55 (2016).

US-Cert (United States Computer Emergency Readiness Team), *Quarterly Trends and Analysis Report* 2(4) (2007).

Walden, I., and Flanagan, A., "Honeypots: A Sticky Legal Landscape?," 29 *Rutgers Communications and Technology Law* 315 (2003).

Warren, S., and Brandeis, L., "The Right to Privacy," 4 *Harvard Law Review* 193 (1890).

Winn, J., "Are 'Better' Security Breach Notification Laws Possible?," 24(3) *Berkeley Technology Law Journal* (2009).

Wu, T., "Application-Centered Internet Analysis," 85 *Vanderbuilt Law Review* 1163 (1999).

Young, J., "Surfing While Muslim: Privacy, Freedom of Expression and the Unintended Consequences of Cybercrime Legislation," 9 *International Journal of Communications Law and Policy* (2004).

——, "Surfing While Muslim: Privacy, Freedom of Expression and the Unintended Consequences of Cybercrime Legislation—A Critical Analysis of the Council of Europe Convention on Cybercrime and the

Canadian Lawful Access Proposal," *Yale Journal of Law and Technology* 346 (2004–2005).

Websites and Articles Published Online

Abovetopsecret, "Is Serco Behind Stuxnet" (ongoing thread, started September 2010), available at http://www.abovetopsecret.com/forum/ thread615788/pg1 (last accessed February 7, 2011).

ACLU Northern California, "Bank Julius Baer & Co. Ltd. v. WikiLeaks" (March 6, 2008), available at https://www.aclunc.org/our-work/ legal-docket/bank-julius-baer-co-ltd-v-wikileaks.

ACLU Virginia, "In re § 2703(d) Orders," available at https://acluva.org/en/ cases/re-ss2703d-orders.

Anderson, K., "Hacktivism and Politically Motivated Computer Crime" (Ensurve, 2008), available at http://politicalhacking.blogspot.com.

Anonnews, "Operation Rainbow Dark," available at http://anonnews. org/?p=press&a=item&i=1162 (accessed January 5, 2012).

Azsecure, "Other forums," available at http://www.azsecure-data.org/ other-forums.html.

———, "Other data," available at http://www.azsecure-data.org/other-data.html.

Baloch, R., "Android Browser Same Origin Policy Bypass < 4.4—CVE-2014-6041," Rafay Hacking Articles, available at https://www.rafaybaloch. com/2017/06/android-browser-same-origin-policy.html.

Barlow, J. P., "A Declaration of Independence in Cyberspace," 1996, available at http://editions-hache.com/essais/pdf/barlow1.pdf (last accessed December 10, 2011).

Bendrath, R., "Frankfurt Appellate Court Says Online Demonstration is Not Coercion," EDRi, June 7, 2006, available at https://edri.org/edrigram number4-11demonstration/.

Berners-Lee, T., *Net Neutrality: This is Serious Blog* (2006), previously available at www.dig.csail.mit.edu/breadcrumbs/node/144 (last accessed March 3, 2010).

Boydon, C., "Building a Botnet Empire in Two Days," June 30, 2006, available at http://images.google.com.au/imgres?imgurl=http://blog.spywareguide. com/upload/2006/05/ISTAdwareThroughWMVFile/ActiveX-thumb. GIF&imgrefurl=http://blog.spywareguide.com/2006/06/&usg=__aA8hJy 8hCGm0aUesHouq5e9kMzM=&h=97&w=128&sz=10&hl=en&start=13& tbnid=sxNZtB3wnM9qmM:&tbnh=69&tbnw=91&prev=/images%3Fq%3 Ddollarrevenue%2Bpopup%2Bactive%2BX%26gbv%3D2%26hl%3Den.

Brandeis University, "Justice Louis J. Brandeis," Louis D. Brandeis Legacy Fund for Social Justice, available at http://www.brandeis.edu/legacy fund/bio.html (accessed March 17, 2011).

Brenner, S., "Hackback as Self-Defense, CYB3RCRIM3: Observations on Technology, Law and Lawnessness," March 24, 2007, available at http://cyb3rcrim3.blogspot.com/2007/03/hackback-as-self-defense.html (last accessed April 16, 2010).

Chaos Computer Club (CCC), "Chaos Computer Club analyzes government malware," 2011, available at http://ccc.de/en/updates/2011/staatstrojaner.

Clarke, R., "Peer-to-Peer (P2P)—An Overview," 2004, available at http://rogerclarke.com/EC/P2POview.html (last accessed February 6, 2011).

——, "Categories of Malware," September 2009, available at http://www.rogerclarke.com/II/MalCat-0909.html (last accessed February 7, 2011).

Clayton, R., "Missing the Wood for the Trees," comments on ICANN fast-flux-report, February 2009, available at http://forum.icann.org/lists/fast-flux-initial-report/msg00022.html (last accessed February 7, 2011).

Cyberberkut, "CyberBerkut gained access to the documents of Joseph Biden's delegation officials," November 25, 2014, available at http://cyber-berkut.org/en/.

——, "CyberBerkut has blocked German Chancellor and the Bundestag's websites," January 7, 2015, available at http://cyber-berkut.org/en/.

Darknet Market Archives, available at https://www.gwern.net/DNM-archives.

Hacking Alert, "White Hat and Grey Hat Hacking: What is the Real Difference?," previously available at http://www.hackingalert.com/hacking-articles/grey-hat-hackers.php.

Derienzo, P., "Eating its Own: Hack Attack," available at http://pdr.autono.net/message2c.html (last accessed January 5, 2012).

DVLabs, "Owning Kraken Zombies: A Detailed Dischapter," April 2008, available at http://dvlabs.tippingpoint.com/blog/2008/04/28/owning-kraken-zombies (last accessed November 11, 2010).

EDRi, "Frankfurt Appellate Court says online demonstration is not coercion," June 7, 2006, available at https://edri.org/edrigramnumber4-11demonstration/.

E-Li, "Anti-Gay Website Hacked by Anonymous," lezbelib.over-blog.com, June 4, 2011, available at http://lezbelib.over-blog.com/article-anti-gay-website-hacked-by-anonymous-75636306.html (last accessed June 5, 2011).

El Universo, "Website of the Presidency of Ecuador suffered cyber attacks," June 20, 2011, available at http://www.eluniverso.com/2011/06/20/1/1355/pagina-internet-presidencia-ecuatoriana-sufrio-ataque-informatico.html?p=1354&m=638 (last accessed June 21, 2011).

Falliere, N., "Stuxnet Introduces the First Known Rootkit for Industrial Control Systems," Symantec, August 6, 2010, available at http://www.symantec.com/connect/blogs/stuxnet-introduces-first-known-rootkit-scada-devices (last accessed February 7, 2011).

Free Anons, "Interview: Ryan Ackroyd AKA Kayla of LulzSec," April 15, 2014, available at https://freeanons.org/interview-ryan-ackroyd-aka-kayla-lulzsec/.

Generic Names Supporting Organisation, "WHOIS Task Forces 1 2 3," June 7, 2005, available at https://gnso.icann.org/en/meetings/minutes-whoistf-07jun05.html (last accessed November 29, 2018).

Green Voice Of Freedom, "Who are the 'Iranian Cyber Army,'" December 15, 2010, previously available at http://en.irangreenvoice.com/article/2010/feb/19/1236 (last accessed December 16, 2010).

Gutman, P., "The Commercial Malware Industry," available at www.cs.auckland.ac.nz/~pgut001/pubs/malware_biz.pdf (last accessed February 4, 2011).

H4ck3d By 3xp1r3 Cyber Army, Pastebin, February 12, 2012, available at http://pastebin.com/GRAmd7qq.

"Hacker History & Culture," H@cker's Handbook, available at http://www.telefonica.net/web2/vailankanni/HHB/HHB_CH03.htm (last accessed January 5, 2012).

Hackers Media, "Subordinate Court of Bangladesh Hacked," previously available http://www.hackersmedia.com/2011/11/subordinate-courts-of-bangladesh-hacked.html.

Hackerone, "Vulnerability Disclosure Guidelines, Vulnerability Disclosure Philosophy," January 10, 2018, available at https://www.hackerone.com/disclosure-guidelines.

Harrington, J., "Hacktivism: What is the Chaos Computer Club?," Suite101, September 8, 2011, previously available at http://joharrington.suite101.com/hacktivism-what-is-the-chaos-computer-club-a387917.

Himma, K., "Hacking as Politically Motivated Digital Civil Disobedience: Is Hacktivism Morally Justified?," ETHICOMP Conference, Linkoping, Sweden (2005), available at https://papers.ssrn.com/sol3/papers.cfm?abstract_id=799545.

Huang, S., "Same Origin Policy Bypass Vulnerability Has Wider Reach Than Thought on TREND MICRO," *Security Intelligence Blog*, September 29, 2014, available at http://blog.trendmicro.com/trendlabs-security-intelligence/same-origin-policy-bypass-vulnerability-has-wider-reach-than-thought/.

Honeynet Project, "About the Project," available at http://old.honeynet.org/misc/project.html (last accessed November 12, 2010).

——, Riden, J. "How Fast-Flux Service Networks Work," available at http://www.honeynet.org/node/132 (last accessed February 6, 2011).

Honker Union Of China, available at http://replay.web.archive.org/20010405092345/http://www.cnhonker.com/cnhonker.htm.

Luther King, Jr., M., "Letters From a Birmingham Jail" (April 16, 1963), available at The Martin Luther King, Jr. Research and Education Institute.

Available at http://mlkkpp01.stanford.edu/index.php/resources/article/annotated_letter_from_birmingham.

Krebs, B., "Ragebooter: 'Legit' DdoS Service, or Fed Backdoor?," *Krebs on Security*, May 13, 2016, available at https://krebsonsecurity.com/2013/05/ragebooter-legit-ddos-service-or-fed-backdoor/ (last accessed April 20, 2017).

Lara, T., "Hackers Attack Government Website in Ecuador to Protest President's Policies Against Freedom of Expression," Knight Center for Journalism in the Americas, *Journalism in the Americas Blog*, August 10, 2011, available at http://knightcenter.utexas.edu/blog/hackers-attack-news-website-ecuador.

LavaSoft, "Waledac Questions Answered," previously available at http://www.lavasoft.com/mylavasoft/company/blog/waledac-questions-answered.

Mangham, M., "The Facebook Hack: What Really Happened," *Gmangham Blog*, April 23, 2012, available at http://gmangham.blogspot.co.uk/2012/04/facebook-hack-what-really-happened.html (last accessed December 21, 2016).

Martin, M., and Kirschbaum, E., "Pro-Russian Group Claims Cyber Attack on German Government Websites," January 7, 2015, available at https://www.reuters.com/article/us-germany-cyberattack/pro-russian-group-claims-cyber-attack-on-german-government-websites-idUSKBN0KG15320150107.

Martin, P., "Australian Government Website Hacked in Protest," Technorati, February 10, 2010, available at http://technorati.com/politics/article/australian-government-website-hacked-in-protest/ (last accessed February 11, 2010).

National Cyber-Forensics Training Alliance, https://www.ncfta.net (last accessed March 2, 2011).

National Cyber Security Centrum, "Leidraad Responsible Disclosure," 2013, available at https://www.ncsc.nl/actueel/nieuwsberichten/leidraad-responsible-disclosure.html.

Opsahl, K. "Cryptome's Publication of Microsoft's Compliance Manual is a Fair Use," Electronic Frontier Foundation, February 26, 2010, available at https://www.eff.org/deeplinks/2010/02/cryptomes-publication-microsofts-compliance-manual.

Pagerghost, "How to Build a Botnet Empire in Two Days," *Security Lab blog. SpywareGuide*, previously available at http://blog.spywareguide.com/2006/06/building_a_botnet_empire_in_tw_1.html (last accessed May 31, 2010).

Parliament Of Australia, www.aph.gov.au.

Pastebin, "OPCartel Proceeds," November 3, 2011, available at http://pastebin.com/XZRpjUZq.

Pospisilli, J., "Cyber Criminals Turn to P2P for DoS Attacks," July 20, 2007, available at http://tech.blorge.com/Structure:%20/2007/07/20/cyber-criminals-turn-to-p2p-for-dos-attacks? (last accessed July 1, 2010).

QMI Agency, "Hacktivist group shuts down child porn sites," Canoe Technology, October 24, 2011, available at http://technology.canoe.ca/2011/10/24/18871656.html (last accessed October 25, 2011).

Rahm, E., and Hai Do, H., "Data Cleanings: Problems and Current Approach" (2009), available at https://www.betterevaluation.org/sites/default/files/data_cleaning.pdf.RFC 1392 Internet Users Glossary. Available at https://datatracker.ietf.org/doc/rfc1392/.

Rogers, M., "Psychological Theories of Crime and Hacking," December 15, 2006, *Telematic Journal of Clinical Criminology*. Available at https://www.researchgate.net/publication/2438130_Psychological_Theories_of_Crime_and_Hacking.

Romano, M., Rosignoli, S., and Giannini, E., "Robot Wars—How Botnets Work," Window Security, October 20, 2005, available at http://www.windowsecurity.com/articles/Robot-Wars-How-Botnets-Work.html (last accessed June 17, 2010).

Rouse, M., "Definition: Back door," TechTarget, June 2007, available at http://searchsecurity.techtarget.com/definition/back-door (last accessed December 21, 2016).

Sawyer, J., "Tech Insight: The Enterprise Hacks Back!" *Dark Reading*, available at http://darkreading.com/security/attacks/showArticle.jhtml?articleID=223100750.

Schneier, B., "Stuxnet," Schneier on Security, October 7, 2010, available at http://www.schneier.com/blog/archives/2010/10/stuxnet.html (last accessed November 12, 2010).

——, "Crypto-Gram Newsletter, September 15, 2003: Benevolent Worms," available at https://www.schneier.com/crypto-gram/archives/2003/0915.html#8 (last accessed November 12, 2010).

Security Beyond Borders, "Salami technique," available at http://securitybeyondborders.org/global-security-glossary/global-security-glossary-s/ (last accessed March 18, 2011).

Stratfor, "Dispatch: Anonymous' Online Tactics Against Mexican Cartels," November 1, 2011, available at https://worldview.stratfor.com/article/dispatch-anonymous-online-tactics-against-mexican-cartels#ixzz1cj0LSuso.

Sypnowich, C., "Law and Ideology," Stanford Encyclopedia of Philosophy, October 22, 2001 (revised October 24, 2014), available at https://plato.stanford.edu/entries/law-ideology/.

Technofriends, "TechCrunch Hacked? (yes, Techcrunch got hacked)," January 26, 2010, available at http://technofriends.in/2010/01/26/did-techcrunch-got-hacked/ (last accessed November 15, 2010).

The Anonymous Log, Facebook, January 4, 2015, available at https://www.facebook.com/TheAnonymousLog.

"The Complete History of Hacking," Scribd.com, previously available at http://www.scribd.com/doc/48245151/The-Complete-History-of-Hacking-1980-2010 (last accessed January 5, 2012).

"The Gospel According To Tux," republished from newsgroup posting to various websites such as the New Hacker's Dictionary, available at http://www.fullbooks.com/The-New-Hacker-s-Dictionary-version-4-219.html.

The Old Computer, available at http://www.theoldcomputer.com/blog/index.php?start=60.

The Wrong Guy, "Activists hack French ruling party's phone numbers," WhyWeProtest, November 10, 2011, available at http://forums.whyweprotest.net/threads/activists-hack-french-ruling-partys-phone-numbers.96206/.

Tippingpoint, "Kraken Botnet Infiltration," April 2008, available at http://www.dvlabs.tippingpoint.com/blog/2008/04/28/kraken-botnet-infiltration (last accessed Nov. 12, 2010).

Tor Project, "Anonymity Online," available at https://www.torproject.org (last accessed March 17, 2011).

Tyson, J., and Crawford, S., "How Virtual Private Networks Work," April 14, 2011, available at https://computer.howstuffworks.com/vpn.htm (last accessed November 29, 2018).

Von Leitner, F., "Chaos Computer Club Clarifications," Tasty Bits from the Technology Front, February 17, 1997, available at http://tbtf.com/resource/felix.html.

Williams, Jeff, "Dismantling Waledac," Microsoft Malware Protection Centre— Threat Research & Response Blog, February 25, 2010, http://blogs.technet.com/b/mmpc/archive/2010/02/25/dismantling-waledac.aspx.

Zakalwe, C., "Turkish Government Websites Hacked in Protest at Internet Censorship," Stop Turkey—BlogSpot, July 7, 2011, available at http://stopturkey.blogspot.com/2011/07/turkish-government-websites-hacked-in.html.

Zand, J., "Indictment Alleges DDoS Attack on Gene Simmons' Web Site by Anonymous Supporter," Justia Law Blog, December 14, 2011, available at http://techlaw.justia.com/2011/12/14/indictment-alleges-ddos-attack-on-gene-simmons-web-site/.

Zeroday Emergency Response Team, available at https://ipfs.io/ipfs/QmXoypizjW3WknFiJnKLwHCnL72vedxjQkDDP1mXWo6uco/wiki/Zeroday_Emergency_Response_Team.html.

Zorz, Z., "Anonymous shuts down child porn sites, leaks usernames," Help Net Security, October 24, 2011, available at http://www.net-security.org/secworld.php?id=11831&utm_source=twitterfeed&utm_medium=twitter&utm_campaign=s3cb0t (last accessed October 31, 2011).

Chatham House Rules Conference Presentations

Chatham House Organisation, available at http://www.chathamhouse.org. uk/about/chathamhouserule/ (last accessed February 7, 2011).

Chatham House Rules, "Internet Filtering and Censorship Proposal Forum," November 2008, Cyberspace Law and Policy Centre, the University of New South Wales, Sydney, Australia.

Closed panel on Cybercrime at AusCERT 2008 with Chatham House Rules. Law-enforcement agents from the Australian Federal Police, New South Wales, Germany and the Federal Bureau of Investigation attended.

Internet Security Operations and Intelligence 5 (ISOI5), Tallin, Estonia, 2008, Chatham House Rules.

Forensics training by Nick Klein, forensics expert and former member of the Australian Federal Police, "Cybercrime, Cyber Security and Digital Law Enforcement" Sydney, March 2010.

Technical/Industry/Academic Reports

Aycock, J., and Maurushat, A., "'Good' Worms and Human Rights" (2006), *Technical Report* 2006-846-39, Department of Computer Science, University of Calgary.

Balatazar, J., Costoya, J., and Flores, R., "Infiltrating WALEDAC Botnet's Covert Operations" (2009), TREND MICRO.

Centre For Homeland Security, George Washington University, *Into the Grey Zone: The Private Sector and Active Defense Against Cyber Threats Report 2016*, available at https://cchs.gwu.edu/sites/g/files/zaxdzs2371/f/down loads/CCHS-ActiveDefenseReportFINAL.pdf.

Denning, D., "Activism, Hacktivism, and Cyberterrorism: The Internet as a Tool for Influencing Foreign Policy" (2001), available at http://www. nautilus.org/infor-policy/workshop/papers/denning.html.

Hafele, D., "Three Different Shades of Ethical Hacking: Black, White and Grey" (February 23, 2004), available at http://www.sans.org/reading_ room/whitepapers/hackers/shades-ethical-hacking-black-white-grey_1390.

Hancock-White, K., "Ethical Hacking," (2008) available at casper182.atspace. com/HancockWhite_ethics_paper.doc.

Imperva, "Hacker Intelligence Initiative" (October 2011), *Monthly Trend Report #5*.

Kaspersky, E., "Cruncher—the First Beneficial Virus?, " *Virus Bulletin* (1993).

Opennet Initiative, *Internet Filtering in China in 2004-2005: A Country Study*, available at https://opennet.net/studies/china.

Owens, W., Dam, K., and Lin, H. (eds.), *Technology, Policy, Law and Ethics Regarding U.S. Acquisition and use of Cyberattack Capabilities* (National Academic Press, 2009), available at https://www.nap.edu/read/12651/chapter/1.

Perriot, F., and Knowles, D., "W32.Welchia.Worm," *Symantec Security Center* (August 11, 2017), available at https://www.symantec.com/security-center/writeup/2003-081815-2308-99.

Panda Security, Quarterly Report PandaLabs (January–March 2010), available at http://www.pandasecurity.om/img/enc/Quarterly_Report_Pandalabs_Q1_2010.pdf (last accessed June 24, 2010).

Security Spotlight, "Even Governments are not Immune to Hacktivism" (February 8, 2010).

Seltzer, W., "Infrastructures of Censorship and Lessons from Copyright Resistance" (2011), USENIX, available at https://wendy.seltzer.org/pubs/seltzer-censorship.pdf.

Solomon, A., and Evron, G., "The World of Botnets," *Virus Bulletin.* (September 2008).

Symantec, *Report on the Underground Economy* (November 2008), available at http://eval.symantec.com/mktginfo/enterprise/white_papers/b-white paper_underground_economy_report_11-2008-14525717.en-us.pdf (last accessed June 28, 2010).

TrustDefender, "In-Depth Analysis of Mebroot/Torpig Trojan Available," available at http://www.trustdefender.com/trustdefender-labs-blog-in-depth-analysis-of-mebroot-torpig-trojan-available.html (last accessed January 31, 2011).

Wheeler, D., and Larsen, G., "Techniques for Cyber Attack Attribution" (2003), *Institute for Defense Analysis*, available at https://www.research gate.net/publication/235170094_Techniques_for_Cyber_Attack_Attribution.

United States Department Of Justice, Criminal Division, Computer Crime & Intellectual Property Section, Cybersecurity Unit, "A Framework for a Vulnerability Disclosure Program for Online Systems" (July 2017), available at https://www.justice.gov/criminal-ccips/page/file/983996/download.

Briefing Papers/Working Papers/White Papers/Theses/ Research Projects

Barroso, D., "Botnets—The Silent Threat" (2007), European Union Agency for Network and Information Security, available at https://www.enisa.europa.eu/publications/archive/botnets-2013-the-silent-threat (last accessed January 29, 2010).

Brunea, G., "DNS Sinkhole" (August 7, 2010), SANS Institute InforSec Reading Room, 2, available at http://www.sans.org/reading_room/whitepapers/dns/dns-sinkhole_33523 (last accessed February 20, 2011).

Cate, F., "Information Security Breaches: Looking Back & Thinking Ahead," Centre for Information Policy Leadership (2008), available at https://www.repository.law.indiana.edu/cgi/viewcontent.cgi?referer=https://

www.google.com/&httpsredir=1&article=1235&context=facpub (last accessed November 29, 2018).

Clayton, R., "Complexities in Criminalising Denial of Service Attacks" written for the *Legal Subgroup of the Internet Crime Forum* (February 2006), available at www.cl.cam.ac.uk/~rnc1/complexity.pdf.

Clayton, R., "Missing the Wood for the Trees," comments on ICANN fast-flux-report (February 2009), available at http://forum.icann.org/lists/fast-flux-initial-report/msg00022.html (last accessed February 7, 2011).

Connelly, C., Maurushat, A., Vaile, D., and Van Dijk, P., "Cyber-Security Education Research Project" (2010).

Honeypot Project, "Know Your Enemy" series of whitepapers, available at http://old.honeynet.org/papers/index.html (last accessed November 12, 2010).

Krogoth, "Botnet Construction, Control and Concealment: Looking into the Current Technology and Analysing Tendencies and Future Trends" (2008), available at http://www.shadowserver.org/wiki/uploads/Information/thesis_botnet_krogoth_2008_final.pdf (last accessed July 5 2010).

Lessig, L., and Resnick, P., "The Architectures of Mandated Access Controls," available at http://cyber.law.harvard.edu/works/lessig/Tprc98_d.pdf.

Lovet, Guillaume, "Fighting Cybercrime: Technical, Juridical and Ethical Challenges," paper presented at the Virus Bulletin Conference 2009, Geneva, September 23, 2009.

Lumby, C, Green, L., and Hartley, J., "Untangling the Net: The Scope of Content Captured by Mandatory Internet Filtering" (December 2009), report written for Google Australia, available at http://www.saferinternetgroup.org/pdfs/lumby.pdf (last accessed January 3, 2011).

Martin, D. (eds.), *Privacy Enhancing Technologies* (June 30 2005). Vol. 3856 of Lecture Notes of Computer Science. Springer 2005. Available at https://link.springer.com/content/pdf/bfm%3A978-3-540-34746-0%2F1.pdf.

Maurushat, A. "Freedom House Report on Internet Freedom: Australia" (2011).

Nazario, J, "Politically Motivated Denial of Service Attacks," The Virtual Battlefield: Perspectives on Cyber Warefare, Arbor Networks, available at http://www.ccdcoe.org/publications/virtualbattlefield/12_NAZARIO%20Politically%20Motivated%20DDoS.pdf.

Rudesill, D. S., Caverlee, J., and Sui, D., "The Deep Web and the Darknet: A Look Inside the Internet's Massive Black Box" (October 20, 2015), *Woodrow Wilson International Center for Scholars*, STIP 03, October 2015; Ohio State Public Law Working Paper No. 314, 6, available at https://ssrn.com/abstract=2676615 (last accessed November 2018).

Samuelson, P., 'Copyright, Commodification, and Censorship: Past as Prologue—But to What Future?,' Conference on the Commodification

of Information, Haifa University, 1999, available at http://www.people.
ischool.berkeley.edu/~pam/papers/haifa_priv_cens.pdf.

Trend Micro, "Zeus: A Persistent Criminal Enterprise" (March 2010), available at https://www.trendmicro.de/cloud-content/us/pdfs/security-
intelligence/white-papers/wp_zeus-persistent-criminal-enterprise.pdf
(last accessed December 2010).

Van Eeten, M., Bauer, J., Asghari, H., and Tabatabaie, S., "The Role of Internet
Service Providers in Botnet Mitigation: An Empirical Analysis Based
on Spam Data" (2010) *OECD Science, Technology and Industry Working
Papers*, 2010/5, OECD Publishing.

Vaughn, Z., "Hacktivism: Civil Rights Activism in the Digital Age" (2005).
University of Texas at Tyler. Available at http://zaxxon.net/eportfolio/
projects/philo/HacktivismResearch_ZV.pdf [Last accessed 20 April 2011].

Wray, S., "Electronic Civil Disobedience and the World Wide Web of
Hacktivism: A Mapping of Extraparliamentarian Direct Action Net
Politics" (November 1998), available at http://nknu.pbworks.com/f/netak
tivizam.pdf.

Yip, M., and Webber, C., "Hacktivism: a theoretical and empirical exploration
of China's cyber warriors" paper presented at ACM WebSci '11, Third
International Conference on Web Science, Koblenz, Germany, June 14–17,
2011, available at https://dl.acm.org/citation.cfm?doid=2527031.2527053.

Zenz, K., "Cyber Crime Within the Russian Federation," presentation at
AusCERT 2008.

Zhao, X., Howe, D., Nissenbaum, H., and Mazeres, D., "Phantom Access
Agent: a Client-Side Approach to Personal Information Control"
(December 2004), available at https://nissenbaum.tech.cornell.edu/
papers/paa.pdf.

Media Releases

Conroy, Stephen (Senator), "Budget provides policing for Internet safety"
(May 13, 2008), available at http://www.minister.dbcde.gov.au/media/
media_releases/2008/033.

Di Jiang Innovations, "DJI To Offer 'Bug Bounty' Rewards For Reporting
Software Issues" (August 28, 2017), available at https://www.dji.com/
newsroom/news/dji-to-offer-bug-bounty-rewards-for-reporting-
software-issues.

FBI, "Sixteen Individuals Arrested in the United States for Alleged Roles
in Cyber Attacks" (July 19, 2011), available at http://www.fbi.gov/news/
pressrel/press-releases/sixteen-individuals-arrested-in-the-united-states-
for-alleged-roles-in-cyber-attacks (last accessed November 10, 2011).

———, "Member of Hacking Group LulzSec Arrested for June 2011 Intrusion
of Sony Pictures Computer Systems" (September 22, 2011), available at
http://www.fbi.gov/losangeles/press-releases/2011/member-of-hacking-

group-lulzsec-arrested-for-june-2011-intrusion-of-sony-pictures-computer-systems (last accessed October 20, 2011).

——, "Two Men Charged in New Jersey with Hacking AT&T's Servers" (January 18, 2011), available at http://www.fbi.gov/newark/press-releases/2011/nk011811.htm (last accessed November 11, 2011).

——, "Second Member of Hacking Group Sentenced to More Than a Year in Prison for Stealing Customer Information from Sony Pictures Computers" (FBI press release, August 8, 2013), available at https://archives.fbi.gov/archives/losangeles/press-releases/2013/second-member-of-hacking-group-sentenced-to-more-than-a-year-in-prison-for-stealing-customer-information-from-sony-pictures-computers.

Sopho, "Sopho Assists Computer Crime Unit in Bringing Botnet Master to Justice" (June 12, 2008), available at http://www.sophos.com/pressoffice/news/articles/2008/06/bentley-imprisoned.html.

US Attorney's Office, Northern District of California, "Thirteen Defendants Plead Guilty For December 2010 Cyber-Attack Against PayPal" (December 6, 2013), available athttp://www.justice.gov/usao/can/news/2013/2013_12_06_thirteen.guiltyplea.press.html.

US Department Of Justice, Western District of Washington, "California Man Pleads Guilty in 'Botnet' Attack That Impacted Seattle Hospital and Defense Department" (May 4, 2006), available at https://www.justice.gov/archive/criminal/cybercrime/press-releases/2006/maxwellPlea.htm (last accessed November 2018).

US Division—Center, "Soldier Faces Criminal Charges" (July 6, 2010), available at http://www.cbsnews.com/htdocs/pdf/ManningPreferral ofCharges.pdf.

Magazine and Newspaper Articles

Abad-Santos, A., "Susan G. Komen Foundation was Hacked Last Night," *Atlantic Wire*, February 2, 2012, available at http://www.theatlantic wire.com/national/2012/02/susan-g-komen-foundation-website-was-hacked-last-night/48192/.

ABC News, "Japanese Web Sites Hacked," January 25, 2001, available at http://abcnews.go.com/Technology/story?id=99306&page=1 (last accessed November 14, 2011).

Aegerter, G., "13 Alleged Members of Anonymous Hacking Group indicted, accused of Participating in Operation Payback," *NBC News*, November 3, 2015, available at https://www.nbcnews.com/news/world/13-alleged-members-anonymous-hacking-group-indicted-accused-participating-operation-flna8C11332039.

Alizar, A., "AOSP Browser SOP," *Xakep*, September 18, 2014, available at http://xakep.ru/news/aosp-browser-sop/.

Allen, J., "Ethical hacker points out security concerns with using home baby monitors," *7News Denver*, January 28, 2015, available at http://www. thedenverchannel.com/news/local-news/ethical-hacker-points-out-security-concerns-with-using-home-baby-monitors01282015.

Anderson, N., "Vint Cerf: one quarter of all computers part of a botnet," *Ars Technica*, January 26, 2007, available at http://www.arstechnica.com/news. ars/post/20070125-8707.html. (last accessed May 31, 2011).

Andy, 'Sports Streamers, Indexes and Broadcast Tools Hit By DDoS Attacks', *Torrent Freak*, June 11, 2013, available at https://torrentfreak.com/sports-streamers-indexes-and-broadcast-tools-hit-by-ddos-attacks-130611/.

AnonWatcher, "GCHQ Hacked. North Korea Claimed," *AnonHQ*, January 3, 2015, available at http://anonhq.com/gchq-hacked-north-korea-claimed/.

Arthur, C., "Alleged LulzSec hacker of Sony Pictures faces trial data in December," *Guardian*, October 18, 2011, available at http://www.guard ian.co.uk/technology/2011/oct/18/lulzsec-alleged-recursion-hacker-trial.

——, "Hacking Group Claiming to be LulzSec Targets US Military Dating Website," *Guardian*, March 28, 2012, available at http://www.guardian. co.uk/technology/2012/mar/28/hacking-group-lulzsec-dating-website.

——, "LulzSec Hacker Arrested Over Sony Attack," *Guardian*, August 29, 2012, available at http://www.guardian.co.uk/technology/2012/aug/29/ lulzsec-hacker-arrest-sony-attack.

——, "Microsoft and Symantec Take Out Botnet Responsible for More Than $1m of Fraud," *Guardian*, February 7, 2013, available at http:// www.guardian.co.uk/technology/2013/feb/07/microsoft-symantec-botnet-fraud-pcs.

Ashford, W., "Chinese university targeted by Islamic State hacktivist," *Computer Weekly*, January 18, 2016, available at http://www.com-puterweekly.com/news/4500271103/Chinese-university-targeted-by-Islamic-State-hacktivist.

Associated Press, "Panel Says WikiLeaks Suspect is Competent to Stand Trial," *New York Times*, April 29, 2011, A11, available at http:// www.nytimes.com/2011/04/30/us/30brfs-PANELSAYSWIK_BRF. html?_r=1&ref=bradleyemanning.

Australian (The), "'Anonymous' hackers hit Visa, Mastercard and Sarah Palin in WikiLeaks revenge," December 9, 2010, available at http://www. theaustralian.com.au/in-depth/wikileaks/anonymous-hackers-hit-visa-mastercard-in-wikileaks-revenge/story-fn775xjq-1225968083650 (last accessed December 10, 2010).

Bajak, F., "Anonymous Hackers Claim They Were Infiltrated," *Bellingham Herald*, February 29, 2012, available at http://bellinghamherald. com/2012/02/29/2415830/anonymous-hackers-claim-they-were.html.

Baker, K., "Anonymous outs members of alleged Steubenville High School 'Rape Crew,'" *Jezebel*, December 24, 2012, available at http://jezebel.

com/5970975/anonymous-outs-members-of-alleged-steubenville-high-school-rape-crew.

——, "Hacking group Anonymous to target paedophiles using the 'dark web' to carry out child abuse," *Daily Mail*, January 25, 2015, available at http://www.dailymail.co.uk/news/article-2924864/Hacking-group-Anonymous-target-paedophiles.html.

Ball, J., "WikiLeaks Publishes Stratfor Emails Linked to Anonymous Attack," *Guardian*, February 27, 2012, available at http://www.guardian.co.uk/media/2012/feb/27/wikileaks-publishes-stratfor-emails-anonymous.

Baloch, F., "Online Security: Pakistani helps Google avoid privacy disaster," *Express Tribune*, September 20, 2014, available at http://tribune.com.pk/story/764713/online-security-pakistani-helps-google-avoid-privacy-disaster/.

Banyan, "Messiah complicated," *The Economist*, December 7, 2013, available at http://www.economist.com/blogs/banyan/2013/12/hacking-singapore.

——, "Two Steps Back," *The Economist*, February 25, 2014, available at http://www.economist.com/blogs/banyan/2013/06/regulating-singapores-internet.

Barlow, J. P., "Is there a there in Cyberspace?" *Utne Reader*, 1995, available at https://www.utne.com/community/isthereathereincyberspace (last accessed November 2018).

Barakat, A., and Khattab, S. "A Comparative Study of Traditional Botnets Versus Super-Botnet," in INFOSEC 2010.

Bastone, W., and Goldberg, A., "Autistic Hacker Helped FBI Nail Anonymous Boss," *The Smoking Gun*, May 13, 2014, available at http://www.thesmokinggun.com/documents/eekdacat-and-the-fbi-576432 (last accessed March 11, 2014).

Bates, D., "Anonymous threaten to unmask boys who 'drove 17-year-old girl to hang herself after they gang raped her and put photo on web,'" *Daily Mail*, April 11, 2013, available at http://www.dailymail.co.uk/news/article-2307266/Rehtaeh-Parsons-gang-rape-Anonymous-threaten-unmask-boys-drove-girl-hang-herself.html.

Batty, D., "Hacking suspect Ryan Cleary suffers from Autism, Court told," *Guardian*, June 26, 2011, available at http://www.theguardian.com/technology/2011/jun/25/hacker-ryan-cleary-diagnosed-autism (last accessed March 11, 2015).

BBC News, "A-Z Hack Attack," February 11, 2000, available at http://news.bbc.co.uk/2/hi/uk_news/639248.stm.

——, "Baidu hacked by 'Iranian cyber army,'" January 12, 2010, available at http://news.bbc.co.uk/2/hi/8453718.stm (last accessed January 13, 2010).

——, "Questions Cloud Cyber Crime Cases," October 17, 2003, available at http://www.bbc.co.uk/2/hi/technology/3202116.stm (last accessed April 27, 2010).

———, "Stuxnet Worm Hits Iran Nuclear Plant Staff Computers," September 26, 2010, available at http://www.bbc.co.uk/news/world-middle-east-11414483 (last accessed November 12, 2010).

———, "York Facebook hacking student Glenn Mangham jailed," February 17, 2012, available at https://www.bbc.com/news/uk-england-york-north-yorkshire-17079853.

———, "Anonymous hits UK government websites in Assange protest," August 21, 2012, available at http://www.bbc.com/news/technology-19330592.

———, "Anonymous hacking group target police web forum," October 24, 2012, available at http://www.bbc.com/news/uk-20072981.

———, "Lauri Love case: Hacking Suspect Wins Extradition Appeal," February 5, 2018, available at https://www.bbc.com/news/uk-england-42946540.

Bergen, J., "Anonymous hacktivists take down MasterCard.com again in support of WikiLeaks," Geek, June 28, 2011, available at http://www.geek.com/articles/news/anonymous-hacktivists-take-down-mastercard-com-again-in-support-of-wikileaks-20110628/ (last accessed June 29, 2011).

Berinato, S., "Attack of the Bots," Wired, November 1, 2006, Issue 14.11.

Beschizza, R., "LulzSec claims FBI affiliate hacked, users and botnet are exposed," Boing Boing, June 3, 2011, available at http://boingboing.net/2011/06/03/lulzsec-claims-fbi-a.html.

Bloomberg, "An Evolving Crisis," Business Week, April 10, 2008, available at https://www.bloomberg.com/news/articles/2008-04-09/an-evolving-crisis.

Blue, V., "Anonymous Hacks US Sentencing Commission and Distributes Files," ZDNet, January 26, 2013, available at http://www.zdnet.com/anonymous-hacks-us-sentencing-commission-distributes-files-7000010369/.

———, "Feds Stumbling After Anonymous Launches Operation Last Resort," ZDNet, January 30, 2013, available at http://www.zdnet.com/feds-stumbling-after-anonymous-launches-operation-last-resort-7000010541/.

Bray, H., "Rapid7 of Boston warns of Android flaw," Boston Globe, September 15, 2014, available at http://www.bostonglobe.com/business/2014/09/15/rapid-boston-finds-android-flaw/JJ9iHJB6YTcs10a7O9TjpN/story.html.

Brewster, T., "Anonymous Strikes Downing Street and Ministry of Justice," Tech Week Europe, April 10, 2012, available at http://www.techweekeurope.co.uk/news/anonymous-government-downing-street-moj-71979.

———, "Widespread Android Vulnerability 'A Privacy Disaster', Claim Researchers," Forbes, September 16, 2014, available at http://www.forbes.com/sites/thomasbrewster/2014/09/16/widespread-android-vulnerability-a-privacy-disaster-claim-researchers/.

Bright, P., "Android Browser flaw a 'privacy disaster' for half of Android users," Ars Technica, September 17, 2014, available at http://

arstechnica.com/security/2014/09/android-browser-flaw-a-privacy-disaster-for-half-of-android-users/.

Broad, W., Markoff, J., and Sander, D., "Israeli Test Worm Called Crucial in Iran Nuclear Delay," *New York Times*, January 15, 2011, A1.

Broersma, M., "Hacker Pleads Guilty to Abortion Website Attack," *Tech Week Europe*, March 12, 2012, available at http://www.techweekeurope.co.uk/news/hacker-pleads-guilty-to-abortion-website-attack-66295.

——, "Anonymous Claims Home Office Website Takedown," *Tech Week Europe*, April 8, 2012, available at http://www.techweekeurope.co.uk/news/anonymous-home-office-ddos-71886.

Brown, B., "A sinister cyber-surveillance scheme exposed," *Guardian*, June 23, 2011, available at https://www.theguardian.com/commentisfree/cifamerica/2011/jun/22/hacking-anonymous.

Builder, "Metasploit: Major Android Bug is a Privacy Disaster (CVE-2014-6041)," *LinusTechTips*, September 15, 2014, available at http://linustechtips.com/main/topic/216087-metasploit-major-android-bug-is-a-privacy-disaster-cve-2014-6041/.

Burt, J., "Anonymous Defaces Many Chinese Government Websites," *Tech Week Europe*, April 6, 2012, available at http://www.techweekeurope.co.uk/news/anonymous-defaces-chinese-websites-71791.

Camber, R., Collins, L., and Fernandez, C., "British teenager charged over cyber attack on CIA as pirate group takes revenge on 'snitches who framed him'," *Daily Mail UK*, June 22, 2011, available at http://www.dailymail.co.uk/sciencetech/article-2006118/Ryan-Cleary-charged-cyber-attack-CIA-LulzSec-takes-revenge.html (last accessed November 10, 2011).

CBC News, "'Tell Vic Everything' tweets protest online surveillance," February 18, 2012, available at https://www.cbc.ca/news/politics/tell-vic-everything-tweets-protest-online-surveillance-1.1187721.

Chesney, B., "Legislative Hackback: Notes on the Active Cyber Defense Certainty Act discussion draft," *Law Fare Blog* (March 7, 2017), available at https://www.lawfareblog.com/legislative-hackback-notes-active-cyber-defense-certainty-act-discussion-draft.

Chiaramonte, P., and Winter, J., "Hacker Group Anonymous Threatens to Attack Stock Exchange," *Fox News*, October 4, 2011, available at http://www.foxnews.com/scitech/2011/10/04/hacker-group-anonymous-threatens-to-attack-stock-exchange/ (last accessed October 4, 2011).

Cluley, G., "AnonPlus, Anonymous's social network, is hacked," *Naked Security*, July 22, 2011, available at https://nakedsecurity.sophos.com/2011/07/22/anonplus-anonymouss-social-network-is-hacked/.

CNN Tech, "Hackers attack US government Web sites in protest of Chinese embassy bombing," May 10, 1999, available at http://edition.cnn.com/TECH/computing/9905/10/hack.attack/ (last accessed November 10, 2011).

Comlay, E., "Hackers target Mexico government websites," *Reuters*, September 15, 2011, available at http://www.reuters.com/article/2011/09/15/us-mexico-hackers-idUSTRE78E7AC20110915 (last accessed September 18, 2011).

Constantin, L., "Sony Pictures Russian Website Compromised," *Softpedia*, June 6, 2011, available at http://news.softpedia.com/news/Sony-Pictures-Russian-Website-Compromised-204563.shtml.

——, "AntiSec Hackers Hit 77 Law Enforcement Websites," *Softpedia*, August 1, 2011, available at http://news.softpedia.com/news/AntiSec-Hackers-Hit-77-Law-Enforcement-Websites-214555.shtml.

——, "U.K. spy agency attacked hacktivist groups," *Computer World*, February 5, 2014, available at http://www.computerworld.com/article/2487354/cybercrime-hacking/u-k--spy-agency-attacked-hacktivist-groups.html.

——, "Many Android devices vulnerable to session hijacking through the default browser," *Computer World*, September 16, 2014, available at http://www.computerworld.com/article/2684059/many-android-devices-vulnerable-to-session-hijacking-through-the-default-browser.html.

Couts, A., "Citibank hacked, more than 200,000 bank customers at risk," *Digital Trends*, June 9, 2011, available at http://www.digitaltrends.com/computing/citibank-hacked-more-than-200000-bank-customers-at-risk/.

——, "Hackers leak Citigroup CEO's personal data after Occupy Wall Street arrests," *Digital Trends*, August 18, 2011, available at http://www.digitaltrends.com/computing/hackers-leak-citigroup-ceos-personal-data-after-occupy-wall-street-arrests/.

Coyne, A., "How the AFP nabbed an Aussie Anonymous hacker," *It News*, March 20, 2017, available at https://www.itnews.com.au/news/how-the-afp-nabbed-an-aussie-anonymous-hacker-455142.

Currie, R., "Japanese Cyber Security Minister doesn't' know what USB Stick is," *The Register*, November 25, 2018, available at https://www.theregister.co.uk/2018/11/15/japanese_cyber_security_minister_doesnt_know_what_a_usb_stick_is/.

Curtis, S., "China Implicated in Hack of French G20 Files," *Tech Week Europe*, March 7, 2011, available at http://www.techweekeurope.co.uk/news/china-implicated-in-hack-of-french-g20-files-23062.

Daily Pakistan, September 17, 2014, available at http://dailypakistan.com.pk/daily-bites/17-Sep-2014/144263

Davis, J., "LulzSec's CIA hack just one of many high-profile hackings," *International Business Times*, June 15, 2011, available at http://www.ibtimes.com/articles/163678/20110615/google-lulzsec-s-cia-hack-just-one-of-many-high-profile-hackings.htm (last accessed June 20, 2011).

Dawn, "Pakistani researcher reveals privacy flaw in Android browsers," *Dawn*, September 20, 2014, available at http://www.dawn.com/news/1133178/ pakistani-researcher-reveals-privacy-flaw-in-android-browsers.

Desjardin, M., "How a White Hat Hacker Saved Your Facebook Photos," *Reviewed*, February 19 2015, available at https://www.reviewed.com/ cameras/news/how-a-hacker-saved-your-facebook-photos.

Dodd, V., and Halliday, J., "Teenager Ryan Cleary Charged Over LulzSec Hacking," *Guardian*, June 22, 2011, available at https://www.theguardian. com/technology/2011/jun/22/ryan-cleary-charged-lulzsec-hacking.

Ducklin, P., "'Shocking' Android browser bug could be a 'privacy disaster': here's how to fix it," *Naked Security*, September 16, 2014, available at http://nakedsecurity.sophos.com/2014/09/16/shocking-android-browser- bug-could-be-a-privacy-disaster-heres-how-to-fix-it/.

Dunn, J. E., "Alleged LulzSec Hacker 'Kayla' Arrested By UK Police," *CSO Online*, September 2, 2011, available at http://www.csoonline.com/ article/689060/alleged-lulzsec-hacker-kayla-arrested-by-uk-police (last accessed November 10, 2011).

Eleftheriou-Smith, L., "Anonymous calls for activists to help expose international paedophile networks with 'Operation DeathEaters,'" *Independent*, January 23, 2015, available at http://www.independent. co.uk/news/uk/home-news/anonymous-calls-for-activists-to-help- expose-international-paedophile-networks-with-operation-deatheaters- 9998350.html.

Elise, A., "China Hacktivists GreatFire Hit with DDoS Attack Costing Up to $30,000 Per Day," *International Business Times*, March 21, 2015, available at http://www.ibtimes.com/china-hacktivists-greatfire-hit- ddos-attack-costing-30000-day-1854692.

Enigmax, "New 4chan DDoS Targets Hated Anti-Piracy Law Firm," *Torrent Freak*, September 22, 2010, available at https://torrentfreak.com/ new-4chan-ddos-targets-hated-anti-piracy-law-firm-100922/.

Ernesto, "Sports Streaming/Torrent Links Site Victorious in Court," *Torrent Freak*, May 10, 2010, available at https://torrentfreak.com/sports- streaming-torrent-links-site-victorious-in-court-100510/.

Errett, J., "Expecting Anonymous at #TMX," *Now Toronto*, November 7, 2011, available at http://www.nowtoronto.com/news/webjam.cfm?content= 183319 (last accessed November 8, 2011).

Express Tribune, "Credit to our white-hats," September 21, 2014, available at http://tribune.com.pk/story/764925/credit-to-our-white-hats/.

Fan, X., "WikiLeaks accuses Union of 'censorship,'" *Cherwell News*, February 3, 2013, available at http://www.cherwell.org/news/world/ 2013/02/03/wikileaks-accuses-union-of-quotcensorshipquot.

Farberov, S., Pow, H., and Nye, J., "Revealed: Prosecutors turned down Reddit co-founder Aaron Swartz's request for plea deal over MIT hacking case TWO DAYS before his suicide," *Daily Mail*, January 14, 2013, available at http://www.dailymail.co.uk/news/article-2262137/Aaron-Swartz-Reddit-founder-request-plea-deal-turned-Massachusetts-prosecutor.html#axzz2KkIHBHh6.

Farley, M., "Dissidents Hack Holes in China's New Wall," *Los Angeles Times*, January 4, 1999, available at http://articles.latimes.com/1999/jan/04/news/mn-60340.

Fernandez, C., "Second WikiLeaks payback vs. MasterCard: LulzSec or Anonymous?," *International Business Times*, June 29, 2011, available at http://www.ibtimes.com.au/second-wikileaks-payback-vs-mastercard-lulzsec-or-anonymous-1283014 (last accessed June 30, 2011).

Finkle, J., "Zombie Attack Exposes Security Flaws, Experts Say," *Sydney Morning Herald*, February 15, 2013, available at http://www.smh.com.au/technology/technology-news/zombie-attack-exposes-security-flaws-experts-say-20130215-2egpw.html.

Fisher, D., "Flaw in Android Browser Allows Same Origin Policy Bypass," *Threat Post*, September 15, 2014, available at http://threatpost.com/flaw-in-android-browser-allows-same-origina-policy-bypass/108265#comment-317786.

Fletcher, O., "China Hackers Seek to Rally Peers Against Cybertheft," *Wall Street Journal*, September 3, 2011, available at http://online.wsj.com/article/SB10001424053111903895904576546430870651962.html (last accessed September 5, 2011).

Fogarty, K., "Hackers come out of shadows to attack police, support Occupy protests," *IT World*, October 28, 2011, available at http://www.itworld.com/security/217561/hackers-come-out-shadows-attack-police-support-occupy-protests.

Fox News, "Cyberattack Targeted Personal Data of over 100,000 Federal Employees," May 26, 2012, available at https://www.foxnews.com/tech/cyberattack-targeted-personal-data-of-over-100k-federal-employees.

Franceschi-Bicchierai, L., "Anonymous claims first victim in 'Operation Charlie Hebdo,'" *Mashable*, January 11, 2015, available at http://mashable.com/2015/01/10/anonymous-operation-charlie-hebdo/.

Friedman, A., "Android bug called a 'privacy disaster,'" *Phone Arena*, September 16, 2014, available at http://www.phonearena.com/news/New-Android-bug-called-a-privacy-disaster_id60750.

Gallagher, P., "Abortion Website Hacker Caught," *Guardian*, March 11, 2012, available at http://www.guardian.co.uk/world/2012/mar/11/abortion-website-hacker-caught.

Gallagher, S., "Anonymous takes down darknet child porn site on Tor network," *Ars Technica*, October 24, 2011, available at http://arstechnica.com/business/news/2011/10/anonymous-takes-down-darknet-child-porn-site-on-tor-network.ars (last accessed October 31, 2011).

——, "White hat claims Yahoo and WinZip hacked by 'shellshock' exploiters," *Ars Technica*, October 7, 2014, available at http://arstechnica.com/security/2014/10/white-hat-claims-yahoo-and-winzip-hacked-by-shellshock-exploiters/.

Goldman, J., "Indonesian Government Sites Hacked Following Hacker's Arrest," *eSecurity Planet*, January 31, 2013, available at http://www.esecurityplanet.com/hackers/indonesian-government-sites-hacked-following-hackers-arrest.html.

Gover, D., "Anonymous Hackers Threaten Web War Against Hong Kong Police and Government," *International Business Times*, October 2, 2014, available at http://www.ibtimes.co.uk/anonymous-hackers-threaten-web-war-against-hong-kong-police-government-1468220.

Grant, D., "NYSE Hacked! Is The Anonymous Infrastructure Crumbling?," *New York Observer*, October 10, 2011, available at http://www.observer.com/2011/10/nyse-remains-unhacked-is-the-anonymous-infrastructure-crumbling-video/ (last accessed October 10, 2011).

Greenberg, A., "The Streisand Effect," *Forbes*, May 11, 2007, available at http://www.forbes.com/2007/05/10/streisand-digg-web-tech-cx_ag_0511streisand.html.

——, "Chinese Botnet Sells Point-And-Click Cyberattacks," *Forbes*, September 13, 2010, available at https://www.forbes.com/sites/andygreenberg/2010/09/13/chinese-botnet-sells-point-and-click-cyberattacks/#5ccf7aee3070.

Halliday, J., "Gene Simmons gets kiss of death from notorious web forum," *Guardian*, October 14, 2010, available at http://www.guardian.co.uk/technology/blog/2010/oct/14/gene-simmons-anonymous-attack-filesharing.

——, "Anonymous Teenager Hacker Spared Jail over Cyber Attacks," *Guardian*, February 1, 2013, available at http://www.guardian.co.uk/technology/2013/feb/01/anonymous-teenage-hacker.

——, "Briton Lauri Love faces hacking charges in US," *Guardian*, October 29, 2013, available at http://www.theguardian.com/world/2013/oct/28/us-briton-hacking-charges-nasa-lauri-love.

Halliday, J., and Arthur, C., "Anonymous' Release of Met and FBI Call Puts Hacker Group Back Centre Stage," *Guardian*, February 3, 2012, available at http://www.guardian.co.uk/technology/2012/feb/03/anonymous-hack-met-fbi-call.

Huffington Post, "Anonymous Claims Suspect Confessed To Rehtaeh Parsons' Rape," April 12, 2013, available at http://www.huffingtonpost.com/2013/04/12/anonymous-suspect-confession-rehtaeh-parsons-rape_n_3070615.html.

Hughes, M., "This Android Browser Bug Will Make You Upgrade To KitKat," *Make Use Of*, September 25, 2014, available at http://www.makeuseof. com/tag/this-android-browser-bug-will-make-you-upgrade-to-kitkat/.

Hunn, D., "How computer hackers changed the Ferguson protests," *St. Louis Post-Dispatch*, August 13, 2014, available at http://www.stltoday.com/ news/local/crime-and-courts/how-computer-hackers-changed-the-ferguson-protests/article_d81a1da4-ae04-5261-9064-e4c255111c94.html.

IT Security Training, "First State Super in Breach of Privacy Act' June 7, 2012 available at https://www.itsecuritytraining.com.au/articles/first-state-super-breach-privacy-act.

Jardin, X., "Anonymous hacks BART after wireless shutdown; protests planned for Monday," *Boing Boing*, August 14, 2011, available at http:// boingboing.net/2011/08/14/anonymous-hacks-bart-after-wireless-shutdown-protests-planned-for-monday.html.

Jerusalem Post, "Online activists hack into Syrian government websites," September 26, 2011, available at https://www.jpost.com/Middle-East/ Online-activists-hack-into-Syrian-government-websites (last accessed September 27, 2011).

Jha, A. K., "#OpHK aka Operation Hong Kong: Anonymous hacks Chinese Government website," *Tech Worm*, 2014, available at http://www.tech worm.net/2014/10/operation-hong-kong-anonymous-hacks-chinese-government-website.html.

———, "RedHack leaks email id's and password from Turkish Cooperation and Coordination Agency (TIKA)," *Tech Worm*, May 18, 2014, available at http://www.techworm.net/2014/05/redhack-leaks-email-ids-and-password.html.

———, "Pro-Russian Hackers leaks documents from Central Election Commission of Ukraine," *Tech Worm*, May 24, 2014, available at http:// www.techworm.net/2014/05/pro-russian-hackers-leaks-documents.html.

———, "Russian Prime Minister's Twitter account hacked," *Tech Work*, August 14, 2014, available at http://www.techworm.net/2014/08/russian-prime-ministers-twitter-account.html.

Jidenma, N., "Naija Cyber Hactivists Hack EFCC website to protest proposed internet censor in Nigeria," *The Next Web*, September 28, 2011, available at http://thenextweb.com/africa/2011/05/26/nigerian-government-agency-website-hacked-by-cyberhacktivists/.

Jowitt, T. "Anonymous Attacks Polish Websites for ACTA Support," *Tech Week Europe*, January 26, 2012, available at http://www.techweekeurope. co.uk/news/anonymous-attacks-polish-websites-for-acta-support-56450.

Karia, J., "Hacker exposes Three Million Iranian Bank Account Details," *Tech Week Europe*, available at http://www.techweekeurope.co.uk/news/ hacker-three-million-iranian-bank-accounts-73161.

———, "Lebanese Hacktivists Take Down 15 Government Websites," *Tech Week Europe*, available at http://www.techweekeurope.co.uk/news/lebanese-hacktivists-15-government-websites-73313.

Keller, B., "Dealing with Assange and the Wikileaks Secrets," *New York Times*, January 26, 2011, MM32.

Kharel, G. C., "Hactivist Group Gator League Brings Down British GCHQ Website, Takes Blame for N Korean Internet Outage," *International Business Times*, December 24, 2014, available at http://www.ibtimes.co.in/gator-league-brings-down-british-gchq-website-takes-blame-n-korean-internet-outage-618166.

Kirk, J., "Iranian Cyber Army Moves Into Botnets," *PCWorld*, August 25, 2010, available at http://www.pcworld.com/businesscenter/article/208670/iranian_cyber_army_moves_into_botnets.html.

———, "Turkish Hackers Strike Websites with DNS Hack," *PCWorld*, September 5, 2011, available at http://www.pcworld.com/article/239501/turkish_hackers_strike_websites_with_dns_hack.html.

Kopstein, J., "Hacker with a cause," *New Yorker*, November 21, 2013, available at http://www.newyorker.com/online/blogs/elements/2013/11/jeremy-hammond-and-anonymous-hacker-with-a-cause.html.

Kovacs, E, "Anonymous Turns Green and Goes After Polluters," *Softpedia*, November 15, 2011, available at http://news.softpedia.com/news/Anonymous-Turns-Green-and-Goes-After-Polluters-234681.shtml.

———, "French Nuke Company Fined After Hacking Greenpeace," *Softpedia*, November 16, 2011, available at http://news.softpedia.com/news/French-Nuke-Company-Fined-After-Hacking-Greenpeace-234900.shtml.

———, "Anonymous Attacks Anonymous for Being Trolls," *Softpedia*, November 16, 2011, available at http://news.softpedia.com/news/Anonymous-Attacks-Anonymous-For-Being-Trolls-234949.shtml (last accessed November 18, 2011).

———, "Anonymous Threatens Congress Over SOPA," *Softpedia*, November 17, 2011, available at http://news.softpedia.com/news/Anonymous-Threatens-Congress-Over-SOPA-235201.shtml.

———, "NSA Website Disrupted Following PRISM Leak, Hackers Want to Troll Agency," *Softpedia*, June 12, 2013, available at https://news.softpedia.com/news/NSA-Website-Disrupted-Following-PRISM-Leak-Hackers-Want-to-Troll-Agency-360574.shtml.

———, "RedHack begins hack attacks in protest against Turkey's New Internet Law," *Softpedia*, February 10, 2014, available at http://news.softpedia.com/news/RedHack-Begins-Hack-Attacks-in-Protest-Against-Turkey-s-New-Internet-Law-425418.shtml.

———, "RedHack Begins Hack Attacks in Protest Against Turkey's New Internet Law," *Tech Worm*, March 28, 2014, available at http://www.techworm.net/2014/03/redhack-ddoses-turkish.html.

——, "Dangerous "Same Origin Policy" Bypass Flaw Found in Android Browser," *Security Week*, September 16, 2014, available at http://www.securityweek.com/dangerous-same-origin-policy-bypass-flaw-found-android-browser.

Kumar, M., "Sony Music Brazil Gets Defaced!," *Hacker News*, June 5, 2011, available at http://thehackernews.com/2011/06/sony-music-brazil-gets-defaced.html (last accessed June 6, 2011).

——, "Customs Authority of Yemen Hacked for Protests against Government," *Hacker News*, August 5, 2011, available at http://thehack ernews.com/2011/08/customs-authority-of-yemen-hacked-for.html.

——, "Nepal Telecommunications Authority Hacked by w3bd3f4c3r," *Hacking Beast*, August 21, 2011, available at https://thehackernews.com/2011/08/nepal-telecommunications-authority.html (last accessed August 22, 2011).

——, "Operation OpIndependencia: Anonymous hit Mexican government official websites," *Hacker News*, September 16, 2011, available at http://thehackernews.com/2011/09/operation-opindependencia-anonymous-hit.html (last accessed September 30, 2011).

——, "International Foreign Government E-Mails Hacked by TeaMp0isoN," *Hacker News*, November 7, 2011, available at http://thehackernews.com/2011/11/international-foreign-government-e.html.

——, "Anonymous Hackers hack neo-Nazis websites & leak personal info of 16,000 Finns," *Hacker News*, November 8, 2011, available at http://thehackernews.com/2011/11/anonymous-hackers-hack-neo-nazis.html.

——, "Bangladesh Supreme Court website hacked," *Hacker News*, November 11, 2011, available at http://thehackernews.com/2011/11/bangladesh-supreme-court-website-hacked.html (last accessed November 12, 2011).

——, "Operation Brotherhood Shutdown: Multiple Sites taken down by Anonymous Hackers," *Hacker News*, November 12, 2011, available at http://thehackernews.com/2011/11/operation-brotherhood-shutdown-by.html (last accessed November 13, 2011).

——, "Vatican Radio Hacked by Anonymous Hackers," *Hacker News*, March 14, 2012, available at http://thehackernews.com/2012/03/vatican-radio-hacked-by-anonymous.html.

——, "New Android Browser Vulnerability Is a "Privacy Disaster" for 70% Of Android Users," *Hacker News*, September 16, 2014, available at http://thehackernews.com/2014/09/new-android-browser-vulnerability-is.html.

Lawson, L., "You say crackers; I say hacker: A hacking Lexicon," *Tech Republic*, April 13, 2001, available at https://www.techrepublic.com/article/you-say-cracker-i-say-hacker-a-hacking-lexicon/ (last accessed July 28, 2009).

Lemos, R., "Cisco, ISS file suit against rogue researcher Robert Lemos," *SecurityFocus*, July 27, 2005, available at http://www.securityfocus.com/news/11259 (last accessed February 10, 2014).

Lennon, M., "Hackers Used Sophisticated SMB Worm Tool to Attack Sony," *Security Week*, December 19, 2014, available at http://www.security week.com/hackers-used-sophisticated-smb-worm-tool-attack-sony (last accessed December 21, 2016).

Leyden, J., "EU climate exchange website hit by green-hat hacker," *The Register*, July 26, 2010, available at http://www.theregister.co.uk/2010/07/26/climate_exchange_website_hack/ (last accessed July 27, 2010).

——, "Anonymous attacks PayPal in 'Operation Avenge Assange,'" *The Register*, December 6, 2010, available at http://www.theregister.co.uk/2010/12/06/anonymous_launches_pro_wikileaks_campaign/.

——, "Anonymous hackers hacked by Young Turks," *The Register*, July 22, 2011, available at http://www.theregister.co.uk/2011/07/22/anonplus_hacked/ (last accessed July 23, 2011).

——, "German states defend use of 'Federal Trojan,'" *The Register*, October 12, 2011, available at http://www.theregister.co.uk/2011/10/12/bundestrojaner/.

——, "Hackers mistake French rugby site for German stock exchange," *The Register*, November 4, 2011, available at http://www.theregister.co.uk/2011/11/04/french_rugby_site_hacktivist_maul/.

Libbenga, J., "German court to examine Lufthansa attack," *The Register*, April 1, 2005, available at https://www.theregister.co.uk/2005/04/01/lufthansa_ddos_attack/.

Liebowitz, M., "Anonymous releases IP addresses of alleged child porn viewers," *NBC News*, November 3, 2011, available at http://www.nbcnews.com/id/45147364/ns/technology_and_sciencesecurity/t/anonymous-releases-ip-addresses-alleged-child-porn-viewers/#.XAAS7S1L1PM (last accessed November 4, 2011).

——, "Hackers Target Stock Index, Hit Rugby Team Instead," *Security News Daily*, November 4, 2011, available at http://www.securitynewsdaily.com/hackers-stock-index-rugby-team-1309/.

——, "Iranian 'Cyber Warriors Team' takes credit for NASA hack," *NBC News*, May 22, 2012, available at http://www.nbcnews.com/id/47522497/ns/technology_and_sciencesecurity/t/iranian-cyber-warriors-team-takes-credit-nasa-hack/#.XADd5y1L1PM.

Limer, E., "Anonymous follows through on BART hack, organises protest," *Geekosystems*, August 15, 2011, available at http://www.geekosystem.com/anon-hacks-bart/.

Lucas, D., "Exclusive: The Legendary #Anonymous PayPal 14 Speak Out Post-Sentencing," *The Cryptosphere*, October 31, 2014, available at https://thecryptosphere.com/2014/10/31/exclusive-the-anonymous-paypal-14-speak-out-post-sentencing/.

Lynch, D., "Pro-Russian Hacker Group CyberBerkut Claims Attack On German Government Websites," *International Business Times,* January 7, 2015, available at http://www.ibtimes.com/pro-russian-hacker-group-cyberberkut-claims-attack-german-government-websites-1775874.

Madrigal, A., "Ahmadinejad Publicly Acknowledges Stuxnet Disrupted Iranian Centrifuges," *The Atlantic,* November 29, 2010, available at http://www.theatlantic.com/technology/archive/2010/11/ahmadinejad-publicly-acknowledges-stuxnet-disrupted-iranian-centrifuges/67155/# (last accessed February 7, 2011).

Malhotra, S., "Android security flaw affects millions of users," *digit,* September 16, 2014, available at http://www.digit.in/mobile-phones/android-security-flaw-affects-millions-of-users-23921.html.

Mandell, N., "Anonymous hacker group threatens Mexican drug cartel Zetas in online video," *New York Daily News,* October 31, 2011, available at http://www.nydailynews.com/news/world/anonymous-hacker-group-threatens-mexican-drug-cartel-zetas-online-video-article-1.969859#ixzz1d4sAfvE6 (last accessed November 1, 2011).

Martin, A., "How Two LulzSec Hackers Slipped Up," *The Atlantic,* July 20, 2011, available at https://www.theatlantic.com/technology/archive/2011/07/how-two-lulzsec-hackers-slipped/353089/.

Masnik, M., "Collateral Censorship: Oxford Union Replaces Assange Speech Backdrop, Citing 'Copyright' Concerns," *Tech Dirt,* February 4, 2013, available at http://www.techdirt.com/articles/20130204/01405321873/collateral-censorshipoxford-union-replaces-assange-speech-backdrop-citing-copyright-concerns.shtml.

Mccaskill, S., "Anonymous Targets Vatican Website," *Tech Week Europe,* March 8, 2012, available at http://www.techweekeurope.co.uk/news/anonymous-targets-vatican-website-65797.

Mccarthy, T., "Andrew Auernheimer's conviction over computer fraud thrown out," *Guardian,* April 12, 2014, available at https://www.theguardian.com/technology/2014/apr/11/andrew-auernheimers-weev-conviction-vacated-hacking.

Messmer, E., "Symantec vs. Hotbar: Who Won?" *Network World,* January 3, 2006, previously available at http://www.networkworld.com/weblogs/security/011312.html.

Mick, J., "Anonymous Engages in Sony DDoS Attacks Over GeoHot PS3 Lawsuit," *Daily Tech,* April 4, 2011, available at http://www.dailytech.com/Anonymous+Engages+in+Sony+DDoS+Attacks+Over+GeoHot+PS3+Lawsuit/article21282.htm.

Millman, R., "SCO hit by hacker protest," *SC Magazine,* November 29, 2004, available at http://www.scmagazineus.com/sco-hit-by-hacker-protest/article/31510/.

Mills, E., "Hackers taunt Sony with more data leaks, hacks," *CNET*, June 6, 2011, available at http://news.cnet.com/8301-27080_3-20069443-245/hackers-taunt-sony-with-more-data-leaks-hacks/.

——, "AT&T-iPad hacker pleads guilty to computer charges," *Cnet*, June 23, 2011, available at http://news.cnet.com/8301-27080_3-20073791-245/at-t-ipad-hacker-pleads-guilty-to-computer-charges/.

——, "AT&T-iPad site hacker to fight on in court (exclusive)," *Cnet*, September 12, 2011, available at http://news.cnet.com/8301-27080_3-20105097-245/at-t-ipad-site-hacker-to-fight-on-in-court-exclusive/.

Moses, A. "Operation Titstorm: hackers bring down government websites," *Sydney Morning Herald*, February 10, 2010, available at https://www.smh.com.au/technology/operation-titstorm-hackers-bring-down-government-websites-20100210-nqku.html.

——, "Super bad: First State set police on man who showed them how 770 000 accounts could be ripped off," *Sydney Morning Herald*, October 18, 2011, available at http://www.smh.com.au/it-pro/security-it/super-bad-first-state-set-police-on-man-who-showed-them-how--770000-accounts-could-be-ripped-off-20111018-1lvx1.html (last accessed October 18, 2011).

——, "Super sloppy: First State customers kept in the dark," *Sydney Morning Herald*, October 19, 2011, available at http://www.smh.com.au/it-pro/security-it/super-sloppy-first-state-customers-kept-in-the-dark-20111019-1m7g6.html (last accessed October 20, 2011).

Muncaster, P. "Chinese hacktivists launch cyber attack on Japan," *The Register*, September 21, 2012, available at http://www.theregister.co.uk/2012/09/21/japan_china_attack_sites_senkaku/.

——, "US software firm hacked for years after suing China," *The Register*, November 29, 2012, available at https://www.theregister.co.uk/2012/11/29/solid_oak_china_hacked_three_years/.

Muthiyah, L., "Deleting Any Album—How I Hacked Your Facebook Photos," *The Zero Hack*, November 8, 2015, available at https://thezerohack.com/how-i-hacked-your-facebook-photos#articlescroll.

NDTV Correspondent, "Android Browser Security Hole Affects Millions of Users, Says Expert," *Gadgets360*, September 16, 2014, available at http://gadgets.ndtv.com/mobiles/news/android-browser-security-hole-affects-millions-of-users-says-expert-592578.

Neal, D., "Team Poison hacks Blackberry after riots," *The Inquirer*, August 9, 2011, available at http://www.theinquirer.net/inquirer/news/2100557/team-poison-hacks-blackberry-riots.

Nuttall, C., "Chinese protesters attack Indonesia through Net," *BBC News*, August 19, 1998, available at http://connections-qj.org/article/internet-china-civilian-and-military-uses.

Ockenden, W., "Crime Stoppers website hacked, police email addresses published in spying scandal 'payback,'" ABC News, November 27, 2013, available at http://www.abc.net.au/news/2013-11-26/crime-stoppers-site-targeted-by-indonesian-hackers/5116856.

Olson, P., "How Twitter Helped Brazil Become a Hotbed for Hacktivists," *Forbes*, February 27, 2012, available at http://www.forbes.com/sites/parmyolson/2012/02/27/how-twitter-helped-brazil-become-a-hotbed-for-hacktivists/.

Oremus, Will., "No, Seriously, Just Disable Java in Your Browser Right Now," *Slate*, January 14, 2013, available at https://slate.com/technol ogy/2013/01/java-zero-day-exploit-don-t-patch-just-disable-java-in-your-browser.html.

Panda Security, "Lulzsec and Anonymous Blur Lines Between 'Hacktivism' and Criminality, According to PandaLabs Q2 Report," *PR Newswire*, July 6, 2011, available at http://www.prnewswire.com/news-releases/lulzsec-and-anonymous-blur-lines-between-hacktivism-and-crimi nality-according-to-pandalabs-q2-report-125068654.html (last accessed July 8, 2011).

Pauli, D., "Aussies Hacked Pentagon, US Army, and Others," *IT News*, October 29, 2013, available at https://www.itnews.com.au/news/aussies-hacked-pentagon-us-army-and-others-362202.

Pauli, D., "THREE QUARTERS of Android mobiles open to web page spy bug," *The Register*, September 16, 2014, available at http://www.theregister.co.uk/2014/09/16/three_quarters_of_droid_phones_open_to_web_page_spy_bug/.

Penenberg, A., "Hacking Bhabha," *Forbes*, November 16, 1998, available at http://www.forbes.com/1998/11/16/feat.html (last accessed November 11, 2011).

Pfeffer, A, and Yaron, O., "Israel government, security services websites down in suspected cyber-attack," *Haaretz*, November 6, 2011, available at http://www.haaretz.com/news/diplomacy-defense/israel-government-security-services-websites-down-in-suspected-cyber-attack-1.394042 (last accessed November 7, 2011).

Pilger, J., "The War on Wikileaks: A John Pilger Investigation and Interview with Julian Assange," January 13, 2011, available at http://johnpilger.com/articles/the-war-on-wikileaks-a-john-pilger-investigation-and-interview-with-julian-assange.

Pilkington, E., "Jeremy Hammond: FBI directed my attacks on foreign government sites," *Guardian*, November 16, 2013, available at http://www.theguardian.com/world/2013/nov/15/jeremy-hammond-fbi-directed-attacks-foreign-government.

Poh, I., "Hacker who called himself 'The Messiah' jailed 4 years and 8 months," *Straits Times*, January 30, 2015, available at https://www.

straitstimes.com/singapore/courts-crime/hacker-who-called-himself-the-messiah-jailed-4-years-and-8-months.

Poulsen, K., "Ex-Hacker Adrian Lamo Institutionalized, Diagnosed with Asperger's," *Wired*, May 20, 2010, available at http://www.wired.com/2010/05/lamo/.

Poulsen, K. "First 100 Pages of Aaron Swartz's Secret Service File Released," *Wired*, December 8, 2013, available at http://www.wired.com/threatlevel/2013/08/swartz-foia-release/.

Poulsen, K., "Unprecedented 25-year sentence sought for TJX hacker," *Wired*, March 19, 2010, available at http://www.wired.com/2010/03/gonzalez-gov-memo/ (last accessed March 12, 2015).

Protalinski, E., "British student jailed for hacking into Facebook," *Zdnet*, February 18, 2012, available at http://www.zdnet.com/blog/facebook/british-student-jailed-for-hacking-into-facebook/9244 (last accessed December 21, 2016).

Quinn, B., "Interpol Website Suffers 'Anonymous Cyber-Attack,'" *Guardian*, March 29, 2012, available at http://www.guardian.co.uk/technology/2012/feb/29/interpol-website-cyber-attack.

Ragan, S., "CCC is at it again—hands out copies of German Interior Minister's fingerprint," *Tech Herald*, August 1, 2008, available at http://www.thetechherald.com/article.php/200814/581/CCC-is-at-it-again---hands-out-copies-of-German-Interior-Minister-s-fingerprint.

——, "Iranian Cyber Army defaces Voice of America and 93 other domains (Update)," *Tech Herald*, February 22, 2011, available at http://www.thetechherald.com/article.php/201108/6849/Iranian-Cyber-Army-defaces-Voice-of-America-and-93-other-domains.

——, "PBS: LulzSec attack an attempt to chill journalism," *Tech Herald*, May 30, 2011, available at http://www.thetechherald.com/article.php/201122/7215/PBS-LulzSec-attack-an-attempt-to-chill-journalism.

Raman, M., "FBI Cracks Down on 'Anonymous' Over PayPal Hacking, Arrests 14," *International Business Times*, July 20, 2011, available at https://www.ibtimes.com/fbi-cracks-down-anonymous-over-paypal-hacking-arrests-14-300225 (last accessed July 21, 2011).

Rash, M. "Mother, May I?," *Security Focus*, January 23, 2008, available at https://www.securityfocus.com/columnists/463 (last accessed November 2018).

Rashid, F., "Anonymous Beards the Banks to Play Twisted Santa Claus," *Tech Week Europe*, December 21, 2011, available at http://www.techweekeurope.co.uk/news/anonymous-beards-the-banks-to-play-twisted-santa-claus-50922.

——, "Hackers Compromised Yahoo Servers Using Shellshock Bug," *Security Week*, October 6, 2014, available at http://www.securityweek.com/hackers-compromised-yahoo-servers-using-shellshock-bug.

Raywood, D., "Is the Mariposa Botnet Still Functioning?" *It News,* June 24, 2010, available at https://www.itnews.com.au/news/is-the-mariposa-botnet-still-functioning-217678 (last accessed June 26, 2010).

Reuters, "War Hack Attacks Tit For Tat," *Wired,* March 28, 2003, available at http://www.wired.com/politics/law/news/2003/03/58275 (last accessed November 10, 2011).

——, "Government Website Hacked By Anonymous Over Censorship," *Sydney Morning Herald,* February 10, 2010, available at https://www.news.com.au/technology/government-websites-hacked-by-anonymous-over-censorship/news-story/d362c3330a6dfeb5632f74208c8df022.

Reuters HK, "Hackers 'disable' Hong Kong Civil Referendum Website," *Guardian,* March 23, 2012, available at http://www.guardian.co.uk/world/2012/mar/23/hackers-hong-kong-civil-referendum.

Riley, M., "China Mafia-Style Attack Drives California Firm to Brink," *Bloomberg,* November 28, 2012, available at http://www.bloomberg.com/news/2012-11-27/china-mafia-style-hack-attack-drives-california-firm-to-brink.html.

Rising, G., "Cody Kretsinger Arizona College Student Charged in Sony Hacking Case," *Huffington Post,* January 12, 2010, available at http://www.huffingtonpost.com/2011/09/23/cody-kretsinger-arizona-c_n_977490.html.

Romney, L., "Bart drafts new policy on disruption of cellphone service," *LA Times,* October 19, 2011, available at http://latimesblogs.latimes.com/lanow/2011/10/bart-outlines-cell-phone-service-disruption-policy.html (last accessed October 20, 2011).

Ronson, J., "Gary Mckinnon: Pentagon hacker's worst nightmare comes true," *Guardian,* August 1, 2009, available at http://www.theguardian.com/world/2009/aug/01/gary-mckinnon-extradition-nightmare (last accessed March 11, 2015).

Ross, M., "Anonymous Indonesia hacker says RBA, AFP attacks were retaliation for spying scandal," ABC News, November 21, 2013, available at http://www.abc.net.au/news/2013-11-21/hacker-says-rba-afp-attacks-were-retaliation-for-spying-scandal/5108220.

RT, "Anonymous busts Internet pedophiles," November 3, 2011, available at http://rt.com/usa/news/anonymous-child-tor-porn-513/ (last accessed November 15, 2011).

——, "NSA Site went down due to 'internal errors,' not DDoS attack, agency claims," October 27, 2013, available at http://rt.com/usa/nsa-site-ddos-attack-754/.

——, "Eye for eye? N. Korea internet restored after 9.5hr blackout," December 23, 2014, available at http://rt.com/news/216887-north-korea-internet-blackout/.

——, "Hacktivist group 'takes down' GCHQ website, claims N. Korean blackout," December 24, 2014, available at http://rt.com/news/217211-gchq-website-down-hackers/.

——, "Hacktivist leak alleges 'extortion & money laundering' by Ukraine's Right Sector leader," February 1, 2015, available at http://rt.com/news/228387-ukraine-hacktivists-leak-yarosh/.

Rushe, D., "Anonymous Publishes Trove of Emails from Haditha Marine Law Firm," *Guardian*, February 7, 2012, available at http://www.guardian.co.uk/technology/2012/feb/06/anonymous-haditha-killings.

——, "Anonymous Sends Unhappy Valentine's Day Greetings," *Guardian*, February 14, 2012, available at http://www.guardian.co.uk/world/us-news-blog/2012/feb/14/anonymous-hacking-valentines-day-nasdaq.

Russon, M., "Anonymous brings down 30 Chinese government websites to support Hong Kong protesters," *International Business Times*, April 13, 2015, available at http://www.ibtimes.co.uk/anonymous-brings-down-30-chinese-government-websites-support-hong-kong-protesters-1496069.

Saarinen, J., "Aussie Anon sentenced to three years' prison," *IT News*, November 19, 2015, available at https://www.itnews.com.au/news/aussie-anon-sentenced-to-three-years-prison-411978.

Sanchez, F., "Hackers hijack Twitter accounts of Chavez critics," *NBC News*, September 27, 2011, available at http://www.nbcnews.com/id/44689342/ns/technology_and_sciencesecurity/t/hackers-hijack-twitter-accounts-chavez-critics/.

Satter, R., and Sullivan E., "North Korea outage a case study in online uncertainties," *Sydney Morning Herald*, December 25, 2014, available at http://www.smh.com.au/digital-life/digital-life-news/north-korea-outage-a-case-study-in-online-uncertainties-20141224-12dltr.html.

Schroeder, S., "LulzSec Hackers Take Down CIA Website," *Mashable*, June 16, 2011, available at http://mashable.com/2011/06/16/lulzsec-hackers-cia/.

Seltzer, S., "For-Profit Company Oversaw Davis's Execution, Had Prompted Complaint for Illegal Purchase of Lethal Injection Drugs," *Alternet*, August 22, 2011, available at http://www.alternet.org/newsandviews/article/670237/for-profit_company_oversaw_davis%27s_execution,_had_prompted_complaint_for_illegal_purchase_of_lethal_injection_drugs/.

Shane, S., and Burns, J. F., "U.S. Subpoenas Twitter Over WikiLeaks Supporters," *New York Times*, January 8, 2011, available at https://www.nytimes.com/2011/01/09/world/09wiki.html.

Singel, R., "Joining Pro-Wikileaks Attacks Is As Easy As Clicking A Button," *Wired*, October 12, 2010, available at http://www.wired.com/threatlevel/2010/12/web20-attack-anonymous/.

Sky News, "Cyber-Warfare: The New Global Battlefield," October 31, 2011, available at http://news.sky.com/home/technology/article/16099978 (last accessed November 2, 2011).

Smith, P., "Indonesian claims responsibility for RBA and AFP attack," *Australian Financial Review*, November 21, 2013, available at http://www.afr.com/p/technology/indonesian_claims_responsibility_Y8kgaL tlfixvXGV5V6FH3I.

Smoking Gun, "Plea Deal Struck Over Attack on Kiss Web Sites," February 5, 2013, available at http://www.thesmokinggun.com/documents/gene-simmons-ddos-plea-587912.

Smolaks, M., "Anonymous Hits Back Over LulzSec Arrests," *Tech Week Europe*, March 7, 2012, available at http://www.techweekeurope.co.uk/news/anonymous-hits-back-over-lulzsec-arrests-65265.

——, "Two Possible TeaMp0isoN Members Arrested," Tech Week Europe, April 13, 2012, available at http://www.techweekeurope.co.uk/news/teamp0ison-policeteampoison-arrested-72738.

Solon, O. "Anonymous 'hacktivists' attack ISIS—strike down terrorist propaganda and recruitment sites," *Mirror*, February 9, 2015, available at http://www.mirror.co.uk/news/technology-science/technology/anonymous-hacktivists-attack-isis---5130966.

Storm, S., "London court: LulzSec hackers called 'latter day pirates' at 'cutting-edge' of cybercrime," *Computer World*, May 15, 2013, available at https://www.computerworld.com/article/2475432/cybercrime-hacking/london-court--lulzsec-hackers-called--latter-day-pirates--at--cutting-edge--of-cy.html.

Sydney Morning Herald, "Telstra offshoot hires teen hacker 'Akill,'" March 24, 2009, available at http://www.smh.com.au/national/telstra-offshoot-hires-teen-hacker-akill-20090324-97yn.html (last accessed March 11, 2015).

——, "Man Arrested Over Bizarre Hacking Campaign Involving Cat," February 11, 2013, available at http://www.smh.com.au/technology/technology-news/man-arrested-over-bizarre-hacking-campaign-involving-cat-20130211-2e77o.html.

Takver, "European Climate Exchange website hacked," *Independent Media Centre Australia*, July 25, 2010, available at http://indymedia.org.au/2010/07/24/european-climate-exchange-website-hacked (last accessed July 29, 2010).

Talal, S., "Pakistani Researcher Helps Google in Preventing a Massive Security Disaster, *ProPakistani*, 2014, available at http://propakistani.pk/2014/09/23/pakistani-researcher-helps-google-preventing-massive-security-disaster/.

Tarantola, A., "US Nuke Stockpile Control Systems Are 'Under Constant Attack,'" *Gizmodo*, March 21, 2012, available at http://gizmodo.com/5895033/us-nuke-stockpile-control-systems-are-under-constant-attack.

The Age, "The Cyberspace Wars," June 22, 2003, available at http://www.
theage.com.au/articles/2003/06/21/1056119529509.html (last accessed
December 2010).

Tech Herald, "CCC is at it again—hands out copies of German Interior
Minister's fingerprint," April 1, 2008, available at http://www.thetech
herald.com/article.php/200814/581/CCC-is-at-it-again-hands-out-copies-
of-German-Interior-Minister-s-fingerprint (last accessed July 15, 2010).

Ticehurst, J., "HSBC internet sites hacked," *V3*, September 20, 2000, available
at http://www.v3.co.uk/v3-uk/news/2007500/hsbc-internet-sites-hacked.

Urdu Point, September 17, 2014, available at http://daily.urdupoint.com/
livenews/2014-09-17/news-303641.html.

Walker, D., "Android bug allowing SOP bypass a 'privacy disaster,' researcher warns," *SC Magazine*, September 16, 2014, available
at http://www.scmagazine.com/android-bug-allowing-sop-bypass-a-
privacy-disaster-researcher-warns/article/371917/.

Waugh, D., "Rehtaeh Parsons Rape Case Solved by Anonymous in Less
Than 2 Hours Despite 'No Evidence'" *PolicyMic*, April 12, 201, available
at https://mic.com/articles/34491/rehtaeh-parsons-rape-case-solved-by-
anonymous-in-less-than-2-hours-despite-no-evidence#.WX5PGa8pj.

Wecanchangetheworld, "4Chan Hacks Anti Piracy Lawfirm, Leaks Porn
Downloaders' Names," *Buzzfeed*, November 29, 2010, available at http://
www.buzzfeed.com/wecanchangetheworld/4chan-hacks-anti-piracy-
lawfirm-leaks-porn-downlo-1q36 (last accessed November 21, 2011).

Whitcomb, D., "Hacker Gets a Year in Prison for Sony Attack," *Sydney
Morning Herald*, April 19, 2013, available at https://www.smh.com.au/
technology/hacker-gets-a-year-in-prison-for-sony-attack-20130419-
2i4hl.html.

Whyte, S. "Meet the Hacktivist Who Tried to Take Down the Government,"
Sydney Morning Herald, March 14, 2011, available at https://www.smh.
com.au/technology/meet-the-hacktivist-who-tried-to-take-down-the-
government-20110314-1btkt.html (last accessed November 7, 2011).

Wilson, D., "Bank of England turns to 'ethical hackers' to fix financial
security," *Tech Rader*, April 23, 2014, available at http://www.techradar.
com/au/news/internet/web/bank-of-england-turns-to-ethical-hackers-
to-fix-financial-sector-security-1244589.

Wisniewski, C., "Sony BMG Greece the latest hacked Sony site," *Naked
Security*, May 22, 2011, available at http://nakedsecurity.sophos.
com/2011/05/22/sony-bmg-greece-the-latest-hacked-sony-site/.

——, "PBS.org hacked... LulzSec targets Sesame Street?," *Naked Security*, May
30, 2011, available at http://nakedsecurity.sophos.com/2011/05/30/pbs-
org-hacked-lulzsec-targets-sesame-street/ (last accessed May 31, 2011).

——, "Hong Kong stock exchange (HKEx) website hacked, impacts
trades," *Naked Security*, August 10, 2011, available at http://naked

security.sophos.com/2011/08/10/hong-kong-stock-exchange-hkex-website-hacked-impacts-trades/.

——, "Hong Kong stock exchange attacked for second day in a row," *Naked Security*, August 12, 2011, available at http://nakedsecurity. sophos.com/2011/08/12/hong-kong-stock-exchange-attacked-for-second-day-in-a-row/.

Wyss, J., "Political hackers are one of Latin America's newest headaches," *Miami Herald*, November 3, 2011, available at http://www.miamiherald. com/2011/10/31/2481360/political-hackers-are-one-of-latin.html.

Xinhau, "Brazilian presidency's blog hacked in protest of corruption," October 14, 2011, *China Daily*, previously available at http://www.china daily.com.cn/xinhua/2011-10-14/content_4060557.html.

Zetter, K., "Router Flaw is a Ticking Bomb," *Wired*, August 1, 2005, available at https://www.wired.com/2005/08/router-flaw-is-a-ticking-bomb/.

Zorz, Z., "French Hacker and Alleged Anonymous Member Arrested After Bragging on TV," *Help Net Security*, April 13, 2011, available at http://www.net-security.org/secworld.php?id=10895.

Online Videos and Podcasts

"Activists deface Syrian official websites" (Al Jazeera English, September 26, 2011), available at http://www.youtube.com/watch?v=qX30M6gakQ4.

"Anonymous—A Message to Congress on SOPA you will not infringe on our rights" (November 18, 2011), available at http://www.youtube.com/watch?v=9rbyk0h3yeg.

"Anonymous—Antisec—OP PayPal" (July 27, 2011), available at http://www.youtube.com/watch?v=aa-h0HHp908.

"Anonymous attack on MasterCard, discussed on 4 News" (December 8, 2010), available at http://www.youtube.com/watch?v=i4HKk5yB8fU.

"Anonymous Hacks Westboro Baptist Church During LIVE" (February 24, 2011), available at http://www.youtube.com/watch?v=OZJwSjor4hM.

"Anonymous Members Allegedly Unmasked, Involved in Westboro Baptist Church Hacking Incident" (June 21, 2011), available at http://www.you tube.com/watch?v=QBExfh1oZCs.

"Anonymous Message to the Australian Government" (February 14, 2010), available at http://www.youtube.com/watch?v=yK1nsGFsvbo.

"Anonymous Message to the Oakland Police Department and City of Oakland" (January 31, 2012), available at http://www.youtube.com/watch?v=SzDuSaf55ek.

"Anonymous—Operation Brotherhood Shutdown" (November 7, 2011), available at http://www.youtube.com/watch?v=ZnPTBLbazAo.

"Anonymous Operation Last Resort Video" (January 26, 2013), available at http://www.youtube.com/watch?v=WaPni5O2YyI.

Anonymous—Operation Syria (September 12, 2011), available at http://www.youtube.com/watch?v=MGfF1ixk7S0.

"Anonymous—The Aftermath of Operation Brotherhood Shutdown" (November 12, 2011), available at http://www.youtube.com/watch?v=bBe9co3l9wI&feature=related.

"Anonymous to Australia," available at http://www.youtube.com/watch?v=eEc80U46hIQ (last accessed January 13, 2011).

"Anonymous v. Westboro Baptists" (February 22, 2011), available at http://www.youtube.com/watch?v=jUcW_8Ya32Q.

"An open letter from Anonymous to the Government of Israel" (November 4, 2011), available at http://www.youtube.com/watch?v=QNxi2lV0UM0.

"Chinese Regime Suspected in Lockheed Martin Hacking" (NTDTV, June 7, 2011), available at http://www.youtube.com/watch?v=1OXO0xgN1TU.

"DHS Thought Crime Tech, PBS and Lockheed Hacked, West in Libya" (May 31, 2011), available at https://www.youtube.com/watch?v=Rvw03tGwy74.

"EDF Hacking into Greenpeace" (November 10, 2011), available at http://www.youtube.com/watch?v=-70sjmTJlsQ.

Edry, R., "Israel and Iran: A Love Story?" TED Talks, December 2012, available at https://www.ted.com/speakers/ronny_edry.

"German hackers discover government spying" (Al Jazeera English, October 25, 2011), available at http://www.youtube.com/watch?v=lIwa_-jvbDQ.

Grey, P., Risky.biz Podcast, "RB2: AusCERT Podcast: Interview with Moscow-Based Cybercrime Analyst Kimberly Zenz" (May 20, 2009).

——, Risky.biz Podcast, "Interview on Risky Business with Michael Dwyer, Chief Executive of First State Superannuation" (October 14, 2011).

"Happy Hour: Weinergate, PBS Hacked" (June 1, 2011) http://www.youtube.com/watch?v=BiGEIPT8XFQ.

Insight, "Hacktivism" (SBS News, September 27, 2011), available at https://www.sbs.com.au/news/insight/tvepisode/hacktivism.

Kemmer, R. "How to Steal a Botnet and What Can Happen When You Do" (Google Tech Talk, September 2010), available at http://www.youtube.com/watch?v=2GdqoQJa6r4 (last accessed June 26, 2010).

Langill, J., "Stuxnet Worm Detailed Examination by SANS," available on a hacker website http://www.garage4hackers.com/showthread.php?604-Stuxnet-Worm-Detailed-Examination-by-SANS (last accessed February 7, 2011).

"LulzSec hacks Atlanta Infragard and challenges FBI" (June 3, 2011), available at http://www.youtube.com/watch?v=aROWwEIPgJA.

"LulzSec Hacks the CIA" (June 17, 2011), available at http://www.youtube.com/watch?v=QzQMBaIjo_w.

"LulzSec To Take Down CIA" (CNN, June 16, 2011), available at https://www.youtube.com/watch?v=fYNf7HG1SKA.

"Operation Invade Wall Street—A Message to the Media" (October 2, 2011), available at http://www.youtube.com/watch?v=lsLuYnEyFLw.

"Operation Titstorm—Anonymous Wants Their Small Boobs" (February 12, 2010), available at http://www.youtube.com/watch?v=FdPmbiK4JGY.

The Agenda, "Attack of the Hacktivists" (TVO, October 25, 2011).

"Twitter Hacked by Iranian Cyber Army (Poetry Reading)" (December 19, 2009), available at http://www.youtube.com/watch?v=rVHZ4MaCmmQ.

"VOICE of America News Website Hacked By Iranian Cyber Army" (February 22, 2011), available at http://www.youtube.com/watch?v=nDk VveI4G8Q.

"We are Anonymous—Sony hacked" (April 28, 2011), available at http://www.youtube.com/watch?v=370bq3VS5WU.

"Website for BART customers hacked by Anonymous" (ABC News [US], August 15, 2011), available at http://www.youtube.com/watch?v=DjFSq-a TMm8&feature=related.

Wikipedia

"Anat Kamm-Uri Blau Affair," available at http://en.wikipedia.org/wiki/Anat_Kamm-Uri_Blau_affair (last accessed October 20, 2018).

"Anonymous P2P," available at http://en.wikipedia.org/wiki/Anonymous_P2P (last accessed November 12, 2010).

"Application Programming Interface Key," available at https://en.wikipedia.org/wiki/Application_programming_interface_key (last accessed November 2018).

"Bennett Arron," available at http://en.wikipedia.org/wiki/Bennett_Arron (last accessed May 31, 2010).

"Chaos Computer Club," available at http://en.wikipedia.org/wiki/Chaos_Computer_Club.

"Click Fraud," available at http://en.wikipedia.org/wiki/Click_fraud (last accessed June 30, 2010).

"Denial of Service Attack (distributed)," available at http://en.wikipedia.org/wiki/Denial-of-service_attack#Distributed_attack (last accessed June 30, 2010).

"Denial-of-service (unintentional)," available at http://www.en.wikipedia.org/wiki/Denial-of-service_attack#Unintentional_denial_of _service (last accessed June 30, 2010).

"The Gifiles," available at https://wikileaks.org/the-gifiles.html.

"Internet of Things," available at https://en.wikipedia.org/wiki/Internet_of_things (last accessed November 2018).

"IP Address," available at https://en.wikipedia.org/wiki/IP_address (last accessed November 2018).

"Peer-to-peer," available at http://en.wikipedia.org/wiki/Peer-to-peer (last accessed December 2011).

"Skype and the Bavarian Trojan in the middle," available at http://wikileaks.org/wiki/Skype_and_the_Bavarian_trojan_in_the_middle.

"SPAM," available at http://en.wikipedia.org/wiki/E-mail_spam (last accessed June 30, 2010).

United States v. Bradley Manning" http://en.wikipedia.org/wiki/United_States_v._Bradley_Manning (last accessed July 25, 2018).

"URL," available at https://en.wikipedia.org/wiki/URL (last accessed November 2018).

"Virtual Private Network," available at http://www.en.wikipedia.org/wiki/Virtual_private_network (last accessed June 30, 2010).

Appendix: Interview Questions

Question 1: Has there been an erosion of a common hacker ethos or has the ethos merely evolved into many different sets of ethics?

Question 2: In your experience with hackers, does the law offer a deterrent?

Question 3: Based on your experience interviewing hackers, what are their perceptions of the illegality of their activity?

Question 4: What types of hacking activity would you consider "ethical"?

Question 5: Should ethical hacking be exempt from cybercrime provisions, and if so what kinds of ethical hacking?

Question 6: Do you equate some forms of ethical hacking as the electronic equivalent of civil disobedience (sit-ins, protests) and if so, should the current civil disobedience framework apply to the online setting?

Question 7: Is there a need for security research exemption in cybercrime provisions (unauthorised access)?

Question 8: Is there a need for a public interest exemption in cybercrime provisions (unauthorised access)?

Question 9: Is there any advice in general that you wish to impart to those engaged in ethical hacking?

Question 10: Is there any advice in general that you wish to impart to governments and organisations in dealing with ethical hacking?

About the Cover Image and the Artist

Serendipity brought scholarly publishing and cutting-edge art production together when we discovered the work of Phillip David Stearns.

A Brooklyn-based artist, Stearns has worked at the crossroads of technology and creativity, developing, among others, a project entitled *Glitch Textiles*, which explored the intersection of digital art and textile design.

A search for an original visual translation of the hidden digital world inhabited by hackers led us to *Fragmented Memory:* a work of art in which data, software and—stunningly—jacquard woven cotton merge into "hypothetical forms of portraiture," to cite the artist.

"Since 2012," Stearns said, "if anything, I've been seduced by the aesthetics of the algorithm." With the author Alana Maurushat being a self-described ethical hacker and the artist developing a series of "Ethical Hacking workshops for non-technical people," *Fragmented Memory* seemed to us the only possible cover image for this volume.

Law, Technology and Media

Edited by Michael Geist

The *Law, Technology and Media* series explores emerging technology law issues with an emphasis on a Canadian perspective. It is the first University of Ottawa Press series to be fully published under an open access licence.

Previous titles in this collection

Derek McKee, Finn Makela, and Teresa Scassa (eds.), *Law and the "Sharing Economy": Regulating Online Market Platforms*, 2018.

Karim Benyekhlef, Jane Bailey, Jacquelyn Burkell, and Fabien Gélinas (eds.), *eAccess to Justice*, 2016.

Jane Bailey, and Valerie Steeves (eds.), *eGirls, eCitizens*, 2015.

Michael Geist (ed.), *Law, Privacy and Surveillance In Canada in the Post-Snowden Era*, 2015.

Michael Geist (ed.), *The Copyright Pentalogy: How the Supreme Court of Canada Shook the Foundations of Canadian Copyright Law*, 2013.

www.press.uottawa.ca

www.ingramcontent.com/pod-product-compliance
Lightning Source LLC
Chambersburg PA
CBHW070245290326
41929CB00047B/2594